HEBREWS

Sacra Pagina Series

Volume 13

Hebrews

Alan C. Mitchell

Daniel J. Harrington, s.j.
Editor

A Michael Glazier Book

LITURGICAL PRESS
Collegeville, Minnesota

www.litpress.org

A Michael Glazier Book published by Liturgical Press.

1   2   3   4   5   6   7   8   9

Library of Congress Cataloging-in-Publication Data

Mitchell, Alan C.
    Hebrews : Alan C. Mitchell ; Daniel J. Harrington, editor.
      p.   cm. — (Sacra pagina series ; v. 13)
    "A Michael Glazier book."
    Includes bibliographical references and indexes.
    ISBN-13: 978-0-8146-5815-4
    ISBN-10: 0-8146-5815-6
    1. Bible. N.T. Hebrews—Commentaries.   I. Harrington, Daniel J.   II.Title.
  BS2775.53.M58 2007
  227'.87077—dc22

                        2006029017

In Memory of

Blanche V. Mitchell (1919–1991)

Grace J. McGinniss (1930–1994)

James L. Lamm (1929–2001)

and for my father

Albert P. Mitchell

CONTENTS

Introduction

Translation, Notes, Interpretation

Exordium

I. Jesus, Son Crowned with Glory as a Result of His Suffering and Death (1:5–2:18)

II. Jesus, Apostle and High Priest: A Model of Faith and Hope (3:1–6:20)

III. The Message for the Mature: Another Priest Like Melchizedek (7:1–10:39)

EDITOR'S PREFACE

Sacra Pagina is a multivolume commentary on the books of the New Testament. The expression *Sacra Pagina* (Sacred Page) originally referred to the text of Scripture. In the Middle Ages it also described the study of Scripture to which the interpreter brought the tools of grammar, rhetoric, dialectic, and philosophy. Thus *Sacra Pagina* encompasses both the text to be studied and the activity of interpretation.

This series presents fresh translations and modern expositions of all the books of the New Testament. Written by an international team of Catholic biblical scholars, it is intended for biblical professionals, graduate students, theologians, clergy, and religious educators. The volumes present basic introductory information and close exposition. They self-consciously adopt specific methodological perspectives, but maintain a focus on the issues raised by the New Testament compositions themselves. The goal of *Sacra Pagina* is to provide sound critical analysis without any loss of sensitivity to religious meaning. This series is therefore catholic in two senses of the word: inclusive in its methods and perspectives, and shaped by the context of the Catholic tradition.

The Second Vatican Council described the study of the sacred page as the "very soul of sacred theology" (*Dei Verbum* 24). The volumes in this series illustrate how Catholic scholars contribute to the council's call to provide access to Sacred Scripture for all the Christian faithful. Rather than pretending to say the final word on any text, these volumes seek to open up the riches of the New Testament and to invite as many people as possible to study seriously the sacred page.

DANIEL J. HARRINGTON, S.J.

PREFACE

Hebrews is one of the most beautiful and most challenging books of the New Testament. Its elegant Greek captures the complexity of the author's thought by expressing his lofty theological ideas in sophisticated and at times enigmatic language. Anyone who writes a commentary on Hebrews quickly discovers why commentators from ancient to modern times have struggled to explain and interpret its message. Indeed, without the rich tradition of interpretation on which to depend, the task of producing a commentary on Hebrews would be even more daunting. Fortunately, there are many excellent commentaries upon which to rely for help in solving the riddle of Hebrews, and readers of this commentary will note its author's indebtedness to the great scholars who have produced them. Their names appear often throughout the following pages.

As no one can write a commentary without the help of other people, I am pleased to express the gratitude I feel for individuals who have aided me greatly in bringing this project to completion. I would like to thank the Theology Department at Georgetown University for a Senior Landegger Research Grant that supported the initial stages of research and writing. I am grateful to Prof. Dr. Cilliers Breytenbach for his generosity in providing me a place to work and making available the resources of the Institut für Antike und Christentum at the Humboldt University in Berlin during 1996–97. I also thank Dr. Eckhard Plümacher, the then Director of the theological library at Humboldt University, for his gracious assistance and for allowing me the full use of the library's resources. The Georgetown University Research Opportunities Program (GUROP) provided me with an undergraduate research assistant for the Fall 2005 semester, who happened to be one of my students, Kathleen M. Rommel. I thank her for the excellent work she did in collecting many of the more recent bibliographical entries. I also want to express my gratitude to Daniel J. Harrington, s.j., who read the entire manuscript and returned it in record time with excellent suggestions to improve it. My thanks go to the editorial staff at Liturgical Press, especially to Peter Dwyer, to Mary Stommes, Colleen Stiller, and to Linda Maloney for the fine work they have done in the production of this volume.

Last, I could never have completed this book without the love and support of my wife, Julia A. Lamm, and our son, Aidan. Both of them have made many sacrifices to allow me the time to work on this project. Throughout the many months it has taken to put the manuscript into final form, each has admirably exemplified that all-important virtue of Hebrews, "patient endurance." A writer could not ask for a better support team.

Alan C. Mitchell
Georgetown University

ABBREVIATIONS

Biblical Books and Apocrypha

Gen	Nah	1-2-3-4 Kgdms	John
Exod	Hab	Add Esth	Acts
Lev	Zeph	Bar	Rom
Num	Hag	Bel	1-2 Cor
Deut	Zech	1-2 Esdr	Gal
Josh	Mal	4 Ezra	Eph
Judg	Ps (*pl.:* Pss)	Jdt	Phil
1-2 Sam	Job	Ep Jer	Col
1-2 Kgs	Prov	1-2-3-4 Macc	1-2 Thess
Isa	Ruth	Pr Azar	1-2 Tim
Jer	Cant	Pr Man	Titus
Ezek	Eccl (*or* Qoh)	Sir	Phlm
Hos	Lam	Sus	Heb
Joel	Esth	Tob	Jas
Amos	Dan	Wis	1-2 Pet
Obad	Ezra	Matt	1-2-3 John
Jonah	Neh	Mark	Jude
Mic	1-2 Chr	Luke	Rev

Other Ancient Texts

CD	Cairo Genizah copy of the *Damascus Document*
Ep. Aristeas	*Epistle of Aristeas*
Jub	*Jubilees*
LXX	Septuagint
m.	Mishnah
MT	Masoretic Text
NT	New Testament
OT	Old Testament

Par. Jer.	*Paraleipomena Jeremiou*
P. Lond.	*Greek Papyri in the British Museum I–VII*
P. Oxy.	*The Oxyrhyncus Papyri*
1Q20	Qumran Cave 1 *Genesis Apocryphon*
1QS	*Rule of the Community*
4Q'Amram	Qumran Cave 4 *Visions of 'Amram*
4QDeut q	Seventeenth copy of Deuteronomy
11QMelch	Qumran Cave 11 *Melchizedek*
T. Abr.	*Testament of Abraham*
T. Benj.	*Testament of Benjamin*
T. Gad	*Testament of Gad*
T. Job	*Testament of Job*
T. Jos.	*Testament of Joseph*
T. Levi	*Testament of Levi*
T. Mos.	*Testament of Moses*
T. Zeb.	*Testament of Zebulun*
Sib. Or.	*Sibylline Oracles*

Periodicals, Reference Works, Serials, and Books Frequently Cited

AB	Anchor Bible
ABR	*Australian Biblical Review*
ABRL	Anchor Bible Reference Library
AJBA	*Australian Journal of Biblical Theology*
ALGHJ	Arbeiten zur Literatur und Geschichte des hellenistischen Judentums
AnBib	Analecta biblica
ANRW	*Aufstieg und Niedergang der römischen Welt*
ANTC	Abingdon New Testament Commentaries
AsSeign	*Assemblées du Seigneur*
Attridge	Harold W. Attridge, *The Epistle to the Hebrews: A Commentary on the Epistle to the Hebrews.* Hermeneia. Philadelphia: Fortress Press, 1989
AusBR	*Australian Biblical Review*
AUSS	*Andrews University Seminary Studies*
BBR	*Bulletin for Biblical Research*
BDAG	Frederick W. Danker, reviser and editor, *Greek-English Lexicon of the New Testament and Early Christian Literature.* 3rd ed.
BDF	Friedrich Blass, Albert Debrunner, and Robert W. Funk, *A Greek Grammar of the New Testament*
BGU	*Ägyptische Urkunden aus den königlichen Staatlichen Museen zu Berlin. Griechische Urkunden*
Bib	*Biblica*
BibOr	Biblica et orientalia

BibRes	*Biblical Research*
BINS	Biblical Interpretation Series
BJRL	*Bulletin of the John Rylands University Library of Manchester*
Bleek	Friedrich Bleek, *Der Brief an die Hebräer erläutert durch Einleitung, Übersetzung und fortlaufenden Kommentar*. 3 vols. Berlin: Dümmler, 1828, 1836, 1840
Braun	Herbert Braun, *An die Hebräer*. HNT 14. Tübingen: Mohr Siebeck, 1984
Bruce	Frederick F. Bruce, *The Epistle to the Hebrews*. NICNT. rev. ed. Grand Rapids: Eerdmans, 1990
BSac	*Bibliotheca sacra*
BT	*The Bible Translator*
BTB	*Biblical Theology Bulletin*
Buchanan	George W. Buchanan, *To the Hebrews: Translation, Comment, and Conclusions*. AB 36. Garden City, NY: Doubleday, 1972
BullBibRes	*Bulletin for Biblical Research*
BZ	*Biblische Zeitschrift*
BZNW	*Beihefte zur Zeitschrift für die Neutestamentliche Wissenschaft*
CBQ	*Catholic Biblical Quarterly*
CBQMS	Catholic Biblical Quarterly Monograph Series
Charlesworth	James H. Charlesworth, *The Old Testament Pseudepigrapha*. 2 vols. New York: Doubleday, 1983–1985
CSion	*Cahiers Sioniens*
CTQ	*Concordia Theological Quarterly*
de Silva, *Perseverance*	
	David A. de Silva, *Perseverance in Gratitude: A Socio-Rhetorical Commentary on the Epistle "to the Hebrews."* Grand Rapids: Eerdmans, 2000
EBib	*Études bibliques*
EcumRev	*The Ecumenical Review*
EDNT	*Exegetical Dictionary of the New Testament*. Eds. Horst Balz and Gerhard Schneider. 3 vols. Grand Rapids: Eerdmans, 1978–83
EKK	Evangelisch-katholischer Kommentar zum Neuen Testament
Ellingworth	Paul Ellingworth, *The Epistle to the Hebrews*. NIGTC. Grand Rapids: Eerdmans, 1993
EspV	*Esprit et vie*
ExpTim	*Expository Times*
FRLANT	Forschungen zur Religion und Literatur des Alten und Neuen Testaments
GJ	*Grace Journal*
Grässer	Erich Grässer, *An die Hebräer*. 3 vols. EKK 17. Zürich: Benziger; Neukirchen-Vluyn: Neukirchener, 1990–97
Hagner	Donald A. Hagner, *Encountering the Book of Hebrews: An Exposition*. Grand Rapids: Baker, 2002
HAL	Ludwig Koehler and Walter Baumgartner. *The Hebrew and Aramaic Lexicon of the Old Testament* (2001)
Héring	Jean Héring, *The Epistle to the Hebrews*. London: Epworth, 1970

NRSV	New Revised Standard Version
NRTh	*La nouvelle revue théologique*
NTAbh	Neutestamentliche Abhandlungen
NTL	New Testament Library
NTS	*New Testament Studies*
Pfitzner	Victor C. Pfitzner, *Hebrews*. ANTC. Nashville: Abingdon, 1977
PRSt	*Perspectives in Religious Studies*
RB	*Revue biblique*
ResQ	*Restoration Quarterly*
RevExp	*Review and Expositor*
RevQ	*Revue de Qumran*
RSR	*Recherches de science religieuse*
RSV	Revised Standard Version
RTR	*Reformed Theological Review*
SacDoc	*Sacra Doctrina*
SB	Sources bibliques
SBLAB	SBL Academia Biblica
SBLDS	SBL Dissertation Series
SBLMS	SBL Monograph Series
SBLRBS	SBL Resources for Biblical Study
SBLSBS	SBL Sources for Biblical Study
SBLSCS	SBL Septuagint and Cognate Studies
ScC	*La scuola cattolica*
SE	*Studia evangelica I, II, III*
SémiotBib	*Sémiotique et Bible*
SNTSMS	Society for New Testament Studies Monograph Series
SP	Sacra Pagina
SPAW	Sitzungsberichte der preussischen Akademie der Wissenschaften
Spicq	Ceslas Spicq, *L'Épître aux Hébreux*. 2 vols. *EBib*. Paris: Gabalda, 1952–53
ST	*Studia theologica*
Str-B	Hermann L. Strack and Paul Billerbeck, *Kommentar zum Neuen Testament aus Talmud und Midrasch*
TBei	*Theologische Beiträge*
TBT	*The Bible Today*
TD	*Theology Digest*
TDNT	*Theological Dictionary of the New Testament*. Eds. Gerhard Kittel and Gerhard Friedrich
TGl	*Theologie und Glaube*
TJ	*Trinity Journal*
TJT	*Toronto Journal of Theology*
TLZ	*Theologische Literaturzeitung*
TRu	*Theologische Rundschau*
TS	*Theological Studies*
TTZ	*Trierer theologische Zeitschrift*
TY	*Tantur Yearbook*
TynBul	*Tyndale Bulletin*

VC	*Vigilae christianae*
VD	*Verbum domini*
VEccl	*Verbum et Ecclesia*
VF	*Verkündigung und Forschung*
WBC	Word Biblical Commentary
Weiss	Hans-Friedrich Weiss, *Der Brief and die Hebräer*. KEK 13. Göttingen: Vandenhoeck & Ruprecht, 1991
Westcott	Brooke F. Westcott, *The Epistle to the Hebrews*. London: Macmillan, 1889, reprinted Grand Rapids: Eerdmans, 1977
WestTheolJourn	*Westminster Theological Journal*
WMANT	Wissenschaftliche Monographien zum Alten und Neuen Testament
WUNT	Wissenschaftliche Untersuchungen zum Neuen Testament
ZNW	*Zeitschrift für die neutestamentliche Wissenschaft und die Kunde der älteren Kirche*

INTRODUCTION

The task of any biblical commentary is to attempt to explain the text in a cogent and coherent manner. Hebrews, by its own admission, sets the bar for this task rather high, as it contains many things that are difficult to explain (5:11). Still, the ambiguities and anomalies of Hebrews make that endeavor not only challenging, but interesting as well.

This commentary follows the standard historical critical approach. Given the difficulties that Hebrews poses, it is essential to understand it on its own terms and in its historical setting. After a brief introduction, treating the usual elementary questions, the commentary conforms to the format of the Sacra Pagina series by offering a translation, notes, interpretation, and short bibliography for each section of the text. The translation is based on the New Revised Standard Version, with modifications that seek to provide a precise rendering of the Greek text into English. On the whole, the translation is a literal one. I have made occasional changes to the translation of the NRSV, which I believe suit the meaning of the words, phrases, or idioms in question, and which bring out nuances to the Greek that help the reader appreciate the sentiment of the author of Hebrews in these instances. The translation choices I have made were done only for scholarly purposes and not simply to change the readability of the NRSV in certain contexts. Hence they are not paraphrases of the NRSV. In my opinion, these changes reflect the range of meaning possible in the original Greek of Hebrews without dramatically changing the overall meaning chosen by the translators of the NRSV. The types of changes I have made to the NRSV translation of Hebrews are basically two: (1) Given the possibility that a Greek word, phrase, or idiom offers a translator several possible choices of English translation, I have sometimes chosen a translation that seems appropriate to the context of the verse in question. (2) The third edition of the standard NT Greek Lexicon (BDAG) was published in 2000, nine years after the publication of the translation of the NRSV. Hence in some instances I have chosen a translation that reflects advances in the lexicography of NT Greek, based on the range of meanings offered in BDAG.

The notes explain the translation and attend to textual, philological, and grammatical matters that are of interest and are necessary for understanding the meaning of Hebrews. The notes also contain references to other ancient literature that may help to elucidate the text. Special attention has been paid to the Septuagint, Hellenistic Jewish writings (notably from Josephus and Philo), and selected Greek and Roman authors, in an effort to locate Hebrews in the thought world, religious milieu, and cultural background of its author and audience. Unless otherwise noted the translations of Greek and Roman authors are taken from the volumes in the Loeb Classical Library. All translations of OT texts are taken from the NRSV. The interpretation looks to the larger picture of the developing arguments in Hebrews in order to understand its meaning and message for its first audience as well as for readers today. The bibliographies supply additional reading that may offer a more in-depth treatment of the text or an interpretation alternative to the one given in this commentary.

1. AUTHORSHIP

The debate over the authorship of Hebrews has focused mainly on whether it should be numbered among the letters of Paul. In the Eastern churches, confidence that Hebrews was authentically Pauline facilitated its inclusion in the canon, whereas in the West uncertainty over the identity of its author inhibited its easy reception. The earliest advocate of Pauline authorship was Pantaenus of Alexandria in the second century C.E. (Eusebius, *Church History* 6.14.4). The earliest extant manuscript of Hebrews, $\mathfrak{P}^{46}$, a witness to the Alexandrian text type, places it after Romans, reflecting the Eastern understanding of it as Pauline. Generally in other manuscripts Hebrews is placed among the letters of Paul or immediately after them, as in many printed editions of the Greek New Testament (Bruce Metzger, *A Textual Commentary on the Greek New Testament* [London and New York: United Bible Societies, 1971] 661–62).

Still, in antiquity the question of the authorship of Hebrews was unsettled. Origen's opinion, quoted by Eusebius (*Church History* 6.25.11-14), illustrates the problem well. Commenting on the style of Hebrews, Origen distinguishes it from Paul's style by describing it as less rude and written in a more elegant Greek. In his opinion the thought of Hebrews is similar to Paul's, but its style is not. He concludes that Hebrews was written by someone, perhaps a disciple of Paul, who had later recalled his teacher's thought and written it down. Curiously, Origen commends churches that attribute the authorship of Hebrews to Paul, and then claims that in truth only God knows who wrote it.

It has become standard for modern commentators to quote this agnostic opinion as representative of Origen's view on the authorship of Hebrews, although in some of his writings he attributes Hebrews to Paul (*First Principles* 1.2.5; 3.1.10, 2.4; 4.1.24, 27; *Against Celsus* 3.53; 7.29). Origen even challenges those who dispute Pauline authorship of Hebrews and claims an interest in proving otherwise (*Letter to Africanus* 8). Despite that challenge, Eusebius reports that Origen entertained the possibility of other authors, i.e., Clement of Rome and Luke (*Church History* 6.25.14). Another Eastern witness, Clement of Alexandria, shared the view that Luke had a role in the composition of Hebrews, as the translator of Paul's original Hebrew version into Greek (Eusebius, *Church History* 6.14.2).

In the West, Pauline authorship was not favored until the time of Augustine (*City of God* 16.22; *On Christian Doctrine* 2.8.13). Jerome acknowledged the difficulties of ascribing authorship to Paul, due to the difference in the style of Hebrews from the other Pauline letters. Nevertheless, he believed that Paul was its author and suggested that he could not put his name on the letter because it was written to Hebrews, who held Paul in disrepute. Like Clement of Alexandria, Jerome claimed that Paul originally wrote in Hebrew, which was translated into Greek by someone else, accounting for the stylistic differences from Paul's letters, which he had originally composed in Greek (*Lives of Illustrious Men* 5.59).

The consensus among commentators today is that Hebrews is non-Pauline, although advocates for Pauline authorship are still to be found. David Alan Black has reexamined the evidence for Pauline authorship and concluded that the internal evidence argues against it, whereas the external evidence argues for it. Regarding the external evidence of Origen's claim that only God knows who wrote Hebrews, Black takes Origen to mean that the secondary author, i.e., "the penman" is unknown. Filling in Origen's blank, Black concludes that Paul was the primary author of Hebrews with the help of Luke, as amanuensis ("Who Wrote Hebrews? The Internal and External Evidence Reexamined," *Faith and Mission* 18 [2001] 3–26).

Whereas Black's proposal is interesting, it is not conclusive. There is enough internal evidence from the style, vocabulary, and theology of Hebrews to raise serious doubts about Pauline authorship (Attridge, 2–3; Ellingworth, 7–12). Also, the external evidence reflects a common assumption among Alexandrian patristic writers that Paul authored Hebrews, an opinion that appears to rest more on an attempt to reconcile two opposing views regarding Pauline authorship than on any hard evidence (see Simon Kistemaker, "The Authorship of Hebrews," *Faith and Mission* 18 [2001] 58).

Black's suggestion that Eusebius' agnosticism over the authorship of Hebrews refers only to someone who acted as Paul's amanuensis is further complicated by the fact that there are clear instances in Eusebius where the verb *graphein*, "to write," refers both to authorship and to actual penning

(*Church History* 2.13.2; 2.17.16, 23; 2.22.6; 3.4.2; 3.4.7; 3.36.6, 11; 3.39.15; 4.7.9; 4.8.3, 5; 4.18.8). There are also places in the *Church History* where Eusebius prefers a compound of *graphein*, when he refers to actual writing alone (2.5.6; 2.8.1; 2.13.5; 2.16.1; 2.17.22; 2.22.6; 2.23.20; 3.3.3; 3.24.7; 3.38.2; 4.7.15). Black's distinction between author and amanuensis cannot be maintained in light of this evidence.

After Paul himself, individuals associated with him have also been proposed as the author of Hebrews. In the West, where Pauline authorship was not readily accepted, Tertullian had suggested Barnabas (*On Modesty*, 20; Jerome, *Lives of Illustrious Men* 5.59). His Cypriot background and status as a Levite made him a candidate, as someone who might have been interested in the ritual themes of Hebrews and the priesthood of Christ. A fair number of commentators from the nineteenth and twentieth centuries have sought to establish him as the author of Hebrews, but not recently (see Spicq 1:199–200, n.8).

Paul's coworker Apollos has garnered a fair amount of interest as a possible author of Hebrews since the time of Martin Luther. Luther was of the opinion that the Alexandria-trained Apollos possessed both the knowledge of the LXX and the rhetorical skill needed to compose a document as refined as Hebrews. He cites Luke's assessment of Apollos as "mighty in the Scriptures" and notes that the "ornamental style of Hebrews" makes non-Pauline authorship plausible (*Sermons* 6.167). Later commentators continued to consider Apollos an appealing candidate because of his Alexandrian background, his connection to the Pauline circle, and his reputation as a powerful preacher whose style could be distinguished from Paul's. Among more recent commentators on Hebrews, Apollos is favored by Paul Ellingworth (*The Epistle to the Hebrews*, 21); Donald A. Hagner, (*Encountering the Book of Hebrews*, 23) and Victor C. Pfitzner (*Hebrews*, 26).

George H. Guthrie has seriously reexamined three centuries of evidence presented in favor of Apollos as the author of Hebrews and has categorized it in a helpful way ("The Case for Apollos as the Author of Hebrews," *Faith and Mission* 18 [2001] 41–56). He classifies the pro-Apollos arguments under three types: (1) no other NT personage fits the bill; (2) there are firm correspondences between what can be known about Apollos and the style and content of Hebrews; and (3) there are questionable correspondences between Apollos and Hebrews that rest more on speculation than on evidence (ibid. 49–54). In a refreshingly honest appraisal, however, Guthrie admits that although one may not be able to certify Apollos as the author of Hebrews he may be "as close as we are going to get" (ibid. 54).

At the beginning of the twentieth century Adolf von Harnack broke new ground in the debate over the authorship of Hebrews by proposing Paul's coworker Priscilla for the role ("Probabilia über die Adresse und den

Verfasser des Hebräerbriefes," *ZNW* 1 [1900] 16–41). Against the likelihood of her as author stands the masculine singular participle *diēgoumenon*, "telling," at 11:32, referring to the author. Still, in recent times Priscilla's authorship has been espoused by Ruth Hoppin (*Priscilla's Letter: Finding the Author of the Epistle to the Hebrews* [Fort Bragg, CA: Lost Coast Press, 1997], first published in 1997 by Christian Universities Press).

Hoppin's argument rests largely on a construct of femininity, which she finds in the letter; this indicates that the author was a woman, someone who was able to "identify with women." The evidence she culls from Hebrews, however, is ambiguous and relies on an assumed view of what characterizes the "feminine mind" over the "masculine mind." Hoppin identifies things like empathy, compassion, an interest in human weakness, and gentle tact and diplomacy as feminine, as if men were incapable of such emotions and conduct. The psychological portrait she draws of the author of Hebrews is tendentious to the extent that once she has defined the "feminine mind" she has no choice but to declare that the author is a woman. Hoppin employs a similar psychological construct to show that the author identifies with women, a claim that rests on the presupposition that the inclusion of women among the "Heroes of Faith" in Hebrews 11 demonstrates a "generosity" toward the portrayal of women that is characteristic of a "feminist."

Complicating the picture further is Hoppin's assumption that great pains were taken to hide the fact that the author was a woman. So, for example, she claims that the masculine accusative participle at 11:32, *diēgoumenon*, differs only by one letter from the feminine accusative, *diēgoumenēn*. Since Hoppin presupposes that changing one letter would not be difficult at all, she asserts that the feminine form was altered to the masculine in order to hide the true identity of the author. She cites Col 4:15 and Rom 16:7 as precedents for such a change. In those instances, however, the feminine form is either supported by manuscript evidence or grammatical ambiguity, neither of which applies to Heb 11:32. In the end Hoppin has presented an imaginative and creative attempt to vindicate Harnack's hypothesis, but her proposal is unconvincing.

The attempts at a precise identification of the author of Hebrews try to account for external and internal evidence to make the best possible determination of who may have written the sermon. In the history of its interpretation as many as thirteen individuals have been suggested as the author (see Ellingworth, 3). Not every one of those names merits equal attention, and much of the evidence brought forth to support the more likely candidates is speculative. Sometimes arguments based on internal evidence that some commentators amass to support Pauline authorship are used by other commentators to argue against Pauline authorship. External evidence does not always agree and cannot always be coordinated with internal evidence.

In the end, one can legitimately question the need to identify the author of Hebrews precisely. The consensus of contemporary commentators indicates correctly that Hebrews is non-Pauline and anonymous.

2. DESTINATION

A variety of geographical locations has been proposed for the destination of Hebrews. Even the greeting in 13:24, "Those from Italy send you greetings," which holds the only internal clue to the possible destination of the sermon, has been interpreted to identify Italy as the place of origin or as the destination for Hebrews. Still other cities have been favored for the location to which Hebrews was sent.

In ancient Christianity, because of the author's interest in the Jewish Law and cult, Jerusalem was thought to be the destination of Hebrews (Chrysostom, *Homilies on the Epistle to the Hebrews, Argument and Summary,* 2; Jerome, *On Illustrious Men,* 5). Some modern commentators have preferred Jerusalem or some other place in Palestine as the location of the community to which Hebrews was addressed (Buchanan, 255–56; Hughes, 19; Spicq 1:220–52; Westcott, xli). Against Jerusalem as the sermon's destination stands the absence of concrete references to the Temple and its cultic rituals. All the author's arguments relative to the Jewish priesthood and ritual practices are drawn from Scripture. Even if a later date for Hebrews, a time after the destruction of the Temple, were proposed, one might expect some reference to its destruction and to the end of sacrifice in Jerusalem. Such references, however, are lacking in Hebrews.

Apart from Jerusalem, commentators have preferred Rome as the sermon's destination. Although the salutation of "those from Italy" (13:24) has been cited as strong evidence that the letter is destined for Rome, the fact that Hebrews is quoted for the first time in a Roman document of the late first or early second century, *1 Clement,* may offer firmer evidence that the capital of the empire is the sermon's destination. In support of Rome commentators have also cited similarities between Hebrews and 1 Peter (Raymond E. Brown and John P. Meier, *Antioch and Rome: New Testament Cradles of Catholic Christianity* [New York: Paulist, 1984] 140–51).

One of the strongest modern proponents of a Roman destination is William L. Lane, who sees the following evidence as pointing to a Roman location for the recipients of Hebrews. Lane interprets "Those from Italy greet you" (Heb 13:24) as a reference to Italians living outside of their homeland who are sending greetings to a house church in Rome (1:lviii). He supports the claim with four additional reasons: (1) allusions to the community's generosity (6:10-11 and 10:33-34) are consistent with what is known of the history of Roman Christianity as described by other ancient Christian sources like Ignatius of Antioch and Dionysius of Corinth; (2) the reference to the community's suffering (10:32-34) reflects the situation of the Roman church at the time of the Edict of Claudius, which expelled Jews and Jewish Christians from Rome in 49 C.E.; (3) the term used for the "leaders" of the community, *hēgoumenoi* (13:7, 17, 24), is found in Christian literature associated with Rome (*1 Clem* 36:1-6; Hermas, Vis. 2.2.6; 3.9.7); and (4) Clement of Rome is the first author to quote Hebrews, in his letter to Corinth (*1 Clem* 36:1-6) (Lane 1:lviii; "Social Perspectives on Roman Christianity during the Formative Years from Nero to Nerva: Romans, Hebrews, *1 Clement*," in Karl P. Donfried and Peter Richardson, eds., *Judaism and Christianity in First-Century Rome* [Grand Rapids: Eerdmans, 1998] 196–244).

In addition to Jerusalem and Rome as possible destinations for Hebrews, other cities have been proposed: Alexandria (Charles P. Anderson, "The Epistle to the Hebrews and the Pauline Letter Collection," *HTR* 59 [1966] 429–38), Antioch (J. Vallance Brown, "The Authorship and Circumstances of Hebrews," *BSac* 80 [1923] 505–38; Vacher Burch, *The Epistle to the Hebrews: Its Sources and its Message* [London: Williams and Norgate, 1936] 137), Corinth (Montefiore, 11–30), Colossae (Thomas W. Manson, "The Problem of the Epistle to the Hebrews," *BJRL* 32 [1949–50] 1–17), and Ephesus (J. Vernon Bartlet, "The Riddle of the Epistle to the Hebrews," *Expositor* 5 [1913] 548–51). The consensus among commentators today is that Rome is the sermon's destination (Attridge, 11; Bruce, 14; Ellingworth, 29; Koester, 49–50; Weiss, 76).

3. DATE

The earliest manuscript of Hebrews, $\mathfrak{P}^{46}$, dates from the third century C.E. and the first clear mention of it in early Christian literature occurs in *1 Clement*, which is dated to ca. 96 C.E. While that must serve as the upper limit for the date, the lower limit is much debated. Not many would date it before 60 C.E., although some would because there is no reference to the destruction of the Temple in Hebrews, yet cultic activity seems to be referred to in the present tense. These commentators would argue that the Temple was still standing when Hebrews was written. That does not really prove much, however, since the cultic activity in Hebrews is restricted to the Levitical sanctuary and is not related to the Temple itself. Also, as several commentators point out, post-70 authors and literature such as Josephus, Clement of Rome, and *Diognetus* sometimes refer to the practice of the Levitical cult in the present tense (e.g., Attridge, 8; Koester, 53).

The internal evidence most often brought forth to support a date in the 60s is the references to the community's hardships (10:32-34; 12:4; 13:3).

Assuming a Roman destination, some commentators maintain that the suffering in 10:32-34 points to the expulsion of Jews and Jewish Christians from Rome under Claudius in 49 C.E. (Lane 1:lviii; Ellingworth, 31; Koester, 51). The mention of verbal abuse and afflictions along with imprisonment and the loss of possessions is thought to have been associated with the hardships Jews and Christians suffered under Claudius. Problematic for the assignment of these hardships to 49 C.E. is the paucity of evidence for exactly what kinds of suffering Jews and Jewish Christians endured at that time. Suetonius, for example, does not mention imprisonment (*Claudius* 25.4). It is likely that not all Jews and Jewish Christians were expelled from Rome by Claudius, so there is no telling whether his edict actually affected members of the community to which Hebrews was addressed (E. M. Small-wood, *The Jews Under Roman Rule* [2nd ed. repr. Leiden: Brill, 2001] 216). Roman Christianity in the first century C.E. seems to have comprised a number of relatively independent house churches with no centralized authority (Lane 1:lix–lx). This could mean that some Christian churches suffered more than others, since Claudius' action appears to have been targeted to those who were creating the disturbances over "Chrestus."

The later references to suffering make clear that none of the community members had shed their blood (12:4), but some were imprisoned (13:3). Commentators who see the earlier references as pointing to the time of Claudius date the later references to the time of Nero, or just prior to his actions against Christians. They conclude to a date for Hebrews in the mid- to late 60s (e.g., Bruce, 22; Lane 1:lxvi; Ellingworth, 33). It is possible, however, that Nero's persecution of Christians may have lasted even longer, continuing perhaps as late as 67 C.E., which would associate it with the events of the Jewish war (John R. Donahue, "Windows and Mirrors: The Setting of Mark's Gospel," *CBQ* 57 [1995] 21–22).

At a still later time, after the destruction of the Jerusalem Temple in 70 C.E., Jews and Jewish Christians in Rome were subject to harassment and social dislocation due to the Roman victory in the Jewish War (Brown and Meier, *Antioch and Rome*, 201; Paula Fredriksen, *From Jesus to Christ: The Origins of the New Testament Images of Jesus* [2nd ed. New Haven: Yale, 2000] 50–52). Josephus vividly describes the triumphal victory procession of Vespasian and Titus through the streets of Rome, where pictorial representations of the various campaigns were so realistically re-created on stages that the war was relived by those who had not witnessed it firsthand, as though the events were unfolding before their very eyes (*War* 7.145-46). He says further that the most conspicuous of the spoils were those taken from the Jerusalem Temple, including a copy of the Torah (*War* 7.148-52). Included in the procession were captives from Judea, among whom was a general, Simon son of Gioras, who was then publicly executed (*War* 7.155). The suffering of Christians addressed by Mark's gospel is the likely object of this kind of abuse (see Brian J. Incigneri, *The Gospel to the Romans: The Setting and Rhetoric of Mark's Gospel*. BINS 65 [Leiden and Boston: Brill, 2003] 208–52; Ivan Head, "Mark as a Roman Document from the Year 69: Testing Martin Hengel's Thesis," *JRH* 28 [2004] 240–59).

Ellen Bradshaw Aitken's hypothesis that Hebrews was written in Rome during the aftermath of the destruction of the Temple and within the context of the Flavian triumph may well be correct ("Portraying the Temple in Stone and Text: The Arch of Titus and the Epistle to the Hebrews," in Gabriella Gelardini, ed., *Hebrews: Contemporary Methods—New Insights*. BINS 75 [Leiden and Boston: Brill, 2005] 131–48). The connections she makes between the text of Hebrews and the Flavian propaganda, which sought to use the Judean victory as a means of solidifying its rule, are indeed suggestive. They are not, however, conclusive as they lack exegetical demonstration from Hebrews itself. The suggestion, for example, that the Flavian triumph and apotheosis of Titus are intentionally replaced by the exaltation of the Son in Hebrews is tantalizing. But this proposal remains speculative and overlooks the fact that the exaltation of the Son is not exclusive to Hebrews in the NT, and that Hebrews employs many of the standard NT features of interpreting Psalm 110 to support his exaltation. Likewise the idea that the priesthood of Jesus was meant to critique the ideology of divine rule expressed in triumphal sacrifices is not really supported from evidence within Hebrews itself. Aitken can only point to an indirect typological reflection on the ritual of the Day of Atonement to make the point. She never really explains how the treatment of the Levitical rites becomes "the rhetorical site for resistance to the Roman imperial ideology." Finally, the comparison between the prominence of the spoils from the Jerusalem Temple in the Flavian propaganda and the mention of the appointments of the Tabernacle in Heb 9:2-5 would be more convincing had the author of Hebrews restricted himself only to those items that were actually mentioned in Josephus' account (*War* 7.148-50). Hebrews does not include all the appointments of the Tabernacle, but it features many more items than were displayed as part of the Flavian triumph. It would seem that the description in Hebrews is an attempt to represent the Tabernacle as it is described in Scripture. It becomes less likely, then, that the author's purpose was to offset the Flavian propaganda with a triumphal statement of his own. Nevertheless, Aitken is correct about the date of Hebrews and the Roman environment in which it was composed, albeit for a purpose other than the one she envisions.

A post-70 date for Hebrews cannot be ruled out, and there are good reasons to think the sermon was written after the destruction of the Temple. Chief among them are the lack of specific references to the Temple cult in Hebrews and the development of the high-priestly christology, which may have been facilitated by the end of the Jewish priesthood in Jerusalem. In addition to these reasons there is the absence of a Temple in the new

Jerusalem in Hebrews. This last detail is similar to what one finds in Rev 21:22. Hebrews rather focuses on the heavenly sanctuary where the singular High Priest, Christ, serves.

Yet another reason for seriously considering a post-70 date for the composition of Hebrews is the way it complements Mark's gospel. Hebrews can be viewed as a development of the christological tradition of the Roman churches as articulated in the Gospel of Mark. Mark's emphasis on the Passion of Christ runs throughout his gospel and may have determined why he ended his gospel on a note of fear (Mark 16:8). In its portrayal of the suffering and death of Christ, Hebrews acknowledges the Markan stress on Jesus' suffering, characterized as an agony with prayers, supplication, loud cries, and tears (Mark 14:33-35; 15:34; Heb 5:7-8). Moreover, Jesus' self-offering as High Priest is completed when he brings his own blood into the heavenly sanctuary (Heb 9:12). Like Mark, Hebrews understands Christ's death as a redemption (*lytron*: Mark 10:45; *lytrōsis*: Heb 9:12). Hebrews, however, proclaims the exaltation of Christ and his session at the right hand of God at the moment when he made purification for sins by means of his death (Heb 1:3). Thus it goes beyond the Markan presentation of Jesus, which ends with the notice of the empty tomb.

Raymond E. Brown catalogued the similarities between Mark and Hebrews on the matter of Jesus' suffering. Curiously, he claimed that Hebrews was not dependent on any of the canonical gospels (*The Death of the Messiah: From Gethsemane to the Grave.* 2 vols. [New York: Doubleday, 1994] 1:225, 227, 229, 234), even though he favors a date in the 80s (*An Introduction to the New Testament.* ABRL. [New York: Doubleday, 1997] 697). He notes in particular the use of *peirasmos*, "test," in Mark 14:38 and *peirazein*, "to test," in Heb 4:15; the fact that Mark's Jesus claims that God has the power to remove the cup from him (Mark 14:36; Heb 5:7); the way Jesus faces his death alone and feeling apparently abandoned (Mark 15:34; Heb 5:8); the notice that he died outside of Jerusalem (Mark 15:20; Heb 13:11-13); the variant reading of Codex Bezae for Mark 15:34, where "abandon" is replaced by "revile" (Heb 13:13; cf. 10:33; 11:26); and the traditions of the Temple veil in Mark 15:38 and Heb 6:19-20 and 10:19-20 (ibid. 1:26, 124, 231; 2:1057, 1107). Like Brown (ibid. 232), Craig Koester believes that biblical traditions of prayer as found in Psalm 116 (LXX: 114 and 115) may serve as a better source for Heb 5:7. The language of the psalm cannot be related any more precisely to Hebrews than can the language of Mark's gospel, apart from the use of *eisakouein*, "to hear" (Ps 114:1a), *deēsis*, "prayer" (Ps 114:1b; note that Hebrews adds *hikēteria* for "supplication"), and *dakruōn*, "tears" (Ps 114:8b).

In addition to these places where the description of Jesus' suffering in Hebrews seems to presuppose Mark's portrayal of his suffering and death, there are other apparent points of contact between the two Roman documents. Hebrews 12:25-29 may be linked to Mark 13:5, 9, 23, 25, 33 in the use of the imperative *blepete*, "see that," and the verb *saleuein*, "to shake" (see the Interpretation below at 12:25-29). There is also a certain affinity between Hebrews and Mark for some of the ideas associated with "tribulation" and "falling away," notably in the Parable of the Sower. Both refer to "land," *gē* (Mark 4:5, 8, 20; Heb 6:7), "thorns," *akantha* (Mark 4:7, 18; Heb 6:8), and "producing," *pherō/ekpherō* (Mark 4:8; Heb 6:8) (see Incigneri, *The Gospel to the Romans*, 357 n.128). The mention of "scorching," *kaumatizein/kausis* (Mark 4:6; Heb 6:8) is likewise found in both texts.

Given the number of possible points of contact between the Gospel of Mark and Hebrews it seems reasonable to assume that the author of Hebrews knew some form of Mark's gospel. It is possible, too, that the author understood his own christology to complement or develop some of the aspects of the basic Markan christology. One has to wonder also whether the later addition of Mark 16:19-20, with its reference to the session of Christ at the right hand of God, as well as the mention of the "confirmation of the message" by "signs," was actually influenced by the proclamation of the exaltation of Christ (10:12) and the claim of God's confirmation of the message by "signs" in Heb 2:3-4 (see the Interpretation below at 2:5-9). It is quite possible that Hebrews was first influenced by the Gospel of Mark and that the later editor who added Mark's longer ending was influenced by Hebrews.

Commentators who favor a post-70 date for the composition of Hebrews look to the impact the loss of the Temple and the priesthood may have had on the community to which Hebrews was addressed. The fact that Hebrews appears to address a later generation of Christians who are flagging in fervor (3:14; 5:11-14; 6:1-6; 13:7; 12:12) may also indicate the appropriateness of a post-70 date (e.g., Braun, 3; Grässer 1:25; Weiss, 76–77; Pamela M. Eisenbaum, *The Jewish Heroes of Christian History: Hebrews 11 in Literary Context*. SBLDS 156 [Atlanta: Scholars, 1997] 7; idem, "Locating Hebrews within the Literary Landscape of Christian Origins," in Gelardini, ed., *Hebrews: Contemporary Methods—New Insights*, 224–31). Some of these commentators place the date of Hebrews in the 80s or 90s, but given the context of the suffering or persecution the recipients seem to be enduring, it may be preferable to consider a time in the early 70s.

4. AUDIENCE

The few clues Hebrews offers to the identity of its audience point to a second generation of Christians (2:3-4; 13:7) that has suffered in the past (10:32-34) and is undergoing another form of persecution, perhaps not as severe and more along the lines of social dislocation (12:3-6, 12-13). Initially they appear to have made a serious effort at practicing their faith through service of one another (6:9-12). In light of the confidence the author expresses in the audience, it would seem that they had derived some initial benefit from their early instruction (10:34).

Why they are now lagging in their practice is not fully evident, but they appear not to be making the kind of progress the author expects of them (5:11–6:3). Perhaps they are threatened by the dire situation of Jews in Rome after the failure of the First Jewish Revolt and the destruction of the Temple in Jerusalem. Some have even stopped attending the common gathering, perhaps because of their malaise or because they do not want to be associated with an assembly that may be under increased scrutiny from their Roman neighbors after the Jewish war with Rome (10:25). Romans, who knew the origins of Christianity in Judaism, would easily have associated Christians with Jews and treated them with similar disdain. Such treatment need not have taken on the official status of a governmental persecution, and most likely it did not.

Perhaps, as a result of such treatment, the recipients of Hebrews wondered whether remaining Christian was to their advantage or at all worthwhile. In any event, the possibility of apostasy is very real in the sermon (6:4-8; 10:26-31). Exhortations to "hold fast" (4:14; 10:23) attempt to shore up the faith of the recipients so that they do not "drift away" (2:1). The presentation of the example of biblical figures who have endured hardship and suffering seems also to be intended to bolster the faith of those who are flagging in their practice (11:1-40).

There is no way to tell what the makeup of the audience of Hebrews is. Roman Christianity had been largely Jewish in its inception, but an increasing Gentile population became part of it after Claudius had expelled some Jewish Christians from Rome in 49 C.E. (James C. Walters, "Romans, Jews and Christians: The Impact of the Romans on Jewish/Christian Relations in First Century Rome," in Donfried and Richardson, eds., *Judaism and Christianity in First-Century Rome*, 175–95). By the time Paul wrote Romans, Jewish Christians were again more present in Roman Christian house churches. It was common in the past to assume that the audience was Jewish Christian because of the sermon's prescript, "To the Hebrews." Often, in view of that understanding, the situation of the audience was taken to be that some of its members were no longer confident in the atoning death of Christ and so were contemplating a return to Judaism. This, then, would have been the author's purpose in exhorting his listeners not to apostasize and to stay the course (Bruce, 382; Ellingworth, 78–80; Barnabas Lindars, *The Theology of the Letter to the Hebrews* [Cambridge: Cambridge University Press, 1991] 4–15; William R. G. Loader, *Sohn und Hoherpriester: Eine traditionsgeschichtliche Untersuchung zur Christologie des Hebräerbriefes*. WMANT 53 [Neukirchen-Vluyn: Neukirchener, 1981] 258; Spicq 1:5–8). This hypothesis is questionable in light of the evidence from Hebrews itself, which does not suggest that its readers are contemplating a return to Judaism. Any arguments in Hebrews that rely on a comparison with Judaism are confined to select scriptural texts from the LXX. Since the comparisons with Judaism deal mostly with its ritual and priesthood, and since there is nothing really to tie those comparisons to actual Jewish practice at the time Hebrews was written, the sermon is probably not directed to a group of Jewish Christians who wish to return to their synagogue(s).

The quality of Greek composition of Hebrews and the high literary level of the sermon suggest that the individuals who received it were educated. In that case they may have been of a higher social standing than some other Roman Christians (James S. Jeffers, "Jewish and Christian Families in First Century Rome," in Donfried and Richardson, eds., *Judaism and Christianity in First-Century Rome*, 128–50). Other than that slim bit of evidence, there is really nothing else in the sermon to indicate the social makeup of the audience.

Regarding the organization of the community the evidence is equally thin. They have had past "leaders" (13:7) and have present ones (13:17). Presumably there were teachers, since there is reference to their initial instruction (6:1-2). One might assume, too, that there were preachers in the community since the author of Hebrews seems to represent that office in the composition of his sermon. The author, of course, may be a teacher if the teaching/preaching functions were combined. There is no mention of apostles, prophets, bishops, presbyters, or deacons. Since the Roman Christians seem to have been grouped in a number of house churches without central organization, it is likely that Hebrews was addressed to one of those house churches. Whether the sermon had a wider circulation in Rome cannot be determined. Certainly it was known by Clement, who referred to it in his own writing ca. 96 C.E.

5. GENRE

Hebrews eludes easy classification as an example of a particular genre because of the anomalies of literary form that beset it. Lacking an epistolary salutation and thanksgiving, which most NT letters contain, Hebrews does not appear to be a letter. Although it does have an epistolary postscript, not every commentator has been confident that it was part of the original document. The issue is further compounded by the traditional placement of Hebrews among the letters of Paul in the canon. In its transmitted form Hebrews appears to be more of an essay or a treatise than a letter. Consequently it is easier to describe Hebrews than to classify it.

a. *Letter/Epistle*

From an early date Hebrews was included in collections of Pauline letters. Formally, however, it does not easily fit within the form of a letter. The most obvious reason is the opening, which lacks the standard elements of a letter: a salutation along with the names of the sender and recipients and a thanksgiving. The title "To the Hebrews" is found in some early manuscripts of Hebrews, as a superscription, but it may not have been part of the original sermon (Koester, 172). To complicate matters, Hebrews does conclude like a typical letter, which frequently ends with some kind of closing remarks, benediction, and farewell. It is the opposite of James, which begins like a letter but does not end like one. Then again there is 1 John, which neither begins nor ends like a letter. All other NT letters have these opening and concluding elements. So the problem of assigning the letter form to Hebrews derives from the discrepancy between its opening and the closing.

Through the years scholars have tried to offer suggestions that might overcome the problem of defining the genre of Hebrews and place it among other New Testament letters. So, for example, a few have claimed that the epistolary prescript has been lost, while others have challenged the authenticity of the epistolary conclusion. Adolf Deissmann made the distinction between a letter and an epistle. Although he treated Hebrews as an epistle, hence a literary artistic letter, he claimed that it might just as easily have been an oration or a diatribe (Deissmann, *Light from the Ancient East* [London: Hodder and Stoughton, 1910] 244). More substantial defenses of Hebrews as an epistle note the inclusion of expository and hortatory sections in the body of Hebrews that are typical of epistles (Spicq 1:21–22). Some commentators argue that the fact that Hebrews was sent to a concrete community indicates that it was meant to function in some way as a letter. So even if it does not contain all the formal characteristics of a letter, the epistolary elements it replicates in chapter 13 should be seen to contribute to its function as a letter (Ellingworth, 62; Lindars, *Theology*, 6–7, Spicq 1:21–22). John Dunnill designated Hebrews an "encyclical letter" because he identified in it a mixture of personal and general elements, which he believes is characteristic of NT encyclicals (*Covenant and Sacrifice in the Letter to the Hebrews*. SNTSMS 75 [Cambridge: Cambridge University Press, 1992] 22).

b. *Homily*

The work of Hartwig Thyen on the form of the Jewish-Hellenistic synagogue homily opened up a new area of genre studies in the study of Hebrews (*Der Stil des jüdisch-hellenistischen Homilie.* FRLANT 47 [Göttingen: Vandenhoeck & Ruprecht, 1955]). Thyen found examples in Philo's commentary on Genesis, *1 Clement*, 4 Maccabees, Stephen's speech in Acts 7, *Barnabas*,

Hermas, and the Wisdom of Solomon. He identified in Hebrews so many of the characteristics of the diaspora synagogue homily, as he reconstructed it from Jewish sources, that he actually claimed Hebrews was "the only example of a completely preserved homily" (ibid. 106). Those characteristics include homiletic language marked by a communal tone, the use of the LXX as a source, the introduction of scriptural citations with rhetorical questions, and the use of paraenesis and exhortation.

Thyen's work was well received by some scholars (Braun, 1; Erich Grässer, "Der Hebräerbrief 1938–1963," *TRu* 30 [1964] 153; Albert Vanhoye, *Homilie für haltbedürftige Christen: Struktur und Botschaft des Hebräerbriefes* [Regensburg: Pustet, 1981] 11; Michel, 24). Others, however, thought the category of sermon or homily was too vague and ill-defined to apply to Hebrews with certitude (Helmut Koester, *Introduction to the New Testament*, vol. 2: *History and Literature of Early Christianity* [New York and Berlin: DeGruyter, 1982] 273; Karl P. Donfried, *The Setting of Second Clement in Early Christianity*. NovTSup 38 [Leiden: Brill, 1974] 26).

c. *Exhortation*

By its own description in 13:22, Hebrews is "a word of exhortation." Judging from the highly paraenetic nature of the book, that is a rather accurate description. The term "a word of exhortation" occurs elsewhere in the NT in Acts 13:15, where Paul and Barnabas visit the synagogue in Antioch of Pisidia and are invited by the officials to offer a word of exhortation, if they have one, after the reading from the Law and the prophets. This example associates "a word of exhortation" very closely with a synagogue homily, and one wonders whether a distinction between the two can be drawn. It must be noted, however, that Hebrews is more than just exhortation. The paraenesis (hortatory material) of Hebrews is integrated into the overall argument of the book. The hortatory sections in Hebrews usually alternate with expository sections, and they are designed to function in relation to the exposition of the main argument. Therefore one has to wonder if the category of homily or exhortation is capable of accurately describing the genre of Hebrews.

In response to the criticism of Thyen's thesis as too vague, the challenge of defining Hebrews as a homily or exhortation was met by a fresh generation of studies that sought to vindicate the essence of Thyen's thesis. Lawrence Wills, for example, undertook a serious study that used the text of Acts 13 to demonstrate the consistent features of an oral sermon, which he labeled "a word of exhortation" ("The Form of the Sermon in Hellenistic Judaism and Early Christianity," *HTR* 77 [1984] 277–99). He attempted to specify the distinction between the vague categories of synagogue homily and "word of exhortation." The peculiarities of the genre are evident in

Acts 13:16-41, where they are discerned in a three-part structure consisting of (a) exempla, (b) conclusions drawn from the exempla and applied to the audience, and (c) exhortation. In Acts 13, Luke begins with biblical examples drawn from the history of Israel, then he concludes to the application of the salvation promised to the ancestors now to the audience Paul addresses and ends with an exhortation that takes the form of a warning drawn from Hab 1:5 (ibid. 278–79). Simply put, then, this oral sermon proceeds from example to conclusion to exhortation, a pattern Wills finds in many early Christian documents, notably Hebrews. Several commentators agree that Hebrews is a sermon in the style of a synagogue homily (e.g., Attridge, 14; Lane, 1:lxxv; Weiss, 40).

Recently, Gabriella Gelardini has maintained that not only is Hebrews a synagogue homily; it is a particular type of synagogue homily that was prescribed for part of the Palestinian Triennial Cycle, in which the Torah was read continuously over three years ("Hebrews, an Ancient Synagogue Homily for Tisha be-Av: Its Function, Its Basis, Its Theological Interpretation," in eadem, ed., *Hebrews: Contemporary Methods—New Insights*, 107–27). Gelardini's analysis of Hebrews as a synagogue homily in the context of a sabbath gathering is indeed interesting and suggestive. The evidence she presents, however, is drawn primarily from the Babylonian Talmud and the Mishnah and is rather late in relation to the dating of Hebrews. Hebrews certainly does appear to be an exhortation or a homily of some sort, but to claim that it is a synagogue homily for Tisha be-Av, as Gelardini does, may be an exercise in overdetermination.

d. *Midrash*

Commentators have called attention to midrashic elements in Hebrews and have suggested that certain passages of the sermon are themselves *midrashim*. By midrash they mean a method of Jewish scriptural exegesis that was common in rabbinic Judaism. In its origin the term "midrash" did not refer to a distinct literary form but rather to a marginal gloss or explanatory note on some part of a scriptural text. In its most general sense in rabbinic Judaism midrash is a form of study directed to a particular question or issue. It is therefore an actualization of the biblical text, applied to a particular situation that occasioned it. A common feature of midrash is the citation of one or more biblical texts.

George W. Buchanan maintained that the first twelve chapters of Hebrews are a homiletic midrash on Ps 110 (*To the Hebrews*. AB 36 [Garden City, NY: Doubleday, 1972] xxi–xxii). His classification has not been widely adopted by later commentators (Ellingworth, 61). Elke Tönges sees Hebrews as a "Jesus Midrash," which means that although the author of Hebrews employs a Jewish method of scriptural interpretation, his midrashic exposition is distinct from Jewish midrash because it is christological ("The Epistle to the Hebrews as a 'Jesus-Midrash,'" in Gelardini, ed., *Hebrews: Contemporary Methods—New Insights*, 89–105). Tönges acknowledges that the biggest obstacles to her hypothesis are a lack of documentary evidence to support this kind of midrash within a synagogue worship service and the lack of conformity of Hebrews to the later midrashic form of a homily. Consequently, her conclusion is tentative: if Hebrews is a Jesus-midrash, it may possibly be a version of a homiletic form that originated in a first-century Hellenistic synagogue service (ibid. 103–104).

The suggestions by Gelardini and Tönges make valuable contributions to a more precise definition of the genre of Hebrews. It would seem, however, that much more work on the synagogue homily needs to be done before one can comfortably classify Hebrews as an example of that genre and locate its *Sitz im Leben* within a synagogue worship service. Nevertheless, Hebrews may be classified as some kind of homily or sermon, though perhaps not specifically one whose *Sitz im Leben* was a synagogue. It may represent a homily that was written or delivered to a Christian house church in Rome, for a group made up mostly of Gentile Christians. Such a homily, characterized by a fair amount of hortatory material, would fit the author's designation of Hebrews as a "word of exhortation" (13:22).

6. STRUCTURE

The structure of Hebrews continues to be an unsettled issue, and one that is highly complicated by the variety of proposals that have been made over the years. For the most part the suggestions fall into two categories: thematic and non-thematic (Attridge, 14–15). Albert Vanhoye labels these categories "conceptual" and "literary" (*La Structure Littéraire de L'Épître aux Hebreux* [Paris: Desclée de Brouwer, 1963] 11–32).

(a) Thematic Structure: A typical thematic structure divides Hebrews into blocks according to a theme identified within these blocks by the commentator. Philip E. Hughes (*Hebrews*, 3–4), for example, divides Hebrews into six parts, with the superiority of Christ the main theme of the entire work: (I) Christ superior to the prophets (1:1-3); (II) Christ superior to the angels (1:4–2:18); (III) Christ superior to Moses (3:1–4:13); (IV) Christ superior to Aaron (4:14–10:18); (V) Christ superior as a new and living Way (10:19–12:29); (VI) Concluding Exhortations, Requests, Greetings (13:1-25).

The problem with thematic structure is that it is very subjective, depending on how well a given commentator can identify the theme in a particular section of the book. For this reason thematic outlines vary quite a bit one from the other, making it very difficult indeed to make structural sense out of Hebrews. The reader is apt to question whether the theme is actually present in the sermon or whether the commentator has read the theme into it. As Attridge notes, thematic approaches often concentrate only on certain sections of Hebrews and do not necessarily deal with the letter in its entirety. Frequently they emphasize the expository sections, giving the impression that the work is largely dogmatic (Attridge, 14). George H. Guthrie points out rightly that thematic approaches are not altogether flawed and do have the virtue of emphasizing the relationship between structure and content (*The Structure of Hebrews: A Textlinguistic Analysis*. NovTSup 73 [Leiden: Brill, 1994] 28).

(b) *Non-Thematic Structure:* One way of overcoming some of the limitations of thematic organizations of Hebrews is to take a non-thematic approach, which looks more at the language of the sermon and analyzes it according to principles of literary, rhetorical, or linguistic criticism. In the last forty years this approach has dominated structural studies of Hebrews. Perhaps the best known literary analysis is Albert Vanhoye's.

Literary analysis attends to the literary features of a text, such as the use of distinctive vocabulary, transitions from one section to another, standard ancient literary techniques like *inclusio*, in which a section begins and ends with similar words, grammatical devices, or expressions, or chiasm, in which elements of a text are arranged in reverse parallel form around a central idea. Internal allusions and repetition are other literary features that may give some clue to the author's intended organization of a text.

Vanhoye, for example, paid much attention to the use of hook words (*mots crochets*; see Léon Vaganay, "Le plan de l'épître aux Hébreux," in *Mémorial Lagrange* [Paris: Gabalda, 1940] 269–77), *inclusio*, and chiasm. "Angel" in 1:4 and 1:5, "faithful" in 2:17 and 3:2, and "high priest" in 4:14-16 and 5:1-2 are examples of hook words that demarcate and connect sections of the sermon. Hebrews uses *inclusio* often, and one clear example comes in the framing of the unit from 7:1-10 where the name Melchizedek occurs in v. 1 and v. 10. Hebrews 13:14 is arranged as a chiasm, helping the author to compare present earthly existence with future heavenly existence:

> For here we have no lasting city,
>> but we are seeking the city which is to come.

In the form of a Greek chi (X), the elements are paralleled in reverse order, with the noun "city" as the central idea. What the readers now have, an earthly city, is compared with what they seek, a heavenly city. The common notion of the city anchors the author's attempt to show what is transient and what is permanent. On the basis of literary features such as these

Vanhoye assembled an elaborate five-part structure for Hebrews arranged concentrically around the central section from 5:11–10:39, which deals with sacrifice and the perfection of Jesus as High Priest. Thus he was able to map out the following scheme (Vanhoye, *Structure*, 85):

Division		Subject	Dominant Genre	Corresponding Section
a.	1:1-4	Introduction		z.
I.	1:5–2:18	The name superior to the angels'	Exposition	V.
II.	A. 3:1–4:14	Faithful Jesus	Paraenesis	IV. B.
	B. 4:15–5:10	Jesus the compassionate High Priest	Exposition	IV. A.
III.	p. 5:11–6:20	Preliminary exhortation: Jesus, the High Priest	Paraenesis	III. f.
	A. 7:1-28	According to the order of Melchizedek	Exposition	III. C.
	B. 8:1–9:28	Perfected	Exposition	Center
	C. 10:1-18	Cause of eternal salvation	Exposition	III. A.
	f. 10:19-39	Final exhortation	Paraenesis	III. p.
IV.	A. 11:1-40	The faith of the ancients	Exposition	II. B.
	B. 12:1-13	The necessary endurance	Paraenesis	II. A.
V.	12:14–13:19	The peaceful fruit of justice	Paraenesis	I.
z.	13:21-25	Conclusion		a.

Although Vanhoye's proposal has been criticized by some (see James Swetnam, "Form and Content in Hebrews 1–6," *Bib* 53 [1972] 368–85; "Form and Content in Hebrews 7–13," *Bib* 55 [1974] 333–48; Koester, 83–86), other commentators have adopted his basic scheme while trying to improve on it (see Attridge, 17–20). Attridge is correct to point out that the problem of finding the structure of Hebrews stems from the fact that it is such a literarily rich document, containing many structural signs, that arranging them in some coherent scheme is very difficult. Any attempt at a structural arrangement usually results in providing only part of the puzzle (ibid. 16).

Other non-thematic structural proposals have looked to ancient rhetoric for clues. These organize individual units of the sermon or its entirety into a coherent rhetorical pattern based on the elements of an ancient speech. Rhetorical handbooks from antiquity play a role in identifying the major divisions of a speech: (1) *proemium* or *exordium*, (2) *narratio* with *propositio*, (3) *argumentatio* with *probatio* and *refutatio*, (4) *peroratio*, and (5) *postscriptum*

(Cicero, *On Invention* 1.1-109). But even here commentators do not agree on what belongs in any of these divisions, nor do they agree on exactly what type of rhetoric Hebrews is. Is it epeideictic (expository) rhetoric, or is it deliberative (persuasive) rhetoric? Or is it a combination of both?

Craig Koester finds a rhetorical structure for Hebrews satisfying because he believes the author's argument is more linear than circular. His structural scheme for Hebrews is as follows (*Hebrews*, 84–85):

I. Exordium   (1:1–2:4)

II. Proposition   (2:5-9)

III. Arguments   (2:10–12:27)

    A. First Series   (2:10–6:20)
        1. Argument: Jesus received into glory through faithful suffering—a way others are called to follow (2:10–5:10)
        2. Transitional Digression: Warning and Encouragement (5:11–6:20)

    B. Second Series   (7:1–10:39)
        1. Argument: Jesus' suffering is the sacrifice that enables others to approach God (7:1–10:25)
        2. Transitional Digression: Warning and Encouragement (10:26-39)

    C. Third Series   (11:1–12:27)
        1. Argument: God's people persevere through suffering to glory by faith (11:1–12:24)
        2. Transitional Digression: Warning and Encouragement (12:25-27)

IV. Peroration   (12:28–13:21)

V. Epistolary Postscript   (13:22-25)

This structure is clean and accounts for all the sections of Hebrews in a coherent way. One quickly sees, however, that it does not conform exactly to the divisions of an ancient speech. Also, by locating the paraenetic sections under the heading "transitional digression" Koester, like previous commentators, favors the expository sections over the paraenesis. One advantage to Koester's structural arrangement is that it shows how the sermon's core is made up of three series of arguments that match the example of Jesus' suffering in the first series with the readers' suffering in the third. The second series of arguments provides the rationale for making that connection between the two. Consequently, the structure of the sermon helps the author to achieve his goal in preaching to the extent that it helps the readers to identify with Jesus.

More recent structural analysis has looked to "linguistic discourse" analysis, or "text-linguistic" analysis. George Guthrie prefers a "text-linguistic" or a "discourse" analysis, in part because it can incorporate some of the methodology of rhetorical and literary analysis. The work as a whole is understood to be a "discourse," whereas an individual part contributing to the whole is called an "embedded discourse." The "embedded discourse" is composed of smaller units called "paragraphs." "Paragraphs" are made up of "cola," at which level the individual words, grammar, and style of the author function. "Text-linguistic" analysis tries to understand the relationships between the sections of a given discourse by first examining each "colon" so that each of the "paragraphs" can be understood for how it relates to the entire "discourse." It is the "paragraphs" that express the author's meaning, and so the "text" can only be understood by grasping the significance of the relationship between the "paragraphs" that make it up (Guthrie, *Structure*, 46–48). Guthrie's structure falls into two main parts: 1:5–4:13, and 4:14–13:19, with the Exordium (1:1-4), the Benediction (13:20-21), and the Conclusion (13:22-25) framing the overall arrangement. (For a fuller schematic outline showing the "embedded discourses" see Guthrie, *Structure*, 144.)

This commentary favors a five-part structure of Hebrews that modifies Vanhoye's proposal. Following Swetnam's suggestion that paraenetic sections come more naturally after expository sections in Hebrews ("Form and Content," 385), the structure of the sermon is arranged thus:

> 1:1-4   Exordium

I. Jesus, Son Crowned with Glory as a Result of His Suffering and Death (1:5–2:18)

II. Jesus, Apostle and High Priest: A Model of Faith and Hope (3:1–6:20)

III. The Message for the Mature: Another Priest Like Melchizedek (7:1–10:39)

IV. Heroic Faith and the Discipline of Suffering (11:1–12:13)

V. Warnings and Exhortations (12:14–13:19)

> 13:20-25   Postscript

7. ESCHATOLOGY

Hebrews employs a combination of realized and future eschatology to achieve its purpose of impressing on its readers the full effect of the salvific work of Christ the High Priest. Having been himself perfected through suffering, Christ became the source of eternal salvation for others (5:9), who are brought to glory along with him (2:10). Consequently, eschatology and soteriology are closely related in the sermon (Attridge, 28). As the pioneer of salvation (2:10), Jesus has passed through the heavens (4:14) to enter the heavenly sanctuary as a forerunner (6:20) who, now in exaltation (1:13; 7:26; 8:1; 12:2), has made it possible for others to receive an eternal inheritance (9:15) as well. The eschatological pattern established in his death, resurrection, and exaltation can be replicated for those who follow him (10:19-22). As the readers run their own race they must fix their gaze on the one who has gone before them (12:2).

From the beginning of the sermon it is clear that the author understands the end times to have been inaugurated, as he addresses his audience "in these last days" (Heb 1:2). This designation is contrasted to the former times (1:1), the time of previous generations (3:16). It is equally clear that the final destination of the audience has not yet been reached, as they journey toward their ultimate goal to find "rest" (Heb 4:1, 6, 9, 11). The location of that rest is a present reality, since the readers have already come to a heavenly city (Heb 12:22) and are receiving an unshakeable kingdom (Heb 12:28). Still, the author proclaims that they have no lasting city here, but look forward to the future city that is to come (11:16; 13:14). Spanning the tension of present and future is "today" (Heb 3:13-15; 4:7), the opportune time to prepare for the ultimate destination.

The eschatological challenge for the readers of Hebrews is to live in the present with an eye to the future. They have already "tasted" the "heavenly gift," the "goodness of the word of God," and "powers of the age to come" (6:4-5). Proleptically they have already been sanctified by Christ's once for all self-offering (10:14), and still they have yet to realize the full assurance of hope to the very end (6:11), as they must await the day when Christ will return to save them (9:28). Since, however, they live in an interim period when not all of Christ's enemies have been put under his feet (10:13), the fullness of his salvific work will not be realized until he returns (10:37-39). To this end the author exhorts his readers to hold fast to their confession (3:6; 4:14; 10:19-22), to approach God with confidence (4:16; 10:19, 22), and to avoid sin that will result in a judgment (6:4-8; 12:14-17, 25-29; 10:26-31).

The problem for the modern reader of Hebrews is to discern the relationship of the three eras addressed in the sermon's eschatology. In particular the ambiguity created by the coincidence of present and future allows for the possibility of confusion over the sermon's eschatological teaching. The tension between present and future corresponds to a tension between earth and heaven. It would be fine if those living in the present earthly realm were confined to that sphere. A problem arises when one tries to understand how the once for all self-offering of Christ in history has inaugurated the future age in the heavenly realm, so that those living in the present earthly realm are already benefiting from the effects of his salvific death, resurrection, and exaltation. According to Hebrews they transcend the present to share in the benefits of the future. The present age may ultimately be redeemed, but those living in it must await final salvation with the return of Christ.

8. CONSCIENCE/CONSCIOUSNESS OF SIN IN HEBREWS

Hebrews expresses the efficacious work of the sacrificial death of Christ as the "perfection of the conscience," *syneidēsis*, which alone enables the worshiper to have access to God. Thus the once for all self-offering of Christ effected what could not be accomplished under the old covenant and through the ritual acts of the Levitical priesthood (7:11). "Perfection" in this sense is a hallmark of the new covenant written on the heart, and captures the sense of interior purification, more complete than any purification sought under the old covenant. The stress on the once for all nature of Christ's own perfection, which is the basis for the perfection of believers, indicates that in one sense the purification of the conscience has already happened. Therefore nothing more need be done to bring about this kind of purification.

Still, one finds warnings against sinning and reminders of the possibility of "falling away" throughout the sermon. These warnings indicate that the author does not see the purification of the conscience of the worshiper as something that precludes the possibility of further sinning. Rather, what was won in the purification of the conscience was freedom from the guilt of one's past sins; this freedom, in turn, facilitated the ability of the believer to worship God in full confidence. Christ has opened the way for the worshiper to approach the throne of God, whose grace strengthens the heart. Whereas Christ, as High Priest, has removed the consciousness of sin by purifying the conscience of guilt, the reader is not freed of sin in the final sense until the end of time.

Hebrews 9:9 makes it clear that sacrifices under the old covenant could not perfect the conscience of the worshiper. In contrast with that assertion stands 9:14 with its promise that the blood of Christ will purify the conscience of the readers from dead works. Again at 10:2 the author refers to the "conscience," this time as the "consciousness of sin," which theoretically should not have existed were the sacrifices of the Levitical system able to cleanse the worshiper. The opposite seems to be true: repetitive sacrifices stand as a reminder of sin (10:3). Under the new covenant, the sacrifice of Christ effected the purification that was unattainable under the old covenant and made possible the access to God that worshipers now have, because through the agency of his blood they have been sprinkled clean from an evil conscience and washed with pure water (10:22).

The teaching of Hebrews, then, is that through baptism the believer's consciousness of past sins, the evil conscience, is removed (10:2, 14, 17-18, 22). This removal of guilt was secured by the death of Christ, whose blood atoned for all sin, once for all. The realization of the complete nature of Christ's atoning death substantiates the author's claim in 10:26 that there no longer remains a sacrifice for sins, something he has already demonstrated in his discussion of the inability of the Levitical system to perfect the conscience of the worshiper.

Hebrews thus emphasizes that atonement for sin was accomplished once for all in the sacrificial death of Christ (1:3; 2:17; 7:27; 9:26, 28; 10:10, 12; 13:12). Yet it warns of the possibility of sin after one's initial repentance (3:13; 10:26) and knows of the temptation to sin (4:15). This possibility applies especially to the sin of apostasy (6:6). The purification of the conscience of the worshiper, then, does not preclude the possibility of sinning again. Still, under the new covenant sin will not be regarded by God, as it had been under the old (8:12; 10:6, 17). The critical distinction is that under the new covenant sins are forgiven without repeated atoning sacrifices (10:18), and sin can be avoided through endurance (12:1, 4; 13:13).

9. THE PRIESTHOOD OF CHRIST AND THE MINISTERIAL PRIESTHOOD

The christology of Hebrews is unique for the way it introduces the notion of Christ as High Priest. By portraying Jesus as a priest the author stresses a new means of access to God through the mediation of Christ, who offers himself as an atoning sacrifice. It is clear in Hebrews that Christ is the singular High Priest. Unlike the Levitical priests, who were many in a succession of one after the other, Christ is the eternal High Priest whose sacrifice is once for all. Consistent with this christology, Hebrews does not attribute the title of priest to any Christian minister. If there are such in the community to which Hebrews was addressed, they are called "leaders." Albert Vanhoye makes this point especially when he distinguishes Hebrews from 1 Peter and Revelation, where the title "priest" is extended to the baptized collectively (*Old Testament Priests and the New Priest* [Petersham, MA: St. Bede's Publications, 1986] 235, 311–18).

In Roman Catholicism, Hebrews has been enlisted to ground the ministerial priesthood of bishops, priests, and deacons. The Council of Trent cited Heb 7:12 as the foundation for a new eternal priesthood, a change from the old (*De Sacramento Ordinis*, 1). The Second Vatican Council made an explicit connection between the eternal priesthood of Christ (Heb 5:1-10; 7:24; 9:11-28) and the ministerial priesthood of those who are consecrated in his image in the sacrament of Orders (*Lumen gentium*, 28). Elsewhere

Vatican II alluded to Hebrews in support of the ministerial priesthood (*Presbyterorum ordinis*, 3) and the priesthood shared by all the baptized (*Lumen gentium*, 10).

Whether Hebrews makes a connection between the high priesthood of Christ and ministerial priesthood might be better established were there clear evidence in the sermon concerning the celebration of the Lord's Supper. Some commentators have taken the references in 6:4 to the heavenly gift that had been "tasted," in 9:2 to the "bread of the Presence" and the "table," and other references to the "new covenant" (8:8, 13; 9:15; 12:24) to be speaking of the Eucharist (Paul Andriessen, "L'Eucharistie dans l'Épître aux Hébreux," *NRTh* [1972] 269–77). James Swetnam, in particular, has argued consistently for the sermon's interest in the Eucharist and has made a link between Christ as High Priest and Christian ministerial priesthood (see "Christology and the Eucharist in the Epistle to the Hebrews," *Bib* 70 [1989] 74–95; "'The Greater and More Perfect Tent': A Contribution to the Discussion of Hebrews 9,11," *Bib* 47 [1966] 91–106). The consensus of commentators still maintains, however, that Hebrews is not specifically concerned with the Christian Eucharist (see Ronald Williamson, "The Eucharist and the Epistle to the Hebrews," *NTS* [1975] 300–12).

In the absence of any explicit mention of ministerial priesthood one is hard pressed to say exactly how Hebrews would link that institution to the priesthood of Christ. Some fruitful avenues have been explored by John M. Scholer (*Proleptic Priests: Priesthood in the Epistle to the Hebrews.* JSNTSup 49 [Sheffield: Sheffield Academic Press, 1991] 200–207) and John Dunnill (*Covenant and Sacrifice*, 239–60), who highlight the function of Christ's priesthood in Hebrews as effecting "communion" between believers and God. Still their conclusions speak more to a priesthood of believers than to a particular form of ministerial priesthood in Hebrews. Daniel J. Harrington has interestingly observed, however, that studies such as these can provide a context for understanding Christian priesthood and sacrifice as institutions grounded in a reality similar to what Scholer and Dunnill hold for a priesthood of believers, the paschal mystery of Christ. Any form of priesthood, corporate or ministerial, must have as its basis a participation in the salvific effects of Christ's life, death, and resurrection (*What Are They Saying About the Letter to the Hebrews?* [New York and Mahwah, NJ: Paulist, 2005] 87).

10. HEBREWS AND ANTI-SEMITISM

The stress in Hebrews on a "new" and "better" covenant (7:22; 8:6-13; 9:15; 10:16-17, 29; 12:24; 13:20) has contributed to the view that not only has the priesthood and sacrifice of Christ replaced the sacrifices and the priesthood of the "old" covenant, but that Christianity has somehow replaced

Judaism. If the language and intent of Hebrews are not understood properly in the context of its first-century C.E. setting, it could be seen as contributing, at the very least, to "anti-Judaism," if not to "anti-Semitism." If, however, Hebrews is understood as a sermon to a Roman Christian house church, some time after the destruction of the Temple, which had brought an end to the priesthood and sacrifice in Judaism, its words may appear to be somewhat less polemical.

One has to wonder, indeed, whether a portrait of Jesus Christ as a heavenly High Priest could have been drawn by any Christian author as long as the Temple was still standing and its institutions were still in place. For a pastor preaching to a group within Christianity itself, in the wake of the terrible destruction wrought on Jerusalem and its most sacred shrine by the Romans, a group that was doubtless dealing with the effects of the horror inflicted on its parent religion and perhaps some collateral effects of its association with Judaism, the encouragement and consolation Hebrews offers may have a different and less strident ring.

Christianity in the city of Rome seems always to have valued its Jewish roots and to have been stamped by a certain Jewish character. In his letter to the Romans, Paul himself tried to show the close bond Gentile Christians shared with their Jewish brothers and sisters, while stressing that the salvation of Israel was a part of God's plan (Romans 9–11). The "mystery of Israel" might have resonated so deeply in the hearts of Roman Christians that the sufferings of Roman Jews in the aftermath of the failure of the First Revolt may have been felt as if they were their own. Who knows what kinds of questions about God's plan for Israel were raised in their own minds or what kinds of fears for what the Romans were capable of doing to them took up residence in their own hearts? One need not assume, then, that the presentation of Jesus as a heavenly High Priest, ministering in a heavenly sanctuary, had to signify the loss of Judaism itself on top of everything else that had been lost after 70 C.E.

If this scenario rings true, one has to assume first that Hebrews was a sermon written for and delivered to Christians alone. As an in-house document it could not have been intended to make a public and definitive statement on the status of Judaism at the time it was composed. Addressed to a Roman house church, probably dominated by Gentile Christians, it seems intended rather to stress what Christians have in Christ and what is worthwhile holding on to, rather than what Jews had lost in the failure of the First Revolt. The author's logic appears to be so focused on presenting how Christians have access to God through Christ that, in creating the High Priest christology he became so caught up in the comparison with the Levitical priesthood and the Tabernacle that he drew conclusion after conclusion, albeit deliberately, without necessarily intending his composition to be detrimental to Judaism (see Knut Backhaus, *Der Neue Bund und das Werden*

*der Kirche: die Diatheke-Deutung des Hebräerbriefes im Rahmen der frühchrist-
lichen Theologiegeschichte.* NTAbh n.s. 29 [Münster: Aschendorff, 1996] 275–
82). After all, his arguments are all drawn from Jewish Scripture and are
confined to a historical period in the life of Israel before there was a Temple.
Were the author's arguments so constructed because he believed that the
Temple never had any legitimacy, or out of respect for the fact that it was
no longer standing? Were his arguments shaped to show the insufficiency
of an old cultic system, or to address a question in the minds of his listeners
about what kind of access to God was now possible in an age when familiar
means of mediation were no longer available? When he speaks of a new
covenant, which stresses the interior over the exterior, is it because he
wishes to challenge the efficaciousness of the old covenant, or is it because
the disappearance of the external means of the "old" now make interiority
a necessity?

Surely these are impossible questions to answer with certitude, but they
may be able to place Hebrews in a broader context of inclusiveness by trying to show where the "new" is the logical completion of the "old" when
the usual institutions of the "old" are no longer available to accomplish
their intended goals. We simply do not know enough about what kind of
distance there was between Jews and Christians in Rome in the last third
of the first century C.E. In this light it must be remembered that the concept
of a "new" covenant, which Hebrews adopts, came from Jewish Scripture
as well (Jer 31:31-34), a text that speaks more about the renewal of Judaism
than the replacement of it.

Hebrews is a sermon for individuals who are wavering in their faith
and appear to be somewhat diffident about their practice. We may never
know the extent or depth of their malaise or what had brought it about.
What we do know is the remedy the author of Hebrews proposed, a remedy
that places the mediation of Jesus Christ as the heavenly High Priest at the
center of his preaching and promises his listeners that their access to God
is fully available because of what Christ has done on their behalf. Comparison is always based on continuity and discontinuity, so if Hebrews speaks
of the discontinuity between the "old" and "new" covenants, it presupposes
first the continuity between them. Nowhere in the sermon does the author
suggest that what God had done in Christ was done to disadvantage Israel,
and any images of past judgment or notice that previous generations did
not receive the fulfillment of the promises are designed to exhort his Christian listeners to stay on track in order to reach their goal of entering into
God's rest. The author rather believes that Jews and Christians will share
a common destiny in the reception of promises fulfilled (11:39-40).

As Hebrews is silent on the relationship of Jews and Christians in Rome
at the time of its composition, it would be unfortunate if later problems and
divisions between the two groups were retrojected back onto it so as to give

the impression that Roman Christians then were inherently "anti-Jewish" or "anti-Semitic." It would be equally unfortunate if Hebrews were enlisted for an "anti-Semitic" purpose today. Hebrews was written by a Christian for Christians, to help them appreciate the salvation that is theirs in Christ. Any attempt to use it against Jews is inappropriate, unwarranted, and unfounded.

FOR REFERENCE AND FURTHER STUDY

Brändle, Rudolf, and Ekkehard W. Stegemann. "The Formation of the First 'Christian Congregations' in Rome in the Context of the Jewish Congregations," in Karl P. Donfried and Peter Richardson, eds., *Judaism and Christianity in First-Century Rome*. Grand Rapids: Eerdmans, 1998, 117–27.

Bruce, Frederick F. "To the Hebrews: A Document of Roman Christianity," *ANRW* II.25.4. (1987) 3496–3521.

Caragounis, Chrys C. "From Obscurity to Prominence: The Development of the Roman Church between Romans and 1 Clement," in Donfried and Richardson, eds., *Judaism and Christianity in First-Century Rome*. Grand Rapids: Eerdmans, 1998, 245–79.

Isaacs, Marie. *Sacred Space: An Approach to the Theology of the Epistle to the Hebrews.* JSNTSup 73. Sheffield: JSOT Press, 1992.

Kraus, Wolfgang. "Neuere Ansätze in der Exegese des Hebräerbriefes," *VF* 48 (2003) 67–80.

Lampe, Peter. *From Paul to Valentinus: Christians at Rome in the First Two Centuries.* Minneapolis: Fortress Press, 2003.

Schenck, Kenneth. *Understanding the Book of Hebrews: The Story Behind the Sermon.* Louisville: Westminster John Knox, 2003.

Swetnam, James. "On the Imagery and Significance of Hebrews 9:9-10," *CBQ* 28 (1966) 155–73.

_____. "Hebrews 9:2 and the Use of Consistency," *CBQ* 32 (1970) 205–21.

11. GENERAL BIBLIOGRAPHY

1. *Commentaries*

Attridge, Harold W. *The Epistle to the Hebrews: A Commentary on the Epistle to the Hebrews.* Hermeneia. Philadelphia: Fortress Press, 1989.

Bleek, Friedrich. *Der Brief an die Hebräer erläutert durch Einleitung, Übersetzung und fortlaufenden Kommentar.* 3 vols. Berlin: Dümmler, 1828, 1836, 1840.

Braun, Herbert. *An die Hebräer.* HNT 14. Tübingen: Mohr Siebeck, 1984.

Bruce, Frederick F. *The Epistle to the Hebrews.* NICNT. Rev. ed. Grand Rapids: Eerdmans, 1990.

Buchanan, George W. *To the Hebrews: Translation, Comment and Conclusions.* AB 36. Garden City, NY: Doubleday, 1972.

de Silva, David A. *Perseverance in Gratitude: A Socio-Rhetorical Commentary on the Epistle "to the Hebrews."* Grand Rapids: Eerdmans, 2000.

Ellingworth, Paul. *The Epistle to the Hebrews*. NIGTC. Grand Rapids: Eerdmans, 1993.

Gench, Frances T. *Hebrews and James*. Louisville: Westminster John Knox, 1996.

Grässer, Erich. *An die Hebräer*. 3 vols. EKK 17. Zürich: Benziger; Neukirchen-Vluyn: Neukirchener, 1990–97.

Hagner, Donald A. *Encountering the Book of Hebrews: An Exposition*. Grand Rapids: Eerdmans, 2002.

Héring, Jean. *The Epistle to the Hebrews*. London: Epworth, 1970.

Hughes, Philip E. *A Commentary on the Epistle to the Hebrews*. Grand Rapids: Eerdmans, 1977.

Isaacs, Marie E. *Reading Hebrews and James: A Literary and Theological Commentary*. Macon, GA: Smyth and Helwys, 2002.

Koester, Craig R. *Hebrews: A New Translation with Introduction and Commentary*. AB 36. New York: Doubleday, 2001.

Lane, William L. *Hebrews*. 2 vols. WBC. Dallas: Word, 1991.

Long, Thomas G. *Hebrews*. Interpretation. Louisville: Westminster John Knox, 1997.

März, Claus-Peter. *Hebräerbrief*. Die Neue Echter Bibel 16. 2nd ed. Würzburg: Echter, 1990.

Michel, Otto. *Der Brief und die Hebräer*. KEK 13. 6th ed. Göttingen: Vandenhoeck & Ruprecht, 1966.

Montefiore, Hugh. *A Commentary on the Epistle to the Hebrews*. HNTC. New York: Harper & Row, 1964.

Pfitzner, Victor C. *Hebrews*. ANTC. Nashville: Abingdon, 1977.

Spicq, Ceslas. *L'Épître aux Hébreux*. 2 vols. *EBib*. Paris: Gabalda, 1952–53.

⸻. *L'Épître aux Hébreux*. SB. Paris: Gabalda, 1977.

Weiss, Hans-Friedrich. *Der Brief an die Hebräer*. KEK 13. Göttingen: Vandenhoeck & Ruprecht, 1991.

Westcott, Brooke Foss. *The Epistle to the Hebrews*. London: Macmillan, 1892; repr. Grand Rapids: Eerdmans, 1977.

Wright, Nicholas T. *Hebrews for Everyone*. London: S.P.C.K.; Louisville: Westminster John Knox, 2004.

2. *Studies*

Aitken, Ellen Bradshaw. "Portraying the Temple in Stone and Text: The Arch of Titus and the Epistle to the Hebrews," in Gabriella Gelardini, ed., *Hebrews: Contemporary Methods—New Insights*. BINS 75. Leiden and Boston: Brill, 2005, 131–48.

Anderson, Charles P. "The Epistle to the Hebrews and the Pauline Letter Collection," *HTR* 59 (1966) 429–38.

Andriessen, Paul. "L'Eucharistie dans l'Épître aux Hébreux," *NRTh* (1972) 269–77.

Backhaus, Knut. *Der Neue Bund und das Werden der Kirche: die Diatheke-Deutung des Hebräerbriefes im Rahmen der frühchristlichen Theologiegeschichte*. NTAbh n.s. 29. Münster: Aschendorff, 1996.

Bartlet, J. Vallance. "The Riddle of the Epistle to the Hebrews," *Expositor* 5 (1913) 548–51.

Black, David Alan. "Who Wrote Hebrews? The Internal and External Evidence Reexamined," *Faith and Mission* 18 (2001) 3–26.

Brown, J. Vernon. "The Authorship and Circumstances of Hebrews." *BSac* 80 (1923) 505–38.

Brown, Raymond E. *An Introduction to the New Testament*. ABRL. New York: Doubleday, 1997.

_____. *The Death of the Messiah: From Gethsemane to the Grave*. 2 vols. New York: Doubleday, 1994.

Brown, Raymond E., and John P. Meier. *Antioch and Rome: New Testament Cradles of Catholic Christianity*. New York: Paulist, 1984.

Burch, Vacher. *The Epistle to the Hebrews: Its Sources and Its Message*. London: Williams and Norgate, 1936.

Charlesworth, James H. *The Old Testament Pseudepigrapha*. 2 vols. New York: Doubleday, 1983–1985.

Cody, Aelred. *A History of Old Testament Priesthood*. AnBib 35. Rome: Pontifical Biblical Institute, 1969.

_____. *Heavenly Sanctuary and Liturgy in the Epistle to the Hebrews: The Achievement of Salvation in the Epistle's Perspectives*. St. Meinrad, IN: Grail Publications, 1960.

Collins, Raymond F. *First Corinthians*. SP 7. Collegeville, MN: Liturgical Press, 1999.

_____. *I & II Timothy and Titus: A Commentary*. NT Library. Louisville: Westminster John Knox, 2002.

Cosby, Michael R. *The Rhetorical Compositions and Function of Hebrews 11 In Light of Example Lists in Antiquity*. Macon, GA: Mercer, 1988.

D'Angelo, Mary Rose. *Moses in the Letter to the Hebrews*. SBLDS 42. Missoula, MT: Scholars, 1979.

Davies, W. D. "A Note on Josephus, *Antiquities* 15.136," *HTR* 47 (1954) 135–40.

Deissmann, Adolf. *Light from the Ancient East*. London: Hodder and Stoughton, 1910.

de Silva, David A. *Despising Shame: Honor Discourse and Community Maintenance in the Epistle to the Hebrews*. SBLDS 152. Atlanta: Scholars, 1995.

Donahue, John R. "Recent Studies on the Origin of 'Son of Man' in the Gospels," *CBQ* 48 (1986) 484–98.

_____. "Windows and Mirrors: The Setting of Mark's Gospel," *CBQ* 57 (1995) 21–22.

Donfried, Karl P. *The Setting of Second Clement in Early Christianity*. NovTSup 38. Leiden: Brill, 1974.

Dunnill, John. *Covenant and Sacrifice in the Letter to the Hebrews*. SNTSMS 75. Cambridge: Cambridge University Press, 1992.

Eisele, Wilfried. *Ein unerschütterliches Reich: die mittelplatonische Umformung des Parusiegedankens im Hebräerbrief*. Berlin and New York: de Gruyter, 2003.

Eisenbaum, Pamela M. "Locating Hebrews within the Literary Landscape of Christian Origins," in G. Gelardini, ed., *Hebrews: Contemporary Methods—New Insights*. Leiden and Boston: Brill, 2005, 224–31.

_____. *The Jewish Heroes of Christian History: Hebrews 11 in Literary Context*. SBLDS 156. Atlanta: Scholars, 1997.

Elledge, Casey. "Exegetical Styles at Qumran: A Cumulative Index and Commentary," *RevQ* 82 (2004) 165–208.

Elliott, John K. "Is Post-Baptismal Sin Forgivable?" *BT* 28 (1977) 330–32.

————. "When Jesus Was Apart from God: An Examination of Hebrews 2,9," *ExpTim* 83 (1972) 339–41.

Emmrich, Martin. *Pneumatological Concepts in the Epistle to the Hebrews: Amtscharisma, Prophet, and Guide of the Eschatological Exodus.* Lanham, MD: University Press of America, 2003.

Feld, Helmut. "Der Hebräerbrief: Literarische Form, religionsgeschichtlicher Hintergrund, theologische Fragen," *ANRW* II.25.4 (1987) 3522–3601.

Feuillet, André. "Le 'commencement' de l'économie chrétienne d'après He ii.3-4; Mc i.1 et Ac i.1-2," *NTS* 24 (1977–78) 163–74.

Filson, Floyd V. *"Yesterday"; A Study of Hebrews in the Light of Chapter 13.* Naperville, IL: A. R. Allenson, 1967.

Fiore, Benjamin. *The Function of Personal Example in the Socratic and Pastoral Epistles.* AnBib 105. Rome: Pontifical Biblical Institute Press, 1986.

Fitzmyer, Joseph A. *Romans: A New Translation with Introduction and Commentary.* AB 33. New York: Doubleday, 1993.

————. *The Acts of the Apostles: New Translation with Introduction and Commentary.* AB 31. New York: Doubleday, 1998.

————. *The Genesis Apocryphon of Qumran Cave 1 (1Q20): A Commentary.* BibOr 18B. Rome: Pontifical Biblical Institute, 2004.

Frankowski, Janusz. "Early Christian Hymns Recorded in the New Testament: A Reconsideration in Light of Heb 1,3," *BZ* 27 (1983) 183–94.

Fredriksen, Paula. *From Jesus to Christ: The Origins of the New Testament Images of Jesus.* 2nd ed. New Haven: Yale University Press, 2000.

Gelardini, Gabriella. "Hebrews, an Ancient Synagogue Homily for Tisha be-Av: Its Function, Its Basis, Its Theological Interpretation," in eadem, ed., *Hebrews: Contemporary Methods—New Insights.* Leiden and Boston: Brill, 2005, 107–27.

Georgi, Dieter. "Hebrews and the Heritage of Paul," in G. Gelardini, ed., *Hebrews: Contemporary Methods—New Insights.* Leiden and Boston: Brill, 2005, 239–44.

Gheorghita, Radu. *The Role of the Septuagint in Hebrews: An Investigation of Its Influence with Special Consideration to the Use of Hab 2:3-4 in Heb 10:37-38.* WUNT 2nd ser. 160, Tübingen: Mohr Siebeck, 2003.

Gleason, Randall C. "Angels and Eschatology of Heb 1–2," *NTS* 49 (2003) 90–107.

Goulder, Michael D. "Psalm 8 and The Son of Man," *NTS* 48 (2002) 18–29.

Grässer, Erich. "Der Hebräerbrief 1938–1963," *TRu* 30 (1964) 138–236.

Gray, Patrick. *Godly Fear: The Epistle to the Hebrews and Greco-Roman Critiques of Superstition.* SBLAB 16. Atlanta: Society of Biblical Literature, 2003.

Guthrie, George H. "The Case for Apollos as the Author of Hebrews," *Faith and Mission* 18 (2001) 41–56.

————. *The Structure of Hebrews: A Textlinguistic Analysis.* NovTSup 73. Leiden: Brill, 1994.

Hanson, Anthony T. "The Reproach of the Messiah in the Epistle to the Hebrews," *SE* 7 (1982) 231–40.

Harnack, Adolf von. "Probabilia über die Adresse und den Verfasser des Hebräerbriefes," *ZNW* 1 (1900) 16–41.

Harrington, Daniel J. *What Are They Saying About the Letter to the Hebrews?* New York and Mahwah, NJ: Paulist, 2005.

Hay, David M. *Glory at the Right Hand: Psalm 110 in Early Christianity*. SBLMS 18. Nashville: Abingdon, 1973.

Head, Ivan. "Mark as a Roman Document from the Year 69: Testing Martin Hengel's Thesis." *JRH* 28 (2004) 240–59.

Hofius, Otfried. *Der Vorhang vor dem Thron Gottes: Eine exegetisch-religionsgeschichtliche Untersuchung zu Hebräer 6,19f. und 10,19f.* WUNT 14. Tübingen: Mohr Siebeck, 1972.

_____. *Katapausis: Die Vorstellung vom endzeitlichen Ruheort im Hebräerbrief.* WUNT 11. Tübingen: Mohr Siebeck, 1970.

Hoppin, Ruth. *Priscilla's Letter: Finding the Author of the Epistle to the Hebrews*. Fort Bragg, CA: Lost Coast Press, 1997. First published 1997 by Christian Universities Press.

Iersel, Bas van. *The Bible on the Living God*. De Pere, WI: St. Norbert Abbey Press, 1965.

Incigneri, Brian J. *The Gospel to the Romans: The Setting and Rhetoric of Mark's Gospel*. BINS 65. Leiden and Boston: Brill, 2003.

Jaeger, Werner. *Early Christianity and Greek Paideia*. Cambridge, MA: Belknap Press, 1961.

Jeffers, James S. "Jewish and Christian Families in First Century Rome," in Karl P. Donfried and Peter Richardson, eds., *Judaism and Christianity in First-Century Rome*. Grand Rapids: Eerdmans, 1998.

Jones, E. D. "The Authorship of Hebr. xiii," *ExpTim* 46 (1934–35) 562–67.

Käsemann, Ernst. *The Wandering People of God: An Investigation of the Letter to the Hebrews*. Minneapolis: Augsburg, 1984.

Kasteren, J.-P. van. "L'Épilogue Canonique du Second Évangile (Mr. 16, 9-20)," *RB* 11 (1902) 240–55.

Kistemaker, Simon. *Psalm Citations in the Epistle to the Hebrews*. Amsterdam: van Soest, 1961.

_____. "The Authorship of Hebrews," *Faith and Mission* 18 (2001) 57–69.

Klauck, Hans-Josef. "Kirche als Freundesgemeinschaft? Auf Spurensuche im Neuen Testament," *MTZ* 42 (1991) 1–14.

Koester, Helmut. *Introduction to the New Testament*. 2 vols. New York and Berlin: DeGruyter, 1982.

_____. "'Outside the Camp': Hebrews 13:9-14," *HTR* 55 (1962) 299–308.

Lane, William L. "Social Perspectives on Roman Christianity during the Formative Years from Nero to Nerva: Romans, Hebrews, 1 Clement," in Karl P. Donfried and Peter Richardson, eds., *Judaism and Christianity in First-Century Rome*. Grand Rapids: Eerdmans, 1998, 196–244.

Lenker, John Nicholas, ed. *Sermons of Martin Luther*. Vols. 5 and 6. Grand Rapids: Baker Books, 1995.

Lindars, Barnabas. "The Rhetorical Structure of Hebrews," *NTS* 35 (1989) 382–406.

_____. *The Theology of the Letter to the Hebrews*. Cambridge: Cambridge University Press, 1991.

Llewelyn, S. R. *New Documents Illustrating Early Christianity*. Vol. 6. North Ryde, N.S.W.: Ancient History Document Research Centre, Macquarie University, 1992.

Loader, William R. G. *Sohn und Hoherpriester: Eine traditionsgeschichtliche Untersuchung zur Christologie des Hebräerbriefes*. WMANT 53. Neukirchen-Vluyn: Neukirchener, 1981.

Löhr, Hermut. *Umkehr und Sünde im Hebräerbrief*. BZNW 73. Berlin and New York: de Gruyter, 1994.

Malherbe, Abraham J. *Moral Exhortation: A Greco-Roman Sourcebook*. Library of Early Christianity 4. Philadelphia: Westminster, 1986.

_____. *The Cynic Epistles*. SBLSBS 12. Missoula, MT: Scholars, 1977.

_____. *The Letters to the Thessalonians: A New Translation with Introduction and Commentary*. AB 32B. New York: Doubleday, 2000.

Malina, Bruce J. *The New Testament World: Insights from Cultural Anthropology*. Louisville: Westminster John Knox, 1993.

Manson, Thomas W. "The Problem of the Epistle to the Hebrews," *BJRL* 32 (1949–50) 1–17.

Matera, Frank. *Galatians*. SP 9. Collegeville, MN: Liturgical Press, 1992.

Meeks, Wayne A. *The First Urban Christians: The Social World of the Apostle Paul*. New Haven: Yale University Press, 1983.

Meier, John P. "Structure and Theology in Heb 1, 1-14," *Bib* 66 (1985) 168–89.

Metzger, Bruce. *A Textual Commentary on the Greek New Testament: A Companion Volume to the United Bible Societies' Greek New Testament*. 3rd ed. London and New York: United Bible Societies, 1971.

Miller, James C. "Paul and Hebrews: A Comparison of Narrative Worlds," in G. Gelardini, ed., *Hebrews: Contemporary Methods—New Insights*. Leiden and Boston: Brill, 2005, 245–64.

Mitchell, Alan C. "Greet the Friends by Name: New Testament Evidence for the Greco-Roman *Topos* on Friendship," in John T. Fitzgerald, ed., *Greco-Roman Perspectives on Friendship*. SBLRBS 34. Atlanta: Scholars, 1997, 225–62.

_____. "Holding on to Confidence: *PARRHESIA* in Hebrews," in John T. Fitzgerald, ed., *Friendship, Flattery, and Frankness of Speech*. NovTSup 82. Leiden: Brill, 1996, 203–36.

_____. "The Use of *prepein* and Rhetorical Propriety in Hebrews 2:10," *CBQ* 54 (1992) 681–701.

Neyrey, Jerome H. "'Despising the Shame of the Cross,'" *Semeia* 68 (1994) 113–37.

Overbeck, Franz. *Zur Geschichte des Kanons: Zwei Abhandlungen*. Chemnitz: Schmeitzner, 1880.

Peterson, David G. *Hebrews and Perfection: An Examination of the Concept of Perfection in the "Epistle to the Hebrews."* Cambridge: Cambridge University Press, 1982.

Robinson, Donald W. B. "The Literary Structure of Hebrews 1:1-4," *AJBA* 2 (1972) 178–86.

Rose, Christian. *Die Wolke der Zeugen: eine exegetisch-traditionsgeschichtliche Untersuchung zu Hebräer 10,32-12,3*. WUNT 2nd ser. 60. Tübingen: Mohr Siebeck, 1994.

Schierse, Franz Josef. *Verheisssung und Heilsvollendung: Zur theologische Grundfrage des Hebräerbriefes*. Munich: Karl Zink, 1955.

Scholer, John M. *Proleptic Priests: Priesthood in the Epistle to the Hebrews*. JSNTSup 49. Sheffield: Sheffield Academic Press, 1991.

Smallwood, E. Mary. *The Jews Under Roman Rule*. 2nd ed. repr. Leiden: Brill, 2001.

Stambaugh, John E., and David L. Balch. *The New Testament in its Social Environment*. Library of Early Christianity 2. Philadelphia: Westminster, 1986.

Stowers, Stanley K. *Letter Writing in Greco-Roman Antiquity*. Library of Early Christianity 56. Philadelphia: Westminster, 1986.

Swetnam, James. "Christology and the Eucharist in the Epistle to the Hebrews," *Bib* 70 (1989) 74–95.

_____. "Form and Content in Hebrews 1–6," *Bib* 53 (1972) 368–85.

_____. "Form and Content in Hebrews 7–13," *Bib* 55 (1974) 333–48.

_____. "'The Greater and More Perfect Tent': A Contribution to the Discussion of Hebrews 9,11," *Bib* 47 (1966) 91–106.

Theissen, Gerd. *Untersuchungen zum Hebräerbrief*. Gütersloh: Gütersloher Verlagshaus Gerd Mohn, 1969.

Thompson, James. *The Beginnings of Christian Philosophy: The Epistle to the Hebrews*. CBQMS 13. Washington, D.C.: Catholic Biblical Association of America, 1982.

Thurén, Jukka. *Das Lobopfer der Hebräer: Studien zum Aufbau und Anliegen vom Hebräerbrief 13*. Åbo: Åbo Akademi, 1973.

Thyen, Hartwig. *Der Stil des jüdisch-hellenistischen Homilie*. FRLANT 47. Göttingen: Vandenhoeck & Ruprecht, 1955.

Tönges, Elke. "The Epistle to the Hebrews as a 'Jesus-Midrash,'" in G. Gelardini, ed., *Hebrews: Contemporary Methods—New Insights*. Leiden and Boston: Brill, 2005, 89–105.

Torrey, Charles C. "The Authorship and Character of the Epistles to the Hebrews." *JBL* 30 (1911) 137–56.

Vaganay, Léon. "Le plan de l'épître aux Hébreux," in *Mémorial Lagrange*. Paris: Gabalda, 1940, 269–77.

Vanhoye, Albert. *Homilie für haltbedürftige Christen: Struktur und Botschaft des Hebräerbriefes*. Regensburg: Pustet, 1981.

_____. *La Structure Littéraire de L'Épître aux Hébreux*. Paris: Desclée de Brouwer, 1963.

_____. *Old Testament Priests and the New Priest*. Petersham, MA: St. Bede's Publications, 1986.

Walters, James C. "Romans, Jews and Christians: The Impact of the Romans on Jewish/Christian Relations in First Century Rome," in Karl P. Donfried and Peter Richardson, eds., *Judaism and Christianity in First-Century Rome*. Grand Rapids: Eerdmans, 1998, 175–95.

Williamson, Ronald. "The Eucharist and the Epistle to the Hebrews," *NTS* (1975) 300–12.

_____. *Philo and the Epistle to the Hebrews*. ALGHJ 4. Leiden: Brill, 1970.

Wills, Lawrence. "The Form of the Sermon in Hellenistic Judaism and Early Christianity," *HTR* 77 (1984) 277–99.

Winston, David. *The Wisdom of Solomon: A New Translation With Introduction and Commentary*. AB 43. New York: Doubleday, 1979.

Wray, Judith H. *Rest as a Theological Metaphor in the Epistle to the Hebrews and the Gospel of Truth: Early Christian Homiletics of Rest*. SBLDS 166. Atlanta: Scholars, 1998.

TRANSLATION, NOTES, INTERPRETATION

Exordium

1. *A God Who Speaks* (1:1-4)

1. At various times in the past and in a variety of ways God spoke to the ancestors through the prophets. 2. In these last days, however, God has spoken to us through a Son, whom he appointed heir of all things and through whom he made the universe. 3. The Son, as the reflection of God's glory and the exact representation of God's essential being, sustaining all things by the power of his word, when he made purification for sins, sat down at the right hand of the Majesty on high, 4. having become as far superior to the angels as the name which he has inherited is more excellent than theirs.

Notes

1. *At various times in the past and in a variety of ways:* The opening verses form a programmatic statement to the entire sermon, yet they are not without ambiguity. The joining of *polymerōs kai polytropōs* by the author of Hebrews has been the subject of much study. Probably these adverbs were chosen because each begins with the Greek letter *pi* (cf. Koester, 93). Such alliteration, not uncommon in Hellenistic texts (Attridge, 37), rendered a text pleasant to the ear when read aloud (Abraham J. Malherbe, *The Letters to the Thessalonians: A New Translation with Introduction and Commentary.* AB 32B [New York: Doubleday, 2000] 106–107). The beauty of the author's diction does not necessarily render his thought unambiguous, as the difficulty of translating the two opening adverbs shows. Just as the English word "polymer" signifies a substance consisting of many similar molecules bonded together, *polymerōs* connotes that the past revelation of God consisted of many parts. The parts, however, cohere because of their similarity. So one ought to be careful not to conclude that what God spoke in the past was made up of vastly differing parts. Nor would it be accurate to think of the revelation as fragmentary or partial. The second adverb, *polytropōs*, carries the sense

of something that subsists in many ways. Subsistence here connotes the sense of continued existence and has an organic dimension to it, rendering the word of God as something living. Both words are not really synonyms (Attridge, 37), as some commentators have suggested (see Weiss, 138); they get at what God's speech was in the past and how it was communicated. If this was written for a Roman community, one wonders whether the recipients heard an echo of Rom 9:4-6:

> 4. They are Israelites, and to them belong the adoption, the glory, the covenants, the giving of the law, the worship, and the promises; 5. to them belong the patriarchs, and from them, according to the flesh, comes the Messiah, who is over all, God blessed forever. Amen. 6. It is not as though the word of God had failed.

Judaism consists of the various things mentioned in this text, which is written in the present tense to show continuity with the past. Paul adds in v. 6 that God's word to Israel is still succeeding. Perhaps one ought not to draw the contrast between past and present too sharply in Hebrews, as the author seems quite interested in showing how God's speech in a Son is compatible with the ways God had spoken, through prophets, in the past. Thus the first two words of the text of this exordium direct the reader to its main point: in the Son God has now spoken in a way that is consistent with God's past speech, but moving in another direction.

God spoke to the ancestors through the prophets: The singularity of God as the speaker here contrasts with the religious world in which Hebrews was written, where many gods communicated by means of dreams, oracles, visions, and the like (Koester, 183). While divination was practiced in ancient Israel, the prophetic oracle became a standard vehicle for God's speech. The important point is that, whereas the time and manner of God's speaking have changed, God remains the same. The noun "ancestors" is the plural of the word "father" (*patēr*) and is the standard designation for Israel's ancestral generation in the LXX (BDAG, 786; Josephus, *Antiquities* 14.255). In chapter 11 the term will be covered by the word for "elders," *presbyteroi* (11:2). "Prophets" is a general term that may include other individuals from the past who were considered to be prophets. Hebrews treats the Psalms as oracles (3:7; 4:7; 5:5-6), and there seems to have been a tradition of seeing David as a prophet (Acts 2:30; Philo, *On Agriculture*, 50).

2. *In these last days, however, God has spoken to us through a Son:* Not only have the time and manner of God's speech changed, so also has the audience. "Last days" is an eschatological term that extends the present time of the author and readers into the expected future (Acts 2:17; 2 Tim 3:1; Jas 5:3; 1 Pet 1:5, 20; 2 Pet 3:3; Jude 18). The author makes God's revelation personal for his readers by the inclusion of "to us." The first audience, "the ancestors," was undoubtedly Israel. But there is ambiguity here, too. The ancestors of the recipients are Roman Jewish Christians, and prophecy played a role in early Christianity as well. The current audience, the readers, are second generation Roman Christians. Despite the fact that the author wants to convey an important sense of continuity in God's speaking, the changes in time, manner, and audience suggest discontinuity (cf. Lane 1:11).

The remainder of the exordium will qualify the difference as the author turns his attention to the Son, who is the subject of important comparisons in the material that follows (1:4, 5, 14; 2:2-3, 18; 3:1-6; 5:5).

whom he appointed heir of all things: Although *klēronomos* does carry the sense of a legal heir, it is obvious that here the Son does not inherit in the usual way (Koester, 178). Commentators call attention to an allusion to Ps 2:8, where a royal descendant inherits the nations. William Lane (1:12) relies on Hugolin Langkammer's suggestion that the allusion is more properly to Gen 17:5, where after receiving a change of names Abraham is designated (*tetheika*) the father of many nations. Thus the investiture of Abraham, marking the beginning of redemptive history in Genesis, parallels the investiture of the Son, marking a new stage of redemptive history. The argument may not be that compelling, however. Abraham is not the heir of God in Genesis 17, but is rather the father whose children will inherit what God promised him. Moreover, the Son in Hebrews is not given a new name. The Son's role as heir seems to function in a different way in this verse. The term shows the relationship of the Son to the Father, a relationship that is qualitatively different from that shared by God and the prophets in the past. The remainder of this section demonstrates why the revelation by means of the Son is definitive for the author's purpose.

through whom he made the universe: The second determinative clause defining the Son's role appeals to the wisdom tradition. Wisdom's role at the beginning of creation serves to establish the link between Father and Son, much as the term "heir" does (Prov 8:22). The Son's preexistence is implied without the specificity of the Johannine author's placement of the *logos* with God from the beginning. The work of the Son at creation sets him apart from the prophets, through whom God had spoken in the past. In this way he is more than a mere prophet.

The noun *aiōn* has this same meaning in the LXX (Tob 13:7; Ps 65:78; Wis 13:9; 14:6; 18:4; Sir 36:17). In Matt 13:22 it refers to this world. The verse speaks of the process of creation by God's word (LXX: Gen 1:3, 6, 9; Ps 32:6; Wis 9:1; NT: John 1:3; Philo, *The Sacrifices of Cain and Abel* 65; Hermann Sasse, *aiōn, aiōnios*, *TDNT* 1:197–209). Unclear in this text is whether *aiōn*, translated as "universe" but meaning "ages" or "worlds," should be taken as a spatial or a temporal term. Some commentators prefer not to distinguish the two meanings in this verse (Bruce, 47; Ellingworth, 96; Koester, 178; cf. Attridge, 41; Grässer 1:59).

3. *The Son, as the reflection of God's glory:* The noun "reflection" is *apaugasma*. In the LXX this term is reserved for Wisdom, "For she is a reflection of eternal light, a spotless mirror of the working of God, and an image of his goodness" (Wis 7:26). As such, Wisdom reflects the image and work of God (cf. Philo, *On Creation* 146; *Special Laws* 4.123; Gerhard Kittel, *augazō, apaugasma, TDNT* 1:507–508). This reflection may be interpreted as a "radiance" either streaming outward from the Son's own glory or reflecting back the glory of God (Attridge, 42; Grässer, 1:60; Koester, 180). The Greek reads literally "the radiance of glory" (indeterminate). Given that the pronoun *autou* comes at the end of the sentence, it is likely to be taken with the nouns that precede it, *apaugasma* and *hypostasis*. Thus the glory and the substance are both attributed to God. The images drawn from the LXX text must have impressed the author of Hebrews as appropriate for

describing the relationship of the Son to the Father. The author's modifications are telling, too. Wisdom is a reflection of eternal light, but the Son is a reflection of God's glory. In the Hebrew Bible God's glory is sometimes described as light (Isa 60:1) or fire (Exod 24:17). But in Exod 33:18-19 Moses asks God to show him the divine glory and God replies: "I will make all my goodness pass before you," thus, associating the two, as in Wis 7:26.

the exact representation of God's essential being: Whereas Wisdom, working with God at the creation, is a mirror of the "working of God," the Son is an "exact representation of his essential being." Philo uses *charactēr*, "exact representation," in the Platonic sense of an imprint. He writes of "presentation," *phantasis*, imprinting the soul like a ring or a seal that is pressed into wax. It stamps the image on the ring or seal into the wax (*On the Unchangeableness of God*, 43; Ulrich Wilckens, *charactēr*, *TDNT* 9:418–23). If that is the sense in Hebrews, then the Son is the reflection of God's glory and the representative image of the essential nature of God. In this context that is so because he, too, is capable of a powerful performative word that sustains all things. The word *hypostasis*, "substance," can have the same meaning as *ousia*, "being" (Helmut Koester, *hypostasis*, *TDNT* 8:572–89). In later Christian theology the two will be distinguished, and *hypostasis* will acquire the meaning of "person" (Attridge, 44; Koester, 180). As a philosophical term it can refer to the "essence" of something (Diogenes Laertius, *Lives of Eminent Philosophers* 7.135; 9.91; Philo, *On Dreams* 1.188; *On the Eternity of the World* 88, 92). The LXX attests the meanings "property" (Deut 11:6; Jer 10:17), "argument" (Deut 1:12), "hope" (Ruth 1:12; Ezek 19:5), "length of life" (Ps 88:48), "sustenance" (Judg 6:4; Wis 16:21), "existence" (Pss 68:3; 138:15; Job 22:20). In Hebrews the term also means "confidence" (3:14) and "assurance" (11:1). Here "substance" or "being" is an appropriate choice.

sustaining all things by the power of his word: The verb *pherein* normally means "to carry" or "to bear" (LXX: 2 Kgdms 8:2, 6; NT: Mark 1:32; 2:3; 7:32; 8:22; 9:17; Acts 5:16; Josephus, *War* 1.669; *Antiquities* 8.321); hence some translations prefer "bearing," as in "carrying." The usage here is unusual, coming from a transferred sense of "to bear" that means "to endure," on the analogy of Rom 9:22 "to sustain" or "to hold up" (Konrad Weiss, *pherō, ktl.*, *TDNT* 9:56–87). An interesting parallel is found in Sir 43:26: "Because of him each of his messengers succeeds, and by his word all things hold together" (NRSV).

Since the instrument of sustenance is the powerful word of God, the sense is that the universe continues to exist because of the powerful word, which caused it to exist in the first place (Genesis 1). The difference, of course, is that here it is the Son's word that does the sustaining, so he has been given the role of the creator God in keeping all things in existence. This verse offers yet another example of how Hebrews identifies the Son and the Father closely in the exordium.

when he made purification for sins: An important theme developed later in the sermon is introduced here. Christ as High Priest, who accomplishes what the Levitical priesthood was unable to do, brings "purification" of the conscience (9:14, 22, 23; 10:22; 12:24). The noun "purification," *katharismos*, as a designation for the result of Christ's self-offering, is used here and 2 Pet 1:9. Elsewhere in the NT (Mark 1:44; Luke 2:22; 5:14; John 2:6; 3:25) it refers to "purification" under the Jewish Law.

sat down at the right hand of the Majesty on high: Another major theme of Hebrews, Christ's exaltation and session at the right hand of God, is introduced. The allusion is to Psalm 110 (109 LXX), which will be cited or alluded to throughout the sermon at key points (1:13; 5:6; 6:20; 7:17, 21; 8:1; 10:12; 12:2).

4. *having become as far superior to the angels:* Hebrews has a penchant for comparison and the author likes the word *kreittōn*, "better" or "superior" (1:4; 6:9; 7:7, 19, 22; 8:6; 9:23; 10:34; 11:16, 35, 40; 12:24). Angels are another important theme introduced in the exordium. The main function of the comparison here must be seen in relation to what follows in 1:5-14, where a catena of scriptural texts will develop the comparison. The point here is to show that as Son he not only surpassed the previous prophetic messengers of God's word but was also superior to the angels, who should be looked upon as familiar mediators between God and humans. If there is an allusion in this to the Law having been mediated through angels, then perhaps the superiority of Christ to them says something about the word spoken in him as compared with the Law.

Some important manuscript witnesses ($\mathfrak{P}^{46}$ B) and *1 Clem.* 36:2 omit the article before angels, although the majority of them include it. As Ellingworth (106) has noted, the use of the article with "angels" in 1:5, 7a, and 13 may be intended to communicate something that was already known, because those verses look back to the reference to angels here in 1:4. This cannot explain the use of the definite article in v. 4, however, because there is no explicit mention of angels earlier in the exordium. The solution proposed is that the article was included by the author of Hebrews to make this form fit better with the later mention of "the angels" in 1:5. The author may have had in mind another stage of revelation that was mediated by angels, between the prophets and the Son.

as the name he has inherited is more excellent than theirs: Exactly what name Jesus inherited is ambiguous here. Is it Lord? Or, as Albert Vanhoye suggested, "High Priest" (*Old Testament Priests and the New Priest* [Petersham, MA: St. Bede's Publications, 1986] 85–86)? Since the Son is at the center of this exordium it is likely that this is the name he is given. The point will be drawn out in the question in 1:5, which reinforces the Son's superiority to the angels: "To which of the angels did he say: 'You are my son, today I have begotten you?'" Being called Son is what sets him apart from them, so it is all the more likely that the name he had been given was precisely for that function and was therefore "Son."

If the recipients are Roman Christians one ought not to miss the similarities between the opening of Romans and the exordium of Hebrews. Romans not only refers to God's promises given through prophets in Scripture but also mentions that Jesus was declared to be the Son of God (Rom 1:2-3). Abraham was also given a name as part of the promise (Gen 12:1-3).

Interpretation

Hebrews opens with one of the most rhetorically polished statements in the New Testament. Although such stylistic elegance is characteristically displayed throughout Hebrews, the exordium shows clearly that the author has mastered the principles of advanced rhetorical composition. Its effect on the readers is compelling and persuasive. The original Greek, all one sentence, pleases the ear with its alliteration and cadence. No less are the mind and spirit satisfied by the carefully structured phrases, leading the reader and/or listener to grasp ideas that are central to the exposition that follows. The significance of the nature of God as Speaker/Revealer and the definitive establishment of the Son as Speech/Revelation are established through pairings and parallels carefully subordinated to permit the explanation of the central ideas of the main clause, that God has spoken anew. The implication is that what has been said is effective because of the means of God's speech, which is more closely bound to the Speaker than any previous vehicles, because he is none other than God's Son.

Speech in Hebrews reveals the character of God and is an integral aspect of the sermon's theology. One cannot help but wonder if such an accomplished author as this one did not have a special appreciation of God as a communicator. The portrait of God as a speaker shows interest in fundamental principles of oratory: good oratory in the ancient world appealed to the *pathos* of the audience and demonstrated the *ethos* or character of the speaker. The most effective speech managed to achieve a balanced harmony between the two. Thus in Hebrews the very nature of God is to speak, to disclose, to reveal. To accomplish these ends, there are a variety of media at God's disposal. The opening verse mentions the prophets as a prelude to the manner of speech that is of special interest to the author, namely the Son. In the next chapter communication between God and humans will include the mediation of angels (Heb 2:2). So the author of Hebrews speaks of the manifold attempts on God's part to communicate through the ages, suggesting that God's desire for self-communication is an ongoing process of self-disclosure, which culminates in the revelation of the Son.

The exordium is structured in three parts: (1) v. 1: God's speech in the past; (2) v. 2: God's speech in these last days; and (3) vv. 3-4: a summary of the place and role of the Son. These verses function to introduce the main theme of the sermon, and they may serve as a summary of the christology of Hebrews. The Son is introduced as the new means of God's communication and is described with terms spanning his preexistence to his exaltation. At the heart of that description is the central tenet of Hebrews that Christ made purification for sins. The author will develop the elements of this brief description in what follows, in order to show how effective was God's speech in the Son by portraying him as the mediator of a better covenant.

The goal of showing what is new and different in the manner of God's speech is dramatically accomplished by the shift of subject from God to the Son in the second verse. Vanhoye (*La Structure Littéraire de L'Épître aux Hébreux* [Paris: Desclée de Brouwer, 1963] 65–68) has shown how this shift creates an interesting inversion of emphases, with the second half of the unit dominating the first, despite the fact that both halves of the exordium are centered on its most important part, the opening of v. 2, "In these last days, however, God has spoken to us through a Son."

The latter two verses, 3 and 4, are rich in content. As relative clauses, they depend on the first half of the exordium (1:1-2). Thus grammatical subordination highlights the importance of the central statement while defining the role of the Son in terms of his functions, which themselves will be expanded on throughout the sermon: his nature, his role in creation, his atoning once for all self-offering, and his exaltation.

The opening verse of the exordium eludes easy interpretation. Some commentators have suggested that the two adverbs, *polymerōs kai polytropōs*, imply that the author understood God's revelation to Israel through the prophets as incomplete, whereas the revelation in the Son is complete (Attridge, 37; Bruce, 46; Hughes, 36; Lane, 1:10; Montefiore, 33–34). Hebrews does show an interest in completeness and fullness elsewhere (2:10; 5:9; 7:19, 28; 9:9; 10:1, 14; 11:40; 12:23) and the author's use of comparison supports such an interpretation (1:4; 5:14; 6:9; 7:7, 19, 22; 8:6; 9:11, 23; 10:34; 11:16, 35, 40; 12:24). The manifold nature of the revelation, however, need not connote incompleteness (Koester, 176). Moreover, what may be more important for the author is the time and manner of what God has done. Hebrews also shows interest in the present time as an opportunity (1:5; 3:7, 13, 15; 4:7; 5:5; 13:8) and the means of salvation offered by the Son. The contrast of what God has done in the past through the prophets and has now done in Christ fits well with the sermon's hortatory function to encourage the readers not to lose confidence at the present moment. The vehicle of God's present revelation, the Son, is the ground of their confidence in this sermon.

The conclusion of v. 2 introduces the important series of qualifications that suit the Son for his work. The reference to his being heir of all things is frequently seen by commentators as an allusion to Psalm 2, where the kings inherit the land (Attridge, 40; Koester, 178; Lane, 1:6). The association of this notion of inheritance, and the extension of it from the land to the universe, not only applies a royal motif to the Son but also draws a comparison between the Son and previous royal figures of the LXX tradition. Implicit in the comparison is the difference between the royal Son's inheritance and theirs. Drawing such comparisons becomes a staple of the way the author of Hebrews argues. The entire exordium makes a series of these comparisons, and that tactic will be continued in the remainder of the sermon.

The beginning of v. 3 underscores the nature of the Son as capable of communicating the *realia* of God. Difficult as it may be to understand the meaning of the terms used here, the affinity of the Son with God is at the heart of the attribution "as the reflection of God's glory and the exact representation of God's essential being." To say that the Son reflects the glory of God is not the same as saying that he is the exact representation of God's essential being. So the author does not merely express one idea through these two clauses, but tries to give distinct content to the way he sees the relation of the Son to God in the work the Son must do as bearer of God's final revelation, now spoken through him. With what seems to be a clear reference to Wis 7:26, "For she is a reflection of eternal light, a spotless mirror of the working of God, and an image of his goodness," the author further qualifies the identity of the Son. The fact that the word "reflection" is paralleled with the expression "spotless mirror" in this LXX text may lead us to think that the author of Hebrews understood the reflection of the Son in some way to mirror the reality of God. The LXX text makes a further synonymous parallel attributing to Wisdom the "image" of God's goodness. The author of Hebrews chose not to reproduce this part of the LXX verse, preferring to call the Son the "exact representation" of God's essential being. The Greek word *charaktēr*, "exact representation," carries the meaning of a "stamp" or an "imprint," so the idea is not far from that of an image. What may be decisive here, however, is the dependent noun. In the LXX text Wisdom is the "image of God's goodness," whereas in Hebrews the Son is the "exact representation of God's essential being." One may rightly question whether this goes further than what the LXX author attributes to Wisdom herself, since "goodness" may be a metaphor for the whole nature of God. In his interpretation, however, the author of Hebrews seems deliberately to have spelled out how he understands the Son to carry the imprint of God. The word "nature," *hypostasis*, means "essential being" or "reality," what makes things what they are. That a child should somehow be a representation or reflect the character of the parent is part of the tradition of Hellenistic Judaism as seen in 4 Macc 15:4: "In what manner might I express the emotions of parents who love their children? We impress upon the character of a small child a wondrous likeness both of mind and of form" (NRSV). As both the "reflection of God's glory" and the "exact representation of God's essential being" the Son is eminently qualified for the role he must play as the vehicle of God's revelation.

The continuation of v. 3 brings into play the Son's function in sustaining the universe, which he shared in creating. Commentators usually call attention to the loose connection of this verse to the wisdom tradition, in the absence of any clear textual parallels. Frequently cited are Wis 7:24, 27, which mention that Wisdom not only has the power to do all things but renews them as well, and 8:1, where Wisdom orders all things. Attridge refers to the Philonic tradition, where the Logos guides "all things on their course" (*The Migration of Abraham* 6), is portrayed as a "pillar" (*On Noah as a Planter* 8), or is described as a "bond" that holds all things together (*On Flight and Finding* 112; Attridge, 45; see also Ronald Williamson, *Philo and the Epistle to the Hebrews*. ALGHJ 4 [Leiden: Brill, 1970] 95–103).

A closer biblical parallel is found, however, in Sir 43:26, where toward the end of an extended wisdom meditation on the glory of God manifested in creation the author proclaims: "Because of him each of his messengers (*angeloi*) succeeds, and by his word all things hold together" (NRSV). The LXX author most likely intends to refer the pronouns in both prepositional phrases to God, but it is possible for the second phrase to refer back to the immediately preceding noun "messenger." The author of Hebrews may have taken advantage of this ambiguity and extended this function of sustaining all things to the Son. If this is the case, the allusion to Sir 43:26 still falls within the wisdom tradition. The subject of the allusion, however, is different and makes a still closer identification of the Son with God in his designated role as the means of God's spoken word. The point is that the Son is no mere messenger of God's word, as the further qualifications of the exordium will demonstrate. An allusion to Sir 43:26 with its mention of the messenger (*angelos*) might also help to explain why the comparison with the angels in v. 4 is important for the author. This comparison will be developed further in the next section (1:5-14).

The following clause introduces the priestly function of the Son, which will become one of the major themes of Hebrews. At this point the wisdom tradition of the previous verses gives way to the tradition of Jesus' sacrificial death. Here the stress on purification for sin anticipates the attention the author will give to this aspect of the Son's priestly function in the central section of the sermon (8:1–10:18). The fact that only this aspect of the priesthood of the Son is mentioned in the exordium indicates something the author felt needed to be addressed. It is important, then, that as the major motifs are introduced in the exordium, the reader's attention be drawn to the Son's self-offering, which qualified him to be a High Priest. The placement of this aspect of the qualifications of the Son in the center of vv. 3 and 4 gives it the prominence the author wanted it to have in the structure of the exordium.

At the end of v. 3 the author mentions yet another important motif in the sermon, the exaltation of the Son and his heavenly enthronement. Allusions to Psalm 110 play a major role in the christology of Hebrews. Later in this chapter (1:13) a similar allusion will help make the comparison of the Son with the angels. In 8:1 the psalm will again be evoked to highlight the heavenly enthronement of Christ as High Priest. In 10:12 the session at the right hand of God follows on the unique sacrifice for sins, which Christ has made. In this last instance we have a close parallel to 1:3, which announces what will later be claimed for the qualitatively different priesthood of Christ in Hebrews.

The author of Hebrews is, of course, not unique in the appropriation of Psalm 110 to help develop his christology. Other allusions to the psalm in christological contexts are found elsewhere in the New Testament, indicating that this is a firm element of early Christian tradition (Matt 22:44; 26:64; Mark 12:36; 14:62; 16:19; Luke 20:42; see David M. Hay, *Glory at the Right Hand: Psalm 110 in Early Christianity*. SBLMS 18 [Nashville and New York: Abingdon, 1973]). In a number of instances an allusion to this psalm comes in a context where either Christ's death (Luke 22:69) or his resurrection (Acts 2:34; Eph 1:20; Col 3:1) relates to his exaltation. In Rom 8:34 and 1 Cor 15:25 Paul brings all three together. Lack of direct attention to or extensive discussion of Christ's resurrection in Hebrews suggests that the author has done something similar in joining it to his exaltation. In a related vein it may be that the author of Hebrews joins Christ's death to his resurrection in the context of his exaltation (Attridge, 46).

The inclusion of the Son's session here emphasizes his glory above all things. The very definite act of sitting down at the right hand of God is an unmistakably powerful biblical image. As Hay (*Glory at the Right Hand*, 86–87) points out, this is not done at the expense of the power and glory of God, but nonetheless underscores the unsurpassable exaltation of the Son after his having undergone the humiliation of death on a cross.

It is frequently asked whether Heb 1:3 derives from an ancient hymnic source. The explanation of this part of the exordium as earlier hymnic material is, however, beset with many problems. In general the identification of hymnic material in the New Testament is itself questionable. The usual texts grouped under this category are John 1:1-18; Phil 2:6-11; Col 1:15-18; 1 Tim 3:16; 1 Pet 3:18-19. The formal characteristics of these New Testament hymns vary one from another, so it is not easy to typify what exactly constitutes formally hymnic material (Lane 1:7). To complicate matters further, commentators do not agree on the limits of the hymnic material in the exordium of Hebrews. Some include the last part of v. 2 because they believe the form of the relative clause to be especially hymnic (Lane 1:8). Still others believe the exordium to be integral in itself and look skeptically on the suggestion that this part of it was taken from earlier hymnic material (Grässer 1:49; Janusz Frankowski, "Early Christian Hymns Recorded in the New Testament: A Reconsideration in Light of Heb 1,3," *BZ* 27 [1983] 183–94; John P. Meier, "Structure and Theology in Heb 1, 1-14," *Bib* 66 [1985] 168–89; Donald W. B. Robinson, "The Literary Structure of Hebrews 1:1-4," *AJBA* 2 [1972] 178–86). The abrupt change of subject from God to the Son, the use of the extended relative constructions, the fact that the author uses several words here (*apaugasma* and *charaktēr*) that are not used elsewhere in the sermon, the notice that the author diverges from the text of Psalm 110 in the choice of the preposition *en* in the expression "at the right hand," when it is correctly cited in 1:13 as *ek*, have fueled speculation that these anomalies all point to the appropriation of hymnic material that antedates Hebrews itself. Some commentators (Ellingworth, 97–98), not convinced by these lines of argumentation, point out that the so-called anomalies can all be reasonably explained within the context of Hebrews to show that the verse is well integrated into the exordium and does not show signs of earlier material deriving from an ancient Christian hymn. Craig Koester, on the other hand, entertains the possibility that the exordium contains traditional elements (179).

The last verse of the exordium turns to the matter of the Son's name, which unequivocally is superior to that of the angels. Naming plays an important role in the biblical tradition, whether it has to do with the naming of a newborn or the change of a name already given. In Hellenistic Judaism the interest in the significance of the name is grasped in Philo's treatise on the changing of names. The verse claims that the Son became superior to the angels to the extent that he had received a name that is more excellent than theirs. Noticeable here is the stress that it is not only in name that Christ is superior to the angels. The name signifies his superiority, which derives from his status as Son. Obviously the author understands the verse as a transition to the next section, 1:5-18, which will make a formal comparison between the Son and the angels.

The name is not specified here, but many commentators understand it to be "Son," the only term by which Christ is designated in the exordium. The circular composition of the exordium supports this assumption, as "Son" is the critical term in 1:2a and the subject of the exordium as a whole (Meier, "Structure and Theology," 188–89).

Some commentators note that the exordium ends on a note of comparison similar to the way it begins. At its opening the comparison focused on the superiority of God's revelation in a Son over what had preceded it through the prophets. In its conclusion the view shifts to the comparison between the Son and the angels. Ostensibly it appears that prophets and angels have little to do with one another. In the context of an announcement about God's revelation, however, one may find a common ground.

Commentators also note that the Hellenistic Jewish tradition that angels mediated the revelation of the Law may come into play in this verse, supplying yet another stage in the ways God communicated before the definitive way announced in the opening of the exordium: through a Son. They point to Heb 2:2 for support, on the assumption that the "word spoken by angels there" is none other than the Jewish Law. A problem with that view is that even though the Hellenistic view of such angelic mediators of the Law postdates the prophetic era in biblical history, what they reveal, the Law, predates it. Thus in the exordium the sequence of revelation does not follow a linear development. One way out of the dilemma may be to understand the wider role of angelic mediators in Hellenistic Judaism to be at work here (*Jub* 1:27, 29; 2:1; Philo, *On Dreams* 1.141-43; *On Abraham* 115; Josephus, *Antiquities* 15.136; Acts 7:30, 38, 53; Gal 3:19; Attridge, 65), which would then provide yet another means of revelation between the prophets and the Son. Such a tradition may lie behind the synonymous use of "angels" and "prophets" in Philo (*On Abraham* 113; *Questions on Exodus* 2.16). This option is attractive not only because it preserves a sequential order, but also because it may explain the anomaly of the definite article, which precedes the word "angels" in the text.

The exordium of Hebrews briefly presents the main theme of the sermon in the role articulated for the Son, first as the means of God's final revelation and then as the one who makes complete purification for sins, i.e., purification of the conscience of the worshipers (9:14; 10:22) and is exalted at the right hand of God. Thus he is the eternal Son and eternal High Priest (2:9-10; 9:12-15; 13:20-21) who mediates access to God in a way superior to those of the past.

For Reference and Further Study

Abernathy, David. "'God Has Spoken Through His Son': The Theology of Sonship in Hebrews 1," *DavarLogos* 3 (2004) 23–35.

Ellingworth, Paul. "Paul, Hebrews and 1 Clement: Literary Dependence or Common Tradition?" *BZ* n.s. 23 (1979) 262–69.

Garuti, P. "Il prologo della lettera agli Ebrei (Eb 1,1-4)," *SacDoc* 34 (1989) 533–56.

O'Neill, J. C. "'Who Is Comparable to Me in My Glory': 4Q491 Fragment 11[4Q491C] and The New Testament," *NovT* 42 [2000] 24–38.

Ulrichsen, Jarl H. "*Diaphorōteron onoma* in Hebr. 1.4: Christus als Träger des Gottesnamens," *ST* 38 (1984) 65–75.

I. Jesus, Son Crowned with Glory as a Result of His Suffering and Death (1:5–2:18)

2. *The Son and the Angels* (1:5-14)

5. For to which of the angels then did God ever say: "You are my Son, today I have begotten you"? And again, "I will be a father to him and he will be a Son to me"? 6. And again, when he brings the firstborn into the world he says: "Let all the angels of God bow down before him." 7. And of the angels, he says, "Who makes his angels spirits and his servants flames of fire." 8. And of the Son, "God, your throne is forever and ever, and the scepter of righteousness is the scepter of your rule. 9. You loved righteousness and

hated lawlessness, because of which God, your God, has anointed you with the oil of gladness more than your comrades." 10. And, "You, O Lord, established the earth, and the heavens are the works of your hands; 11. they will perish—but you remain; and everything will grow like an old garment; 12. like a mantle you will roll them up, and as a garment they will be changed. You, however, are the same and your years are without end." 13. To which of the angels did he ever say, "Sit at my right hand, until I put your enemies under your feet like a footstool"? 14. Are they not ministering spirits sent out for service on behalf of those awaiting the inheritance of salvation?

Notes

5. *For to which of the angels then did God ever say: "You are my Son, today I have begotten you":* The author introduces a catena of scriptural citations with a rhetorical question implying that God has never spoken in this way to any angel. But angels are sometimes referred to as "sons of God" in the Hebrew Bible (Gen 6:2, 4; Ps 29 (28):1; 82 (81):6; 89 (88):7; Job 1:6; 2:1; 38:7; Dan 3:25). The LXX changes "sons" to "angels" in Job 1:6; 2:1; and 38:7. The only instance of a singular "son of God" is found in Dan 3:25 (LXX 3:92), where the LXX has "angel of God." Thus the status of the Son is enhanced. The unit is framed by this question and the similar one posed in v. 13. Picking up on the sermon's opening verse, the author supplies the content of God's speech, now to the Son himself, who is the vehicle of that speech in the prologue.

The author applies Ps 2:7 to the Son. In the psalm the one designated "son" is the king, who as a royal heir receives an inheritance of the nations (Ps 2:8). This text may have informed the author's description of the Son as the "heir of all things" (1:2). In 5:5-6 the author will join this verse of the psalm to Ps 110:2 to make an important point about Jesus as an eternal High Priest. Its context here, in a discussion of the Son's eternity, fits well with the author's theology.

When the "begetting" of the Son took place is subject to a wide range of interpretations. Some commentators specify a moment outside of time, perhaps at creation (Michel, 110; Montefiore, 44), whereas others look to the Son's incarnation (Spicq 2:16) or to his exaltation (Attridge, 54–55; Braun, 35; Ellingworth, 114; Hughes, 54; Koester, 191; Weiss, 161; Westcott, 21). Given the context, which has already proclaimed the exaltation of the Son, the author most likely understands this moment of begetting as the moment of the Son's exaltation. The psalm text is so linked in other NT writings (cf. Acts 13:33). To focus on exaltation, however, need not preclude preexistence and the eternal generation of the Son (Attridge, 55; Bruce, 54; Aelred Cody, *Heavenly Sanctuary and Liturgy in the Epistle to the Hebrews: The Achievement of Salvation in the Epistle's Perspectives* [St. Meinrad, IN: Grail Publications, 1960] 90–91).

And again, "I will be a father to him and he will be a Son to me": The author uses the word "again" to introduce biblical quotations in 1:6; 2:13; 4:5; and 10:30. The second citation here is from the LXX of 2 Sam 7:14, repeating the relationship of the Father and the Son, now as if it were a future reality. As part of the *Oracle of Nathan* it has that future meaning in relationship to the immediate and remote heirs of David. Thus it was later open to messianic interpretation, a meaning likely to carry over into Hebrews. Jesus' sonship in Hebrews is connected with his status as Messiah (see Heb 11:26). The Messiah was called "son" in Jewish tradition (cf. 2 Esdr 7:28-29).

6. *And again, when he brings the firstborn into the world he says:* In the LXX, the verb "to bring" (*eisagein*) is used for God's leading the people of Israel into the land of Canaan (Exod 3:8; 6:8; 23:20; 33:3). The noun *oikoumenē* usually means an inhabited place or the inhabited world (BDAG, 699; Philo, *On The Unchangeableness of God* 175, 176; *On Agriculture* 35, 143; *The Migration of Abraham*, 217; *On Dreams* 2.180; *On Abraham* 226; etc.). In Exod 16:35 it refers to the land of Canaan. Hebrews uses it in 2:5 to refer to the "world to come." As the author usually employs the word *kosmos* for this world (4:3; 9:26; 10:5; 11:7, 38), *oikoumenē* here probably refers to eternity. Thus the bringing of the firstborn into that world signifies the Son's exaltation rather than his incarnation (Grässer 78; Lane 1:27; Koester, 193; Weiss, 162–63). This interpretation is corroborated by the remainder of the text, which speaks of angels worshiping him and of his eternal throne.

Let all the angels of God bow down to him: The third quotation from the LXX appears to come from Ps 96:7, which has changed the MT's "all gods bow down before him" to "all his angels worship him." Another possible source is the LXX of Deut 32:43, "And let all the sons of God worship him," which is paralleled with "and let all the angels of God strengthen him." Unfortunately, the verse does not appear in the MT of Deut 32:43. Radu Gheorghita (*The Role of the Septuagint in Hebrews: An Investigation of Its Influence with Special Consideration to the Use of Hab 2:3-4 in Heb 10:37-38*. WUNT 2nd ser. 160 [Tübingen: Mohr Siebeck, 2003] 40–41, 53) provides a variant Hebrew version from Qumran, 4QDeut^q, as a possible source, as does Koester (193). Thus they posit an alternate Hebrew text that was the source of the LXX version. The Qumran text, however, is ambiguous since it reads *kl-ʾlhym*, which is found in the MT of Ps 97:7. Gheorghita claims that the mention of angels in the LXX text was likely the reason the author selected and conflated it to the form he inserted into the chain of scriptural citations (*The Role of the Septuagint*, 53). Yet a third source may be found in the *Odes*, which were appended to the Greek Psalter. The second ode is a translation of Deuteronomy 32, and v. 43 of this ode corresponds exactly to formulation in Heb 1:6, "Let all the angels of God bow down before him." Lane believes that Hebrews chose the text of this ode for its appropriateness in 1:6 (Lane 1:28). Gheorghita, however, discounts *Odes* 2:43 as the source of the citation because of its origin, the question of its availability to the author of Hebrews, and probable Christian editing (*The Role of The Septuagint*, 42; Ellingworth, 118).

7. *And of the angels, he says, "Who makes his angels spirits and his servants flames of fire":* Some commentators (Koester, 190) prefer to translate *pros men tous angelous* "to the angels" because of a similar expression in 1:13. It would seem that "of" or "concerning" is more appropriate here and in 1:8 in reference to the Son, as what follows is more a statement about both than speech directed to them.

This fourth scriptural quotation is taken from LXX Ps 103:4, where it has the meaning that God has turned angels into wind or spirits. The Greek word *pneuma* can mean either (BDAG, 832–36). The MT is ambiguous and may have the meaning given it by the LXX translator or an alternate meaning: God turns winds or spirits into his mediators, i.e., angels. A similar problem arises with the ambiguity of the MT, "and he makes his servants flames of fire," where it can mean that God makes flames of fire into his servants or turns his servants into flames of fire. The LXX is clear that the meaning is the latter. Taken with the first part of the psalm verse, the author's meaning emerges. In contrast to the Son, angels and servants are passing like winds and flames of fire, whereas the Son endures forever, as the next verse indicates.

8. *And of the Son, "God, your throne is forever and ever, and the scepter of righteousness is the scepter of your rule:* This verse from LXX Ps 44:7 can easily be translated "Your throne, O God, is forever and ever." The predicate nominative is preferred here to the nominative as a vocative, so that God is not directly addressing the son as "God." Another reason for preferring this translation is the parallel between throne and scepter in what follows. The scepter is a symbol of a ruler's authority. The Greek word *euthytētos* means "uprightness," but it is a synonym for *dikaiosynē*, "righteousness" (BDAG, 406).

9. *You loved righteousness and hated lawlessness, because of which God, your God, has anointed you with the oil of gladness more than your comrades:* The author continues with the Psalm citation by including v. 8. It is almost exactly the same as in the LXX. In the previous section the Son was described as someone ruling with the scepter of righteousness. Here he possesses the virtue of righteousness (*dikaiosynē*) itself, and therefore is qualified to be an excellent ruler (Koester, 194–95).

Anointing is common in the ancient world. Kings in particular were anointed, and the context here suggests a royal anointing. "Oil of gladness" occurs once in the MT at Isa 61:3. In the LXX it appears in the form cited here in Ps 44:8. The LXX Greek of Isa 61:3 differs from that of the psalm. "Gladness" is commonly associated with sound or the voice in the Hebrew Bible. It is the mark of a festival or a victory and is not usually associated with oil, so it is a peculiar metaphor. Most commentators take it to mean that anointing, especially that of a king, is a glad and joyous occasion, a celebration (Koester, 195). Here "oil of gladness" is a particular reward for the Son, distinguishing him from others because of how he has loved righteousness. There is a double distinction here. Not only is he anointed; he is also set apart from his comrades because he receives the oil of gladness.

10. *And, "You, O Lord, established the earth, and the heavens are the works of your hands:* The sixth LXX quotation, from Ps 101:26-28, begins on a note of ambiguity. To whom is it addressed, to God or to Christ? Curiously, Koester (195) has the first part of the verse referring to Christ and the second to God. Although in the LXX context, as in the MT, the title "Lord" would be used for God, it is probably referring to the Christ here, as it does elsewhere in Hebrews (2:3; 7:14; 12:14). In 13:20 the application to Jesus is explicit. Yet in eleven other places in Hebrews the term "Lord" is used for God (7:21; 8:2, 8, 9, 10, 11; 10:16, 30; 12:5, 6). After the previous LXX quotation addressed to the Son, it is reasonable to conclude that this one addresses him as well. The remainder of the section builds toward the second rhetorical question about the status of the Son. His work at the creation

has already been introduced in the prologue (1:2) and here it is specified and qualified by its extent.

11–12. *they will perish—but you remain; and everything will grow like an old garment; like a mantle you will roll them up, and as a garment they will be changed:* As the psalm and text continues, so also the comparison of the Son, now to the creation. It is a perishable entity whereas he is eternal; thus he remains. That the author envisions the creation perishing as an act of God may be inferred from his reference to what "remains" in 12:28. There, by an eschatological act, "creation" is shaken, and it is contrasted to what remains, i.e., "what cannot be shaken" (see the Notes at 12:28). So also does the Son differ from the creation he was instrumental in bringing about. Joined to this image is another of transience. The metaphor of clothing wearing out appears elsewhere in the Hebrew Bible (Deut 8:4; Neh 9:21; Isa 50:9; 51:6), and that seems to be the sense here. In Isa 51:6 the earth is likened to a garment that grows old.

The image of deterioration and destruction continues. In the judgment oracle of Isa 34:4 the heavens will be "rolled up" like a scroll, although the verb differs from what we find in Ps 102(101) and in Hebrews. The sense is that they have served their usefulness, like a scroll that one is finished with. Here, just as one rolls up a cloak when done with it, so the heavens and the earth will perish at an appointed time, having accomplished the purpose for which they were created. The author envisions a part of the heavens that was created and a part that was eternal. It is the created part of the heavens that perishes (12:26). The Son, however, endures forever, something confirmed in the next part of the verse.

You, however, are the same and your years are without end: The psalm verse originally applied to God now applies to Christ and will be echoed later in Heb 13:8. An important element of the author's christology is the eternity of the Son, which is developed throughout the sermon (5:6, 9; 6:20; 7:3, 16-17, 21, 24, 28; 9:12, 14; 13:20).

13. *To which of the angels did he ever say, "Sit at my right hand, until I put your enemies under your feet like a footstool":* The second rhetorical question framing this catena of LXX quotations reminds the reader that the contrast between the Son and the angels has been at the heart of the author's purpose in this section. The text in question, Ps 110 (109):1, has already played a role in the exordium (1:3). The right side was the position of honor (LXX: 1 Kgdms 2:19; Pss 15:8; 45:9; 2 Esdr 2:42) and friendship. Sirach (12:12) counsels that an enemy ought never to be placed at one's right side, for he might try to displace the individual. In Zech 6:13 (LXX) a priest sits to the right of the throne where the high priest, Joshua, is to be enthroned. Hebrews has selected this psalm verse, which is a favorite of NT authors, precisely to delineate the position and status of the Son as compared with the angels and creation. The image of enemies being transformed into a footstool indicates that the Son has been given power in exaltation. It speaks of vindication as well, for the Son is not actually subduing his enemies. Rather, God does this for him.

14. *Are they not ministering spirits sent out for service on behalf of those awaiting the inheritance of salvation?* Earlier in the catena (1:7), the angels were called "spirits" and "ministers." Here the two concepts are joined to reprise that sentiment and

to complete the force of the rhetorical question in v. 13. Since no angel has been given the power of the Son in exaltation, they must have a different function. They serve not the throne of God as angels sometimes do in the Hebrew Bible, but they are placed in service to those who await the inheritance of salvation. The participle, "those who await," signals an eschatological context, as the verb *mellein* sometimes refers to the awaited end time (Matt 3:7; 12:32; Luke 13:9; Rom 5:14; 8:38; 1 Cor 3:22). The author will use this verb in a similar sense in 2:5; 6:5; 10:27. The exordium described the Son as the heir of all things (1:2). The faithful followers of the Son are the ones who stand to benefit here. His inheritance, as described in this comparison, makes theirs possible.

Interpretation

This second section is composed of a series of biblical quotations whose purpose is to elaborate on the status of the Son as proclaimed in the exordium. Framing the text with an *inclusio* expressed by the rhetorical question "To which of the angels did God ever say?" in vv. 5 and 13, the author collects seven texts from the LXX, mostly from Psalms, in order to illustrate authoritatively the importance of the revelation given through the Son. Adverbial and prepositional phrases hold the seven citations together. Whereas most of the citations refer to the Son (vv. 5, 6, 8-9, 10, 13), two refer to the angels (vv. 7 and 14).

Several commentators have shown how these biblical citations correspond to the statements made about the Son in the exordium. Meier, for example, has argued that the ring formation of the exordium continues here in 1:5-14 and has tried to show how each of the biblical quotations matches one of the statements in 1:1-4. Although the correspondence between the two sections of the first chapter is not exact, the function of this collection of texts from the LXX helps the author to expand on the characteristics of the Son mentioned in the exordium.

The immediate reference to the angels in v. 5 picks up on the comparison of the Son with angels in v. 4 (Vanhoye, *La Structure*, 68; Koester, 197–98). Implicit in the comparison is the understanding that what set Jesus apart from them was that he had obtained a more excellent name than they. Although the name itself is not specified, it is most probably that of "Son." Therefore in the opening verses of this section the author has selected LXX texts that highlight the Father/Son relationship.

The first text is taken from Ps 2:7 and is reproduced exactly, though in a different context. In the psalm itself the text refers to the Judean king, whom the Lord established as such over the people. Originally the proclamation was made by the king himself, with the introduction, "The Lord said to me, 'You are my son. . . .'" Hebrews applies the text directly to the Son, giving it a christological twist. There is much talk of intertextuality in biblical studies today, the understanding of how differing contexts are used to reinterpret texts within the biblical tradition itself. In the New Testament this is the case where LXX texts have been appropriated for other purposes and have been given a new function by virtue of their new setting. This is a perfectly legitimate hermeneutical move. Gheorghita (*The Role of the Septuagint*, passim) has shown that the author of Hebrews selects LXX texts that fit his purpose and modifies them to develop his christological claims. This amounts to a "re-scripturing" of texts, whereby the author appropriates the tradition and actualizes it in a new context.

Critical in "re-scripturing" is the discovery of a meaning for a biblical text that can be applied to the situation of the readers, which the author is addressing. This involves a certain encoding that the author applies to key terms of the original text to render it anew. For the author of Hebrews the expression "my son" functions as a multivalent term in the citation from Ps 2:7. Now pressed into service as evidence for the sonship of Christ, the text is differently encoded by the author. How the readers would have understood this cannot be known for certain, but the extension of the biblical tradition here must have had an impact on their understanding of the proclamation of Christ's sonship in his exaltation. This is precisely the point the author wished to make.

Joined to this psalm citation is a text taken from 2 Sam 7:14: "I will be a father to him and he will be a son to me." The connection of the two texts is made on the basis of the mention of the word "son" in both. Another link is the context of royal sonship, which both texts originally shared. This text from 2 Samuel 7 forms part of Nathan's oracle to David, which refers directly to his son and heir, Solomon. The oracle promises the perpetuity of Davidic kings on the Judean throne. Whether the two citations ought to be construed as messianic is open to question. It may be possible that they were given messianic interpretation in first-century Judaism. Some commentators point to John 7:42: "Has not the scripture said that the Messiah is descended from David and comes from Bethlehem, the village where David lived?" as evidence that among Christians the text had already gained that status (Gheorghita, *The Role of the Septuagint*, 51). The reference to the seed of David links both texts.

The third citation (Ps 97[96]:7) follows the temporal reference to the time when the firstborn is brought into the world in v. 6. Exactly what is meant here is not immediately clear and is rather obscured by the expression "and again." Elsewhere in Hebrews it has the meaning of doing something again, which would then carry the meaning here that the Son is being reintroduced into the world. The word "again" (*palin*) occurs ten times in Hebrews (1:5, 6; 2:13[bis]; 4:5, 7; 5:12; 6:1, 6; 10:30). In 4:7 it refers to God doing something additional, and in 5:12 it underscores the need for the readers to learn first principles again. In 6:1 a similar meaning is evoked when the author suggests that they not repeat the basics. In all the other instances it is used as a formula to introduce yet another scriptural citation after one has already been given. Here it has the same function. So the Son is not being introduced again into the world, but rather the author is adding more evidence for his case by citing another biblical text where God is addressing the Son: "and again." The case for this interpretation is strengthened by the occurrence of the word *oikoumenē* for "world" in this text. When the author refers to this world he uses the noun *kosmos*, but when he refers to the heavenly world or the world to come he uses *oikoumenē* (1:6 and 2:5). Here the Son is being introduced into the heavenly realm and the occasion on which God speaks to him in this way is his exaltation.

In order to stress the importance of the Son's exaltation the comparison with the angels is resumed by the introduction of a text from Deut 32:43, "Let all the angels of God worship him." The older LXX witnesses have "let the sons of God worship him," and other witnesses add "let the messengers (*angeloi*) of God be strengthened." As indicated in the Notes above, this text may have been part of the liturgical heritage Jewish Christians brought with them from the synagogue to early Christianity (see Rev 15:3, where there is a reference to the singing of the Hymns of Moses, the source of this text, in heaven). Perhaps this context allowed an easy shift for the author to have the angels worship the Son.

The second grouping of LXX citations in vv. 7-12 expands the contrast of the angels with the Son. The reference from Ps 104(103):4 shows the subordination of the angels, created by God as winds and flames of fire. The images connote the swiftness of movement that characterizes these divine messengers. Another way the author draws the contrast is simply by varying the amount written about each. The two verses (vv. 7, 14) about the angels pale in comparison with the eight verses on the Son (vv. 5-6; 8-13; cf. Lane, 1:28).

The psalm quotation is almost exact with only a minor variation. A shift of meaning had already occurred in the LXX. The MT describes "wind" and "fire" as the messengers and servants of God, whereas the LXX describes the messengers and servants as "wind" and "fire." It may appear to be only a semantic difference, but the emphasis seems to show more clearly the power of God over the angels, as well as their subordination. In addition, the shift of focus also stresses the mutability of angels who are made so by God, and who, as created beings, can change like the wind or flames of fire. The point is that the Son is immutable (Heb 13:8).

The contrast of v. 8 underscores the superiority of the Son, who does not belong to the created order of the angels. With the aid of a quotation from Ps 45(44):7-8, Hebrews shows the parity the Son has with God. What is more, the application of this quotation to the Son underscores why he should be worshiped by angels, since he rules over an eternal kingdom. The mention of the throne hearkens back to the exordium and the all-important session of the Son at the right hand of God. The contrast motif of mutability/

immutability forms an important dimension of the author's presentation of Christ in Hebrews. Immutability as a mark of his eternal nature is a chief characteristic of the Son and his work (6:20; 7:3, 17, 21, 24, 28).

The inclusion of Ps. 45(44):8 has puzzled commentators, since it seems not to have any immediate value for the contrast being drawn between the angels and the Son. The fact that the Son has loved righteousness and hated lawlessness does not imply the opposite for the angels. Several commentators have suggested that it is the mention of the superiority of the Son over his comrades that has attracted the author, who wished to show yet again that the Son is superior to the angels, who may be considered his comrades (Attridge, 60; Ellingworth, 124; Lane 1:30). Without a doubt this has caught the author's attention, but his interest in righteousness is not confined to this verse alone (see 5:13; 7:2; 11:7, 33; 12:11). The mention of the Son's anointing serves to underscore once again that he has been established and appointed as Son and eternal heir by God.

Stressing the permanent nature of the Son, the author draws on Ps 102:25-27 (LXX 101:26-28) to refer back to the mention of his role in creation earlier in the exordium. Here the significance lies not only in the contrast between the created order established by the Son and his own permanence, "they will perish—but you remain"; "you, however, are the same and your years are without end." The original setting of the psalm refers to God's immutable nature. Hebrews applies this directly to the Son, making the connection between the two inescapable. From such an application one may infer the divine nature of the Son, which like the unchangeable and abiding nature of God is superior to that of the transitory world. Furthermore, in the context of the comparison with the angels the selection of this text implies that the role of the Son in the creation of the universe surpassed any attendant role they may have had. In Hellenistic Judaism the angels function as mediators between God and humans, and some texts show their presence even at the creation (Job 38:7).

By means of an *inclusio* in v. 14 the author frames the LXX citations gathered here with a rhetorical question, similar to the one in v. 5. The text comes from Ps 110(109):1. Hearkening back to v. 3 of the exordium, the session theme is reiterated and then followed by an interpretive comment that drives home again the point that the Son is indeed superior to the angels. Having already established by means of the quotation of Ps 104(103):4 that the angels are ministering spirits, the author underscores their subordination to the Son by the fact that they are not seated at the right hand of God as he is. Such a proclamation as "Sit at my right hand . . ." has never been given to any angel; it is reserved for the Son.

As any good preacher would do, the author of Hebrews has explained more fully in this section what he proclaimed in 1:4, that the Son is superior to the angels. The simple rationale, that the Son had been given a superior name to that of the angels, requires elaboration. This the author accomplishes in a "midrashic" style, where a catena of scriptural citations witnesses to the place of the Son in relation to God, in order to show his status precisely as Son. The intertextual nature of this passage demonstrates the author's skill at "re-scripturing" LXX texts for his readers so that they are actualized anew. Today's readers may not be as concerned with the superiority of Christ over angels as were those who first heard this sermon. Still, they can appreciate the author's clarification of the relationship of Christ to God for the way it adds to their understanding of New Testament christology.

For Reference and Further Study

Bateman, Herbert W. *Early Jewish Hermeneutics and Hebrews 1:5-13*. New York: Peter Lang, 1997.
_____."Psalm 45:6-7 and Its Christological Contributions to Hebrews," *TJ* 22 (2001) 3–21.
Brown, Raymond E. "Does the N.T. Call Jesus God?" *TS* 26 (1965) 508–91.
Cockerill, Gareth Lee. "Hebrews 1:6: Source and Significance," *BBR* 9 (1999) 51–64.
Johnson, Luke Timothy. "The Scriptural World of Hebrews," *Int* 57 (2003) 237–50.
Meier, John P. "Structure and Theology in Heb 1:1-14," *Bib* 66 (1985) 168–69.
_____. "Symmetry and Theology in the Old Testament Citations of Heb. 1:5-14," *Bib* 66 (1985) 504–33.
Motyer, Stephen. "The Psalms Quotations of Hebrews 1: A Hermeneutic-free Zone?" *TynBul* 50 (1999) 3–22.
Schenck, Kenneth L. "A Celebration of the Enthroned Son: The Catena of Hebrews 1," *JBL* 120 (2001) 469–85.
Steyn, Gert J. "A Quest for the *Vorlage* of the 'Song of Moses' (Deut 32) Quotations in Hebrews," *Neot* 34 (2000) 263–72.
_____. "A Quest for the *Vorlage* of Psalm 45:6-7 (44:7-8) in Hebrews 1:8-9," *HTSTeolStud* 60 (2004) 1085–1103.
Thomas, Kenneth J. "The Old Testament Citations in Hebrews," *NTS* 11 (1964–65) 303–25.

3. *So Great a Salvation* (2:1-4)

1. For this reason we must pay closer attention to what we have heard, or else we may drift away from it. 2. For if the message announced by angels still holds firm and every violation and refusal to listen received a just punishment, 3. how shall we escape when we neglect so great a salvation, which was first announced by the Lord and attested to us by those who

heard, 4. when God bore witness by signs and wonders and various miracles as well as by the gifts of the Holy Spirit according to his will?

Notes

1. *For this reason we must pay closer attention to what we have heard, or else we may drift away from it:* "For this," *dia touto*, refers back to the previous section as the basis for the warning that forms these verses. Simply stated, the author wants the readers to attend to the message more closely. One of the author's favorite hortatory verbs is *prosechein*, which basically means "pay close attention to" or "take care" (Exod 10:28; 19:12; 23:21; 34:11; Lev 22:2; Num 16:15; Deut 1:45; 4:9, 23; 6:12; 8:11; 11:16; 12:13, 19), especially in hortatory texts. It is also used for "bringing a ship to port" (Herodotus, *Histories* 9.99; LSJ, 1512). In light of the warning not to drift away, the author may be appealing to this verb's "nautical" sense (Koester, 205). Thus the meaning might be to grasp firmly so as not to lose something. The author also uses *katechein*, "hold fast to," in hortatory contexts (3:6, 14; 10:23).

   Attending to "what has been heard" refers to obedient listening in Hebrews (3:7, 15, 16; 4:2). Later, when discussing the rebellion of the wilderness generation (3:7-19), the author will compare their ability to listen to the readers'. That generation was unable to hear properly because they lacked the faith to "listen." For this reason they did not benefit from what they had heard (4:2). The content of the message is not specified. In the immediate context it may refer to all that has thus far been said about the Son (1:1-14). It may also refer to the totality of what God has spoken in the Son (1:2).

   The warning not to "drift away," *pararrein*, may allude to a nautical metaphor (Lane 1:37; Koester, 205; Weiss, 183) for being "unmoored," or it may simply be a general exhortation reinforcing the warning to "hold fast" (cf. Prov 3:21), akin to the warnings about those who have "fallen away" in 6:6, and not to be "carried away by diverse and strange teachings" in 13:9. The author uses the metaphor of an "anchor" in 6:19.

2. *For if the message announced by angels still holds firm and every violation and refusal to listen received a just punishment:* The message or *logos* is the word, now spoken through angels. The definitive word of God is spoken through the Son (1:2). The message spoken by angels must then be less grand. Paul implies as much in Gal 3:19 when he speaks of the Law as inferior to the promise because it was spoken through angels. Traditionally, the Law was seen as mediated by angels (Gal 3:19; Acts 7:53). In Judaism this mediation does not at all affect the importance or stature of the Law. For Paul and the author of Hebrews, however, there is a difference in importance between God's word spoken through a Son and what was spoken by means of angels. The author uses the aorist participle of *akouein* in 4:2 to refer to those in the wilderness generation who "listened" to the word that was heard: in other words, to those who were obedient in contrast to those who failed in obedience. Here the reference is to the message that was heard.

   The adjective *bebaios* has a legal meaning of "in effect" or "valid" (BDAG, 172; MM, 107–108). The author uses it again in this sense in 9:17. The LXX has five instances of this adjective, all with the sense of "firm" (Esth 3:13c; Wis 7:23; 3 Macc 5:31; 7:7; 4 Macc 17:4). Its use in a conditional clause in this verse is not intended by the author to mean anything other than that the word is still in effect. He is not questioning whether it is or is not. The verb *bebaioun* means "to strengthen," "to make firm," or "to confirm" (Pss 41[40]:13; 119[118]:28; 3 Macc 5:42; Mark 16:20; Rom 15:8; 1 Cor 1:6; 2 Cor 1:21; Col 2:7). The author uses this verb again in 13:9 to exhort the readers to be "strengthened" by grace and not foods.

The inability to listen, to heed what is heard, is the subject of the third chapter on the wilderness generation and its disobedience. Already the author is antici-pating the comparison of his audience with that disobedient generation, as they are now warned that they will be held to greater accountability for what they have heard. Paul also uses the noun "transgression," *parabasis*, in Rom 2:23; 4:15; 5:14; and Gal 3:19 to refer to transgressions against the Law. The noun for "refusal to listen," *parakoē*, occurs elsewhere in the NT only in Paul (Rom 5:19; 2 Cor 10:6). The verb *parakouein* does appear in exactly the same sense of "refuse to listen" in Matt 18:17(bis). For Hebrews a refusal to listen is tantamount to disobedience. Effective listening requires compliance with what is heard. This will become clearer in chapter 3.

The noun for "punishment," *misthapodosia*, occurs only in Hebrews, here and again in 10:35 and 11:26. In the other two places it is used to mean a reward, as the first part of the word may indicate. Greek *misthos* can mean a reward, as in the Matthean beatitudes at Matt 5:12 and 1 Cor 9:18. It can also simply mean "wages" as in Rom 4:4; 1 Cor 3:8; Jas 5:4. In Rom 6:23 Paul refers to the wages of sin, close to the meaning in Hebrews. The just deserts for violation and refusal to listen can hardly be a reward and so must be a punishment. In the LXX the combination of *misthos* and *apodidonai* means to pay wages (Deut 24:15; Tob 2:12; Wis 10:17; Herbert Preisker, *misthos, ktl., TDNT* 4:695–706). Koester (96, 206) thinks the coinage comes from the author of Hebrews (see also Lane 1:35). He points to another similar coinage in 11:6 with the noun *misthapodotēs* for someone who gives a reward. Outside of Hebrews, the adjective "just," *endikon*, occurs only in Rom 3:8.

3. *how shall we escape when we neglect so great a salvation:* What they will escape from is not specified, but presumably it is a just punishment like the one men-tioned in the protasis of the sentence. The apodosis is designed to stress the impossibility of escaping that punishment. Later in the sermon at 12:25 (see 10:28-31) a warning will be issued not to refuse the one who is speaking, in words reminiscent of 2:2-3. The parallel with the fate of the ancestors in that text to the punishment the wilderness generation receives here is similar. So is the impossibility of escaping a like fate.

The noun "salvation," *sōtēria*, occurs seven times in Hebrews (1:14; 2:3, 10; 5:9; 6:9; 9:28; 11:7), and the verb "to save" twice (5:9; 7:25). The term carries a broad range of meaning in the New Testament. Here salvation is contrasted with the message announced through angels mentioned in the protasis. That message was its own announcement of salvation, but in the author's a fortiori argument even it cannot compare with the greatness of the salvation now offered to the readers.

which was first announced by the Lord and attested to us by those who heard: The
Greek expression is convoluted: "which taking an origin of speech through the
Lord." The sense seems to be "spoken at first through the Lord." The intention
is once again to contrast the message given through angels with the salvation
proclaimed by the Lord, i.e., the Son. Thus the comparison of the Son with the
angels that pointed to his superiority over them is echoed here with a similar
effect.

On the verb *bebaioun* see v. 2 above. The announcement of the great salvation
was passed on to the author and the readers alike in a reliable fashion. Elsewhere
in the NT *bebaioun* can also mean to strengthen or make firm (1 Cor 1:6, 8; 2 Cor
1:21; Col 2:7). If that is the meaning here, it is a salvation that was first proclaimed by the Lord and reinforced by those who heard it, or him.

The expression "those who heard" is vague and lacks an object. What did
they hear, the word of salvation or the Lord's proclamation of it? Either implied
object will fit the context. Given that there is so much subordination of ideas
within these verses, it is likely that the author has the noun "salvation" in mind
as the antecedent. Thus the qualifications of this salvation are that it was
(1) first announced by the Lord and (2) attested by other preachers, who handed
it on. That way the number of those who heard it is not restricted to the followers of Jesus, those who actually heard him, but includes the generations of
Christians who received the word of salvation up to the time that the writer
and audience did. On the similarities of this verse and the next to Mark 16:19-20
see the Interpretation at 2:5-9.

4. *when God bore witness by signs and wonders and various miracles as well as by the
gifts of the Holy Spirit according to his will:* The peculiar verb *synepimartyrein* is
hapax (a single occurrence) in the NT and is not extant in the LXX. It does occur
in *Ep. Aristeas* 191. A simpler word, *symmartyrein*, is used by Paul in Rom 2:15,
meaning "witness to," and in Rom 8:16, "attest to," a meaning also found in
1 Pet 5:12, but with the Greek verb *epimartyrein*. *Synepimartyrein* appears to
combine both senses for a literal meaning of "attest to with." Whereas piling
up prepositional prefixes may be rare in NT Greek, it is not confined to Hebrews.
Perhaps the author's choice of verbs is influenced by the string of datives in
the remainder of the verse, which serve as the verb's indirect objects. The variant *symmartyrein* is attested in Vaticanus, probably a scribal correction for the
odd choice of word. The genitive absolute here carries the meaning of "when
God bore witness."

The nouns "signs," "wonders," and "miracles" are stock terms for the mi-
raculous in the biblical tradition. In the MT and the LXX the pairing of "signs
and wonders" often refers to the plagues of the Exodus tradition and other
positive acts of God on behalf of Israel (Exod 7:3; Deut 4:34; 6:22; 7:19; Ps
135:9[LXX]; Wis 8:8; Isa 8:18; 20:3; Jer 39:20 [LXX]; Dan 4:37 [LXX, Old Greek]; 6:28
[LXX, Θ]). The expression "signs and wonders" can refer negatively to God's
punishment of Israel, as in Deut 28:46. In the NT "signs and wonders" are often
placed in an apocalyptic or eschatological context (cf. Mark 13:22). In Acts 4:30
the pairing refers to miracles done in Jesus' name, or acts of power done by the
apostles (5:12) or granted by the Lord through the action of apostles (14:3; 15:12).
Although the author of the Fourth Gospel distinguishes Jesus' miracles in his

gospel vis-à-vis the Synoptics by using the term "signs" rather than "miracles," the terms seem interchangeable in general.

"Miracles" here is the standard NT term, *dynameis*, "deeds of power," which in the NT refers to Jesus' miracles (Matt 11:20, 21, 23; 13:54, 58; Mark 6:2; Luke 10:13) or simply the power at work in Jesus (Matt 14:2; Mark 6:14) or heavenly power (Matt 24:29; Mark 13:25; Luke 21:26). In Acts, *dynameis* is used for the miracles done through the apostles and Paul (8:13; 19:11). Paul includes "miracles" among the gifts of the Holy Spirit (1 Cor 12:28-29). He also refers to miracles done among the Galatians by the Holy Spirit (Gal 3:5). Interestingly, in the LXX the term most often refers to the ability to make war or to armies (2 Chron 26:11; 1 Macc passim; 2 Macc passim; Ezek 27:27; Dan 11:25). The phrase "by the gifts of the Holy Spirit" translated literally is "by the divisions of Holy Spirit," or "by the distributions of Holy Spirit."

The final expression "according to his will" may refer only to the "divisions of the Holy Spirit" or to all the elements of the series. The noun for "will" (*thelēsis*) is *hapax* in the NT, although it does occur in the LXX for "the will of God" (Tob 12:18; 2 Macc 12:16). Elsewhere Hebrews uses the more usual term *thelēma* (10:7, 9, 10, 36; 13:21).

INTERPRETATION

The style of these verses is hortatory, marked by imperatives and rhetorical questions that shift away from the expository style used thus far in the sermon. The first verse issues the warning and the following three present its rationale in the form of an a fortiori argument. At the heart of this passage lies the question, "How shall we escape when we neglect so great a salvation?" (v. 3). This great salvation has already been declared in the exordium and the expansion on it in the remainder of the first chapter. It is none other than the word of God finally spoken through the Son. The logic builds on the comparison between the Son and the angels that immediately precedes this section. When it is accepted that he has been given a greater name and status than the angels, and that indeed he is exalted at the right hand of God, it follows that the salvation available through him is worthy of credence. The underlying premise in the author's argument is that if all that has already been said about the place of the Son is true, then the message declared by God must be more carefully observed.

It is not clear, however, whether the exhortation to pay closer attention implies that the situation addressed is the opposite. Is it simply a matter of the excellence of the message that warrants the closest possible attention, or have the readers hitherto not given it the attention it deserves? In favor of the first possibility is the use of the comparative adverb *perissoterōs*, which is synonymous with the comparative adverb *mallon*, "more" (cf. BDF §60[3]). The use of the comparative suggests that the paraenesis is general, although it could imply that the readers were paying less attention than they should have. In favor of the latter is the context and other references in the sermon where the readers are exhorted to "hold fast" (3:6, 14; 10:23) and to stay the course, as if they have already drifted away (Attridge, 64; Ellingworth, 235).

Why the message of salvation deserves this kind of adherence rests on an a fortiori argument. If the message already declared through angels (the Law) was a valid message, for which just punishment was rendered for deviations or refusals to hear, then how much more would one expect a just punishment for the same behavior in face of the message declared by God through the Son? If transgression against the former warranted just punishment, then certainly transgressions against the latter will. The previous message so described is the Jewish Law, which was understood to have been mediated by angels. The author not only affirms the validating origin of the Law, but also confirms the power of the Law to punish those who violated it.

What renders the message declared through the Son valid and authoritative is a similar validating origin, but one that may be still stronger because it was declared not through angels, but rather without any mediation by God's self. The Middle Platonic thought world of the author would see such an unmediated message, coming directly from God, as stronger than one mediated by angels. The author does not say one is more valid than the other, but merely implies that the direct message from God warrants closer attention and that transgression against it may be more severely punished.

The author does not describe the content of the message. He merely refers to it as "what we have heard." At the very least this is a general description of the revelation of God treated in the exordium as something God spoke through the Son. The image of God as speaker is prominent in Hebrews, as is the notion of revelation as a spoken entity. Whether one can reasonably assume that the "gospel" is being referred to here is something that is not entirely out of the question. One caution, however, must be observed if that interpretation requires a contrast between Law and Gospel, which otherwise is not extensively treated in Hebrews. The word "gospel" (*euangelion*) does not occur in Hebrews at all. This would not preclude, however, that the general term "what we have heard" refers to the early Christian "kerygma."

The consequence of "drifting away," if attention is not paid to this message of salvation, conjures up the image of being at sea and losing sight of one's goal, or straying off course. In light of the sermon's own teleological bent this is not out of the question (cf. Koester, 206).

The second verse established one element of the comparison needed to conclude reasonably to the author's point that the message declared through the Son carries sanctions of its own with it. The reference to the validity of the message first declared by means of angelic mediators seems to allude to the popular belief in Hellenistic Judaism that angels played some role in the reception of the Law. If a scriptural tradition lies behind this idea it derives most likely from the mention of the "holy ones" whom Moses in Deut 33:2 says accompanied God to Sinai. The argument is strengthened with help from the LXX version of this text, which has the description of angels at the right hand of God at the moment when God delivered the Law to Moses. In nonbiblical Hellenistic Jewish literature one can find mention of the mediatory role of angels in Moses' reception of the Law in *Jubilees* 1:27; 2:1; 26–27. Josephus in *Antiquities* 15.136 writes that the holiest part of the Law was delivered through the embassy of angels. Paul himself may be a witness to such a view among first-century Jews. In Gal 3:19 he refers to the Law as "ordained by angels through an intermediary." Luke, too, seems to know of some association of angels with the Sinai tradition. In Acts 7:53 Stephen says that the Law was "ordained by angels," perhaps referring to his earlier mention of an angel who spoke with Moses on Sinai (Acts 7:38). Granted, there is no clear textual connection between these New Testament references and Deut 33:2 or Heb 2:2. Paul's meaning in Gal 3:19 is open to interpretation (Frank Matera, *Galatians*. SP 9 [Collegeville: Liturgical Press, 1992] 133) and translation problems obscure the clarity of Luke's meaning in Acts 7:38, 53 (Joseph A. Fitzmyer, *The Acts of the Apostles: New Translation with Introduction and Commentary*. AB 31 [New York: Doubleday, 1998] 380, 386; cf. W. D. Davies, "A Note on Josephus, *Antiquities* 15.136," *HTR* 47 [1954] 139). Still, these texts may count as evidence for the continued belief in first-century Judaism that angels played some role in the giving of the Law.

Important to the author's argument is the emphasis that even if the Law was mediated by angels it was still spoken by God and was therefore still in effect (*bebaios*). For this reason, when it was transgressed, a punishment was justly exacted. In an a fortiori development the main point of the argument becomes evident. This being the case, there is no excuse and there can be no escape from the retribution of God if the message delivered through the Son is itself neglected. The question posed at the beginning of v. 3 requires a negative answer.

What constitutes neglect is unclear, nor is it said that the neglect has already occurred. Other warnings in Hebrews express a similar concern for adherence (3:1-6, 12-19; 4:1-2, 11-13, 14-16; 5:11–6:8; 10:23-31; 12:12-13, 14-17, 25-29; 13:1-6, 7-16). So it seems there has been some kind of erosion in the way the readers lived their faith from the time of their conversion. The author exhorts them to "pay closer attention" to what was preached to them lest they "drift away," i.e., grow lax. Later, in 10:23-25, the appeal not to waver will be made explicitly, with an added example of some community members failing to meet together with the others (v. 25). The antidote to wavering is to attend more closely to the preached message.

The importance of what they should more closely attend to is expressed by the phrase "so great a salvation." The noun "salvation" is polyvalent, expressing salvation itself and the message of salvation as it had been given by God through the Son. How the readers are to avoid neglecting salvation will unfold in the constellation of expository and hortatory sections that make up the author's sermon. In this section the author establishes the importance of salvation as a reason for not neglecting it.

The greatness of this salvation is characterized by the quality of witnesses to it. "First announced by the Lord" echoes the exordium's evaluation of the word spoken "in this final time" through the Son. Earlier in the sermon the author gave an elaborate comparison of the Son to the angels. Here the superiority of the Son to the angels is accomplished more subtly through the parallelism of expression formed by vv. 2a and 3b: "the message announced by angels" is juxtaposed to the "salvation which was first announced by the Lord."

In addition to the declaration by the Lord, the greatness of this salvation was attested by earthly witnesses. Here the mediatory role has to do not with angels, or the Son himself, but rather with those who themselves may have heard him and then passed on what they had heard to others, perhaps to some in the community being addressed. In an effort to shore up even further the value and validity of this message the author presents it in a continuity of proclamation that reaches back to God and down to the current generation of hearers who are willing to receive it. He does not specify who these people are. Presumably they are the deceased individuals referred to in 13:7, who had first instructed the readers in the Gospel. Some commentators think they may have been eyewitnesses who had heard Jesus preach (Ellingworth, 141; Hughes, 77; Lane 1:39; Montefiore, 53). They seem simply to belong to a category of "those who heard." It has been suggested that the vagueness of their identity is one way the author focuses on the message itself and not on those who witnessed to it (Attridge, 67; Braun, 49–50; de Silva, *Perseverance*, 107; Grässer 1:106–107; Koester, 207).

If that were not enough to substantiate the validity and unsurpassed worth of this message of salvation, the author goes on to say that God witnessed to it through signs and wonders and by the gifts of the Holy Spirit. "Signs and wonders" is a technical term in the Old Testament, especially in the Exodus tradition, for the theophanic elements accompanying revelation. The status of the message given through the Son qualifies for a revelation then, too, as it was attested by divine "signs and wonders." What these are and when they took place is not specified. Equally vague is the designation "various miracles." How should we distinguish among signs, wonders, and miracles?

The last category of divine attestation, gifts of the Holy Spirit, is perhaps easier to determine, as Paul refers to gifts of the Holy Spirit in 1 Cor 12:4, 11. Here, however, a different Greek word is used. Curiously, Paul includes miracles under the gifts of the Holy Spirit (1 Cor 12:28-29; Gal 3:5), whereas this author treats them separately. The "gifts" are not the Pauline *charismata*, but are rather *merismoi*, "divisions." Some commentators prefer the word "distributions" (Koester, 207; cf. Lane 1:34). Interestingly, Luke portrays the bestowal of the Holy Spirit as something divided or distributed (*diamerizomenoi*) among those gathered in the upper room at the first Christian Pentecost (Acts 2:3). Perhaps in Hebrews these "divisions" ought to be read as epexegetic, explaining and interpreting signs, wonders, and miracles.

The warning contained in this section establishes two things. First, it shows how much the author values the salvation he believes to have come in God's word spoken by means of the Son. Second, it shows his concern for his readers, that they may benefit from having heard that word. The comparison with the Law helps to support his view of the importance of salvation, which he attempts to show is a more valuable message than what was first declared by angels. The exhortation to pay closer attention to the message declared by the Son places the responsibility for adherence on the shoulders of the readers. As with other similar exhortations in the New Testament, the estimable value of salvation makes it incumbent on the readers, and indeed on all Christians, to heed the word of the Lord.

For Reference and Further Study

Bachmann, Michael. "'. . . gesprochen durch den Herrn' (Hebr 2,3): Erwägungen zum Reden Gottes und Jesu im Hebräerbrief," *Bib* 71 (1990) 365–94.

Grässer, Erich. "Das Heil als Wort: Exegetische Erwägungen zu Hebr 2,1-4," in Heinrich Baltensweiler and Bo Reicke, eds., *Neues Testament und Geschichte*. Tübingen: Mohr Siebeck, 1972, 261–74.

Oberholtzer, Thomas K. "The Eschatological Salvation of Hebrews 1:5–2:5," *BSac* 145 (1988) 83–97.

Vanhoye, Albert. *Situation du Christ: Hébreux 1–2*. LD 58. Paris: Cerf, 1969.

4. *Subjecting All Things* (2:5-9)

5. Now God did not subject the coming world, about which we are speaking, to angels. 6. But someone has testified somewhere, "What is man that you remember him, or son of man, that you care for him? 7. You have made him for a little while lower than the angels; you have crowned him with glory and honor, 8. subjecting all things under his feet." Now in subjecting all things (to him), God left nothing outside his control. As it is, we do not yet see everything in subjection to him, 9. but we do see Jesus, who, for a little while, was made lower than the angels, now crowned with glory and honor because of the suffering of death, so that apart from God he might taste death for everyone.

NOTES

5. *Now God did not subject the coming world, about which we are speaking, to angels:* The Greek particle *gar* does not resume the previous section, but rather introduces a new part of the argument (see 4:12; 7:1; 10:1; cf. Attridge, 69). The tradition of God subjecting the world to angels was current in Hellenistic Judaism, as the LXX of Deut 32:8 shows (Attridge, 70; Lane 1:45). The future world, however, was not to be placed under their control, and the author echoes that sentiment (Bruce, 71–72; Ellingworth, 146–47).

"The coming world," *oikoumenē*, is the "inhabited world." In 1:6 the noun refers to the heavenly world, where the angels are commanded to bow down before the Son. The same sense applies in this verse, where the noun is qualified by the participle *mellousan*, "that which is about to happen" or "coming." The verb *mellein* is eschatological in most of the places it occurs in Hebrews (1:14; 2:5; 6:5; 9:11; 10:1, 27; 13:14; cf. 8:5; 11:8, 20). Here the future heavenly world is subjected to the Son (Attridge, 70; Ellingworth, 146; Koester, 213; Lane 1:43; Weiss, 193).

6. *But someone has testified somewhere:* As in 4:3-4, this use of the Greek adverb *pou*, "somewhere," leaves the impression that the author does not know exactly where the text he has in mind is cited. This way of introducing scriptural quotations or allusions is not peculiar to Hebrews. Philo uses it, for example (*The Unchangeableness of God* 74). It appears to be a literary device and may be a common homiletic practice (Attridge, 70–71). The author, so familiar with the LXX, especially the Psalms, would surely know that the citation comes from Psalm 8. The use of *diamartyreisthai* is in keeping with the author's preference for authenticating the word of God by using legal metaphors, as in the previous section (2:4).

"What is man that you remember him, or son of man, that you care for him? 7. You have made him for a little while lower than the angels; you have crowned him with glory and honor, 8. subjecting all things under his feet": The citation follows the LXX (Ps 8:5-7) fairly closely, except for the omission of the placement of humans over the created order in v. 7a. This verse is included in some NT manuscripts (א A C D* P Ψ 0243. 0278. 6. 33. 81. 104. 365. 629. 1050. 1739. 1881. 2464 *al* lat [sy^{ph**}] co), but it is likely that a scribe would have added it to bring the text more in conformity with the LXX, and so the shorter text is preferred.

More recent translations like the NRSV prefer to drop the word "man" for "human beings" and to change the singular pronouns in the citation to the plural, "them." The Greek *anthrōpos* is collective and carries the meaning of humans or humanity. Here it is likely that it refers not only to humans but also to Christ, as it alludes to the comparison of Christ with the angels in the previous chapter.

The verb *mimnēskesthai* is in the subjunctive, with the sense of "might" or "should" remember, communicating the distance between the creature and the creator. "Remembering" in the Hebrew Bible is an important divine function that suggests more than merely calling to mind. When God "remembers," the word carries a sense of obligation on God's part to do something for someone or for Israel as a whole. Often it means to remember the covenant and therefore to act out of a duty on behalf of Israel, God's covenanted people (see Gen 8:1; 19:29; 30:22; Exod 2:24; 20:24; Num 10:1; 1 Sam 1:19; Ps 98:3).

The formulation "son of man" in the psalm causes problems for a smooth interpretation. The psalm, lacking the definite article, does not reflect the usual NT formulation, "the son of the man." This may impede a christological interpretation of the psalm in Hebrews, although it need not disqualify such an interpretation. In the MT and LXX the expression "son of man" can simply mean a human (cf. Num 23:19; Jdt 8:16; Ps 143:3; Job 16:21; 25:6; Sir 17:30; Jer 2:6; 27:40; 28:43; 30:12; 30:38; Ezekiel [passim 96 instances]; Dan 7:13). The problem, of course, is how the expression appears in the NT, where it is determinate and not absolute as in the MT and LXX. At issue is whether and when "son of man" took on a titular status, and if in Hellenistic Judaism such a title had already been interpreted to refer to a coming Messiah. Some commentators maintain that the only clear non-Christian messianic use of "son of man" is found in *1 Enoch* (46:3; 48:2; 69:27-29; 70:1; 71:14, 17; Attridge, 73; Koester, 215).

The titular use of "son of man" seems first to have occurred in the NT. Although one does not find it in Paul, it is applied regularly to Jesus in the Synoptics and John. Some argue that Jesus used the expression himself as a circumlocution for the first person singular pronoun, "I" (Matt 8:20). Where the gospel pericopes include the vision of Dan 7:13, commentators are divided over whether it is already a messianic title in the Hebrew Bible that is then applied to Jesus by the early church (John R. Donahue, "Recent Studies on the Origin of 'Son of Man' in the Gospels," *CBQ* 48 [1986] 484–98). Inescapable in these passages is the apocalyptic context of the Daniel citation (Matt 26:64; Mark 13:26; 14:62; Luke 21:27; John 1:51).

Since the definite article is missing in Heb 2:6, the author is not using the term as a title. The correspondence between "man" in the psalm quotation and "son of man" would suggest that the meaning here should be nontitular, a human being (cf. Koester, 215–16). There is no doubt that the author uses the ambiguity of the psalm in order to make a connection between the humans mentioned in it and Jesus (2:9).

The verb "to care for," *episkeptein*, means "to look after" in the positive sense of coming to one's aid (Jas 1:27), and so it parallels the notion of God's remembering in the previous verse. The LXX frequently has God as the subject of this verb (Gen 21:1; 50:24; Exod 3:16; 4:31; Sir 46:14; Jdt 8:33; BDAG, 378).

In the LXX the adjective *brachy* has the simple meaning "a little," as in a quantity (1 Sam 14:29, 43), but it may also have a spatial meaning, as in "a short distance" (2 Sam 16:1) or a temporal sense, as in "a short while" (Pss 93(94):17; 118:87). The temporal meaning is found elsewhere in the NT at Luke 22:58 and Acts 5:34. In view of the author's use of the adjective in 2:9 the translation "for a little while" seems appropriate in the psalm citation in order to make the application to Jesus.

The verb *ellatoun* means "lower in status" or "lessen." The expression "made him for a little while lower than the angels" is parallel to "crowned him with honor and glory" in the next verse, making both roughly synonymous. This meaning seems paradoxical, as "honor and glory" are antithetical to "lowering." The psalm, however, gives tribute to the role humans play in creation (Gen 1:26,

28), even if they rank below angels in the created order. The "honor and glory" of humans is confirmed by the notice that all things are subjected to humans. In the psalm this cannot refer to anything more than earthly reality.

Now in subjecting all things (to him), God left nothing outside his control: The author resumes his thought begun in v. 5. If it was not to angels that the world to come was subjected, he now supplies the answer to the question his readers may have asked themselves: "Then to whom did he subject the world to come?" Here begins the application of the psalm to Jesus, as it is paraphrased in a way that is reminiscent also of the quotation of Psalm 110 (109) in 1:13, reintroducing the theme of the Son. Some manuscripts ($\mathfrak{P}^{46}$ B d v vg^{mss} bo^{ms}) omit "to him" (*autō*). Commentators note that since the text cited does not have the pronoun, the more original reading would also lack it, and it was probably added by a scribe to make the application to Jesus more explicit (Attridge, 69; Koester, 216).

God is not specified in the text as the subject of the verb "leave to," *aphienai.* The Greek adjective *anypotaktos* occurs elsewhere in the NT to refer to people who cannot be controlled (1 Tim 1:9; Titus 1:10). The negative *ouden* produces the opposite effect to create the redundancy that interprets all things being subjected to him to mean that there is nothing that cannot be subject to him. The dative *autō*, now expressed in the text, is unclear. To whom does the author refer it? If it refers to humanity in the psalm, then it merely paraphrases the sentiment there. If it looks forward to Christ, it anticipates the explanation of how what the psalm recounted was not fully achieved by humans, as the next verse would indicate.

As it is, we do not yet see everything in subjection to him: The ambiguity continues. Does this verse refer to the failure of the present world to be subjected to humans or to the future world not yet subjected to Christ? The adversative *de* of the next verse suggests that the author has humans in mind here. The present world is not completely subjected to humans.

9. *but we do see Jesus:* Now the hermeneutical focus of the quoted psalm becomes explicit: It was meant to interpret the salvific work of the Son. Attridge notices the artistry of the verses (71). Framing the name Jesus with reinterpreted allusions to the psalm makes the author's exegetical purpose evident. Not only is the death of Jesus placed at the center, but his incarnation and exaltation are given their due as well (Attridge, 72–73). Later in the sermon the author will invite the readers "to look to Jesus" as they run the race (Koester, 217). Here they also see him in his exalted state, even if the total subjection of all things has yet to occur. The fact that he is exalted attests to the ultimate subjection of all things.

who, for a little while, was made lower than the angels: The humanity proclaimed in the psalm is none other than that of the Son, who in the incarnation participated in the lowered state of humanity, and as a result was even lower than the angels. Unlike the psalm itself, the author's application of this verse to Jesus is intended as an antithesis to what follows. The psalm is then actualized in a new way for the readers.

now crowned with glory and honor because of the suffering of death: Christ's exaltation results not merely from the incarnation but from the acceptance of humanity to its limits, suffering, and death. The allusion to the psalm is further explained; the way to glory was through death. It is tempting here to see echoes of the Gospel of Mark, another document of the Roman church, which proclaims that the only way to glory is through the cross (Mark 8:34; 9:35; 10:35-45). The reference to the "suffering of death" makes clear that the author has interpreted the psalm to apply to Jesus, whose exaltation must be understood in terms of his suffering and death. Jesus can only be exalted because he was first lowered (Attridge, 75). For this reason he is not identified as Christ in this verse, but is called Jesus. It is the human face of Jesus that the author wants his audience to see. Later in the sermon the actual suffering of Jesus will be graphically described in terms of prayers, supplications, loud cries, tears, and fear (5:7). His shameful death marked by "reproof" takes place "outside the camp" (12:2; 13:12), signifying the "lowering" he had undergone.

so that apart from God, he might taste death for everyone: There is some debate about the placement of this clause. Otto Michel thinks it is misplaced, since the crowning has already been mentioned (*Hebräer*, 139). Some commentators rightly believe it modifies everything that precedes it in v. 9 (Attridge, 76; Peterson, *Hebrews and Perfection*, 55). Most translations follow the majority of manuscript witnesses, which have "so that with the grace of God." There are a few manuscripts, however, that preserve the reading "apart from God," and this was the patristic understanding of the text (cf. Koester, 217–18). The difference in Greek is the difference between *chariti theou* and *chōris theou*. The minority witness is preferred because it makes sense in light of what is being exposed here. The author is talking about the suffering of Jesus as a human, i.e., how he suffered in his human nature. In Hebrews Jesus' suffering is proclaimed as real suffering, reminiscent of Mark's gospel (Heb 5:7-8; 12:2; 13:12-13). Some commentators prefer "apart from God" as the more difficult reading (Braun, 57; Ellingworth, 155–56; John K. Elliott, "When Jesus Was Apart from God: An Examination of Hebrews 2,9," *ExpTim* 83 [1972] 339–41; Montefiore, 59; Peterson, *Hebrews and Perfection*, 216). Attridge believes the context, which shows God's concern for humanity, prevents the reading "apart from God" (77). Since, however, the author interprets the parallelism in v. 5 of the psalm as antithetical rather than synonymous when applying the psalm to Jesus, the reading "apart from God" does not seem out of place. Ellingworth shows how the context supports such a reading (156).

"To taste death" means to undergo it. The author uses a metaphor for "dying" as in Mark 9:1; John 8:52 (cf. Luke 14:24). The addition of "for everyone," *hyper pantos*, indicates the scope and depth of the "great salvation" referred to in 2:3, of which Jesus is the pioneer (2:10) and the source (5:9).

INTERPRETATION

After the exhortation of 2:1-4 the author returns to the theme of the angels and the Son, now to show yet another way that the Son is superior to the angels. The coming heavenly world will be under his control, not theirs. What practical import this has for the readers is unclear. If they were involved in some form of angel worship or appeasement of angels out of fear (see Randall C. Gleason, "Angels and Eschatology of Heb 1–2" *NTS* 49 [2003] 90–107), the assurance of the author that angels will not have control over eternity places the focus where it belongs. It is the Son who controls eternity. This section of the sermon develops a key aspect of the author's eschatology.

It is somewhat peculiar for the author to engage in a midrash on Psalm 8 to explain why this is the case. The psalm was originally meant to celebrate the dignity of humans in the created order by highlighting God's effective remembrance and care for them as God's crowning achievement. The placement of the psalm in this section of the sermon is, however, not completely unintelligible. The midrash on Psalm 8 allows the author to make a significant point about the role Jesus played in bringing the understanding of the psalm to a new level. In effect this amounts to a kind of "re-scripturing" of the psalm. The author wants to show how the dignity of humans was elevated by what God did through the human agency of the Son and what the eschatological effect of the Son's role is. By applying the psalm verse to Jesus the author explains how he completes the divine plan for humans, as the representative human (Julius Kögel, *Der Sohn und die Söhne: eine exegetische Studie zu Hebräer 2, 5-18* [Gütersloh: Bertelsmann, 1904] 55; Ernst Käsemann, *The Wandering People of God: An Investigation of the Letter to the Hebrews* [Minneapolis: Augsburg, 1984] 128). The question raised by the psalm about whether God has anything to do with humans anticipates God's involvement in the way Jesus perfects humanity. Thus this part of the argument will prepare the reader for what follows in 2:10-18 (Alan C. Mitchell, "The Use of *prepein* and Rhetorical Propriety in Hebrews 2:10," *CBQ* 54 [1992] 695).

The psalm enables the author to stress how, at the time of creation, God elevated the dignity of humans. Its inclusion at this point in the argument functions in two ways. First, it serves not only to point out that, despite humans' subordination to angels, they had received honor and glory and were given a cooperative role with God in creation. Creation was subjected to them (Gen 1:26), as v. 6 of the psalm observes. In this way humans entered into a relationship with God, who had placed them at the head of creation. After the Fall, however, that relationship was broken and stood in need of repair (Gen 3:24). It was never fully realized and remained incomplete. Second, it also shows that the one to whom the future world would be subjected had a real share in humanity, but his elevation to glory was based on the way he embraced the human condition to the point of suffering and death (Albert Vanhoye, *Situation du Christ, Hébreux 1–2* LD 58 [Paris: Cerf, 1969] 261). In his example, obedience facilitated the completion of the relationship with God that had been broken in the Fall. As a result everything that had been subjected to humans in creation was now subjected to him in a new way, which is proleptic, since it awaits further eschatological fulfillment (Attridge, 75; Peterson, *Hebrews and Perfection*, 51, 126–30). This sense is made clear when the author says that although the readers can see Jesus they are unable to see everything subjected to him (2:9).

The author emphasizes the human Jesus in his suffering prior to exaltation here, because he is preparing for the next section of the chapter that will argue for the propriety of Jesus' death as the cause for leading others to glory. Here he is crowned with glory and honor because of his death, something that qualifies him to bring others to glory (2:10). Is this not foreshadowed in the expression "that he might taste death for everyone"?

How does Jesus taste death for everyone? In 1 Corinthians the resurrection of Christ is spoken of as the down payment on or firstfruits of the resurrection of all believers (1 Cor 15:20, 23). In Hebrews, despite the exalted language in reference to the Son, Jesus dies a real death; he participates fully in humanity. Perhaps this is the legacy of the Roman church anchored in the Gospel of Mark.

So all things are subjected to the Son rather than to angels. This, of course, is not immediately evident. Do the readers see this subjugation? No. What they see is Jesus, to whom the psalm is now applied. He is the one who in his incarnation took on full humanity in a state that was, for a while, lower than the angels. In the real time of their worlds the readers are engaged in the day-to-day life of humans that involves suffering of their own. The example of Jesus is then instructive. He was lowered, but was exalted and became a model because he accepted the limits of the human condition unto death. The result was that he, like humans in the psalm, was crowned with honor and glory. What in the psalm is synonymous, being made lower than the angels and yet crowned with honor in glory, in its application to Christ is antithetical.

Critical in the author's interpretation of the psalm is the stress on the temporal sense of "a little while," *brachy ti*, and the changes made to the psalm as he elaborates on it in his text. When the author reiterates this expression in v. 9 the placement of "a little while" is moved forward, giving it prominence. He then changes the tense of the participles from the aorist active of the original psalm to the perfect passive. The aorist addresses what God did in the past when humans were created, whereas the perfect shows the completed action of God in Christ (Simon Kistemaker, *Psalm Citations in the Epistle to the Hebrews* [Amsterdam: van Soest, 1961] 105–106; Gheorghita, *The Role of the Septuagint*, 106).

Does the author, in citing and reinterpreting Psalm 8, develop a "Son of Man" christology here? As the expression "son of man" is anarthrous, he is not using the term in a titular sense, but rather wants to connect Jesus with all humanity by means of a generic understanding of the term. Thus the term "man" of the psalm provides a basis for the reflection on Jesus' humanity. The author's use of the psalm is intended to address the incarnation and exaltation of the Son in light of his suffering.

What is the source of this reflection by the author of Hebrews? Michael Goulder has argued that the author introduced this interpretation of Dan 7:13 into the NT, as it is not present in Paul ("Psalm 8 and The Son of Man," *NTS* 48 [2002] 18–29). He suggests that Mark created the titular use of Son of Man out of the tradition he had gotten from Hebrews. Since Hebrews was written after Mark, however, it would seem better to argue that the trajectory runs in the opposite direction: Hebrews got the tradition from Mark. The author of Hebrews was familiar with the traditions of the Roman church, which included not only Paul's sermon to the Romans, but the Gospel of Mark as well. It makes better sense to argue that Hebrews was written after the destruction of the Temple, and that Mark's Gospel was already in place in Rome when the sermon was written. Hebrews presupposes a narrative of the life and death of Jesus, and the Gospel of Mark fits that narrative well. Mature reflection on the death of Jesus and the consequences of that death for all humans is clear in Hebrews.

If Hebrews were written before the Gospel of Mark, then it is likely that the Gospel of Mark would have been markedly different in its composition. One conjectural example may suffice to illustrate this claim. The longer ending of Mark (16:9-20) may have come under the influence of Hebrews in at least two places. First, Mark 16:19 narrates that after Jesus was taken up into heaven he sat down at the right hand of God (*ekathisen ek dexiōn tou theou*; v.l.: *ekathisen en dexią tou theou* [C Δ *pc* it; Ir^lat]). The only other NT text that has this formulation is Heb 10:12, "But when Christ had offered for all time a single sacrifice for sins, 'he sat down at the right hand of God'" (*ekathisen en dexią tou theou*; v.l.: *ekathisen ek dexiōn tou theou* [A 104]). Second, Mark 16:20 refers to the attestation (*bebaiountos*) of the message (*logos*) by signs (*dia sēmeiōn*). Hebrews 2:3-4 is the only other NT text where the verb *bebaioun*, "attest to," and the noun *sēmeia*, "sign," occur together to explain how the message of salvation (*logos*) was attested (*ebebaiōthē*) by those who heard, and witnessed by God (*synepimartyrein*) through signs (*sēmeiois*).

Commentators usually attribute the similarities between Heb 10:12; 2:3-4; and Mark 16:19-20 to common early Christian traditions each author drew upon independently of the other, without claiming that Hebrews may have influenced the composition of the longer ending of Mark (David M. Hay, *Glory at the Right Hand: Psalm 110 in Early Christianity*. SBLMS 18 [Nashville: Abingdon, 1973] 83–84; Hughes, 69; William R. G. Loader, *Sohn und Hoherpriester: Eine traditionsgeschichtliche Untersuchung zur Christologie des Hebräerbriefes*. WMANT 53 [Neukirchen-Vluyn: Neukirchener, 1981] 16–21; Michel, 130). J.-P. van Kasteren believed that the similarities between Mark 16:19-20 and Heb 10:12; 2:3-4 were best explained by positing that the author of Hebrews knew the Gospel of Mark. He did not think, however, that the longer ending of Mark could have been influenced by Hebrews ("L'Épilogue Canonique du Second Évangile [Mr. 16, 9-20]," *RB* 11 [1902] 249, n.1). Ceslas Spicq affirmed that the longer ending of Mark "represents the same theological and apologetic ideas as Hebrews" (1:96, n.1), but he proposed a date of 67 C.E. for Hebrews and placed the longer ending of Mark in the apostolic era, earlier than many would (John R. Donahue and Daniel J. Harrington, *The Gospel of Mark.* SP 2 [Collegeville: Liturgical Press, 2002] 463; cf. André Feuillet, "Le 'commencement' de l'économie chrétienne d'après He ii.3-4; Mc i.1 et Ac i.1-2," *NTS* 24 [1977–78] 168–69). It would appear, then, that none of these authors believes that Hebrews could have influenced the author of the longer ending of Mark, either because the traditions exemplified in both texts had already gained the status of common early Christian traditions or because the longer ending of Mark was already appended to the original gospel by the time Hebrews was written. If one posits a post-70 C.E. date for Hebrews and a second-century date for the longer ending of Mark the picture looks somewhat different. Even some who have observed the similarities between both texts had a hard time attributing them to chance or coincidence (Feuillet, "Le 'commencement,'" 165; van Kasteren, "L'Épilogue Canonique," 246). It seems reasonable, then, in view of a post-70 C.E. date for Hebrews, to conclude that the author of the longer ending of Mark was influenced by Hebrews when composing Mark 16:19-20.

The historical circumstances of Hebrews and its christology point to the strong possibility that the Gospel of Mark predates Hebrews. First, Mark written a few years before Hebrews is closer to the time of the destruction of the Temple. The lack of explicit references to the Temple in Hebrews suggests that it was probably written in the aftermath of the fall of Jerusalem. Second, whereas Hebrews shares the view of Mark that Jesus died a real death, it lacks the concentrated focus on the suffering of Jesus that the Gospel of Mark witnesses to. Hebrews is already making arguments for the meaning of Christ's death that the Gospel of Mark could not have made. The High Priest christology of Hebrews could only come after the lower christology of Mark (see Introduction, 3. *Date*).

FOR REFERENCE AND FURTHER STUDY

Brady, Cora. "The World to Come in the Epistle to the Hebrews," *Worship* 39 (1965) 329–39.

Elliott, John K. "When Jesus Was Apart from God: An Examination of Hebrews 2:9," *ExpTim* 83 (1971–72) 339–41.

Harnack, Adolf von. "Zwei alte dogmatische Korrekturen im Hebräerbrief," SPAW (1929) 63–73.

Steyn, Gert J. "Some Observations about the *Vorlage* of Ps 8:5-7 in Heb 2:6-8," *VEccl* 24 (2003) 493–514.

Vanhoye, Albert. "L'*oikoumenē* dans L'Épître aux Hébreux," *Bib* 45 (1964) 248–53.

5. *A Merciful and Faithful High Priest* (2:10-18)

10. It was fitting that God, for whom and through whom all things exist, in bringing many children to glory should make the pioneer of their salvation perfect through sufferings. 11. For the one who sanctifies and those who are sanctified all stem from a single source. For this reason he is not ashamed to call them brothers and sisters, 12. saying, "I will proclaim your name to my brothers and sisters; in the midst of the congregation I will praise you." 13. And again, "I will put my trust in him." And again, "Here am I and the children whom God has given me." 14. Since, therefore, the children shared flesh and blood, he himself likewise shared the same things, so that through death he might destroy the one who has the power of death, that is, the devil, 15. and free those who all their lives were held in slavery by the fear of death. 16. For it is clear that he did not take hold of angels, but the descendants of Abraham. 17. Therefore he had to become like his brothers and sisters in every respect, so that he might be a merciful and faithful high priest in matters pertaining to God, to make a sacrifice of atonement for the sins of the people. 18. Because he himself was tested by what he suffered, he is able to help those who are being tested.

Notes

10. *It was fitting that God, for whom and through whom all things exist, in bringing many children to glory should make the pioneer of their salvation perfect through sufferings:* The notion of propriety, *to prepon*, here is complex. In the milieu of Hellenistic Judaism it may not have been seen as proper for God to be involved with human suffering (Attridge, 82). The author seems to think otherwise and shows the appropriateness of God's direct involvement in the suffering of the Son. For the notion of rhetorical propriety in this text see Alan C. Mitchell, "The Use of *prepein* and Rhetorical Propriety in Hebrews 2:10," *CBQ* 54 (1992) 681–701.

God is described by the double prepositional phrase "for whom and through whom all things exist." In response to those who claimed the world was un-originate, Philo countered with a restatement of the biblical image of God as the origin of all creation. In one place he wrote about God as the divine architect, who without the aid of anyone else created the entire universe (*On the Creation* 17–25), yet in another he addressed the distinction among the various forms of causality, expressed by the prepositional phrases similar to those used in this verse. In Philo's considered opinion "by which" expresses the efficient cause of something, "from which" the material cause, "through which" the instrumental cause, and "for which" the final cause. He goes on to say that in creation the instrumental cause was the logos, God's Word (*On the Cherubim* 124–28). In this verse "for whom," *di' hon*, means that God is the end of creation and "through whom," *di' hou*, means that God was the instrumental cause, through which creation came about. Earlier the Son was described by *di' hou*, as the instrumental cause of creation (1:2) in a role similar to that played by Philo's *logos*.

God is also described as "bringing many children to glory." The subject of the participle *agagonta* is ambiguous, as it could refer to Christ (Gerhard Delling, *archē, ktl., TDNT* 1:488; Käsemann, *The Wandering People of God*, 43) or to God (Attridge, 82; Bruce, 77; Grässer 1:128; Ellingworth, 159; Koester, 227; Michel, 147–48; Weiss, 206). A more natural reading of the verse would take God as the subject, whose purpose in perfecting the Son is to bring many others to glory. The Greek has "sons" rather than children, which captures the allusion to the perfection of the one Son that will effect the perfection of "many sons." The mention of glory here recalls the glory with which the Son was crowned in v. 9.

Jesus will be called "pioneer" or "leader" later in 12:2, where he is described as "the pioneer and perfecter of our faith." Elsewhere in the NT the Greek term *archēgos* is applied to him in Acts 3:15 and 5:31. In Hebrews the term captures the beginning point of the full range of his work. As pioneer, he is the one who goes ahead to open the way, just as he was the first to taste death in 2:9. If later he is the pioneer of faith, here he is the pioneer of salvation because through his suffering and death not only will he himself be perfected, but he also will make possible the perfection of others as the mediator of a new covenant (9:15).

"Perfection" is a central concept in Hebrews, describing not only what happens to Jesus but also what his self-offering has done for all believers (9:11-14). The Greek term "perfect," *teleios*, means "be complete" or "be mature" (BDAG, 995–96). In the LXX death becomes a means of perfection in Wis 4:13-14 (Peterson, *Hebrews and Perfection*, 26). Hebrews goes beyond that notion to suggest that suffering is an appropriate method of bringing to completion, and lays the foundation for later Christian tradition in this regard (Attridge, 86). The act of perfecting plays the role of qualifying Jesus for his ministry as High Priest (5:9; 7:28). His "perfection" enables him to minister in a "more perfect" tent (9:11).

11. *For the one who sanctifies and those who are sanctified all stem from a single source:* The verb "sanctify," *hagiazein*, means "set apart" or "dedicate" when things are its object (LXX: Gen 2:3; Exod 13:2, 12; 19:23; 29:27, 37, 44) and "make holy" or "consecrate" when referring to persons (LXX: Exod 19:14, 22; 28:41; 29:1, 27, 33; Sir 33:12; 45:4; BDAG, 9–10). The language of sanctification is cultic, anticipating the end of the passage, where Jesus is called the merciful and faithful High Priest (2:17). The singular active participle, "the one who sanctifies," and the plural passive participle, "those who are sanctified," effectively join Jesus to all of humanity, later described in a fraternal relationship with him. "Sanctification," a cleansing or purification of the conscience, in Hebrews results from Jesus' self-offering as High Priest as this notion is developed in later chapters

(see Introduction, 8. *Conscience/Consciousness of Sins in Hebrews*). It is what makes the ritual of the new covenant more effective than that of the old (9:13; 10:10, 14, 29; 13:12).

Some translations interpret the Greek *ex henos*, "out of one," to mean "having the same Father." Whereas the union of Jesus and humanity spoken of here does stem from God, the ambiguity of the text has led ancient and modern commentators to propose other sources such as Adam or Abraham (Attridge, 88–89). Koester makes a distinction between the theological and anthropological meanings of the term (220). The theological sense fits best here.

For this reason he is not ashamed to call them brothers and sisters: Confirming the familial relationship of Jesus with all humans, the author emphasizes the solidarity of Christ with fellow human beings. He is not ashamed to be counted as part of humanity. The idea of Jesus being ashamed to be associated with his followers originated in another Roman document. In Mark 8:38 Jesus warns his followers that those who are ashamed of him will find the Son of Man ashamed of them when he enters into his glory. Hebrews is not necessarily countering this claim but is rather stressing the union of Jesus with fellow human beings. This is an important point to establish here because of the role solidarity will play in his function as heavenly High Priest. Fictive kinship was a common motif in early Christianity, so the reference to "brothers and sisters" is traditional here. The Greek word *adelphos* covers both males and females, much like the German *Geschwister* (Hans-Josef Klauck, "Kirche als Freundesgemeinschaft? Auf Spurensuche im Neuen Testament," *MTZ* 42 [1991] 10–11).

12. *saying, "I will proclaim your name to my brothers and sisters; in the midst of the congregation I will praise you":* The participle "saying," *legōn*, introduces the quotation from Psalm 22(21). Just as Mark has put the first verse of this psalm on the lips of Jesus before his death (Mark 15:34), Hebrews has Jesus proclaim its twenty-third verse (LXX: MT: v. 22). The psalm is reproduced faithfully here with one exception. The LXX has the verb *diegesthai*, "tell" or "narrate," whereas in Hebrews the verb is *apangelein*, "proclaim" or "announce." Either the change was already in the author's source or he changed it himself (Gheorghita, *Role of the Septuagint*, 62; Attridge, 90). The psalm itself divides into two parts, lamentation and praise. Whereas other NT authors focus on the lamentation in interpreting Christ's death (Rom 5:5; Matt 27:35, 39, 43, 46; Mark 15:24, 29, 34; Luke 23:34, 35; John 19:24, 28) the author of Hebrews quotes from the praise section. It is likely that he does this in view of the word "glory" and the citation of Psalm 8 in the previous section.

13. *And again, I will put my trust in him:* The source of the citation is unclear. It may derive from 2 Sam 22:3, or from Isa 8:17 or 12:2. The author has rearranged the first two words. In the possible source texts the adverb *pepoithōs* precedes the future verb *esomai*. He also adds a subject in the form of the first person singular personal pronoun, *egō*, "I."

And again, Here, am I and the children whom God has given me: The quotation is from Isa 8:18 and its presence here may answer the question about the source of the previous LXX citation. Most likely it, too, comes from Isa 8:17. This time the author reproduces the LXX exactly. "Children" are now the collective children of God and not only the "brothers and sisters" mentioned above. Whereas Jesus proclaims God's name to his brothers and sisters in the assembly, now he stands with them in that assembly sharing a common confidence and faith in God.

14. *Since, therefore, the children shared flesh and blood, he himself likewise shared the same things, so that through death he might destroy the one who has the power of death, that is, the devil:* Another part of the argument begins here (Attridge, 91). Picking up on the word "children" cited from Isaiah in the previous verse, the author returns to the notion of Jesus' solidarity with humanity. As humans share "blood and flesh," so also does he. The verb *metechein* means "share," or "participate in" (BDAG, 642), and it is used similarly in the LXX (1 Esdr 5:40; 8:70; Prov 5:17; Wis 16:3; 19:16). The author will use this verb again in 5:13 and 7:13.

    By means of his incarnation, Jesus' sharing of "blood and flesh" was purposeful. Notably through his death, the devil is destroyed. In the Hebrew Bible the devil is not necessarily a personification of evil (1 Sam 29:4; 2 Sam 19:23; 1 Kgs 5:18; Ps 109:6; cf. Job 1:6). The Hebrew word *sātan* means "adversary" or "opponent" (HAL, 918). The identification of the devil with death is biblical and traditional (Wis 2:23-24; 1 Cor 15:26, 55; Rev 20:14). It is not clear what the power of death is in the author's mind. In context it would seem to be the ability death has to prevent some of the "sons and daughters" from coming to glory, through fear of death itself. Christ's death has obviated that.

15. *and free those who all their lives were held in slavery by the fear of death:* Fear of death was a form of "slavery" for many in antiquity, as it can be today. Philosophers and orators addressed the issue because it was so prevalent, but they saw it stemming from superstition and counseled that death is really nothing to be feared (Epicurus, *Letter to Menoeceus* 125; 133; *Principal Doctrines* 11; 20; Dio Chrysostom, *Orations* 6.42; Plutarch, *On Superstition* 166F; *On Tranquility of Mind* 476A-B; Seneca, *Epistles* 24.22-23; 82.16; 102.26). In the Hebrew Bible death was seen as the natural end to a full life (Gen 3:19; 25:8; Deut 34:7; 2 Sam 14:14; Job 42:17). It was also seen, however, as a separation from God (Isa 38:18-20; Pss 6:5; 30:9-10; 88:10-12) and something to be feared (Ps 102:23-24; Eccl 12:1-8).

16. *For it is clear that he did not take hold of angels, but the descendants of Abraham:* Angels are not the object of Jesus' concern, but rather humans, the descendants of Abraham. The verb *epilambanesthai* means "take hold of" (BDAG, 374). In the LXX the verb can mean "support" (1 Kgdms 6:6; Ezek 41:6) or "help" (Sir 4:11). In Jer 38:32 it is used for God's taking Israel by the hand to lead them out of Egypt. The sense is not clear in Hebrews, but in light of what follows, perhaps a similar sense of "help" or "rescue" is intended. The children of Abraham are, of course, Jews (Isa 41:8; Jer 33:26; 4 Macc 6:17, 22). Christians saw themselves as children of Abraham and believed they would have a share in the promises made to him (Luke 1:55; Gal 3:16). The descendants of Abraham must be the "sons" and "brothers and sisters" alluded to earlier (Koester, 232).

17. *Therefore he had to become like his brothers and sisters in every respect:* The verb *homoiuon* can mean "make like" or "compare" (BDAG, 707). In Acts 14:11 it describes the perception by the people of Lystra that Paul and Barnabas had become like gods. Perhaps this verse is a further elaboration on 2:11, offering yet

another expression of the solidarity between the Son and other humans. Becoming like his brothers and sisters qualifies the Son as the perfect mediator between God and humans (2:9-10). The verse also anticipates 2:18, where Jesus is tested as they are.

so that he might be a merciful and faithful high priest in matters pertaining to God: A purpose clause introduced by the Greek particle *hina* sets out the theme that will dominate the next sections of the sermon beginning in 3:1 with the call to consider the fidelity of Jesus as apostle and High Priest, and developed in 4:14–5:10 (Vanhoye, *Structure*, 84). Hebrews alone in the NT calls Jesus a High Priest (4:14, 15; 5:5, 10; 6:20; 7:26; 8:1; 9:11), and a large part of the sermon's central argument (8:1–10:18) will be devoted to comparing him with the Levitical high priest.

Priests and high priests in Israel performed a variety of functions. Their oracular function was exercised through the casting of the sacred lots, the Urim and Thummim (Lev 16:8; Deut 33:8). They were in charge of the sanctuary (Num 3:38) and regulated ritual purity (Leviticus 13, 14, 15). They also offered sacrifices (Lev 16:6, 15; Deut 33:10), although non-priests were able to offer sacrifices as well (Gen 15:10; Lev 17:3, 5; Judg 13:19). The usual location of their activity was the sanctuary (Aelred Cody, *A History of Old Testament Priesthood*. AnBib 35 [Rome: Pontifical Biblical Institute, 1969] 29; 51–52; 190). On priests in the Hebrew Bible and Hellenistic Judaism see Albert Vanhoye, *Old Testament Priesthood and the New Priest: According to the New Testament* (Petersham, MA: St Bede's Publications, 1980) 19–59.

Mercy and fidelity are two important aspects of Jesus' priesthood, which cover his obligations to humans and to God in that service as a mediator between both. The fidelity of the Son will be discussed in 3:2-6 and his ability to sympathize with human weakness will be taken up in 4:15-16. That qualities of "fidelity" and "mercy" contribute to the mediatory role Jesus plays as High Priest is shown by the appeal at the end of each of these two texts to "hold on to confidence" (3:6 and 4:16).

"Matters pertaining to God," *ta pros ton theon*, occurs three times in the LXX. In Exod 4:16 God describes Moses' relationship to Aaron, saying that Moses shall be as god (*ta pros ton theon*) to Aaron. In Exod 18:19 Jethro, Moses' father-in-law, tells him that he must be as God (*ta pros ton theon*) to the people. Finally, in Deut 31:27 Moses warns the people of a worse rebellion after his death, since they have been so rebellious and stubborn about things concerning God (*ta pros ton theon*) while he was among them. In the first two instances Moses represents God, and in the last, although it is vague in meaning, the suggestion is that the people have been disobedient in observing their duties toward God. In Romans, Paul reminds his audience that he had a right to boast in Christ in matters pertaining to God (*ta pros ton theon*), after which he goes on to describe his work as a "minister," *leitourgos*, of Christ Jesus to the Gentiles in priestly service to the Gospel (Rom 15:17). The expression *ta pros ton theon* describes the proper sphere of Paul's ministry. Similarly in this verse it pertains to the sphere of Jesus' ministry.

to make a sacrifice of atonement for the sins of the people: The author anticipates what will follow in the explication of the work of Jesus as High Priest. Like any high priest, he will offer sacrifice for atonement of sins (8:3). The difference is that his sacrifice was "once for all" (7:27). The verb "atone," *hilaskesthai*, means "propitiate," "expiate" (BDAG, 473–74). Most of the instances of this verb in the LXX have to do with removal of sin (4 Kgdms 5:18 [bis]; 24:4; Pss 24:11; 64:3; 77:38; 78:9; Dan 9:19).

18. *Because he himself was tested by what he suffered, he is able to help those who are being tested:* The first OT instance of the verb "test," *peirazein*, refers to God testing Abraham (Gen 22:1). The theme of testing plays a role in the formation of the wilderness generation (Exod 15:25; 16:4; 17:2, 7; 20:20; Num 14:22), which the author takes up in chapter 4. Jesus is also tested in the wilderness by the devil (Matt 4:1-11; Mark 1:13; Luke 4:2-13). In this verse the test comes through suffering, which assures the solidarity of Jesus with his brothers and sisters. So he is able to help because he has shared their condition.

Interpretation

The central argument of Hebrews is found in 8:1–10:18. It focuses on Jesus as the High Priest of a new and better covenant. In order to prepare for the exposition of Jesus' role as High Priest, the author avails himself of the opportunity to explain how Jesus was qualified to mediate between God and humans. He has already established the superiority of the Son over other mediators like the angels (1:5-14; 2:5-9). Now he undertakes an examination of how Jesus' perfection through suffering rendered him able to mediate in a new and better way.

This section (2:10-18) divides into four parts: (1) God's propriety and purpose in perfecting the Son (2:10); (2) the solidarity of the Son with humans, based on common origin (2:11-13); (3) the destruction of death's power and deliverance from fear of death (2:14-15); and (4) how solidarity with humans rendered Jesus a merciful and faithful High Priest (2:16-18). In these verses the author expands on the argument in 2:5-9, where Jesus completed the glory of humans by having tasted death for all.

The argument about the propriety of God's perfecting Jesus through suffering functions in several ways. First, it involves God with Jesus' suffering and death in a way that was not expected in Hellenistic philosophy, or in Hellenistic Judaism for that matter. Second, highlighting the propriety of Jesus' death at this point in the sermon prepares for the fuller argument regarding his priesthood later in 8:1–10:18. Third, from a rhetorical standpoint propriety and persuasion are linked, so when the author says "it was fitting" he means not only that it was appropriate but that the way Jesus suffered and died was also more persuasive (Mitchell, "The Use of *prepein*," 681–94). This has ramifications for the quality of his mediation as High Priest.

The application of Psalm 8 to Jesus in 2:5-9 performed an important function in showing that God's plan for humans was not frustrated, but was brought to fulfillment in the Son's death. As the author proclaimed at 2:9, in death Jesus was "crowned with honor and glory." According to the psalm, humans were already the crowning achievement of God in creation. Were that the end of the story, enough would be said. There was need, however, for a new human to be "crowned with honor and glory" because the relationship between God and humans established at the time of their creation had been broken in the Fall. The relationship was repaired when Jesus tasted death for all (2:9). Thus he completed the glory God had originally intended for humans at the time of creation, and now "all things" are subjected to him, not only those things mentioned in Ps 8:7-8. Hebrews, of course, has omitted these final verses of the psalm.

Completing the glory of humans was made possible because of the solidarity Jesus had with them. First that solidarity is described in terms of common origin (2:11), because of which Jesus is not ashamed to be numbered among mortals (2:12). This solidarity is, then, further expounded by means of a midrash on Ps 21:23 and Isa 8:17-18a, where there is a stress on what Jesus shared with humans, namely "blood and flesh" (2:14). Finally, the ultimate meaning of this solidarity is exposed: he was able to free humans from the fear of death by destroying the one who wielded death's power, i.e., the devil.

The process of "re-scripturing" the texts of Ps 21:23 and Isa 8:17-18a obscures the "time." The actions described there no longer refer to the past, to the prophet and his children, but are brought into the present. Jesus stands in the midst of the assembly (*ekklēsia*), where he makes his proclamation to his brothers and sisters.

Drawing on traditional understandings of the victory of Christ over death, the author's eschatological perspective emerges in the final verses of this section. It was hinted at in 2:8-9. We cannot see the final eschatological moment in its full glory, but what we can see is the humiliation of the Son, which led to his glorification. He was able to taste death for everyone (2:9) because he shared the same "blood and flesh" with his brothers and sisters. Thus they are freed from fear of death, but not finally, as that moment is still unfolding.

Fear of death was common in the ancient world. The Epicureans were experts at helping people overcome it. Myths of heroic figures who had overcome death were abundant (Attridge, 79–82; Koester, 239). In language reminiscent of Paul's to the Corinthians (1 Cor 15:54-56), the author of Hebrews proclaims the victory of Christ over death and the power of death. At this point he actualizes the text for his readers. Jesus did not do this for angels, but for the children of Abraham, for human beings. Here the language of solidarity meets the real human situation, addressing the needs of the readers.

If, as High Priest, Jesus was to make effective atonement for sins, he had to play two roles. First, he had to identify with humans, those on whose behalf he would make an offering for atonement. Second, he had to attend to the things of God (2:17). In this way he could fulfill the obligations of atonement, which were expiation and propitiation (Koester, 241).

But he goes beyond merely those two aspects of his high priestly ministry. Verse 18 describes yet another consequence of his solidarity with humans. He too was tested, tried by what he suffered, as are all human beings. Therefore he is the one who can offer genuine help for those who are now undergoing a test. The text is actualized for the readers, who can turn to the example of Christ in his fidelity to God as they experience their own trials and tribulations. In this way, too, the author is able to set up the next exhortation that follows immediately in 3:1-6.

In this section the author has provided valuable information that will help the readers later to grasp the large central argument of his sermon (8:1–10:18). There Jesus' atoning work as High Priest will be engaged in an extended exposition of comparisons with the Levitical priests. The author will conclude with the confident assertion that Jesus' once for all self-offering has perfected for all time those who are sanctified (10:14). The underlying reasons for the author's bold claim are presented here in the exposition of the solidarity Jesus has with humans, based on his completion of the glory that God intended them to have from the moment of their creation. When the author returns to the exposition of Jesus as High Priest, little will have to be said of the mechanism of mediation, since the author has explained how his intercession works here, on the basis of his having shared the origin and nature of his humanity.

For Reference and Further Study

Carlston, Charles E. "The Vocabulary of Perfection in Philo and Hebrews," in R. A. Guelich, ed., *Unity and Diversity in New Testament Theology*. Grand Rapids: Eerdmans, 1978, 133–60.

Gray, Patrick. *Godly Fear: The Epistle to the Hebrews and Greco-Roman Critiques of Superstition*. SBLAB 16. Atlanta: Society of Biblical Literature, 2003.

Gudorf, Michael E. "Through a Classical Lens: Hebrews 2:16," *JBL* 119 (2000) 105–108.

Knauer, Peter. "Erbsünde als Todesverfallenheit: Eine Deutung von Röm 5,12 aus dem Vergleich mit Hebr 2,14f.," *TGl* 58 (1968) 153–58.

Kögel, Julius. *Der Sohn und die Söhne: Eine exegetische Studie zu Hebräer 2:5-18*. Gütersloh: Bertelsmann, 1904.

McCruden, Kevin B. "Christ's Perfection in Hebrews: Divine Beneficence as an Exegetical Key to Hebrews 2:10," *BibRes* 47 (2002) 40–62.

Seeberg, Alfred. "Zur Auslegung von Hebr. 2:5-18," *NJDT* 3 (1894) 435–61.

Swetnam, James. "A Merciful and Trustworthy High Priest: Interpreting Hebrews 2:17," *Pacific Journal of Theology* 21 (1999) 6–25.

Thompson, James W. "The Appropriate, the Necessary, and the Impossible: Faith and Reason in Hebrews," in Abraham J. Malherbe et al., eds., *The Early Church in Its Context: Essays in Honor of Everett Ferguson*. NovTSup 90. Leiden: Brill, 1998, 302–17.

Vanhoye, Albert. "Le Christ, grand-prêtre selon Héb. 2, 17-18," *NRTh* 91 (1969) 449–74.

II. Jesus, Apostle and High Priest: A Model of Faith and Hope (3:1–6:20)

6. *Worthy of More Glory than Moses* (3:1-6)

1. Therefore, holy brothers and sisters, partners in a heavenly calling, consider that Jesus, the apostle and high priest of our confession, 2. was faithful to the one who appointed him, just as Moses also "was faithful in [all] God's house." 3. Yet Jesus is worthy of more glory than Moses, to the extent that the builder of a house has more honor than the house itself. 4. (For every house is built by someone, but the builder of all things is God.) 5. Now Moses was faithful in all God's house as a servant, to testify to the things that would be spoken later. 6. Christ, however, was faithful over God's house as a son, and we are his house if we hold firm the confidence and the pride of hope.

Notes

1. *Therefore, holy brothers and sisters, partners in a heavenly calling:* "Brothers and sisters" is common terminology for fellow-Christians in the NT. It is not clear whether the adjective *hagioi*, "holy," should be taken with what precedes or what follows. Nestle-Aland[27] takes it with *adelphoi*, but it could easily be placed with *metochoi*, "partners." Given the distance between it and *metochoi*, the adjective more naturally modifies *adelphoi*, which encompasses both brothers and sisters (Klauck, "Kirche als Freundesgemeinschaft," 5, 10–11). The author uses *metochoi* to identify fellow Christians (3:14; 12:8). Later he will refer to them as "saints" (6:10; 13:24), echoing the identity of "the one who sanctifies" and "those who are sanctified" (2:11). Hebrews understands the community to share in the life of Christ together, as Christ has shared in their lives (2:14). Their calling is from heaven, stressing that it is not earthly. Coming from heaven implies that either its source or its goal is God. The language is reminiscent of prophetic callings in the Hebrew Bible. The heavenly realm is of particular interest to the author of Hebrews (6:4; 8:5; 9:23; 11:16; 12:22).

"Calling," *klēsis*, is the normal word used in the NT for an "invitation" (Rom 11:29; Eph 1:18; 2 Tim 1:9) or a "condition," i.e., the state of having been called (1 Cor 7:20; BDAG, 549; Helmut Traub, *ouranos* (NT), *TDNT* 5:513–43). Paul uses "call from above" in Phil 3:14, where the adverb *anō*, "upward," qualifies the noun. The noun is ambiguous, since it can mean the origin of the invitation or its destination. Other uses of "heavenly" in Hebrews favor the sense of destination (6:4; 8:5; 9:23; 11:16; 12:22), but the sense of origin is also present (6:4). Perhaps the author intends both (Koester, 242).

consider that Jesus, the apostle and high priest of our confession: The verb "consider," *katanoein*, simply means "notice" or "observe." But it also means "contemplate" or "think about" (BDAG, 522). Hebrews uses it here and in 10:24 to encourage readers to think carefully about something. Nowhere else in the NT is Jesus called an apostle. Rather, he calls apostles (Matt 10:2; Mark 3:14; Luke 6:13) and sends them (Luke 22:35). Combining both terms, the author presents him as a High Priest who was sent. He has already been described as a messenger in 2:12 (Attridge, 107). Apostles function differently from high priests: the former primarily preach and the latter sanctify and sacrifice. Placing the terms together captures the two aspects of Christian worship, preaching and sacrifice, i.e., eucharist. It is clear in the NT that, without having to be called an apostle, Jesus is sent from God (Matt 10:40; 15:24; Mark 9:37; Luke 10:16; John 3:17; 5:36). Only Hebrews ascribes to him the role of High Priest. The noun *archiereus* was introduced in 2:17 and will be applied to Jesus again throughout the sermon (4:14, 15; 5:5, 10; 6:20; 7:26; 8:1; 9:11).

The noun "confession," *homologia*, is rare in the LXX, where it translates *nᵉdhabhah*, "free will offering" (Deut 12:6, 17; 1 Esdr 9:8; Amos 4:5; Ezek 46:12) or *nedher*, "vow" (Lev 22:18; Jer 51:25). Philo has it in the sense of "confession" (*Allegorical Interpretation* 82; *On the Unchangeableness of God* 25; *On Abraham* 203; *On Joseph* 185), as does Josephus (*Antiquities* 18.154). Here the author uses it as he does in 4:14 and 10:23. Most commentators take it to be a reference to the content of the community's faith rather than the experience of faith. The use of the definite article here supports that interpretation (Koester, 243).

2. *was faithful to the one who appointed him, just as Moses also "was faithful in [all] God's house":* The fidelity of Jesus has already been established in 2:17, where he conformed himself to the will of God. In light of what follows, the fidelity of Jesus may be seen as the antithesis of the infidelity of the wilderness generation (3:17-18). The adjective "faithful," *pistos*, unifies the entire section, occurring three times in the passage (3:1, 2, 5). In this passage "faithful" should be understood as "worthy of trust," which means that the priest can speak for God as Moses does in Num 12:6-8 (Vanhoye, *Old Testament Priests*, 96). For this reason the author cites the text of Num 12:7 to underscore the authority of Moses.

The verb *poiein* means basically "make," but it can mean "appoint" (1 Sam 12:6 [LXX]; Mark 3:14; Acts 2:36). Some commentators opt for the meaning "make," which suggests that Jesus was faithful to God, who created him (Braun, 79; Grässer 1:165). In light of Moses' appointment by God in 1 Sam 12:6 (LXX), and since the author is comparing Jesus and Moses, the meaning "appoint" is preferred here (Weiss, 246).

The text of Num 12:7 specifies that Moses was faithful in all God's house. The word "all," however, does not appear in all NT manuscripts of Hebrews (cf. 𝔓¹³·⁴⁶ᵛⁱᵈ B vgᵐˢ Ambr). Yet later, in v. 5, when the author cites Num 12:7, "all" is included and there are no manuscripts without it. It is likely, then, that the NT manuscripts that include "all" preserve the original text. How it may have dropped out of some is a matter of speculation.

The noun *oikos* can mean "house" or "household," but it can also refer to a "dynasty" (2 Sam. 7:11; BDAG, 698–99). As Moses was trustworthy in leading the people of Israel, "house" here refers to the collective Israel under his leadership (Exod 16:31; 40:38; Lev 10:6; 17:8, 10; 22:18; Num 20:29).

3. *Yet Jesus is worthy of more glory than Moses:* Jesus' glory is mentioned in 1:3 as the reflection of God's glory. He is crowned with glory in 2:9 on account of his sufferings, and glory is attributed to him in the final praise of 13:22. In Exod 33:22 Moses asks God to show him God's glory and in 40:34 he is in the presence of God's glory, which fills the tabernacle. Sirach speaks of Moses in equally high terms and of how God not only revealed glory to him but glorified him before kings (45:1-3). To say that Jesus is worthy of more glory than Moses presupposes that Moses, too, is worthy of glory, but the author does not spell it out. It can be that Moses was worthy to come into the presence (glory) of God. In context it could also be that God had appointed him over his house, as Num 12:7 would indicate.

to the extent that the builder of a house has more honor than the house itself: It stands to reason that someone who designs and builds a house receives more "honor" than the finished product. Philo says something similar in relation to one who receives property as being better off than the property itself, on the analogy that the one who has created something is better than the creation (*On Noah As A Planter* 68; Weiss, 248; Koester, 245). One should not look for an exact correspondence between the elements of the comparison, which would make Jesus the builder of a house. The question is of the proportional honor that renders Jesus superior to Moses.

4. *(For every house is built by someone, but the builder of all things is God):* This parenthetical remark seems like an afterthought, but it actually contributes to the argument. The verb "build," *kataskeuazein*, can also mean "prepare" or "furnish" (BDAG, 526–27). In addition to its use in the previous verse, it occurs elsewhere in Hebrews at 9:2, 6 in relation to furnishing the sanctuary and at 11:7 in reference to the ark built by Noah.

Lane (1:77) notices the chiastic structure of vv. 3-4 forming an ABB'A' structure:

A   Jesus is worthy of more glory than Moses

    B   just as the builder of a house has more honor than the house itself

    B' For every house is built by someone

A'   but the builder of all things is God.

The author has deliberately arranged the verses to explicate the argument. It runs thus: Jesus' honor is greater than Moses' in a way that is comparable to how God's honor is greater than the honor of the Creation.

5. *Now Moses was faithful in all God's house as a servant, to testify to the things that would be spoken later:* The text of Num 12:7 is repeated here, perhaps indicating that this is what the author had in mind when speaking of Moses' fidelity earlier in v. 2. The reason for Moses' appointment over the house of Israel is spelled out, so that he might testify to things that would be spoken later. How exactly and in what form Moses' testimony would be given is not specified, and no words of testimony are brought forth. It is the example of Moses' trustworthiness that testifies, as it looks forward to a greater trustworthiness on the part of the Son. So for the author of Hebrews, Moses is a witness to Christ, and because he is an authoritative spokesman for God his testimony is trustworthy. Just as the Law foreshadowed things to come (10:1), so does the one who gave that Law to Israel. Similarly in 11:26 the author projects Moses' sufferings forward as a foreshadowing of the sufferings of Christ. Still, Jesus is not a new Moses in Hebrews as he is in Matthew. As Moses was considered a prophetic figure, he falls among those through whom God had spoken in the past before speaking definitively in the Son (1:1-2).

The comparison of Moses and Jesus accounts for the significant differences between them. Moses was a servant and not a son. The noun "servant," *therapōn*, is distinct from the word for "slave," *doulos*, thus giving Moses more honor than a mere slave. The term is applied to Moses elsewhere in the LXX (Exod 4:10; 14:31; Num 11:11; Deut 3:24; Josh 1:2; 8:31, 33). Here it is drawn from the LXX of Num 12:7, so perhaps not too much should be made of the author's terminology (Attridge, 111).

Hebrews uses the verb "testify," *martyrein*, to convey the sense of "witnessing" (7:8, 17; 10:15; 11:2, 4, 5, 39). Only here does the author use the noun *martyrion*, which is used extensively in the LXX (e.g., Gen 21:30; 31:44; Josh 22:27, 28, 34; 3 Kgdms 2:3).

6. *Christ, however, was faithful over God's house as a son:* This is the first use of *Christos* in Hebrews. As it is indeterminate, the author probably does not intend it as a title, but as part of Jesus' name (Koester, 247).

The identity of Jesus as Son has already been well established. The comparison of Jesus to the angels in the first chapter provides the basis for understanding why now, when the contrast is drawn between Jesus and Moses as that between a "son" and a "servant," the readers should readily grasp its import. The angels were servants of God's message, too (1:14). Jesus' appointment over God's house and his trustworthiness in that role will be developed throughout the sermon and come to expression in 10:21, "and since we have a great priest over the house of God."

And we are his house if we hold firm the confidence and the pride of hope: As is his wont, the author includes himself in the exhortations (2:1; 4:1, 14; 6:1; 10:39; 12:1). The actualization of Num 12:7 now gives a different composition to the house of God. It is not only Israel, whom Moses led, but it now includes the readers.

The author uses several terms to express this notion of "holding on." In 2:1 a nautical metaphor (*prosechein*) gave the sense of not letting a boat "drift" away. Here the verb is *katechein*, which also appears in 10:23. In 4:14 and 6:18 one finds the synonym *kratein*. It can mean to hold on to the "word" as in Luke 8:15.

The noun *parrhēsia*, "boldness," or "confidence," is a virtue of friendship, i.e., frank speech. It is also the right of the free citizen to speak in the city assembly (Horst Balz, *parrhēsia*, EDNT 3:45-47; Heinrich Schlier, *parrhēsia*, TDNT 5:871–86). As such it has a subjective and an objective aspect (Käsemann, *The Wandering People*, 42–43): subjective because the person who possesses the virtue practices it, objective because it is grounded in the rights established by friends or by political rule. In Hebrews the word connotes the confidence to speak openly and frankly with God. Hence it is the virtue of access to God. It is objectively constituted by God, who makes this access possible through Christ (Alan C. Mitchell, "Holding on to Confidence: *PARRHĒSIA* in Hebrews," in John T. Fitzgerald, ed., *Friendship, Flattery, and Frankness of Speech*. NovTSup 82 [Leiden: Brill, 1996] 203–36). Ultimately this confidence is eschatologically oriented, as it is concerned with future expectation (Erich Grässer, *Der Glaube im Hebräerbrief* [Marburg: Elwert, 1965] 16–17, 36, 109).

The double object of "holding on" includes *kauchēma*, the word for "boasting." It occurs elsewhere in the NT only in Paul (Rom 4:2; 1 Cor 5:6; 9:15-16; 2 Cor 1:14; 9:3; Gal 6:4; Phil 1:26; 2:16). The author introduces here the important virtue of "hope," which will be developed throughout the sermon (noun: 6:11, 18; 7:19; 10:23; verb: 11:1). "Hope" will enable the readers to approach God and to enter the sanctuary. It is as important as the "boldness" that is required to do that.

Interpretation

Comparison is a critical tool in the author's approach to bringing his readers to see his perspective on the Christian confession. After having compared the Son to angels, he now turns to a comparison with Moses. The fact that he remains positive in this comparison, not calling attention to the fact that Moses failed in his fidelity (Num 20:12), suggests that he, and perhaps the community to which he writes, held Moses in high regard. Moses is recalled in chapter 11 as one of the great heroes of faith. If there is any question of Moses' fidelity, the author leaves it unexpressed and only obliquely brings it into the picture. In 3:7–4:13 there is no mention of Moses, but it can be inferred from 4:8 that Moses was among those who heard but did not listen.

The analogy drawn between the Son and Moses makes three important points. First, the Son was appointed to a position of leadership, as was Moses. Second, the Son was faithful in the exercise of that leadership, as was Moses. Third, the Son was worthy of more glory than Moses, precisely because he was Son, and not servant as was Moses.

The development of the exhortation begins with a consideration of Jesus as the faithful high priest sent by God (3:1-2). It then is shaped largely under the influence of the text of Num 12:7. Once the author recalls that Moses "was faithful in [all] God's house," the choice of what to highlight in the comparison is quite dependent on the language of that OT verse.

Moses' fidelity is explained in terms of what he owed God, who appointed him (3:2). By analogy Jesus exhibits a similar fidelity. Here the author is stressing the continuity between the two. Moses was esteemed in Hellenistic Judaism (Lane 1:74), and so drawing this positive point of comparison would bring equal esteem to the Son.

There is, however, discontinuity between Moses and the Son as there was discontinuity in the various forms of speech by means of the prophets and the definitive speech of God in the Son (1:1-2). The exposition of the allusion to Num 12:7 shows why Jesus is worthy of more glory than Moses. That claim can only be furthered with the aid of an example from daily life. The one who builds the house has more honor than the house itself. The creative work of the builder who constructs the house is worth more consideration than the finished product. The author ultimately grounds the comparison in the relationship of God to creation. No one would challenge him on the fact that God is worthy of more glory for his handiwork in creation than is the creation itself. By the same measure, then, Jesus' glory outscales Moses' in the way God's glory outscales the creation's.

Not ending the argument there, the author draws yet another distinction between Moses and the Son, on the analogy of the distinction between a "servant" and a "son." Spatial terminology enhances the comparison as the author notes that Moses was a servant "in" the house of God (3:2), but the Son was "over" the house (3:6).

Moses as servant was subordinate to the Son not merely by status, but by virtue of the fact that he himself testified to things that would later be spoken of the Son. At this point the author need not elaborate on the content of that testimony. It is enough to show Moses as one who mediated God's word in the past, a word the author believes pointed to the Son. Later the author will claim that Moses' sufferings anticipated the sufferings of the Son (11:26).

The practical import of the comparison is developed in the last verse of the exhortation. The author is not engaged in comparison for the sake of comparison, but rather is showing that the glorification of the Son by God, i.e., his exaltation, opened the way for the believers themselves. His aim is to persuade his readers that holding on to the confession is worthwhile. He can do that by holding up that goal as something the recipients too will receive. The eschatological goal accomplished in Christ is the goal for the community. When the author proclaims "we are his house" (3:6), he completes the purpose of the comparison he has drawn.

The term "house," however, is not univocal. First, when referred to Moses it signifies the house of Israel. In relation to the Son, however, it refers to the household composed of the ones he leads to glory (2:10). To actualize this meaning among his readers he makes the explicit connection between them and the "house."

Sharing in the glory of the Son requires a steadfast trustworthiness similar to that exhibited by Moses and the Son. If the readers are to reach the appointed eschatological goal, they must hold on to confidence and not waver in their own hope of accomplishing that goal.

For Reference and Further Study

D'Angelo, Mary Rose. *Moses in the Letter to the Hebrews.* SBLDS 42. Missoula: Scholars, 1979.
Hay, David M. "Moses Through New Testament Spectacles," *Int* 44 (1990) 240–52.
Marrow, Stanley B. "*Parrhēsia* and the New Testament," *CBQ* 44 (1982) 431–46.
Schreiber, Stefan. "Eine neue *varia lectio* zu Hebr 3,4b?" *BZ* 44 (2000) 252–53.
Vanhoye, Albert. "Jesus '*fidelis ei qui fecit eum*' (Hebr 3,2)," *VD* 45 (1967) 291–305.

7. *Rebellion in the Wilderness* (3:7-19)

7. Therefore, as the Holy Spirit says, "Today, if you hear his voice, 8. do not harden your hearts as in the rebellion as it was in the day of wilderness testing, 9. where your ancestors tested me despite having seen my works 10. for forty years. Therefore I was angry with that generation, and I said: 'They always go astray in their hearts, and they have not known my ways.' 11. As I swore in my wrath, 'They shall never enter into my rest.'"

12. Be careful, brothers and sisters, lest there be in any of you an evil and unbelieving heart, that turns away from the living God. 13. Rather, exhort one another each day, as long as it is called "today," so none of you may be hardened by the deceitfulness of sin. 14. For we have become partakers of Christ, if we hold fast our initial confidence until the end. 15. As the saying goes, "Today if you hear his voice, do not harden your hearts as in the rebellion." 16. Who were those who heard and rebelled? Were they not all whom Moses led out of Egypt? 17. With whom was he angry for forty years? Was it not those who sinned, whose bodies fell in the wilderness? 18. To whom did he swear that they shall never enter into his rest, if not those who disobeyed? 19. We see, then, that they were not able to enter because of their unbelief.

NOTES

7. *Therefore, as the Holy Spirit says:* Hebrews refers to Scripture as the witness of the Holy Spirit in two places in the homily (9:8; 10:15). The author may mean that the Holy Spirit is the authority behind Scripture or its source, perhaps by means of inspiration (Attridge, 114; Braun, 85; Bruce, 95; Montefiore, 75; Spicq 2:72; Westcott, 80). Others stress the present experience of the readers, who hear the words of Scripture anew as they are mediated by the Holy Spirit (Martin Emmrich, *Pneumatological Concepts in the Epistle to the Hebrews: Amtscharisma, Prophet, and Guide of the Eschatological Exodus* [Lanham, MD: University Press of America, 2003] 29; Hughes, 141; Koester, 254; Lane 1:84). The exhortation is conditioned on the ability of the readers to hear the word of God. The verb "say," *legein*, is in the present, so it is as if the Holy Spirit is speaking directly to the readers.

Today, if you hear his voice: Psalm 95:7-11 in the Hebrew Bible differs from the LXX (Ps 94:7-11) in its introduction, where the former expresses a wish, "Today if you would hear his voice," and the latter a condition, "Today, if you hear his voice." Hebrews shares with the LXX the urgency of the word "today," *sēmeron*, as the author wishes to actualize the psalm text for his readers. This sense of "today" is found elsewhere in the LXX (Exod 14:13; Deut 5:3; 6:2, 6, 24; 9:1, 3, 6, etc.), where it is equivalent to the emphatic "on this day," *en tē hēmera tautē* (Deut 5:1; 4:20, 39; 26:16; 27:9; Josh 3:7) and "today," *en tē sēmeron hēmera* (Josh 5:9). In the NT it is shared especially by Luke (2:11; 4:21; 19:9; 23:43).

8. *do not harden your hearts as in the rebellion as it was in the day of wilderness testing:* The rebellion and testing of which the psalm speaks refers to Meribah ("quarrel," *rîb*, in Hebrew) and Massah ("testing," *nissāh*, in Hebrew). The place names refer to the quarrel the Israelites had with Moses over a lack of water in the wilderness after the Exodus from Egypt (Exod 17:1-7; Num 20:2-13). Moses interpreted their action as a testing of God. The psalm concurs with this assessment, as indicated by vv. 9b-11. That the psalm is referring to this incident is somewhat clearer in the MT than in the LXX, where the place names Meribah and Massah were not retained, but were rather translated with the Greek words for "rebellion" and "testing" respectively.

9. *where your ancestors tested me despite having seen my works* 10. *for forty years:* The psalm alludes to Moses' question to the people in Exod 17:2, "Why do you test the Lord?" (cf. 17:7; Ps 78[77]:41, 56; Jdt 8:12) and to Num 14:22, where the Lord tells Moses that the people have tested him ten times despite all the glory and the signs the people had seen in Egypt. Normally it is God who tests Israel (Exod 15:5; 16:4; 20:20; Deut 8:2; 13:3; 33:8; Jdt 8:25, 26).

Therefore I was angry with that generation: The verb "be angry," *prosochthizein*, occurs only here and in 3:17 in the NT. In the LXX it has the sense of "be offended" (Gen 27:46; Num 21:5), "abhor" (Lev 26:15, 30, 43, 44), "detest" (Ps 21:25), and "feel disgust for" (Ps 94:10; Ezek 36:31; Sir 25:2; 38:4; 50:25). Hebrews has punctuated v. 10 differently than did the authors of the MT and LXX. Those versions of Psalm 95(94) begin a new sentence at verse 10: "Forty years I was angry with that generation . . ." whereas Hebrews ends the previous sentence with the expression "forty years." The effect changes the meaning of the psalm, which indicates that the Lord was angry for forty years. In Hebrews the people test the Lord despite having seen his works for forty years. Consequently the author had to insert the Greek particle *dio*, "therefore," to explain the Lord's anger resulting from the wilderness generation's lack of appropriate response to the Lord's works for forty years. The responsibility for the Lord's anger is thus shifted to the wilderness generation. Curiously, in v. 17 the author reverts to the psalm's original meaning, that God was angry for forty years.

and I said: 'They always go astray in their hearts, and they have not known my ways': The verse continues to follow the psalm quite closely. "They always go astray in their hearts, and they have not known my ways" may express the offense as a *hendiadys*, i.e., one thing and not two. The wilderness generation strayed in their hearts by not knowing the Lord's ways. The verb "go astray," *planan*, means basically "wander" (e.g., Gen 21:14; 37:15; Exod 14:3; 23:4; Pss 58(57):3; 95(94):10; 107(106):4, 40; 119(118):110, 176). The lack of knowledge of the Lord and the ways of God forms part of the prophetic critique against Israel (cf. Hos 2:8; 4:1, 6; 6:6; 11:3; Mic 4:12; Hab 2:14; Zech 2:9, 11).

11. *As I swore in my wrath, 'They shall never enter into my rest':* The Greek particle *hōs*, which begins this verse, must have a consecutive sense. As a result of the people's failings the Lord swore that they would not enter into his rest. The denial is a strong one here. "Rest," *katapausis*, occurs nine times in Hebrews (3:11, 18; 4:1, 3, 4, 5, 8, 10, 11). The concept of "rest" is very important for the author, but it is difficult to grasp. "Rest" in Hebrews is usually drawn in some fashion from the LXX, either in Gen 2:2 or Ps 95:11, as here in 3:11. Is "rest" a location or a state? Is it spatial or temporal? Those who see here allusions to Num 14:30 find a parallel in the expression "You will certainly not enter the land." The land is understood as a place of rest. As a state, "rest" most often refers to God's rest, or something analogous to it. It signifies a condition that is proper to God, but that the readers may participate in. As a temporal term, "rest" may actually span the past in its reference to God's Sabbath rest, the present as a state the readers enter into, and the future as their eschatological goal (Thomas G. Long, *Hebrews*. Interpretation [Louisville: Westminster John Knox, 1997] 55).

Ernst Käsemann stressed the importance of the notion of "rest" as a final goal of redemption, influenced by Gnosticism rather than by the Hebrew Bible (*The Wandering People of God*, 74–75). His view has not gone unchallenged. Otfried Hofius questioned the Gnostic derivation of "rest," finding it instead in Jewish apocalyptic (*Katapausis: Die Vorstelling vom endzeitlichen Ruheort im Hebräerbrief*, 59–101). Harold Attridge also called into question the Gnostic background of the term "rest" by noting that often Hellenistic Jewish motifs are mistakenly identified as Gnostic (128). Judith H. Wray challenged Käsemann's view, claiming that, while rest is a theological metaphor used to shore up the notion of fidelity in the sermon's rhetoric of encouragement, its scope is more limited than Käsemann would grant. The lack of sustained usage of the metaphor in Hebrews leads Wray to conclude that its purpose is illustrative. "Rest" functions in relation to the sermon's christology and encourages a kind of participation in the work of Christ. The advantage of the metaphorical sense of "rest" is that it need not then indicate a place (land) or a time (Sabbath) and can properly signify a state, as it does regarding God in the Hebrew Scriptures (*Rest as a Theological Metaphor in the Epistle to the Hebrews and the Gospel of Truth: Early Christian Homiletics of Rest*. SBLDS 166 [Atlanta: Scholars, 1998] 90–94).

As a state, then, "rest" has a final sense in that it is the eschatological goal of Christians (11:10, 16; 12:22-24; 13:14). It also has a present sense to the extent that the readers participate in God's rest, in anticipation of its future fulfillment (3:12-15; 4:3, 9-11; 10:19-22). In a course on Hebrews at Yale in the Fall 1979 semester Nils A. Dahl suggested that one meaning of "rest" in Hebrews was associated with the idea of living in the "eighth day." By that he meant that the author understood Christians to live in the period of the "eighth day," the time when the work of God's creation has been completed. Therefore "rest" embraces the "already" and the "not yet," like other eschatological terms in Christianity (Attridge, 128).

12. *Be careful, brothers and sisters, lest there be in any of you an evil and unbelieving heart, that turns away from the living God:* The warning to "be careful" appears twice in Hebrews (see 12:25) and introduces an exhortation to watchfulness, as the nuance of the verb "see," *blepein*, indicates. The imperative *blepete* is here followed by the negative particle *mēpote* and the future of the verb "to be," *estai*. The combination of all three in Greek indicates a strong sense of apprehension about the condition in the dependent clause (BDF §370[2]). In this case the author warns against the presence of anyone in the community who is unfaithful and "turns away from the living God" because of an "evil and unbelieving heart." In the Hebrew Bible "doing evil in the sight of God" is the equivalent of idolatry (Deut 4:25; 9:18; 17:2; 31:22; Judg 2:11; 3:7, 12; 4:1; 6:1; 10:6; 13:1), which provokes God to anger. The opposite is to do what is right in the sight of the Lord (Judg 17:6; 21:25; 1 Kgs 11:33, 38; 14:3; 15:5, 11; 2 Chr 14:2; 20:32; 25:2; 29:2). In the Deuteronomic perspective both dispositions reflect the condition of the heart (Deut 4:29; 6:5; 10:12; 11:13; 13:3; 26:16; Josh 22:5; 1 Sam 7:3; 12:20, 24). The expression "evil heart" is found in the LXX (Prov 26:23; 2 Esdr 3:21) and is a condition linked to alienation from God (2 Esdr 7:48).

Infidelity is qualified by a particular means, "turning away from the living God." The verb "turn away from," *aphistanai*, is the same one used of the wilderness generation in Num 14:9, where rebellion was characterized as "turning away from the Lord," standard language for idolatry and rebellion (Deut 13:10; 32:15; Josh 22:18, 23, 29). Psalm 95 speaks of those who rebelled as having "hardened their hearts." Hebrews links the condition of rebellion to the hearts of the readers and cautions against turning away from God, which is manifested in their infidelity. The exhortation beginning in this verse follows directly on the psalm and must be understood in light of it. "The living God" is a biblical notion (Bas van Iersel, *The Bible on the Living God* [De Pere, WI: St. Norbert Abbey Press, 1965]). See also 1 Thess 1:9, where the expression signifies the goal of conversion, i.e., to turn from idols and to the living God.

13. *Rather, exhort one another each day, as long as it is called "today," so none of you may be hardened by the deceitfulness of sin:* Following that line of reasoning, the author exhorts the readers to understand what "today" in the psalm means for them.

It is a time of opportunity, when they can avoid sin and remain faithful by remaining with God. The expression "as long as it is called" carries the sense of the urgency the author feels for his readers. How long can "today" last? The author does not have a punctiliar notion of time here, but the sense is that there is a limited space of time in which to conform to the exhortation.

The verb "harden," *sklērynein*, is the same as in the psalm citation in v. 8. The author now actualizes the psalm for his readers by applying it to them. "Hardening" results from "the deceitfulness of sin." "Deceit," *apatē*, rarely occurs in the LXX (Jdt 9:3, 10, 13; 16:8; Eccl 9:6 [S]; 4 Macc 18:8), where the verb "deceive," *apatan*, is more frequent. The noun is attested elsewhere in the NT (Matt 13:22; Mark 14:9; Eph 4:22; Col 2:8; 2 Thess 2:10; 2 Pet 2:13).

14. *For we have become partakers of Christ, if we hold fast our initial confidence until the end:* In secular Greek the noun *metochoi* means a partner, as in people who have business together (BDAG, 643; MM, 406). The term also has political connotations for residents of the city. Partnership with Christ is a result of the "confidence" the readers have (3:6). Such "partnership" is a form of "friendship" (Erich Grässer, *Der Glaube im Hebräerbrief*. MTS 2 [Marburg: N. G. Elwert, 1965], 98; on friendship in the NT see Alan C. Mitchell, "Greet the Friends by Name: New Testament Evidence for the Greco-Roman *Topos* on Friendship," in John T. Fitzgerald, ed., *Greco-Roman Perspectives on Friendship*. SBLRBS 34 [Atlanta: Scholars, 1997] 225–62). Some commentators translate the genitive "of" as a dative, "in" or "with," as the latter conforms better to English usage.

The author expresses the notion of "holding fast" with different Greek verbs throughout the sermon. Here, as in 3:6 and 10:23, *katechein*, "hold in possession" is used. In 4:14 one finds *kratein*, "hold on to." The exhortation to maintain oneself faithfully, either by holding on to confidence or to the confession, plays a central role in the sermon's paraenetic sections (see the Notes at 3:6). The repetition of the exhortation reinforces the centrality of the author's concern that the readers maintain their fidelity. Here the object is the initial confidence they had experienced, which supplied them with the assurance they needed. Not unlike the confidence they are exhorted to hold on to in 3:6, this foundational experience is what had anchored them in the past. The noun "confidence," *hypostasis*, is difficult to translate in Hebrews, as it may carry an objective sense as in 1:3 or a combination of objective/subjective senses as in this verse and in 11:1 (see the Notes at 1:3 and 11:1).

15. *As the saying goes, 'Today if you hear his voice, do not harden your hearts as in the rebellion':* An articular infinitive introduces the quotation from Ps 95:7-8. Commentators are divided over whether this verse serves as a summary of vv. 12-14 (cf. Lane 1:88) or whether it is an introduction to what follows in vv. 16-19 (Braun, 98; Weiss, 266; Ellingworth, 228; Grässer 1:192; Koester, 261). Attridge sees it as the resumption of the argument in v. 13 that had been interrupted by the digression of v. 14 and so places it with what precedes (119–20). Despite the grammatical awkwardness of the syntax, stylistically the verse is more like what precedes it than the diatribal style that follows. After the digression in v. 14, which serves as a motivating clause, the author concludes the argument mounted in vv. 12-13 by completing the exhortation with an echo of the psalm verse cited in v. 7 and an explication of whom the psalm had in mind.

16. *Who were those who heard and rebelled? Were they not all whom Moses led out of Egypt?:* In diatribal style the author poses five questions that explicate the citation from Psalm 95. Playing on the key words of the psalm itself, he asks about those who "heard" and "rebelled." Curiously, the answer makes it seem as though none of the wilderness generation had been faithful. Numbers 14 does say that the whole congregation rebelled and that God swore that none of them would see the promised land. Within that same chapter, however, an exception is made for Caleb, who followed God with his whole heart, his descendants (Num 14:24), and Joshua (Num 14:30), who had not rebelled.

17. *With whom was he angry for forty years? Was it not those who sinned, whose bodies fell in the wilderness:* The author still has Psalm 95 in mind where it states that God was angry with the wilderness generation for forty years. The verb "be angry with" is the same as that quoted earlier in 3:10 (see the Notes above). Numbers 14:33-34 calculates God's displeasure with the wilderness generation as forty years, one year for each of the forty days that Israel spied out the promised land. The author seems to have forgotten, however, that in v. 10 he had rearranged the "forty years" of Ps 95:10 so that it applied to the time of the rebellion rather than to the duration of God's anger (see the Notes at v. 10).

    Returning to the narrative of Num 14:29-33, the author reminds his readers that the disbelief of the wilderness generation had catastrophic results. The verb "fall," *piptein*, means literally "fall down," but is used figuratively for "perishing" (Pss 10:10 [9:31]; 18[17]:38; 27[26]:2; 36[35]:12; Prov 11:28; Sir 1:30; 2:7; etc.; Acts 5:5, 10; 1 Cor 10:8; BDAG 815). In Num 14:29 the Lord swears that the dead bodies of those who rebelled shall fall in the wilderness. Leaving bodies unburied was prohibited in Israel's Law except in the case of the unrighteous. According to Deut 28:26 the exposed corpses of those who are disobedient and not observant will be food for birds and wild animals. The fate of those who rebel against God is the same in Isa 66:24.

18. *To whom did he swear that they shall never enter into his rest, if not those who disobeyed?:* Another reference to Ps 95:11 keeps before the readers' eyes the power of a divine oath. The author's method for actualizing the psalm for his readers has been to take the first part of each verse of the psalm and answer it rhetorically with the negative example of the rebellious wilderness generation. Here it is a question of their disobedience. The verb "disobey," *apeithein*, is related to the noun "disbelief," *apistia*, in the next verse. In Hebrews, as in the LXX (Exod 23:21; 26:15; Deut 1:26; 9:23; 32:51; Josh 5:6; Isa 30:12), disobedience is connected to a refusal to hear the word of the Lord or to a hardening that prevents adherence to it (Sir 30:12). The refusal to heed what they have heard originates with the fact that they had not been persuaded by what they had heard (Attridge, 121).

19. *We see, then, that they were not able to enter because of their unbelief:* Following up on the previous mention of the nature of Israel's rebellion, the author makes the point even more explicit by saying that it was precisely unbelief that prevented some of the wilderness generation from entering the promised land. The hardening of heart in the psalm quoted at 3:8, the testing of God, the errors of the heart (3:10), and the lack of knowledge of God (3:10) are the manifestations of disobedience that stemmed from an inability to believe.

Interpretation

The previous section of the sermon (3:1-6) engaged the readers in a comparison of the fidelity of Jesus with that of Moses. It closed with an exhortation to "hold fast" their confidence so they might be true members of God's household (3:6). In this section the author continues to elaborate on the quality of fidelity by returning to the time of Moses and the negative example of those who followed him out of Egypt on the way to Sinai. The period of rebellion was marked by wandering, which turned into going astray. In an effort to prevent his own readers from sharing the attitude of the wilderness generation, the author issues an exhortation designed to help them understand how fidelity related to holding fast their confidence.

This exhortation divides into three parts: (1) vv. 7-11, a citation from Ps 95(94):7-11; (2) vv. 12-15, a warning against becoming like those prevented from entering God's rest; and (3) vv. 16-19, a series of rhetorical questions in diatribal style that actualizes the psalm and concludes with a warning against disobedience. Together with 4:1-10, 11-13 these verses form the first of three parts that discuss a theme important to the author's purpose, i.e., entering into God's rest.

The psalm citation is introduced with a formula that directs it as if it were the words of the Holy Spirit spoken to the readers. By allowing the Spirit to speak through the psalm, the author permits the words of the psalm to unfold to the point of the ominous oath that the rebellious generation would not enter the promised land (3:11). The cause of God's anger in the psalm, i.e., hearts gone astray and a lack of knowledge of God, spells out the nature of Israel's rebellion and disobedience (3:10). The consequences of that rebellion are then explicitly stated. The oath sworn here, in all its horror, will be offset with consideration of the oath God swore to Abraham in response to his fidelity and endurance (6:13-20). Perhaps in anticipation of that more positive image of God's oath, the author presents a negative one in the prevention of the wilderness generation from entering into God's rest.

The notion of rest is introduced in this passage and will be elaborated on in the next chapter. The exhortations to enter into God's rest show that it is possible, by remaining faithful, to reach the goal that eluded the wilderness generation. It will become clear in 4:8-10 that the offer of entering God's rest was not closed to everyone by the disobedience of the wilderness generation. Equally clear, however, is that disobedience can still prevent one from entering into God's rest (4:11).

The author keeps the possibility of disobedience alive for his readers in the exhortation beginning in v. 12, making them aware of the consequences of "an evil and unbelieving heart." By recalling the opening verse of Psalm 95 he actualizes the psalm for his readers, introducing the possibility that some of them may share symbolically in the rebellion of Israel by possessing erring hearts themselves. Later in the sermon the heart will be featured as the locus of the new covenant (8:10; 10:16), and in another section that has affinities with this one the readers will be exhorted to approach God with a "true heart" and, once again, to hold fast their confidence (10:23). In view of the author's interest in the heart and its proper disposition, the warning against an evil and unbelieving heart becomes more poignant.

A two-pronged strategy for maintaining the community and preventing assimilation to disobedience is then recommended. Mutual exhortation is the first remedy proposed for guarding against unbelief, so that their own hearts may not be hardened. Such exhortation must be honest and frank, lest they be deceived. In ancient psychagogy individuals sought the advice of a wise person who would provide such frank criticism. The Epicureans practiced mutual correction in a communal way. It is something along these lines that the author would like to see practiced by his readers.

In addition to mutual exhortation, adherence or fidelity is advised by means of the encouragement to hold fast to their initial grounding. The recipients have been reminded that they have become partners in Christ. Thus like any good partner they cannot back out of the deal. If the author has a commercial metaphor in mind (Koester, 260), then the sense of obligation is clear and informs the nature of holding fast. If he is employing a political metaphor, then the obligation is based on the allegiance partners owe to one another. In any event it is clear that obligation on the basis of partnership is what the author appeals to here.

The verse from Psalm 95 repeated in v. 15 looks back to the warning against hardening of hearts in v. 13, and there is a note of urgency: the opportunity to respond is not open-ended. "Today" is a limited period of time within which the response must be made, as stated in v. 13.

Emerging in the remainder of the exhortation, the theme of *apistia*, "unbelief," reminds the readers of the cause of the wilderness generation's disobedience. Here it is not only the psalm that informs the author's thinking. Numbers 14 plays an important hermeneutical role in making the necessary connections he seeks among disobedience, rebellion, and unbelief. This intertextuality has already taken place in the arrangement of the psalm itself, but the author gives the Numbers narrative a more explicit role in the questions he frames in vv. 16-18.

Picking up on the word "rebellion" at the end of the psalm quotation, the author does not miss an opportunity to capture his audience's attention by implicitly comparing them to the wilderness generation. The question in v. 16 is answered by the one that immediately follows it. Likewise in v. 17 one question answers the other. The culminating question contains its own answer. In all instances the rebellion is the failure on the part of the wilderness generation to hold fast to its initial grounding, thus producing evil and unbelieving hearts. For the hardness of their hearts, deriving from their unbelief, those of the wilderness generation provoked God to swear that they would never enter the promised land.

In a tour de force that shows the effective exemplary power of the failures of the wilderness generation the author concludes the section with the statement that they were not able to enter because of their unbelief. This conclusion looks forward to the next section of the sermon, where the narration of what happened to the wilderness generation will be more fully actualized for the readers. In 4:1-13 the author will directly apply the prohibition to enter into the promised land to his audience as he develops the notion of a promised rest and warns that unbelief will have the same effect on the audience that it had on the wilderness generation.

With the ancient readers of Hebrews, today's readers share the concern for fidelity and steadfastness in their own religious lives. Elements of this text may help to remind them of the need for attentiveness and wholehearted-ness in responding to God's word. Just as a lack of persuasion brought about a hardening of hearts among the wilderness generation, so also it is possible for modern hearers of the word to fail to perceive the message of Scripture today.

For Reference and Further Study

de Silva, David A. "Entering God's Rest: Eschatology and the Socio-Rhetorical Strategy of Hebrews," *TJ* 21 (2000) 25–43.

Gleason, Randall C. "The Old Testament Background of Rest in Hebrews 3:7–4:11," *BSac* 157 (2000) 281–303.

Hofius, Otfried. *KATAPAUSIS: Die Vorstellung vom endzeitlichen Ruheort im Hebräer-brief.* WUNT 11. Tübingen: Mohr Siebeck, 1970.

Johnsson, William G. "The Pilgrimage Motif in the Book of Hebrews," *JBL* 97 (1978) 239–51.

Lombard, H. A. "Katapausis in the Letter to the Hebrews," *Neot* 5 (1971) 60–71.

Nardoni, Enrique. "Partakers in Christ (Hebrews 3:14)," *NTS* 37 (1991) 456–72.

8. *Strive to Enter that Rest* (4:1-13)

1. Let us fear, therefore, lest any of you think to fall behind while the promise of entering his rest remains. 2. For the good news was announced to us as it was to them; but the word they heard did not benefit them, because they were not joined in faith with those who listened. 3. We believers are entering into that rest, just as God has said, "As I swore in my wrath, 'They

shall not enter into my rest,'" although his works were completed from the foundation of the world. 4. Somewhere it had said about the seventh day, "And God rested on the seventh day from all his works." 5. And again in this text it says, "They shall not enter into my rest." 6. Since therefore it remains open for some to enter it, and those who formerly received the good news failed to enter because of disobedience, 7. again he designates a certain day "today," saying through David a long time ago, in the words already quoted, "Today, if you hear his voice, do not harden your hearts." 8. For if Joshua had given them rest, God would not speak later about another day. 9. So then, a Sabbath rest still remains for the people of God; 10. for whoever enters God's rest, that one God gives rest from his works as God did from his. 11. Let us therefore strive to enter into that rest, so that no one may fall from the same sort of disobedience.

12. For God's word is living and active, sharper than any two-edged sword, penetrating until it divides soul from spirit, joints from marrow; it is able to judge the thoughts and intentions of the heart. 13. And no creature is hidden from him, but all are naked and incapacitated before the eyes of the one with whom we must finally reckon.

Notes

1. *Let us fear, therefore, lest any of you think to fall behind while the promise of entering his rest remains:* In the Hebrew Bible "fear" connotes the respectful distance separating a creature from God (Gen 3:10; 28:17) and the disposition of the creature before the creator (Gen 18:15; Exod 3:6; Deut 5:5). Fear is also a motivating force that guards against sin (Gen 20:8; Exod 20:20; Num 12:8; Deut 13:11; Josephus, *Antiquities* 2.24). Philo thought that fearing God was not the same as loving God (*On the Unchangeableness of God* 69). Loving God presupposed a nonanthropomorphic view of God, since the individual is paying appropriate honor to God (*theoprepōs*) for God's sake. Only those who fear God hold an anthropomorphic notion of God, since they liken God to a human. The author of Hebrews has already demonstrated that he holds an anthropomorphic notion of God in the opening chapter, where God speaks, and in 10:31, where the living God is portrayed as having hands.

   Whereas the verb *dokein* carries the meanings "seem," "appear," or "be found" (as in a judgment or a verdict), it can also connote thought, thus "think," or "suppose" (Gen 38:15; Exod 25:2; 2 Macc 2:29; 5:6; 7:16; 9:8, 10; 14:14, 40; 3 Macc 5:5, 49; 4 Macc 9:30; 13:14; BDAG, 224–25). As the remainder of the text addresses thoughts and intentions, this meaning fits the context well.

   The verb "fall behind," *hysterein*, suggests "want" or "lack" of something, a deficiency of some sort. The word can also mean to miss an opportunity by omission or commission (BDAG, 1043). If one could not keep pace because of weakness, for example, this verb would express that kind of falling behind. Josephus uses it to describe prophecies that "fall short" of their predictions (*Antiquities* 18.199). In Philo, Jacob imagines Joseph as a "laggard," *hysterēkota*, when he does not return with his brothers after they had sold him (*On Joseph*

182). In another place he associates such "lagging behind" with failure to reach the goal (*On Agriculture* 85). Whereas it is possible for the verb to mean a failure to complete something through omission (Philo, *Moses* 2:233), it is likely the author is warning here against a more deliberate act on the part of the readers.

The author understands the promise to enter God's rest as still in effect. The verb *kataleipein* can mean "remain" in the sense of being "left" or "left over" (BDAG, 521). This sense is attested in the LXX (Gen 7:23; Deut 28:62; 3 Kgdms 19:18; Sir 24:33) and in Hellenistic Judaism (Josephus, *War* 4.338; Philo, *On the Creation* 63; *Allegorical Interpretation* 2.56; 3.20; *Moses* 1.308; 2.264).

Hebrews uses the noun "promise," *epangelia*, and the verb "to promise," *epangellein*, to refer to the promise God made to Abraham (6:13-15; 7:6; 11:9, 17), or more generally of God's promises (8:6; 9:15; 10:36) or the act of God's promising (6:13, 17; 10:23; 11:11; 12:26). The noun also refers to promises the ancestors did not receive (11:13, 39). The notion of God's promise was introduced in Gen 12:1-3 and served as the archetype for God's relationship with Israel prior to the Mosaic covenant. Hebrews, like Paul, believes that even after the Law had been given, the promise was still in effect, and that it had not been nullified (Heb 6:13-20; Rom 4:13-16; Gal 3:17). Here the reference is more general.

On the noun "rest," *katapausis*, see the Notes to 3:11. Here "rest" refers to entering into heavenly reality, which when completed will mean entering into the heavenly city (12:22). The term encompasses both a realized and a future eschatology (Attridge, 128; Koester, 268). A failure to enter God's rest now will result in a failure to enter it later.

2. *For the good news was announced to us, as it was to them:* Hebrews never uses the noun "good news," *euangelion*, but only the verb "announce good news" *euangelizein*, here and in v. 6. In the LXX it means simply "tell good news," which may be synonymous with the announcement of God's salvation (Pss 39:9; 67:12; 95:2; Joel 3:5; Isa 40:9; 52:7). The voice is passive, so presumably God did the announcing. The ambiguity of the term "good news" allows the author to make a link back to Israel's ancestors. Their good news was what God promised them. There is continuity between that promise and the good news preached to Christians, just as the word spoken of old is continuous with the word spoken in the Son.

but the word they heard did not benefit them, because they were not joined in faith with those who listened: Whereas there is continuity in the fact that God has spoken to the ancestors and to the readers (1:1-2), there is discontinuity in the effects of God's word. Because of their disobedience and unbelief (3:18-19), the wilderness generation could not enter into God's rest. Thus they did not benefit from the word they had heard. The verb "benefit," *ōphelein*, means to obtain some help or relief from something or someone (Tob 2:10; Ps 89[88]:22; Prov 10:2; 11:4; Wis 5:8; 6:25; Sir 5:8; Matt 15:5; 16:26; 27:24; Rom 2:25; 1 Cor 13:3; 14:6; Gal 5:2). It occurs again in Hebrews at 13:9.

The last part of the verse is difficult to understand since the participle of *synkerannynai*, "mix with," is attested in a singular (*synkekrasmenos:* א b d vg[cl] sy[p] sa[mss]) and a plural form (*synkekrasmenous:* 𝔓[13vid.46] A B C D* Ψ 0243. 33. 81. 1739. 2464 *pc* vg[st.ww] sy[h] sa[mss]). The singular participle would render the meaning as "it was not joined with faith with those who listened." The subject would be the word that was spoken. The plural changes the meaning to "they were not joined in faith with those who listened," as in the standard Greek edition of the NT. Many commentators prefer the plural because it allows the readers to include themselves among those who listened, in analogy with 11:39-40. For a fuller discussion of the textual problem see Attridge, 125–26, and Koester, 270.

3. *We believers are entering into that rest, just as God has said, "As I swore in my wrath, 'They shall not enter into my rest'":* Those prevented from entering God's rest lacked faith (3:19). Conversely, the possibility of entering into rest is still open for those who believe. The first person plural of the verb "to enter," *eiserchesthai,* makes it possible for the writer and readers to be included among those believing. Caleb and Joshua tried to prevent the rebellion in the wilderness and remained faithful (Num 14:6-10; 14:24-30). Consequently they might serve as an example of believers who could enter into rest. According to 3:16, however, the author includes all who left Egypt with Moses among those who rebelled. It is likely, then, that Caleb and Joshua do not represent "those who listened" in the previous verse, allowing for a more general interpretation of that phrase.

The ingressive sense of the verb "we are entering" indicates a present state that will be completed at a future time. Without saying exactly how those who believe are entering into rest, the author suggests that the process has already begun but has not yet been fully realized. The present tense in Greek can carry the meaning of a future, and so entering into rest has a proleptic meaning (Attridge, 126; Koester, 270; Weiss, 279). When the process will be completed is not specified. On the citation from Ps 95(94):11 see the Notes to 3:11.

although his works were completed from the foundation of the world: "Works" is elliptical in the genitive plural, as is found in the psalm quotation in the next verse for "all the works." "Foundation," *katabolē,* appears in the LXX at 2 Macc 2:29 referring to a whole construction (see *Ep. Aristeas* 129). In the NT the expression "from the foundation of the world" means the creation (Matt 13:35; 25:34; Luke 11:50; John 17:24; Eph 1:4; Rev 13:8). The author will use it again at 9:26.

4. *Somewhere it had said about the seventh day, "And God rested on the seventh day from all his works":* As in 2:6 a Scripture citation is introduced by "somewhere," *pou.* The quotation appears to be from Gen 2:2. This method of quoting is found, for example, in Philo (*On the Unchangeableness of God* 74).

The author has simply written "the seventh," but he means "the seventh day," as the context shows. "The seventh day" was a common substitute for the Sabbath in Second Temple Judaism (Exod 16:30; 2 Macc 12:38). Philo even associates rest with the number seven (*On the Unchangeableness of God* 12). Hebrews adds the preposition *en* to the seventh day to show clearly that it was on the seventh day that God rested. The author also makes God the subject, which is lacking in the LXX (cf. Exod 20:11; 31:17).

5. *And again in this text it says, "They shall not enter into my rest":* The psalm quotation is repeated for emphasis. The repetition of the idea of entering or not entering into rest holds the entire text together. Here it rounds out the first part, before the author moves to a clarification of why some of the ancestors were prevented from entering into God's rest and how the possibility is still open for the readers.

6. *Since therefore it remains open for some to enter it, and those who formerly received the good news failed to enter because of disobedience:* The author reiterates the opening verse of this section, substituting the verb "remain open," *apoleipein*, for "remain," *kataleipein*, which makes his meaning clearer. He will use it again in 4:9 and 10:26. The reference to Moses and others of the wilderness generation, who were prevented from entering the land of Canaan because of their disobedience, creates a desired contrast between the ancestors and the readers. The noun "disobedience," *apeitheia*, is related to the noun for "disbelief," *apistia* (Rudolf Bultmann, *peithō, ktl., TDNT* 6:1–11). The paraenetic force of the verse reminds the readers what is at stake if they fail in faith.

7. *again he designates a certain day "today," saying through David a long time ago, in the words already quoted, "Today, if you hear his voice, do not harden your hearts":* Now is the opportune time for Christians to heed the warning, lest they, too, be prevented from entering into God's rest. In 3:13 the author has indicated that "today" is coterminous with a specific period of time, "as long as it is called today." At 10:25 he describes the day of judgment, which will presumably bring "today" to a close (Koester, 271).

   This time the psalm quotation is introduced with a reference to David, who was traditionally thought to have authored the Psalms (Luke 20:42; Acts 2:25, 34; Rom 4:6; 11:9). The use of Greek *en* with a personal name is common in Second Temple Judaism to introduce a biblical citation (Casey Elledge, "Exegetical Styles at Qumran: A Cumulative Index and Commentary," *RevQ* 82 [2004] 188). Perhaps there is an echo of Heb 1:1 here. It is not clear if, like Luke, the author counts David's words as prophetic (Acts 2:30). Certainly the following quotation from Ps 95(94):7 has the ring of a prophetic warning. The expression "long ago" (lit: "after so long a time") is *hapax* in the NT (cf. Matt 25:19). It is attested in the Pseudepigrapha (*Par. Jer.* 5:18) and in other Greek literature of the time (Lucian, *The Dream,* 5; Josephus, *Antiquities* 1.318).

8. *For if Joshua had given them rest, God would not speak later about another day:* The Greek *Iēsous* translates to Joshua or Jesus. The context prefers the former, although a typological exegesis might yield a reference to Jesus (cf. Attridge, 130; Koester, 272). Joshua 21:43 and 22:4 refer to the people having been given rest after they entered the promised land under the leadership of Joshua. This cannot be the rest the author refers to. There is yet another rest to be entered into, as the remainder of the verse indicates. The argument is similar to those in 7:11 and 8:7, which establish further need.

   Because of the oath sworn against a part of the wilderness generation some, including Moses, did not enter into rest. Still, as noted above, God gave others rest (cf. Deut 31:7). Whatever that "rest" was, it does not qualify for the goal the author speaks of here. He notes that on the basis of Psalm 95 another day was already envisioned. It is to this day and this rest that the readers are invited to respond.

9. *So then, a Sabbath rest still remains for the people of God:* The noun "Sabbath," *sabbatismos*, occurs only here in the NT. It is unattested in the LXX. In the Gospels and Acts (Matt 12:5; Mark 2:27; Luke 23:54, 56; John 5:9, 10, 18; 9:14, 16; Acts 13:27, 42; 15:21; 18:4) one finds the more frequent term *sabbaton*, which is pre-

ferred by the LXX as well (2 Kgdms 4:23; 11:5, 7, 9; 1 Chr 9:32; 2 Chr 23:4; Neh 9:14; 13:18; 1 Macc 1:43; 6:49; 8:27, 28; 2 Macc 12:38; Isa 66:23).

The expression "the people of God" is a biblical designation for Israel, reminiscent of the covenant formulas, "They shall be my people, and I will be their God" (Jer 24:7; 32:38; Ezek 11:20; 14:11; 37:23; Zech 8:8) and "I will be their God, and they shall be my people" (Jer 31:33; Ezek 37:27; 2 Cor 6:16; cf. Rev 21:7). The author will quote this formula in 8:10 from the citation of Jer 31:31-34. Here he includes the recipients in the heritage of Israel under this title.

10. *for whoever enters God's rest, that one God gives rest from his works as God did from his:* According to Gen 2:2 the "works" God rested from were the "works" of creation. The author has cited Ps 102:25 referring to the "work" of God's hands (1:10) and has spoken of God's "works" witnessed by the ancestors (3:9). Although Jewish tradition does not believe that God rested completely from his works, Israel's Sabbath observance required a cessation of all work on the Sabbath except for offering God praise and worship (Koester, 272). In 6:10 the author refers to the "work" of the readers, linked with their love (cf. 10:24). In 13:1-6 they are exhorted to continue to offer hospitality, and their service to prisoners is recalled in 10:34. These stand in contrast to "dead works" (6:1; 9:14). These good works are those the readers will be given rest from, when they finally enter into God's rest (12:22; 13:14).

11. *Let us therefore strive to enter into that rest, so that no one may fall from the same sort of disobedience:* The verb "endeavor," *spoudazein*, means "hurry" or "expedite," but mostly in the NT refers to "making a sincere effort" (BDAG, 939; Günther Harder, *spoudazō, ktl., TDNT* 7:559–68). All the occurrences are in letters (Gal 2:10; Eph 4:3; 1 Thess 2:17; 2 Tim 2:15; 2 Pet 1:10; 3:14; 1 Pet 1:15). The word is infrequent in the LXX. The hortatory subjunctive encourages the readers to make every sincere effort to enter the rest. The author includes himself with the readers in the exhortation, showing the value of making such an effort.

The verb "fall," *piptein*, is used figuratively for how the wilderness generation perished (Num 14:29, 35). In 3:17 the author actualized Num 14:29 for his readers by alluding to it in a rhetorical question about who provoked God to anger in the wilderness. Thus he linked the disobedient ancestors to his readers, who may fall away. On *piptein* see the Notes at 3:17.

The noun *hypodeigma* means an "example," and so it is used positively in the LXX (2 Macc 6:28, 31; 4 Macc 17:23; Sir 44:16; Ezek 42:15), whereas in the NT it may be used positively (John 13:15; Jas 5:10) or negatively (2 Pet 2:6; Heb 4:11). Here it does not refer to an example of disobedience but rather to the disobedience itself and its consequences (BDAG, 1037). Elsewhere in Hebrews it stands for the model of the Temple (8:5; 9:23).

12. *For God's word is living and active, sharper than any two-edged sword, penetrating until it divides soul from spirit, joints from marrow:* Here "God's word" is characterized by its vitality. Hebrews only uses *logos* in the singular. Most often it refers to a word spoken by God (4:2, 12; 6:5; 11:3; 12:9), but it can be a word about God (13:7). Since Scripture embraces both of those meanings it is possible that the author has Scripture in mind, as something that is able to confront the listener or reader (Donald A. Hagner, *Encountering the Book of Hebrews*, 76; Lane 1:102,

105; Koester, 280; Spicq 2:89). In 6:1 *logos* refers to the word of Christ. Finally, it also means the sermon preached by the author to the recipients (13:22).

Only here does the participle "living," *zōn*, modify a noun other than God in Hebrews. The God of Hebrews is a living God (3:12; 9:14; 10:31; 12:22) whose "word" is also characterized as "living." Paired with "living" is the adjective "active," *energēs*, which is a later form of *energos* (Ezek 46:1). *Energēs* also has the sense of "effective." "Living" and "active" are not paired in the LXX, but the two occur together in Xenophon, *Memorabilia* 1.4.4. A weakly supported variant (B Hier[pt]) has "clear" (*enargēs*), which does not fit the context. Paul describes the word of God as something at work (*energeitai*) in the believers (1 Thess 1:13). The author stresses that God's word is dynamic rather than static in order to heighten the sense of the warning he is giving.

The dynamism of the word is expressed under the metaphor of a sword. The image of the sword appears to be drawn from Judg 3:16, where it does not refer to the word of God. The LXX does not characterize God's word as a sword, although it contains references to God's sword (Isa 27:1; 34:5). Perhaps the closest one gets to the image in Hebrews is the metaphor of the mouth of the Servant as a sword in Isa 49:2 and the image of the word leaping from heaven like a warrior carrying the sharp sword of God's authentic command in Wis 18:15-16. Elsewhere in the NT a two-edged sword comes from the mouth of the Son of Man in Rev 1:16, as it does from the mouth of the rider who is called the word of God in Rev 19:15, 21. Philo has the image of God's word as sharp and able to sever things into parts (*Who Is the Heir* 130-31) and portrays God as sharpening the edge of his "all-cutting word" (ibid. 140; cf. 235–236; *The Worse Attacks the Better* 110).

The verb "penetrate," *diïkneisthai*, is rare in Greek and occurs only once in the LXX (Exod 26:28), where it refers to one of the five bars running through the frame of the sanctuary. It occurs only here in the NT. Absent from Philo, the verb is found a few times in Josephus, who uses it figuratively (*War* 1.426) and literally (*War* 3.165; 6.261; *Antiquities* 3.157; 13.96).

In the LXX the "soul" and "spirit" are those faculties that animate the human body. An interesting text from Wis 15:11 speaks of God inspiring humans with "active souls," *psychēn energousan*, and breathing into them "a lifegiving spirit," *pneuma zōtikon*. In 4:12 the author describes God's word as "living," *zōn*, and active, *energēs*. Josephus paraphrases Gen 2:7 and describes God as instilling in Adam "spirit and soul" (*Antiquities* 1.34; cf. 11.240). He also explains the dietary prohibition against consuming an animal's blood as originating in the belief that blood stands for "soul and spirit" (*Antiquities* 3.260; cf. Philo, *The Worse Attacks the Better* 80-83; *Who Is the Heir* 55-57; *Questions on Genesis* 2.59). "Soul" and "spirit" express the vitality of the human being.

The noun "joint," *armos*, is used only here in the NT and occurs just twice in the LXX (Sir 27:2; 4 Macc 10:5). Similar to the usage in Sir 27:2, Josephus has the noun for the joints in the stones of the Temple wall (*Antiquities* 3.118). The usual term in Greek for a joint in the body is *arthron* (4 Macc 9:17; Philo, *Embassy to Gaius* 238; Josephus, *Life* 403). "Marrow," *muelos*, is the standard Greek noun, used metaphorically for the innermost or choicest part of something (Gen 45:19; Job 21:24; 33:24; Josephus, *War* 6.204; Philo, *On the Change of Names* 174; *Moses*

1.291; *Questions on Genesis* 2.3). These images are designed to show the totality of the human and the depth to which the word of God is able to reach as it penetrates the core of the human being. Nothing can be hidden, as the thought continues, from this dynamic word of God.

it is able to judge the thoughts and intentions of the heart: Perhaps this is an allusion to Ps 44:21 (43:22): "For he knows the secrets of the heart." The other function of the "word" is "to judge." The adjective "able to judge," *kritikos*, appears only here in the NT and is not extant in the LXX. After the exhortation of v. 7 not to harden their hearts (3:8; 4:7) and the warning to avoid acquiring an evil heart, the author strengthens his exhortation with a note of accountability. God knows what lies in the human heart (cf. Luke 16:15) and his word has the ability to judge its sentiments.

13. *And no creature is hidden from him:* Here we have an echo of the creation narra-tive, where Adam and Eve unsuccessfully attempt to hide from God (Gen 3:8). The adjective "hidden," *aphanēs*, is rare in the LXX (Job 20:30; 24:20; 41:14; 2 Macc 3:34), where *kryptos* and *kryphaios* are more common. The notion that one cannot hide from God is common in Hellenistic Judaism (Isa 40:27-28; Sir 1:30; 16:17). Philo, for example, says that the sinner "shall never escape the eye of him who sees into the recesses of the mind and treads its inmost shrine" (*On the Un-changeableness of God* 9; cf. *On Providence* 2.35).

but all are naked and incapacitated before the eyes of the one with whom we must finally reckon: An interesting parallel is found in *1 Enoch* 1:5: "Everything is naked and open before your sight, and you see everything; and there is nothing which can hide itself from you" (trans. E. Isaac in Charlesworth 1:17). The verb "incapaci-tate," *trachēlizein*, means to "twist the neck" of a sacrificial animal or to "suffer hardship" (LSJ, 1118). Josephus shows one instance of the verb (*War* 4.375). Philo uses it in relation to a grip that renders one prostrate (*On the Cherubim* 78; *Who is the Heir* 274; *Moses* 1.297; *Every Good Person Is Free* 159). He pairs "be naked," *gynmazein*, and "grasp by the neck," *trachēlizein*, in one place to describe a land worn out and gripped by violence (*On Rewards and Punishments* 153). The meaning of this part of the verse remains obscure (Attridge, 136; Koester, 274; Montefiore, 89).

The sense that individuals will be held accountable by the word of God is strengthened by the last part of this verse, which mentions an "account" or "reckoning." The noun *logos* can mean "an account," and the author uses it with that sense in 13:17 (BDAG, 600–601). The one to whom they must account is most probably God (Attridge, 136).

Interpretation

Having established in the previous section the consequences of disobe-dience for entrance into God's rest, in the warning issued in 4:1-13 the au-thor calls the readers' attention to the possibility of missing the opportunity to enter that rest. The development of the previous ideas forms three sec-tions of this text: vv. 1-5; 6-11; 12-13. Each section is nicely framed.

The first section (4:1-5) begins with a reference to rest and the exhortation not to fail to take the opportunity to enter into it (v. 1). It ends with the oath God swore that those who were disobedient in the wilderness generation would not enter that rest (v. 5). By calling his readers to fear that they might not enter into God's rest the author actualizes the biblical text for them. They may share the fate of the wilderness generation if they, too, fall short of the goal. The author wants his readers to feel that they have something in common with the ancestral generation. Both have heard the word of God, and each must make the appropriate response to that word. Since failure to believe prevented some of the ancestors from entering into the promised rest, were the readers to follow their example they would suffer a fate similar to the one suffered by the wilderness generation.

"Unbelief" is not specified by a particular form or action. The author likens it to the rebellion of the wilderness generation (4:11), but Hebrews gives little evidence of a rebellion among the readers. They are portrayed as sluggish (5:11-14; 12:12-13), immature (6:1-3), in danger of apostasy (6:4-6; 10:26-31), negligent or lax (10:25), weak in confidence (3:6; 10:35), in need of endurance (10:36), and weighted down by sin (12:1). Perhaps "unbelief" constitutes the general state of the believers, evident in the particulars just listed. Clearly it is cause for some concern, as the warning to enter the rest while the promise is still open is issued with a sense of urgency.

Alongside the severe warning the author places some encouragement: "We believers are entering into that rest . . ." (v. 3). He does this elsewhere in the sermon to offset the harshness of some of his words (4:14-16; 6:9-12; 10:32-39). The encouragement functions to draw a contrast between the ancestors and the readers. Those who were unfaithful in the wilderness generation failed to accomplish what they had set out to do; they did not receive the fulfillment of what God had promised them. They were not the beneficiaries of the promise because they had not benefited from the word they had heard. The readers still have a chance as long as "today" remains open.

The completion of God's work of creation (v. 3) did not preclude the wilderness generation from sharing in God's rest, and the possibility that later generations may enter into that rest is still open. The author is somewhat obscure in his thought on this matter. Even though there are two groups of ancestors alluded to, those who listened and those who did not, he focuses only on the disobedient ancestors in order to provide a negative example that should not be followed. One might have expected the idea that the readers should unite themselves in faith with those who listened, in order to enter into the promised rest. Probably the tone of the text is more negative than positive because the author's thought is governed by the citation from Ps 95(94):11. The strong admonition that the disobedient ones would never enter God's rest informs the warning the author issues to his readers. This is a matter of some urgency.

Including himself among the believers who are entering into God's rest, the author wishes to be united in faith with his readers. It appears that he is trying to set an example that would challenge the example of the disobedient wilderness generation. The logic of v. 3, however, does not flow easily. The positive note of entering into rest is offset by the divine oath that the disobedient would not enter into it. The contrast parallels what has already been said. The harsh oath reinforces the author's warning that if it is possible to enter that rest, so also is it possible to be prevented from entering it. Almost as if by free association of ideas he then tacks on the mention of God having completed his work from the foundations of the world. His purpose must be to show that no matter how long ago the rest was established, on the basis of God resting from the work of creation the promise of that rest is still in effect. God finished his work and rested, and yet that rest is still open to those who listen to the word of God.

The mention of the completion of God's work helps the author to introduce the notion of the Sabbath, the basis for any rest at all. Although v. 4 gives the impression of being a bit off the cuff, it is constructed deliberately by the author. He pulls another scriptural text out of the air to explain the meaning of the Sabbath and then offsets it again with the oath from Ps 95:11. The rest that the disobedient are prevented from entering is like God's own rest. That is not to say that the author is suggesting his readers are like God, but only that God established a rest into which he continues to invite people to enter by means of his word.

The transition to the second section (vv. 6-11) begins with the possibility of entering into that rest, with a reminder that some of the wilderness generation were prevented from doing so because of disobedience. It ends with a warning that the recipients may fall like the wilderness generation if they fail through a similar disobedience.

The presence of the Greek *tinas*, "some," in v. 6 shows that the author believes it is still possible for the readers to enter the rest. The warning is reinforced by yet another mention of the fact that those of the wilderness generation who were disobedient failed to enter the rest. Then follows the cause for the author's optimism that the promise of rest is still open. God has designated another day for rest, called "today." "Today" is any opportune day on which the word of God comes to someone. "Today" is a temporal designation for the moment when God speaks. So the author interprets Ps 95(94):7 to mean that the proper response to hearing God's word is to receive it with a generous heart. The psalm is actualized for the readers because of the possibility that the promised rest is still open as long as "today" lasts (Heb 3:13). The second half of this text, then, ends on a note of hope in the midst of dire warnings. It is still "today" and rest is available. If this were not the case, the rest into which Joshua led the people would have been final. As it is, the rest he offered the people was proleptic and could not be final until the promise of rest was renewed in Jesus.

In fact, Joshua did not lead the people into rest alone. He did it together with Caleb. Yet the author does not mention Caleb. Can the omission be deliberate so that only the name Joshua, which is the same as Jesus in Greek, might point to the one who can lead them into God's rest permanently? The movement of the text suits such an interpretation. The rest being spoken of is possible because of God's rest at the completion of his work from the foundation of the world. That very rest was offered to the wilderness generation, but some of them failed to achieve it. As Joshua was instrumental in leading some of that generation to it, although not in a final way, Jesus makes possible the offer of the completion of that rest.

The third section (vv. 12-13) begins a related excursus on the word of God as something vital from which no one can hide and ends with the reminder that no creature can hide from God. The word that is spoken and must be received with a generous heart actually demands the kind of response the author is looking for. One cannot be half-hearted or try to hide oneself from it because it has the power to expose whatever is false and disingenuous. The vital penetrating word plunges into the depths of the human person, confronting one with truth in such a way that the individual necessarily must reckon with God. Since that word can judge the thoughts and intentions of the heart, only the generous and not the hardened heart will pass muster.

For Reference and Further Study

Attridge, Harold. "'Let Us Strive to Enter that Rest': The Logic of Hebrews 4:1-11," *HTR* 73 (1980) 279–88.

Becker, Eve-Marie. "'Gottes Wort' und 'Unser Wort.' Bemerkungen zu Hebr 4,12-13," *BZ* 44 (2000) 254–62.

Lombard, H. A. "Katápausis in the Letter to the Hebrews," *Neot* 5 (1971) 60–71.

Oberholtzer, Thomas K. "The Kingdom Rest in Hebrews 3:1–4:13," *BSac* 145 (1988) 185–96.

Vanhoye, Albert. "La parole qui juge: Hé 4, 12-13," *AsSeign* 59 (1974) 36–42.

9. *A Great High Priest* (4:14–5:10)

14. Since, then, we have a great high priest who has passed through the heavens, Jesus, the Son of God, let us hold fast to our confession. 15. For we do not have a high priest who is unable to sympathize with our weaknesses, but we have one who in every respect has been tested as we are, yet apart from sin. 16. Let us therefore approach the throne of grace with

boldness, so that we may receive mercy and find grace to help in time of need.

5:1. Every high priest chosen from among humans is appointed on their behalf regarding things pertaining to God, in order to offer gifts and sacrifices for sins. 2. He is able to deal gently with the ignorant and wayward, since he himself is subject to weakness; 3. and because of this he must offer sacrifice for his own sins as well as for those of the people. 4. And one does not presume to take this honor, but when called by God, just as Aaron was.

5. So also Christ did not glorify himself in becoming a high priest, but was appointed by the one who said to him, "You are my Son, today I have begotten you"; 6. as he says also in another place, "You are a priest forever, according to the order of Melchizedek." 7. In the days of his flesh, Jesus offered up prayers and supplications, with loud cries and tears, to the one who was able to save him from death, and he was heard because of his reverent submission. 8. Although he was a Son, he learned obedience through what he suffered; 9. and having been made perfect, he became the source of eternal salvation for all who obey him, 10. having been designated by God a high priest according to the order of Melchizedek.

NOTES

14. *Since, then, we have a great high priest who has passed through the heavens, Jesus, the Son of God, let us hold fast to our confession:* Although the Greek is not the same as in this verse, there are two references to the great high priest, *archiereōs megalou*, in the LXX (1 Macc 13:42; 14:27). In the LXX the high priest is called the "great priest," *ho hiereus ho megas* (Lev 21:10; Num 35:25, 28, 32; 2 Kgdms 12:11; 22:4, 8; 2 Chr 24:11; 34:9; Neh 3:1, 20; 13:28; Jdt 4:6, 8, 14; 15:8; Hag 1:1, 12, 14; 2:2, 4; Zech. 3:1, 8; 6:11). The Hebrew of Josh 20:6 has *hakohen haggadol*, lacking in the LXX.

Heavenly journeys are common in the literature of Hellenistic Judaism (e.g., *Apocalypse of Zephaniah; 2 Enoch; Martyrdom and Ascension of Isaiah*). Curiously, the author seems uninterested in the details of the journey, but simply mentions it to qualify the nature of Jesus' priesthood. Ultimately Jesus is a high priest who is "exalted above the heavens" (7:26). He is also one enthroned at the right hand of God in the heavens (8:1), and as High Priest he enters a sanctuary that is "heaven itself" (9:24). Hebrews appeals to the motif of Jesus' entrance into the heavenly sanctuary in several other places (6:20; 8:2; 9:11-12) as a distinctive feature of his high priesthood. And so, it is no incidental detail that he is a High Priest who has passed through the heavens; rather it is something that is constitutive of Jesus' priesthood, and that, along with other distinguishing factors the author develops in subsequent sections of the sermon, sets him apart from earthly high priests.

The preferred title for Jesus in Hebrews is simply "Son." Here (4:14) and in three other instances it is expanded more fully to "Son of God" (6:6; 7:3; 10:29). In the Hebrew Bible the king is sometimes referred to as God's "son" (2 Sam

7:14; 1 Chr 17:13; 22:10; 28:6; Pss 2:7; 89:27). Hebrews joins "Son of God" to the title of high priest, making a connection between this part of the sermon and the earlier chapters focused primarily on the Son. In *T. Levi* 4:2, Levi will become God's son, minister (*therapōn*; cf. Heb 3:5) and priest (*leitourgos*; cf. Heb 1:7; 8:2). Commentators believe that the profession of Jesus as the Son of God was at the heart of the community's faith, especially in light of the attention to the "confession" in this passage (Attridge, 139; Koester, 282).

"Hold fast," *kratein*, means "hold on to" or "cling to something." (BDAG, 564–65). Here it seems not to be a general injunction, but rather a command to maintain a specific set of beliefs. The author is trying to encourage his readers not to let go of the traditional teaching they had received. Earlier (2:1) the author expressed a similar sentiment by means of the verb *prosechein*, a nautical term for keeping a ship on course so that it would not "drift off" (LSJ, 1512). In 3:14 he uses *katechein*, found also in 10:23. He likes to vary terminology for this concept.

On "confession," *homologia*, see the Notes at 3:1. The content of the confession is not specified; the author seems to take for granted that his audience knows exactly what he refers to. The term occurs at 3:1 and 10:23 as well. In 3:1 Jesus is referred to as the "apostle and high priest of our confession" in the context of a discussion of his fidelity. Here the readers are to imitate that fidelity by holding fast to the confession because he is an exemplary High Priest, someone worthy of following in fidelity.

15. *For we do not have a high priest who is unable to sympathize with our weaknesses:* The double negative strengthens the force of the affirmation about the nature of Jesus' high priesthood. "Sympathize," *sympathēsai*, appears only in Hebrews in the NT (cf. 10:34). This verb occurs twice in the LXX. In 4 Macc 5:25 it expresses a quality of God manifested in the fact that the Law was given to humans as an act of God's sympathy. In 4 Macc 13:23 the seven Maccabean brothers are sympathetic toward one another because of their common upbringing and education in the Law. Priesthood in the Levitical tradition is hereditary, and while there may have been expectations of character and behavior, the ability to sympathize with weakness was not required of a priest. Here such sympathy forms a critical part of Jesus' high priesthood. It may be that in light of v. 14, where Jesus' high priesthood is described in exalted terms, the author wants to reassure his readers that Jesus, as High Priest, is not remote or unaware of the human condition.

"Weakness," *astheneia*, can refer to "illness," to "physical limitation" (see Heb 5:2; 11:34), or to "inadequacy" such as "helplessness" (BDAG, 142). Here the term is understood as "helplessness" in resisting temptation to sin.

but we have one who in every respect has been tested as we are, yet without sin: On the "testing" of Jesus see the Notes at 2:18. On Jesus' thorough familiarity with the human condition see the Notes at 2:17. The assertion that Jesus was human and knew human weakness without giving in to temptation is common in the NT. The tradition is invoked here to draw a distinction between any other high priest and Jesus as High Priest. The former was acquainted with human weakness that leads to sin, whereas Jesus knows the human condition without succumbing to the temptation to sin.

16. *Let us therefore approach the throne of grace with boldness:* The verb *proserchesthai* means "approach" in the sense of "draw near to." This term indicates having access to God, and has cultic connotations (Exod 12:48; 19:9; 34:32; Lev 9:5, 7, 8; 10:4, 5; Num 10:3, 4; 16:40; 18:3, 4, 22; Deut 21:5; Heb 7:25; 10:1, 22; 11:6; 12:18, 22) and can mean "come into the presence of a deity" (BDAG, 878; MM, 547). The author uses the hortatory subjunctive here. How do the readers now approach the throne of God? In Solomon's prayer of dedication at the newly built Temple he described how whoever approached the house of God would be heard by God enthroned in heaven (1 Kgs 8:30). Without an earthly temple, Hebrews understands access to the throne of God as through the Son, who has opened up the way to that throne and as High Priest mediates access (10:19-20). In 12:18, 22 this verb will facilitate a contrast between Sinai and the new Jerusalem, the wilderness generation and the readers, who now have access to God in a way that the ancestors did not. On "boldness," *parrhēsia*, see the Notes at 3:6.

   The usual triad in the NT is grace, mercy, and peace (1 Tim 1:2; 2 Tim 1:2; 2 John 3). In the LXX the pairing of grace with mercy occurs only at Wis 3:9 and 4:15. Mercy is joined to peace in Tobit 7:12, but is more frequently paired with truth (Pss 39:11; 61:7; 83:11; 84:10; 88:14, 24; 115:1; 137:2).

5:1. *Every high priest chosen from among humans is appointed on their behalf regarding things pertaining to God, in order to offer gifts and sacrifices for sins:* The reminder that the earthly high priest is human, subject to the human condition, recalls 4:15, where the qualifications of the heavenly High Priest stressed his full acquaintance with the human condition. Sirach 45:16 describes Aaron as having been chosen from among the living. The verb *lambanein*, which at its root means "take," is used to express how the high priest is "chosen from among mortals." The sense is that the high priest is part of the human race, but is then set apart (Philo, *Special Laws* 1.101, 226). This is clear from the meaning of "take" in Lev 8:2 in reference to Aaron and his sons, and then again in Num 8:6 referring to the Levites, who are to be taken from among the Israelites and cleansed.

   The mediatory role of the high priest is stressed in this part of the verse in preparation for the contrast with the kind of mediator the heavenly High Priest is. To be put in charge is to be appointed. The verb *kathizein* commonly means "appoint" someone (cf. 1 Cor 6:4). Since the role was hereditary, being appointed must refer to being charged with sacred duties. Perhaps the author has in mind the ritual of ordination as described in Exodus 29. In the LXX ordination consisted of "filling the hands" of the priests (see Exod 29:22-25, 29 and Lev 8:25-29).

   Regarding "on their behalf," the Greek text translated literally reads "on behalf of humans," *hyper anthrōpōn*. The phrase parallels "from among humans," *ex anthrōpōn*, in the first part of the verse, creating a nicely balanced clause, "taken from among humans and appointed on behalf of humans." The author shows the mediatory role of the high priest and his solidarity with those on whose behalf he offers sacrifice.

   On the expression "things pertaining to God," *ta pros ton theon*, see the Notes at 2:17. The description of the earthly high priest's work of mediation here echoes the description of Christ's atoning work as a merciful and faithful High Priest in 2:17.

The verb "offer," *prospherein*, is a technical term in the LXX for sacrificing. Its object varies according to the kinds of sacrifices offered. Of the eighteen times the verb appears in a cultic sense in the NT, twelve of them occur in Hebrews (5:1, 3; 8:3, 4; 9:7, 9, 25; 10:1, 2, 8, 11; 11:4). This usage reflects the standard understanding in the Pentateuch (Exod 36:3, 6; Lev 2:1, 4, 11, 14; 7:8, 9, 12, 18, 29, 33, 38; 21:6, 8, 17; 23:20; 27:9, 11; Num 3:4; 5:9; 7:12; 15:4; 16:35; 18:15; 26:61; 28:2, 26; Konrad Weiss, *prospherō*, *TDNT* 9:65-68).

Normally in Greek "gifts," *dōra*, and "sacrifices," *thysia*, are distinct. The LXX frequently combines both nouns for a particular offering made before the Lord. The words are interchangeable and do not determine separate kinds of sacrifices (Koester, 285). Hebrews reproduces the LXX language of sacrifice here, where the objects of sacrifice are referred to only in a generic way.

Judaism required "sin offerings" for purification from certain kinds of defilement and for atonement, especially on the Day of Atonement itself (Leviticus 16). Leviticus 6:25-30 specifies the ritual for "sin offerings." Everything about the offering is holy, and it has the power to sanctify anything that comes in contact with it, so that even a garment soiled by its blood has to be washed in a special way (Lev 6:27). The author does not specify the matter here; this is simply a general description of the function of the high priest. Since he had a special role on the Day of Atonement, when, once yearly, he entered the Holy of Holies, the author probably has the ritual of atonement in mind.

2. *He is able to deal gently with the ignorant and wayward, since he himself is subject to weakness:* The verb *metriopathein*, not extant in the LXX, means "moderate one's feelings" (BDAG, 643; Wilhelm Michaelis, *metriopatheō*, *TDNT* 5:938). Philo uses it in this sense (*Allegorical Interpretation* 3:134; *On Abraham* 257; *On Joseph* 26; see Josephus, *Antiquities* 12.128) along with the noun *metriopatheia* (*Allegorical Interpretation* 3.129, 132, 144; *On the Virtues* 195) and the adjective *metriopathēs* (*Special Laws* 3.96). Such control was a philosophical ideal for the Peripatetics (Diogenes Laertius, *The Lives of Eminent Philosophers* 5.31), whereas Cynics and Stoics strove for "indifference" or "freedom from passion," *apatheia* (Epictetus, 4.6.34; Crates, *To Metrocles*; Diogenes, *To Crates*; *To Amynander*, in Abraham J. Malherbe, *The Cynic Epistles*, SBLSBS 12 [Missoula, MT: Scholars Press, 1977] 86, 106, 114; cf. Spicq 2:108). The high priest can moderate his anger with those who are unknowing or who have gone astray. The Greek verb *agnoein* means "be unaware of" or "not understand." According to Lev 5:17 even if someone should commit a sin out of ignorance, guilt is still incurred, so the sin has to be expiated (cf. Lev 22:14). In 1 Macc 13:39 errors (*agnoēmata*) as well as offenses (*hamartēmata*) are equally pardoned by the king.

Regarding the weakness of the high priest, the author uses the verb *perikeisthai*, which means "wrap around" (BDAG 648; Mark 9:42; Luke 17:2) or "surround" (Heb 12:1). In Hellenistic Jewish literature it has the meaning "wear" (Ep Jer 6:24, 58) or "fetter" (4 Macc 12:2 [cf. Acts 28:20]). In Jer 9:25 (LXX) it means "shave." Some commentators have preferred the meaning "wear," since much was made of the elaborate vestments worn by the high priest symbolizing his power, now contrasted by the author with "weakness" (Koester, 286–87). One can also be "bound" by weakness as if it were a "fetter." In 12:1 the author uses the verb with the meaning "surround." Albert Vanhoye prefers the translation "enveloped in weakness" to draw the contrast with the otherwise expected glory of the high priest (Sir 45:7-8) symbolized by his vestments (Exod 28:2; Sir 50:5, 11). Hebrews, on the other hand, stresses the solidarity of the high priest with humanity (Vanhoye, *Old Testament Priests*, 139).

3. *and because of this he must offer sacrifice for his own sins as well as for those of the people:* The antecedent of "this" is "weakness." On the Day of Atonement the high priest was obligated to make sacrifices for his own sins (Lev 16:6; cf. 4:3-12; 9:7), for the sins of his household (Lev 16:6, 11), and for the sins of the people (Lev 16:15; cf. 4:13-21; 9:7), in addition to making atonement for the sanctuary, the tent of meeting, and the altar (Lev 16:16-18, 20, 33).

4. *And one does not presume to take this honor, but when called by God, just as Aaron was:* Looking back to the opening verse of this section where the high priest is "taken" from among humans by God, the author now uses the same verb to stress the point that no person takes this honor upon himself.

   An ellipsis presumes the repetition of the verb "take," *lambanein*, with the expression "when called by God." Priesthood is a call from its inception, as Moses was instructed to "take" Aaron and his sons and anoint them as priests (Exod 28:1-5; Lev 8:12-13). Thereafter, however, it is hereditary (Exod 29:29). Aaron is the prototype of earthly high priesthood, having been appointed by a call from God (Exod 28:1; Num 8:1-2). In Hellenistic Judaism, Aaron was seen as exalted because God had chosen him for the priesthood (Sir 45:6-22).

   The final part of the verse emphasizes that Jesus, like Aaron, was appointed by God to the high priesthood. The author anticipates a problem he will later engage more forcefully, i.e., Jesus did not come from a hereditary line of priests (7:13-14). He will establish Jesus' priestly pedigree otherwise in v. 6.

5. *So also Christ did not glorify himself in becoming a high priest:* Like Aaron, Jesus was called to the priesthood, and just as Aaron did not take it upon himself, neither did Christ. If there is likeness between the way each became a priest, there is difference, too. In v. 4 the priesthood was referred to as an honor. Here it is a matter of glory. Earlier, in 2:9, the author described Jesus as crowned with honor and glory. "Glory and honor" are given to the Lord in the LXX of Ps 95:7, whereas the Hebrew (96:7) has "glory and strength." In Exod 28:2 (LXX) God instructs Moses to make a holy vestment for Aaron "for honor and glory" and in 28:40 tunics and sashes to the same end. First Maccabees 14:21 refers to the "glory and honor" of the high priests and other priests in Israel. Whereas "glory and honor" may have been associated with the office of high priest, in Hebrews the association is with the priesthood of Jesus (Koester, 287).

   "You are my Son, today I have begotten you": This is the second reference in the sermon to Ps 2:7. (See the Notes at 1:5.) The psalm's function highlights yet another difference between the priesthoods of Jesus and Aaron, as the Son is greater than Aaron. The contrasts will be developed more extensively in subsequent chapters (7:11-28; 8:1–10:18).

6. *as he says also in another place, "You are a priest forever, according to the order of Melchizedek":* Parallel to the text of Ps 2:7 is one from Ps 110(109):4. The quotation

is almost exact, apart from the LXX's inclusion of the verb "you are," *ei*, which most manuscripts of Hebrews omit, except for 𝔓⁴⁶ P 629. The idea will be reiterated in 6:20 and the psalm verse cited again in 7:17 and 21, where it is treated as an "oath." In 7:23-24 the author will make clearer how this distinction affects the comparison of Jesus to Aaron. Jesus' priesthood is permanent. The earthly high priest dies (7:16; 23), whereas the Son lives forever (7:24), since his priesthood is founded on "the power of an indestructible life" (7:16).

The reference to the "order" of Melchizedek is unclear, as the author does not explain what an "order" of priests is. The expression is even more problematic in view of the fact that there was no line of priests deriving from Melchizedek in Jewish tradition. Since the author changes "order," *taxis*, to "likeness," *homoiotēta*, in 7:15, this is probably what he has in mind. Jesus is a priest in the likeness of Melchizedek, bringing his priesthood closer in line with Melchizedek's than with Aaron's. The "eternity" of Melchizedek's priesthood is the distinguishing factor. Aaron's priesthood, like that of all priests of the OT, ended with death. Jesus' priesthood continues forever. On the importance and significance of Melchizedek in Hellenistic Judaism see the Notes at 7:1.

7. *In the days of his flesh, Jesus offered up prayers and supplications, with loud cries and tears, to the one who was able to save him from death:* The author turns to the earthly Jesus and his sufferings to further distinguish his priesthood from that of the Levitical priests. The humanity of Jesus has already played an important role in the comparisons made thus far in the sermon in 2:10-18, where the earthly sufferings of Jesus qualified him for his mediatory role as High Priest. In fact, Jesus' humanity seems important to the author only when he speaks of his suffering, so the expression "days of his flesh" really only applies to the days of his Passion and death. This is confirmed by the later mention of "flesh" in 10:20 as the vehicle, the curtain through which believers may enter the "sanctuary of blood."

The noun "prayer," *deēsis*, connotes a sense of urgency in the LXX (3 Kgdms 8:28, 30, 38, 45, 49, 52, 54; Job 8:6; 16:21 [A B S]; 27:9; 36:19; 40:27; Pss 5:2; 6:9; 9:12; et al.), where it is at times synonymous with "supplication." Like Philo (*On the Posterity and Exile of Cain* 169; *The Special Laws* 3.68; *Embassy to Gaius* 227, 239, 276, 290, 331), Luke appears to understand the noun as a Septuagintism, since he uses it only in the opening chapters of his gospel in relation to Jews awaiting the fulfillment of the promises (1:13; 2:37; 5:33). "Supplication," *hikitēria*, is the feminine form of the adjective *hikitērios*, which occurs only twice in the LXX (Job 40:27; 2 Macc 9:18). In the first instance it is paired with "prayers." Otherwise in Hellenistic Judaism one finds the pairing of the two synonymous terms in Philo (*On the Cherubim* 47; *Embassy to Gaius* 276).

The inclusion of "loud cries," (*meta*) *kraugēs ischyras*, and "tears," *dakruōn*, seems to refer to prayers Jesus offered in the Garden of Gethsemane (Matt 26:36-46; Mark 14:32-42; Luke 22:39-46) on the night before he died, and from the cross at the moment of his death (Matt 27:46; Mark 15:34). Elsewhere in the sermon the author has made a point of Jesus' solidarity with humans (2:5-18). Here he echoes the point by stressing the real suffering Jesus underwent. That prayers of desperation were sometimes characterized in a similar way in Hellenistic Judaism is evident from Pss 39(38):12; 116(114):8; 3 Macc 5:6-8.

That God could deliver a person from death was commonplace in the Hebrew Bible (Josh 2:13; Job 5:20; Pss 33:17; 53:13; 68:20; 116:8; Hos 13:13; Acts 2:24) and Hellenistic Judaism (Add Esth 4:8; Sir 48:5; 51:9).

and he was heard because of his reverent submission: The author is confident that Jesus' prayer was heard, yet this part of the verse has caused serious problems of interpretation. If Jesus prayed to be saved from death and his prayer was heard, why did he die? Some have argued that Jesus' prayer in the Garden of Gethsemane was that God's will be done, and it is this prayer that was heard (Spicq 2:117; Peterson, *Hebrews and Perfection*, 92). Others have argued that Jesus prayed to be delivered from the power of death, and that was accomplished through the resurrection (Attridge, 150; Ellingworth, 291; Koester, 288; Vanhoye, *Old Testament Priests*, 128). In light of the tradition in Acts 2:24, the latter option seems preferable.

8. *Although he was a Son, he learned obedience through what he suffered:* One issue here is whether this part of the verse should be taken as the end of v. 7 (deSilva, *Perseverance*, 192) or the beginning of v. 8 (Lane 1:110). Most commentators treat it as part of v. 8. The Hellenistic Greek *paideia* tradition stressed the idea of learning discipline through suffering. Sometimes this was expressed in a gnomic statement, *mathein pathein*, "to suffer is to learn" (Attridge, 152; Ellingworth, 291; Koester, 290; Spicq 2:117). Deuteronomy 21:18 counsels parents on how to handle a disobedient (*apeithes*) son, who does not listen when they try to discipline (*paideuein*) him. Such "disciplining" was a way of learning obedience, something that was valued in the prophetic and wisdom traditions (Jer 7:28; 31:18; Ezek 21:10; Hos 7:12; Prov 3:11; 5:12; 13:1; 19:18). The author is familiar with this tradition; it will form the core of a later exhortation (12:5-11).

9. *and having been made perfect, he became the source of eternal salvation for all who obey him:* The verb *teleioun* in Greek means to be complete, but it is also the verb used to express the idea of ordination of priests in the LXX. In 2:10 the author spoke of the propriety of Jesus being made perfect through suffering, as the pioneer of salvation who brings others to glory. The idea here is not far from that, namely that through his own completion he became a source of salvation for all who obey him. Having learned obedience, he can save others who are likewise obedient. The author wishes to make a connection between the suffering/learning experience of Christ and what his readers must undergo.

10. *having been designated by God a high priest according to the order of Melchizedek:* The verse opens with an aorist participle of the verb "designate," *prosagoreuein*, paralleling the opening of v. 9, which begins with an aorist participle of "perfect," *teleioun*. In proclaiming that the Son has also been designated a "priest," the author may be playing on the verb *teleioun* to disclose a second level of meaning. *Teleioun* means "fulfill," "complete," or "make perfect" (BDAG, 966). This verb is also used in the LXX for "make the hands perfect," in reference to a priest, as part of the ritual of ordination (Exod 29:9, 29, 33, 35; Lev 4:5; 8:33; 16:32; Num 3:3; Vanhoye, *Old Testament Priests*, 187). So it had come to mean "to ordain." Although it is not explicit in the text, there may be a play on the word to suggest that Jesus' suffering was part of his designation by God as a priest. It was not only his being brought to perfection that qualified him to lead

others to salvation. Having been designated a priest also helped him to accomplish that purpose.

The author concludes the section by alluding to the citation of Ps 110:4, but now changing "priest" to "high priest," thus forming an *inclusio* with v. 1, where he spoke of the high priest being taken from among humans.

Interpretation

The form of these verses is paraenesis guided by the hortatory subjunctive, "let us hold on to," in the opening verse. The object of the injunction is that the hearers may remain firm in the "confession," a term already used by the author in the sermon (3:1).

It appears that this exhortation (4:14-16) would fit better immediately after 2:18, which concludes the section on Jesus' perfection through suffering. There, too, the solidarity of Jesus with all of humanity is what qualifies him to be a "merciful and faithful" high priest. Some of these themes provide motivation for this exhortation.

As it is, the exhortation is separated from 2:10-18 by 3:1–4:13, sections that develop the comparison of the Son with Moses and deal with the infidelity of the wilderness generation. The value of an example of fidelity is strengthened by the warning of what might happen to the readers if they are unfaithful. The author offers them an opportunity to compare themselves and their disposition in faith not only with Moses and the wilderness generation, but also with the Son.

Another reason why the author has placed this exhortation here and not after 2:18 is that in 2:10-18 he dealt primarily with the identity of the Son and only mentioned his high priesthood in anticipation of what will begin in 5:1. In 2:10-18 the perfection of the Son through suffering builds on the comparison of the Son with the angels, particularly on the question of the completion of humanity and the reference to Psalm 8. The exhortation (4:14-16) belongs here because it makes a transition from the warning against disobedience (3:7–4:13) and the qualifications of the high priest in 5:1-4.

The motivation for holding fast to the confession comes first from a consideration of what they "have." They indeed have a great High Priest who, like many heroic figures in Hellenistic Judaism, has made a heavenly journey (4:14). They have a High Priest who is not unable to sympathize with their weaknesses (4:15). They have a High Priest who has been tested in every respect (4:15). In 8:1 the author will again remind the readers of what kind of High Priest they have. He will remind them of the confidence they have to enter the sanctuary in 10:1. Paraenesis is always traditional, reminding the listeners of something they have already heard (Malherbe, *1 and 2 Thessalonians*, 82). This is not the first time they have heard about what they have, i.e., a High Priest who can mediate effectively for them with God.

The stress in 4:15 on the Son's ability to sympathize (*sympathēsai*) with their weaknesses contrasts with the earthly high priest's measured anger in 5:2 (*metriopathein*) in relation to those he serves. The latter suggests aloofness and distance, whereas Jesus' sympathetic mediation implies solidarity (Mitchell, "The Use of *prepein*," 697). Because he has been tested fully, apart from sin, the bond between Jesus and those he serves is stronger. As a representative of God who is the Son of God, he is also a more effective mediator because he can address both the divine and the human.

As God's representative, Jesus provides access to God in a way the earthly high priest could not. Earlier he was described as the "pioneer of salvation" (2:10). Later he will be called "the source of salvation for all who obey him" (5:9). In this exhortation he is the one who makes it possible for the listeners to "approach the throne of grace" (4:16). All who do so receive not only expiation for their sins but also mercy and grace in time of need. The author now broaches an important matter for the understanding of Jesus as a High Priest. As he did not come from a priestly lineage, an argument has to be made for his being a High Priest.

Before undertaking a consideration of Jesus' priesthood, the author describes the office of the high priest to establish important points of comparison between the two. First he speaks of the call of the high priest, where he comes from (5:1a). Then he talks about the function of the high priest, what he does (5:1b-c). Next he mentions the disposition of the high priest, how he mediates between God and humans (5:2), and in an *inclusio* ends with the rationale for his sacrificial service, i.e., why he functions in this way. The verses are arranged chiastically (Vanhoye, *Structure*, 107–109):

A   taken from among humans (v. 1a);

    B   to offer gifts and sacrifices for sins (v. 1b);

        C   able to deal gently with the ignorant and wayward (v. 2a);

        C' since he himself is subject to weaknesses (v. 2b);

    B' he must offer sacrifice for his own sins as well as for those of the people (v. 3);

A'   one does not presume to take this honor, but when called by God (v. 4).

Earlier in the sermon it was important to establish Jesus' place as the Son. The author did this by an elaborate comparison with the angels (1:5-14; 2:5-9) and with Moses (3:1-6). Now a link is made between the Son and his priesthood, again by a comparison, this time with Aaron. As with the earlier comparisons there was continuity and discontinuity, so also here. Jesus is like Aaron, who had to offer sacrifices and mediate between God and humans, and he was called, just as Aaron was. He differs from Aaron and all earthly high priests in that he does not offer sacrifices for his own sins, and insofar as he derives from a different order of priests.

Moving to the priesthood of Christ in 5:5, the author shows how he has fulfilled what were set out as requirements for priesthood in 5:1-4. First, his appointment as priest is paralleled with his appointment as Son by the juxtaposition of two psalm verses (2:7; 110:4). Sonship and priesthood are brought together through a common appointment. Jesus was called to each by God. As with the first four verses, these next six are chiastically arranged (Vanhoye, *Structure*, 109–13):

A   Christ was appointed as high priest (vv. 5-6);

    B   He offered prayers and supplications with loud cries and tears (v. 7);

    B'   He learned obedience through what he suffered (v. 8);

A'   Christ was designated by God a high priest (vv. 9-10).

Lest there be any mistake about the efficacy of his mediation, the author reminds his readers that Jesus was in full solidarity with humans through his actual suffering. Here the author is concerned only with the final hours of Jesus' human life, his Passion and death. He alludes to the agony in the Garden of Gethsemane in 5:7. Since he believes Jesus' prayer was heard, he must have understood that Jesus prayed not to be spared from death, but rather to be free of death's power over him. This, of course, is standard traditional language referring to the resurrection (1 Cor 15:20-28; Acts 2:24).

The perfection of the Son through suffering was already mentioned in 2:10. Suffering is not incidental to the priesthood of Jesus, but is constitutive of it (Spicq 2:117; Peterson, *Hebrews and Perfection*, 95; Mitchell, "The Use of *prepein*," 698). Here it plays a role in establishing Jesus' credentials as an effective High Priest. Because he had learned obedience through his suffering, he is able to lead others to salvation (Michel, 229). Here we find another echo of 2:10, where Jesus is described as the pioneer of salvation. Still, how his suffering leads others to salvation is not immediately clear. The image of a pioneer suggests that he had opened the way to salvation. The stress on his obedience suggests the exemplary nature of his suffering. The author calls it his reverent submission (5:7). Others may follow him as a "leader" in this regard by imitating his obedience, to the point of death if need be.

Perhaps in a subtle way the author establishes yet another connection between Jesus' perfection through suffering and his being designated a priest. The link between suffering and priesthood is made structurally as well. The expression "having been made perfect" in 5:9 is paralleled by "having been designated" in 5:10. The author sees these two actions on God's part as constituting the effective priesthood of the Son. The use of Scripture in the citations from Pss 2:7 and 110:4 validates the author's claim.

The author has established the credentials of Jesus' priesthood, showing that he is like the priests of old from Aaron on down but that he differs from them in significant ways. This section of the sermon fills out 4:14-15 by making concrete exactly what constituted the greatness of Jesus' high priesthood. He offers believers greater access to God than was available under the old priesthood. By applying to Christ in 5:5-10 the definition of a high priest in 5:1-4 the author demonstrates how well Christ's person and work qualified him for this all-important role. He has hardly exhausted the topic, as the next section of the sermon will show.

FOR REFERENCE AND FURTHER STUDY

Attridge, Harold. "Heard Because of His Reverence," *JBL* 98 (1979) 90–93.
Ellingworth, Paul. "Just Like Melchizedek," *BT* 28 (1977) 236–39.
Kurianal, James. *Jesus Our High Priest. Ps 110,4 as the Substructure of Heb 5,1–7,28.* European University Studies 23/693. Frankfurt am Main: Peter Lang, 2000.
Swetnam, James. "The Crux at Hebrews 5,7-8," *Bib* 81 (2000) 347–61.
Vanhoye, Albert. "Situation et Signification de Hébreux V.1-10," *NTS* 23 (1976–77) 445–56.
Young, Norman H. "Suffering: A Key to the Epistle to the Hebrews," *AusBR* 51 (2003) 47–59.

10. *Food for the Mature* (5:11–6:3)

11. About this we have much to say that is hard to explain, since you have become dull in understanding. 12. For though by this time you ought to be teachers, you need someone to teach you again the basic elements of the oracles of God. You need milk, not solid food; 13. for everyone who lives on milk, being still an infant, is unskilled in the word of righteousness. 14. But solid food is for the mature, for those whose faculties have been trained by practice to distinguish good from evil.

6:1. Therefore let us go on toward maturity, leaving behind the basic teaching about Christ, and not laying again the foundation of repentance from dead works and faith in God, 2. instruction about cleansings, laying on of hands, resurrection of the dead, and eternal judgment. 3. And we will do this, if God permits.

Notes

11. *About this we have much to say that is hard to explain, since you have become dull in understanding:* An ambiguity in the relative pronoun *hou*, "this," has divided commentators over its antecedent. Some take it as masculine "him," referring it back to Melchizedek (Weiss, 330; Ellingworth, 299). Others take it as neuter, referring to the priesthood treated in 5:1-10 (Attridge, 156; Lane 1:136; Koester, 300). The neuter fits best here, as the previous section dealt not only with Melchizedek, but with the priesthood of Christ as well.

By referring to the difficulty of the topic the author reminds his readers how daunting it is. He will take it up more extensively in subsequent chapters (7:1–10:25). The expression "there is much to say," *polys ho logos*, is a rhetorical commonplace (Dionysius of Halicarnassus, *Roman Antiquities* 1.23.1; *First Letter to Ammaeus*, 3; Lysias, *Against Pancleon* 11; Philo, *Who Is the Heir* 133, 221; cf. Attridge, 157; Lane 1:136; Koester, 300). The difficulty of explaining something may stem from the subject itself, as the Greek adjective *dysermēneutos* suggests (BDAG, 265). It may also have to do with the ability of the audience to hear what is being said, as seems to be the case in the situation being addressed in this paraenetic section of the text.

The expression "dull in understanding," *nōthroi tais akoais*, translated literally, is "sluggish in hearing." It recalls "the word of hearing," *ho logos tēs akoēs*, in 4:2, where the wilderness generation did not benefit from what it had heard. The adjective implies negligence (Sir 4:29; 11:12; MM, 432; Spicq 2:142–43) and appears to have been a term in the language of Epicurean psychagogy for a sluggish person in need of frank speech (Philodemus of Gadara, *On Frank Criticism* Col. XIXa.12). A remedy for the condition, "diligence," will be proposed in 6:12. The tone of this exhortation is in keeping with the author's earlier warning to his readers (2:1; 3:7-8; 4:1-2, 7) about paying close attention to what is heard, and how the failure to do that will lead to dire consequences. The inability to hear, in Hebrews, is tantamount to disobedience (3:16-19).

12. *For though by this time you ought to be teachers, you need someone to teach you again the basic elements of the oracles of God:* The author suggests that the readers are not neophytes and should know more by now than they do. Although it may be ironic, the claim that they should be "teachers" may also indicate that he held them in high enough regard that he expected them to be able to hand on to others what they themselves had already received.

"Teachers" were part of the structure in early Christian communities (Acts 13:1; Rom 12:7; 1 Cor 12:28-29; Eph 4:11; Jas 3:1). In the Pastorals the public reading of Scripture, exhorting, and teaching are the work of the missionary (1 Tim

4:13, 16). Official teachers carried the additional burden of being held to a higher standard, as is suggested by Jas 3:1 (cf. 1 Tim 5:17). The author, however, does not suggest that his readers should exercise a particular office, but rather that they should know as much as teachers know about the faith (Attridge, 159).

By suggesting that the readers need someone to teach them again, the author intimates that they need to "re-learn" the basics of what they had been taught. Apparently the sluggishness referred to above has prevented them from making progress. Concern with "making progress" in moral development is common among Hellenistic philosophical schools (Diogenes Laertius, *The Lives of Eminent Philosophers* 7.91; Epictetus, *Dissertations* 1.4.1-32), something shared by Christian communities (cf. Phil 1:25; 1 Tim 4:15).

"The elements," *stoicheia*, can refer to the alphabet (Diogenes Laertius, *The Lives of Eminent Philosophers* 7.56) and fundamentals of grammar (Xenophon, *Memorabilia* 2.1.1), or to the powers that make up the universe (Gal 4:3, 9; Col 2:8; 2 Pet 3:10, 12). Qualified by "oracles of God," the meaning here is simply the basics of the Christian faith. The noun for "oracles," *logioi*, can refer to prophecy (Isa 5:24; 28:13). In light of the opening of Hebrews (1:1-2), the frequent exhortation to hear and to listen to what has been spoken, and the author's understanding of the prospective nature of some scriptural citations (4:6-10; 7:11-19; 8:8-13), it seems that the author is referring to a basic understanding of God's revelation (Attridge, 159). More particularly, the readers apparently have failed to grasp the meaning of Christ's death as the means of completely removing guilt over past sins. This may be the reason why they are sluggish and stalled in their growth in faith.

You need milk, not solid food: The food metaphor completes the author's idea that the readers "need" to relearn basic teaching. Such metaphors were common in antiquity (Epictetus, *Dissertations* 2.16.39; 3.24.9; Philo, *On Agriculture* 9; *The Migration of Abraham* 29; *On Dreams* 2.9; Attridge, 159; Ellingworth, 304; Koester, 302). In the practice of psychagogy, ancient spiritual direction, the spiritual guide had to tailor the instruction to the ability of the student to receive it (Abraham J. Malherbe, *Moral Exhortation: A Greco-Roman Sourcebook*, Library of Early Christianity 4 [Philadelphia: Westminster, 1986] 48–67). The metaphor is not exclusive to Hebrews, as Paul himself employs it in a more caustic way in 1 Cor 3:1-4, where the situation is quite different. The Corinthians were not as far along as the recipients of Hebrews. The author appears to be trying to shame his audience; it will become clear in 6:1-2 that he really wants them to be able to take solid food. He believes that they are ready to move toward maturity even if they do not think they are capable of doing that.

13. *for everyone who lives on milk, being still an infant, is unskilled in the word of righteousness:* In 1 Pet 2:2 Christians are likened to newborns; they need milk to grow into salvation. The reference here is more negative, meaning the recipients need milk because they are incapable of the "word of righteousness." Exactly what the author intends by that expression is not clear. "Righteousness," *dikaiosynē*, is not used in the same way as Paul uses the term "justification." The noun *logos*, "word," can mean an actual word, a message, or the process of reasoning about something (BDAG, 598–601). To be unskilled in the word of righteousness may mean "unable to speak it" (Attridge, 160) or "unable to think about it" (Koester,

302). Since "milk" is contrasted with "solid food" and "milk" is appropriate for "infants," "solid food" corresponds to "the word of righteousness" in the analogy, i.e., mature teaching (Ellingworth, 307). This interpretation is confirmed by the next verse.

14. *But solid food is for the mature, for those whose faculties have been trained by practice to distinguish good from evil:* In contrast to the "infants," *nēpioi*, stand the "mature," *teleioi*, a distinction found in Hellenistic Judaism (Philo, *The Migration of Abraham* 29; *On Sobriety* 9) and in the NT (1 Cor 13:10-11; Eph 4:13-14). Ephesians refers to this maturity as "the measure of the full stature of Christ" (4:13).

The noun "faculties," *aisthētēria*, refers to faculties of sense (BDAG, 29). In 4 Macc 2:22 the "mind," *nous*, is enthroned among the senses to act as a governor. The training of the "senses" in this way is a means of coming to moral perfection. The verb for "training," *gymnazein*, means "exercise naked" (BDAG, 208; Albrecht Oepke, *gymnos, ktl., TDNT* 1:773–76). Athletic metaphors are common vehicles in antiquity for expressing progress in virtue (Philo, *Moses* 1.48; *On Sobriety* 65; Isocrates, *To Nicocles* 10; Epictetus, *Dissertations* 3.8.1; 3.10.8; 3.12.16; 3.20.11; 4.4.30). They appear elsewhere in the NT at 1 Cor 9:24; 2 Tim 4:7; this author will use one again at 12:11.

The ability to distinguish good from evil is the most basic kind of moral reasoning, the discretionary power to know right from wrong. In Sir 37:18 the mind, like a tree, has four branches: good, evil, life, and death. Obviously, paired in parallels "good" is equated with "life," and "evil" with "death." The reference is to Gen 2:9, 17. To learn what is good and evil among humans is the task of the scribe in Sir 39:4. Among philosophical schools moral training produced the same effect (Attridge, 161).

6:1. *Therefore let us go on toward maturity, leaving behind the basic teaching about Christ:* The Greek verb *pherein* means simply "carry" or "bear," but it has an extensive range of connotations. The author of Hebrews uses the verb five times, demonstrating his grasp of its scope. Here the sense is "move on" as one progresses in spiritual growth or development (BDAG, 1052). "Maturity," *teleiotēs*, is sometimes translated "perfection," but that may be misleading. In 5:14 the author noted that solid food is for the mature. Here he sets out the goal toward which the recipients should work, i.e., "maturity."

In contrast to moving toward maturity, the author enjoins his readers to move away from or leave behind the elementary teaching about Christ. The genitive "of Christ" can be subjective (Christ's own teaching) or objective (the teaching about Christ). As the author rarely refers to the historical Jesus, it is hard to imagine that he intends that they leave behind the teaching of Christ himself, perhaps as found in the gospels. He seems to be encouraging their theological and spiritual development, i.e., that they move to a more mature understanding of Christ than what they had at their initiation into Christianity. The sophisticated high priestly christology of Hebrews would fit that bill.

not laying again the foundation of repentance from dead works and faith in God: "Foundation" can refer literally to the foundation of a building (Josephus, *Antiquities* 11.93; 15.391; cf. Heb 11:10) or, figuratively, to the foundation, i.e., the basis of something (Philo, *Allegorical Interpretation* 2.6, 41, 96; 3.113, 145; *On the Cherubim*

101; *Special Laws* 2.110; *On Rewards and Punishments* 120). Paul uses the word to refer to the preparatory work that missionaries have done before him (Rom 15:20; cf. 1 Cor 3:10). This meaning fits the context here, which refers to the recipients' repentance and basic faith in God at the time of their conversion. There is no need for them to revisit this foundation. Thus the author is urging them to move further on in their development. The expression "dead works," *nekroi ergoi*, occurs again in 9:14. Some commentators have taken it to mean the works of the Jewish Law (Lane 1:140), whereas others take it to mean "sins leading to death" (Attridge, 164; Koester, 304; Hermut Löhr, *Umkehr und Sünde im Hebräerbrief*, BZNW 73 [Berlin and New York: de Gruyter, 1994] 148–52). In 3:12 the author warned the readers about having an "evil, unbelieving heart" that might cause them to fall away from the "living God." The notion of "dead works" stands over against the worship of a living God (Grässer 1:338). The latter is the preferred meaning.

Since the readers' conversion was marked by "faith in God," this, too, refers back to the "foundation of repentance." As such it signifies the positive dimension of their conversion just as "dead works" had signified the negative dimension (Grässer 1:339).

2. *instruction about cleansings, laying on of hands, resurrection of the dead, and eternal judgment:* The word for "cleansings," *baptismos*, is not exclusively used for Christian baptism, as is *baptisma* (BDAG, 165; Albrecht Oepke, *baptismos, baptisma, TDNT* 1:545). The former embraces Jewish ritual washings (Mark 7:4; Heb 9:10; see Josephus, *Antiquities* 18.117, referring to the baptism of John) and Christian baptism (Col 2:12), whereas the latter is extant only in Christian writings. The plural form is problematic, and various interpretations have been proposed. Ceslas Spicq catalogues the possibilities: triple immersions for the Trinity or relative to water, blood, and desire; rebaptisms; outer washings and inner purifications (Spicq 2:148). Some add the distinction between the baptism of John and the baptism of Jesus, and the difference between Christian baptism and Jewish proselyte baptism (Ellingworth, 315). Commentators are divided over the specific meaning, whether the word refers primarily to Christian baptism (Ellingworth, 315; Hughes, 202) or ritual washings (Lane 1:140; Grässer 1:341–42; Weiss, 338). Attridge gathers all the options: pagan lustral rites, Jewish rituals of purification, or a variety of Christian purification rites apart from baptism (Attridge, 164). It may have been the case that these washings were being repeated, unnecessarily in the author's view, since the once for all self-offering of Christ should have precluded them after they were initially performed (Lane 1:140).

In the LXX the laying on of hands signifies a commissioning to authority, as in Num 27:18-23 and Deut 34:9 in reference to the commissioning of Joshua. The use of the gesture in Acts 13:3 approximates this meaning, as Barnabas and Saul are set apart for the work of the mission. Similarly the seven deacons selected in Acts 6:5-6 receive the laying on of hands as part of their commissioning. In Acts 8:17-19 and 19:6 the gesture signifies the reception of the Holy Spirit. Elsewhere in Acts the laying on of hands accompanies healings (Acts 9:12; 17; 28:8). The gesture signifies ordination in 1 Tim 4:14; 5:22; and 2 Tim 1:6. The exact meaning is difficult to determine in this verse. Those who see the previous mention of washings as a reference to baptism claim that the laying on of hands connotes the reception of the Holy Spirit, as in a kind of confirmation. Since the gesture is not exclusively Christian, if one were to take the previously mentioned washings as something other than baptism, the laying on of hands might mean a commissioning to authority or office. How a commissioning might fit with the foundation of repentance is hard to imagine, as one would expect some maturation before such a commissioning were granted. It is likely here that it refers to the communication of the Holy Spirit as an elemental aspect of Christian life.

Two fundamental teachings of Christianity, the "resurrection of the dead" and "eternal judgment," round out the basic foundations the author sees no need to revisit. While both of these teachings are not exclusive to Christianity and are also found in some forms of Judaism, the context of the recipients' initial conversion suggests that they should be seen as Christian teachings. One of the earliest NT discussions of the resurrection of the dead is found in 1 Corinthians 15. The NT speaks more often of "eternal punishment" (Matt 18:8; 25:41, 46; 2 Thess 1:9; Jude 7) than "judgment"; the expression "eternal judgment" is *hapax* here. Perhaps Acts 24:25 is close, but "coming judgment" is not the same as "eternal judgment," which here means a judgment that stands for eternity.

3. *And we will do this, if God permits:* The author presumes his readers will follow his exhortation as he expresses a wish for their conformity to what he has encouraged them to do in 6:1, to "go on toward maturity." Their ability to "go on toward maturity" is predicated on the will of God. The model of the person who follows God's will is Christ (10:9). In Hebrews no transformation of the person can happen apart from God's will (10:10).

INTERPRETATION

After an extensive exposition on priesthood, involving a comparison of Jesus with Aaron, a discussion of the origin of Jesus' priesthood, and his qualifications for it (4:14–5:10), the author breaks for a word of exhortation about the ability of his listeners to grasp the difficult teaching he will impart in subsequent chapters.

More a warning about dire consequences, as were other exhortations up to this point in the sermon, this exhortation both shames and encourages the readers to break free from their spiritual inertia. The author accuses them of being dull in their understanding, but the charge does not get any more specific than that. If his words are related to an actual situation in the community of the readers, it will not be easy to determine exactly what he has in mind.

The unit is structured in two parts: a warning about failing to advance to maturity (5:11-14), and an exhortation to go on to maturity (6:1-3). As with other warnings and exhortations in the sermon (cf. 6:4-12), the first part presents a harsher sentiment than does the second. Both sections function together to help the author move the readers beyond the point where they have ceased to make progress, in order to prepare them for the most difficult part of the sermon in the coming chapters (8:1–10:18). As a preacher, the author knows how to anticipate conditions in his listeners that may impede the reception of his message.

By inference we can assume the author is disappointed with his audience over the lack of progress they have made in the practice of their faith. He says as much when he measures their progress up to the moment (5:12). The point is reinforced by making contrasts between "infants" and "the mature," and "milk" and "solid food." The imagery focuses the readers' attention on what they have failed to accomplish by now. A lack of confidence may have prevented them from making progress to the extent that they do not believe they are really ready for "solid food." The author, however, clearly believes they are ready for it (6:1-2), and so, by echoing their concern (5:12-13) and referring to them as infants, he is shaming them in order to help them move forward.

The previous section of the sermon appealed to the Greek *paideia* tradition to describe the way Jesus was brought to perfection (*teleioun*) by learning through suffering (5:9). This process enabled him to "teach" others and bring them to salvation. By contrast, the readers are not as "mature" (5:13-14) as they should be. The author expects them to be in a position to instruct others, and in order to do that they must be willing to move beyond the basics of the faith, the place where they appear to be stalled in their spiritual development.

Some commentators suggest that the author shows interest in developing an educational scheme of progress in moral growth, not unlike others in the Hellenistic world among the various philosophical schools (Attridge, 158–62; Koester, 308–309). The images and metaphors he employs do have parallels in the nonbiblical world. Lane is right, however, to point out that the author's scheme in Hebrews does not correspond fully to those in the philosophical schools (Lane 1:137), but he goes too far in claiming that "the idea of progressive stages, or of development and growth towards maturity, seems *not* to have been in his mind."

The author need not map out all the stages of moral growth because he is interested in challenging his readers starkly. The suggestion that they return to the basics is rhetorical here and has the function of shaming the readers so that they may move beyond the point in their development where they are stalled. Prodding the readers to maturity is the point here, with a sense of urgency that places the goal before their eyes. They cannot remain at the stage where they are merely repeating the steps they have already been through. Mention of those stages (6:1-2) may refresh their confidence and bring them to the point they should by now have attained. The author calls his readers to accountability and wants them to adopt the practice of mature Christians, which he believes they are ready to do. To this end he has framed the issue well. He would like to tell them more, but what he has to say is difficult to understand and cannot be grasped by those who are not mature (5:11). He returns to this idea in 5:14 by reminding them that "solid food" is for the mature. The "solid food" of his difficult teaching awaits them in this sermon (8:1–10:18), and so he wants to be sure they are able to apprehend what he has to say.

That the author does not really want the readers to return to the elemental teachings and practices becomes clear in the last three verses of this unit. The exhortation to go on to maturity necessarily includes the need to leave something behind, i.e., the "elementary doctrine of Christ." The six things that belong to that catechetical experience, "repentance from dead works," basic "faith in God," "instructions about cleansings," "the laying on of hands," the fundamental teachings about "the resurrection of the dead" and about "eternal judgment," need not be revisited or repeated. In fact, dwelling on these basic teachings seems to be preventing some of the readers from moving toward maturity.

The exhortation in this passage is designed to prepare the audience for what follows. The author has yet to present the "mature" teaching about Christ that will form the central argument of the sermon (8:1–10:18). There he will demonstrate why, once the readers have been initiated in faith, they need not dwell on the basics. Lane is correct to note that the major argument of the sermon builds on the fundamentals mentioned in 6:1-2 (Lane 1:140). Therefore the author's attempt to move the readers toward maturity is also an attempt to prepare them for the more difficult matter of the sermon, which is about to unfold.

The author of Hebrews knows that making progress in spiritual development is slow and sometimes arduous work. There is always the temptation to remain at the level where one is most comfortable. Advancing may involve fear and trepidation simply because the future is always unknown. There are also risks, however, in standing still, for the possibility of becoming spiritually stagnant is real. Coming to mature faith requires direction and self-examination. The author offers direction to his readers and invites them to examine themselves in order to understand their apprehension in moving on toward maturity. He also wishes to prepare them to understand the more difficult teaching he is about to present, which is really only for the mature to grasp.

For Reference and Further Study

Kiley, Mark. "A Note on Hebrews 5:14," *CBQ* 42 (1980) 501–503.
Owen, Huw P. "The 'stages of ascent' in Heb 5.11–6.3," *NTS* 3 (1956–57) 243–53.

Peterson, David G. "The Situation of the 'Hebrews' (5:11–6:12)," *RTR* 35 (1976) 14–21.

Schnackenburg, Rudolf. "Typen der *'Metanoia'* Predigt im Neuen Testament," *MTZ* 1 (1950) 1–13.

Swetnam, James. "Form and Content in Hebrews 1–6," *Bib* 53 (1972) 368–85.

Thüsing, Wilhelm. "'Milch' und 'feste Speise' (1 Kor 3,1f. und Hebr 5,11–6,3): Elementarkatechese und theologische Vertiefung im neutestamentlicher Sicht," *TTZ* 76 (1967) 233–46, 261–80.

11. *Going on to Maturity* (6:4-12)

4. For it is impossible to restore again to repentance those who have once been enlightened, and have tasted the heavenly gift, and have shared in the Holy Spirit, 5. and have tasted the goodness of the word of God and the powers of the age to come, 6. and then have fallen away, since by themselves they crucify the Son of God again, making him a shameful example. 7. Ground that drinks up the rain falling on it repeatedly, and that produces a crop useful to those for whom it is cultivated, shares a blessing from God. 8. But if it grows thorns and thistles it is worthless and close to being cursed; its end is to be burned over.

9. Even though we speak in this way, beloved, we are confident of better things in your case, things that belong to salvation. 10. For God is not unjust, so as to overlook your work and the love you showed for his sake in serving the saints, whom you still serve. 11. And we want each one of you to show the same eagerness with respect to the fullness of hope to the very end, 12. so that you may not become sluggish, but imitators of those who through faith and patience inherit the promises.

NOTES

4. *For it is impossible to restore again to repentance those who have once been enlightened:* Verses 4-6 constitute one of the sermon's most difficult teachings to understand and interpret. Accustomed as modern readers are to think of Christianity as a religion open to repentance at all times and under all circumstances, the sentiment expressed here sounds alien to us. The issue is second repentance rather than initial repentance.

Adynaton in Greek may appear with or without the verb "to be" (BDF §127.2). Here the adjective describes something that cannot be done rather than something that is "powerless" (BDAG, 22; Walter Grundmann, *dunamai, ktl., TDNT* 2:284–317). The verb *photizein* can mean "shine," "illuminate," or "enlighten." It is found in a Roman inscription as a term describing the Roman Christian community as "enlightened by the will of God" (BDAG, 1074). Elsewhere in the NT also it carries the meaning of "enlightened" (John 1:9; Eph 1:18; 3:9). The author uses it again in 10:32 when he recalls the early life of the community after its members were "enlightened." The inability of a person to repent at Qumran is conditioned by the "stubbornness of his heart" (1QS 2:25–3:8).

The adverb *hapax* can mean a one-time occurrence or something that has happened "once for all." The first meaning occurs in Hebrews at 9:7, 28 (9:26 is usually offered as an example, but there it means "once more" [BDAG, 97]). Here the meaning of "once" is appropriate. The author uses *hapax* in a similar way in 10:2.

to restore again to repentance: The verb *anakainizein* occurs only here in the NT. In the LXX it commonly means "renew" (Ps 102:5; 103:30; Lam 5:21), although in Ps 38:3 and 1 Macc 6:9 it carries the meaning of sorrow or suffering that recurs. It has the meaning "repair" in 2 Chr 15:8. The author has spoken of repentance in 6:1 as a turning from "dead works," i.e., turning from sin to God. The meaning is similar here, with the qualification that once one has repented there can be no restoration of repentance should one fall away. Thus the author rules out a second repentance since the earlier enlightenment was "once for all." Their enlightenment refers to their conversion, their initial reception of the word (2:1-3; 4:2), when they became partakers of a heavenly call (3:1). It is also called their first confidence (3:14). To be enlightened may mean to be illuminated by Christ. Ephesians 5:14, which some believe to be a fragment of a hymn that may have been used at baptism, captures the sense well: "Awake, O sleeper! Rise from the dead, and Christ will shine upon you."

4–5. *and have tasted the heavenly gift, and have shared in the Holy Spirit,* 5. *and have tasted the goodness of the word of God and the powers of the age to come:* The sentence begun in v. 4 actually spans three verses and is extended by qualifications added to the phrase "those who have once been enlightened." These are they who have "tasted the heavenly gift," who have "shared in the Holy Spirit" and have "tasted the goodness of the word of God and the powers of the age to come." All these qualifications employ the metaphor of "tasting" or "sharing," with their objects being the spiritual benefits received in baptism. The "heavenly gift" has sometimes been interpreted as the Eucharist. Many commentators take it to mean something more general, such as salvation. Participation in the Holy Spirit is yet another effect of the convert's baptism. The author uses the noun *metochos* to describe his readers as those who share a heavenly call (3:1) and Christ (3:14). He has already referred to the gifts of the Holy Spirit, associated with God's witness on behalf of Christ, at 2:4. Earlier, in 6:2, the reference to the "laying on of hands" probably points to the reception of the Holy Spirit in the community. Thus reminding the readers that their initial enlightenment made them partakers of the Holy Spirit seems quite natural in a discussion of what their lives were like immediately after their conversion. Since the word of God featured so prominently in the beginning chapters of the sermon, it, too, has a place here and is yet another object of the metaphor of tasting, as are the powers of the age to come. Again, these "powers" are mentioned in 2:4 in relation to the initial preaching the members of the community had heard. Here the noun is qualified by the phrase "of the age to come," indicating that the readers have had some glimpse of what they hope for in the *eschaton.*

6. *and then have fallen away:* The verb *parapiptein,* "fall away" is used only here in the NT. In the LXX the word connotes sin or transgression that results from failing to do what one is obligated to do. In Ezek 22:4 it means incurring guilt as the result of bloodshed and idolatry. In Hebrews the sense of apostasy is clear, perhaps echoing the warning in 3:12 about falling away from the living God as a result of unbelief. In this context, however, the act of "falling away" must also include the things that were tasted or shared in the previous verse: the heavenly gift, the Holy Spirit, the good word of God, and the powers of the age to come (Koester, 315). The loss of all these things hints at the consequences of the apostasy.

since by themselves they crucify the Son of God again, making him a shameful example: In the NT the simple verb "crucify," *staurein,* is normally used. Here the compound *anastaurein* presents the interpreter with two choices. Should the prefix *ana-* be taken in its normal meaning of "up," or should one read it as "again"? The first choice would mean that apostates themselves raise the Son of God on the cross, the second that they crucify him again. The problem is complicated by the fact that the verb is *hapax* here. In non-biblical Greek it always has the simple meaning "crucify" (BDAG, 72). The meaning of "crucify again," however, is intriguing, since there is so much stress in the sermon that Christ's self-offering was "once for all" (7:27; 9:12, 28; 10:10). The singularity of his death is also used to contrast with the multiple offerings required under the old covenant (7:27; 9:6). The qualifying participle *paradeigmatizontas,* then, "to disgrace someone publicly," indicates that the author probably means that apostates, in their apostasy, have negated the symbol of the crucified Christ, turning it into an object of shame. What they have negated is the "once for all" nature of his death. They may have done this by seeking the comfort of repeated external rituals, which the author believes are unnecessary (see the Interpretation at 10:1-18). Some take the participles to be temporal; in that case the sense is that as long as people are crucifying the Son of God they are unable to be restored (John K. Elliott, "Is Post-Baptismal Sin Forgivable?" *BT* 28 [1977] 330–32). The temporal sense, however, does not explain the cause of the impossibility of restoration, adding nothing new to what the converts would already know. The sense, then, seems to be causal; the apostates themselves raise the Son of God on the cross in disgrace.

7. *Ground that drinks up the rain falling on it repeatedly, and that produces a crop useful to those for whom it is cultivated:* The image of the ground soaking up rain recalls the description of the land in Deut 11:11-12. There it is a land God looks after. One need not see God as the beneficiary here, since the image is meant as an incentive to the readers. When the cycle of nature works toward its purpose, a useful crop is produced. The farmer receives the bounty of the land as it was intended by God.

shares a blessing from God: It is biblical to connect God's blessing to the land or to an abundant crop. When God promised the land to Abraham in Gen 12:1-3, blessing accompanied the promise. In Gen 26:12-13 Isaac is blessed by God in conjunction with a hundredfold yield on his planting. Deuteronomy 33:13-16, Moses' blessing of Joseph, specified the land as a recipient of God's blessing, manifested in the abundance it produces. Perhaps more relevant for this verse in Hebrews is the counsel of Prov 28:19-20 that anyone who tills the land and is faithful will receive abundant blessings. The verb *metalambanein* is frequently translated "receives," but its first meaning is "share" or "participate in" (BDAG, 639).

8. *But if it grows thorns and thistles:* The verb *ekpherein* means literally "carry out" or "bear." Figuratively it means "grow" or "produce" (BDAG, 311–12). Thorns and thistles are a sign that the land has been cursed. The author may have Gen 3:18 in mind, where Adam's sanction after the Fall is to have to work a cursed land that will produce thorns and thistles.

    it is worthless and close to a curse: The two expressions are synonymous. In the LXX *adokimos*, "worthless," refers to silver that has become dross (Isa 1:22; Prov 25:4). The NT usage often carries the meaning of not passing muster (Rom 1:28; 1 Cor 9:27; 2 Cor 13:5-6, 7). In the Deutero-Pauline letters the adjective describes the "worthless" faith of those who oppose the truth or deny God (2 Tim 3:8). A similar pairing occurs in Aelius Aristides, *Orations* 26.53, where he speaks of something as "helpless and close to being cursed." Does the author think there is still a chance that the land will avoid a curse? The context suggests otherwise.

    its end is to be burned over: Despite the grammatical ambiguity the antecedent of the relative, "whose," must be "land" back in v. 7. Fire is a symbol of divine judgment in Hebrews in 10:27 and 12:29.

9. *Even though we speak in this way, beloved:* The first time the author refers to the recipients as "beloved" comes in an attempt to mitigate the stern warning just issued with an assertion of his confidence in them.

    we are confident of better things in your case, things that belong to salvation: By expressing his confidence in what the readers will gain through their perseverance the author intends to remind them of the course they set out upon at their conversion. "Better things," *ta kreissona*, is used throughout the sermon (1:4; 7:7, 19, 22; 8:6; 9:23; 10:34; 11:16, 35, 40). Here it is epexegetic, spelled out by what follows, "things that belong to salvation."

10. *For God is not unjust so as to overlook:* Already in another document of the Roman church Paul has expressed a similar sentiment on the justice of God (Rom 3:5). There, of course, Paul is grounding the idea of divine judgment. The author uses the expression to mitigate the hard teaching he has just presented about the impossibility of a second repentance. The aorist infinitive *epilathesthai* expresses the effect of God's justice, "so as [not] to overlook."

    your work and the love: Love and "good works" are paired in the exhortation in 10:24. The readers are exhorted to faith and hope in 10:22-23. There follows a section on deliberate sin and the prospect of resultant divine judgment. Here the triad is also present, but in reverse order: love (6:10), hope (6:11), and faith (6:12). These verses are preceded by a section on the impossibility of repentance from apostasy and the judgment that ensues. In light of these similarities between the two texts, it may be that the author is thinking of the early situation of the community described in 10:32-34, where love was demonstrated in the midst of suffering.

that you showed for his sake: The text actually reads "for his name," which if taken literally would mean that their action was done for God. The translation "for his sake" expresses better the sense of purpose the author associated with the love exhibited by community members.

in serving the saints as you still serve: Two participles form the expressions "serving" and "serve," one in the aorist tense and the other in the present. However, the sense of past or completed action, sometimes associated with the aorist, is missing because the main verb on which the participles depend is also in the aorist (BDF §339). Thus the translation, "serving."

11. *to show the same eagerness with respect to the fullness of hope to the very end:* The verb "show" is repeated from the previous verse in reference to their work and love. Here the author wants the readers to manifest their eagerness, by which he refers to the quality of their work and love in the early days following their conversion. "Eagerness" is now heightened by the anticipation of the end time because of the quality of their full hope. The noun "hope" occurs in 3:6, where it is linked to "confidence." Interestingly, in that instance there is very good manuscript evidence for the inclusion of the expression "firm to the end" (𝕏 C D Ψ 0243. 0278. 33. [ˢ 323]. 1739.1881 𝔐 latt sy⁽ᵖ⁾ bo) after the word "hope." In 7:19 the author speaks of a "better hope" enabling the readers to draw near to God, and in 10:23 the readers are exhorted to hold fast to the "confession of our hope." The word "fullness" occurs in 10:22 in relation to "faith," making yet another connection between the text under consideration here and chapter 10. The expression "to the end" is ambiguous. It may mean to the end of their journey, expressing the hope that they will lead faithful lives on earth, or it may mean to the end of time, carrying an eschatological meaning. In either instance counseling perseverance is appropriate.

12. *so that you may not become sluggish, but imitators of those who through faith and patience inherit the promises:* The adjective for "sluggish" appears only in Hebrews in the NT, here and at 5:11. The early use means "sluggish in hearing," whereas here it has more the sense of being "lazy" (BDAG, 683). Cautioning against "sluggishness," the author contrasts the eagerness he counsels in the previous verse. Not leaving the sentiment in the negative, the author proposes a positive counterpart. Rather than becoming sluggish, they ought to become "imitators" of those who acquire what God has promised. Many modern English translations (RSV, NRSV, NAB, NIV, NASV) rightly prefer to stress the part of the participle *klēronomountōn* that means "inheritance." Thus they translate: "those who . . . inherit the promises." Even though when used in the NT the verb often means "acquire, obtain, come into possession" (BDAG, 547), the author's interest in "promise" and "inheritance" warrants a translation of "inherit." The means of inheritance are "faith" and "patience." These virtues are favorites of the author. He closes this exhortation by expressing his desire for his readers' steadfastness, which will translate into the kind of eagerness he sees as characteristic of those who are positioned to receive the "better things of salvation," here expressed simply by "promises."

INTERPRETATION

In 5:11-14 the author began warning his readers about some shortcomings in their spiritual development, reminding them that they were holding themselves back from making progress toward maturity and so were like children who prefer milk instead of solid food. This led into an exhortation to become like the mature. In 6:1-3 that process of coming to maturity was marked by progress that moved beyond the elementary teaching they had received at the time of their conversion. This process was referred to in shorthand as not laying again the foundation of repentance from dead works and of faith in God. Having repented and converted, the readers need not look back, but rather ever forward to the fulfillment of their hope.

In v. 4 the author turns again to the question of repentance and the possibility of repenting after apostasy, almost as if to say that as it is impossible for those who have already repented to return to the foundation of repentance already established, so too is it impossible to restore to repentance someone who, having been enlightened, has committed apostasy. The circumstances are, of course, different, but the two instances are joined by the inability to return to repentance. The mature have no need of it, and the apostate has no chance of it. Thus there is a unity in this section from 5:11–6:12.

The warning about the impossibility of second repentance seems to derive from deliberate disobedience in the form of apostasy. Those in question render counterfeit what they have received in baptism, and by so doing they portray the cross of Christ as a mockery. Both faults constitute a refusal to move forward toward maturity.

The difficult teaching on the impossibility of second repentance presents challenging ideas for believers and pastors alike. Surely no sin is beyond forgiveness and, given the mediatory work of the High Priest Jesus in this sermon, reconciliation and atonement for sin are accomplished in a unique way, according to the author's christology. Therefore the sentiment of these verses should be viewed in terms of a proposed difficulty of second repentance from a subjective point of view. Anyone who has gone so far as to apostasize after having been previously enlightened has made it virtually impossible to repent again. The original repentance and conversion were grounded in the death of Christ. Should they "fall away" from that salvation they would remove its ground, thus rendering repentance meaningless. Acting as if the death of Christ did not have the transformative value in their lives that it actually does prompts the author's harsh language about holding the cross up to ridicule. As the meaning of Christ's death will be developed in the following sections of the sermon, any response of the readers that does not match the fidelity of Jesus to the will of his Father constitutes a grave offense.

Despite the force of the warning against this kind of apostasy it is difficult to ascertain whether it has already occurred in the community. If the author is concerned that a refusal to go "on toward maturity" may contribute to apostasy, his purpose here is to include an extreme example of a definitive rejection of Christ. Therefore it is possible that some of the community members have involved themselves in religious practices that the author sees as a countersign to what he believes was won in the "once for all" self-offering of Christ: unencumbered access to God under the new covenant, which stresses a law written in the minds and hearts of worshipers and the removal of consciousness of sin, even on God's part.

Repeating rituals and instructions associated with initial conversion inhibits the readers from "going on toward maturity" (6:1-2). Once "the foundation of repentance from dead works and of faith in God" has been laid there is no need to establish it again. It is possible that the author envisions a worst-case scenario of his audience's refusal to go on toward maturity: that they will lose confidence completely in what was won for them in Christ and fall away altogether. Therefore he issues a warning against apostasy in the strongest language possible.

Later in the sermon the author will engage the issue of apostasy again in the matter of deliberate sin "after having received the knowledge of the truth" (10:26-27). The expression "there no longer remains a sacrifice for sins" in 10:26, which also speaks of the impossibility of repentance, is matched by "Where there is forgiveness of these [sc. sins], there is no longer any offering for sins" in 10:18. Given the context there about the advantages of the new covenant over the old, the chances are increased that the repetitive rituals that some members of the community were involved in were in some way related to the apostasy, real or potential. At 10:18 these rituals are declared futile in light of Christ's "once for all" self-offering. In 10:26 they are seen as useless in reclaiming anyone who has "spurned the Son of God, and profaned the blood of the covenant" by seeking repeated purification of conscience, which has already been effected by Christ's death.

The purpose of Hebrews is to offer a word of exhortation (13:22) that advances the readers to the fulfillment of what the author hoped for them. His own confidence is here expressed in the fact that he is sure they are capable of receiving the better things of salvation (6:9). Without making progress, however, this goal will not be realized. The combination of negative warnings (5:11–6:8) and positive exhortation (6:9-12) is the author's preferred method for promoting spiritual growth in his readers. Despite the dire warnings, the author reminds his readers of God's justice. Their work and love on behalf of the saints is not forgotten. Apparently their original spirit of service to others was marked by enthusiasm. So the author desires now that they will match that initial eagerness as they pursue the goal of maturity under the signs of a full hope, faith, and patience. In the final exhortation it seems that the real issue is "sluggishness," that they have become lazy and have not pursued their spiritual development with the zeal they initially exhibited.

Were one merely to dwell on the denial of the possibility of second repentance, something contemporary Christians would find offensive, the author's fuller meaning would be lost. The fundamental belief Hebrews presents in the efficacy of Christ's self-offering stresses its once for all nature. Since, in his death, Christ as High Priest has ultimately perfected the consciences of believers, he has made them complete and in need of no further purification. Therefore the apparently harsh teaching in this passage has really to do with the affirmation of what Christ has accomplished for all believers. If the readers lack confidence in the fullness of his self-offering and its power to cleanse their consciences of guilt from past sins, the author considers this a serious offense tantamount to apostasy. Should they involve themselves in purifying rituals and cleansings associated with their initial repentance, so as to suggest that Christ's work was not complete, they effectively attempt to redo what he has already done. This amounts to re-crucifying Christ and holding him up to public spectacle. The author's real aim is to instill confidence in his readers that will prevent them from engaging in practices that he sees as forms of apostasy.

Since many contemporary Christians understand repentance to be an ongoing process that may last a lifetime, the sentiment of this section of the sermon will strike them as alien to the need for continual renewal in one's spiritual life. Opportunities for reconciliation with God in Christ abound for Christians today, a fact that seems directly to contradict the teaching of Hebrews on a second repentance. Still, those opportunities for continual renewal and reconciliation are grounded in the once for all self-offering of Christ, which is unrepeatable. In the final sense reconciliation has been accomplished and ongoing repentance is now seen as the process of appropriating into one's life the fullness of what Christ has accomplished. Therefore the fundamental sentiment behind this passage of the sermon may not be so incompatible with what Christians believe today after all.

For Reference and Further Study

Coley, S. M. "Exegesis of Hebrews 6:4-12," *Faith & Mission* 20 (2003) 99–102.

de Silva, David A. "Hebrews 6:4-8: A socio-rhetorical investigation (Part 1)," *TynBul* 50 (1999) 33–57; "Hebrews 6:4-8: A socio-rhetorical investigation (Part 2)," *TynBul* 50 (1999) 225–35.

Emmrich, Martin. "Hebrews 6:4-6—Again! (A Pneumatological Inquiry)," *WestTheolJourn* 65 (2003) 83–95.

Mathewson, David. "Reading Heb 6:4-6 in Light of the Old Testament," *WestTheol-Journ* 61 (1999) 209–25.

Nongbri, Brent. "A Touch of Condemnation in a Word of Exhortation: Apocalyptic Language and Graeco-Roman Rhetoric in Hebrews 6:4-12," *NovT* 45 (2003) 265–79.

12. *The Surety of God's Oath* (6:13-20)

13. When God made a promise to Abraham, since he had no one greater by whom to swear, he swore by himself, 14. saying, "I will surely bless you and multiply you." 15. And thus Abraham, having patiently endured, obtained the promise. 16. Human beings, of course, swear by someone greater than themselves, and an oath given as confirmation puts an end to all dispute. 17. In the same way, when God desired to show even more clearly to the heirs of the promise the unchangeableness of his will, he guaranteed it by an oath, 18. so that through two unchangeable things, in which it is impossible that God would prove false, we who have taken refuge might have strong encouragement to seize the hope set out as a goal. 19. We have this hope, a sure and steadfast anchor of the soul, that enters the interior place behind the curtain, 20. where Jesus, a forerunner on our behalf, has entered, having become a high priest forever according to the order of Melchizedek.

Notes

13. *When God made a promise to Abraham:* The author appeals to the story of Abraham in Gen 12:1-3. The lxx version does not describe God's words to Abraham as a "promise," *epangelia*. Rather the focus at this point in the narrative is on "blessing," *eulogein* (Gen 12:2 [bis], 3 [bis]; 14:19 [bis]; 22:17; 24:1). In Wis 12:21 God is referred to as one who gave Israel's ancestors "oaths and covenants full of good promises" (*hyposcheseis*). Josephus portrays God as one who makes promises to Moses and to Israel (*Antiquities* 2.275; 3.23; 5.39, 159, 214). The author uses the verb *epangellein* at 10:23; 11:11; 12:16, where God is also its subject. The noun is more frequent (4:1; 6:12, 17, 25; 7:6; 8:6; 9:15; 10:36; 11:9 [bis], 13, 17, 33, 39). God promised that Abraham would receive a blessing, a nation, and a land. Only the blessing and propagation are mentioned explicitly in the next verse, but since the author notes that Abraham received the promise in v. 15 he must have all its elements in view.

    since he had no one greater by whom to swear, he swore by himself: God swears by himself in Gen 22:16, where the verb is in the first person. The author changes that to the third person here since he is narrating what God has done. It is not uncommon for the author to alter the LXX text when he cites it (Gheorghita, *The Role of the Septuagint*, 41). The reference to "no one greater by whom to swear" reflects knowledge of the debate in Hellenistic Judaism over this text. Invoking the name of someone greater was required in making an oath. Since in God's case there can be no one greater, God must swear by himself. In an effort to counter those who would claim that it was inappropriate for God to swear an oath, Philo noted that God swore an oath that was befitting God (*theoprepein*) because he is the best of all things (Philo, *Sacrifices of Cain and Abel* 91–94; *Allegorical Interpretation* 3.203-7; *Abraham* 273; *On Dreams* 1.12; *Questions on Genesis* 4.180). Hebrews sees nothing wrong with God's swearing an oath, as it produces security in the believer.

14. *saying, "I will surely bless you and multiply you":* The author cites Gen 22:17 with a change of the object of the verb "multiply" from "your descendants" in the LXX to "you." God pronounces this blessing in response to Abraham's fidelity in the binding of Isaac. The content of the oath that God swore reflects the original blessing given to Abraham in Gen 12:1-3.

15. *And thus Abraham, having patiently endured, obtained the promise:* The verb *makrothymein*, "endure patiently," recalls the *makrothymia*, "patience" counseled in 6:12. Abraham, therefore, is an example of those "who through faith and patience inherit the promises." The LXX does not portray Abraham as an example of someone possessing *makrothymia*, and neither does Philo. The verb *epitynganein* means "obtain what one seeks" (BDAG, 385). Paul uses the verb in relation to what Israel failed to "obtain" (Rom 11:7). Hebrews uses it also in 11:33 of the great figures of Jewish biblical history, who received the promises.

16. *Human beings, of course, swear by someone greater than themselves:* Turning to the subject of oaths and how they function, the author underscores the security of God's word by a comparison. Philo's treatment of the topic confirms the conventions of swearing oaths in Hellenistic Judaism. Why it is necessary for God to swear is not immediately evident. If the author is thinking along the lines of Hellenistic Jewish tradition, the purpose may be merely to instill greater confidence in the readers (see Philo, *Abraham* 273). The thought is resumed in v. 17.

    and an oath given as confirmation puts an end to all dispute: For a similar thought on the confirming nature of oaths see Philo, *On Dreams* 1.12. The oath works to end disputes by calling on God as a witness (*Allegorical Interpretation* 3.205; *On the Decalogue* 86). Although Philo claims that oaths secure matters that are insecure, he also refers to an oath as a "crutch for human weakness" (*Sacrifices of Cain and Abel* 96). "End," *peras*, can mean a spatial limit or boundary (cf. Matt 12:42; Luke 11:31; Rom 10:18) or the conclusion of a process (BDAG, 797). It occurs in the latter sense only here in Hebrews. An *antilogia* is a "controversy" or "dispute," as in 7:7, or "hostility" or "rebellion" as in 12:3 and Jude 11 (BDAG, 89). The author shows familiarity with the legal terminology of oathmaking current in his day (Attridge, 180).

17. *when God desired to show even more clearly to the heirs of the promise the unchangeableness of his will:* The author now supplies his explanation for why God swore an oath. The verb *epideiknymi* means simply to "show" something (BDAG, 370).

It can also mean "show" in the sense of demonstrating the truth of something (Acts 18:28). The comparative adjective *perissoteron*, "more clearly," qualifies the action of the verb. In one manuscript (B) the adverbial form *perissoterōs* is attested, as it is in Heb 2:1; 13:19. Although the expression "heirs of the promise" may refer to Abraham and his descendants, the author must include his readers also, since they are the immediate object of his concern and are clearly included in the next verse. The appeal to the unchangeableness of God's will stresses the surety of God's oath. The difference between God and humans is sometimes expressed in terms of God's unchangeableness in the Hebrew Bible (see Num 23:19; 1 Sam 15:29). Philo offers evidence for the notion that God's will is unchangeable (*On the Unchangeableness of God* 22–23). He explains his view by noting that humans change and are inconstant because they cannot see into the future. Since, for God, all time is one, God is unchangeable (*On the Unchangeableness of God* 29–32). Any anthropomorphism attributed to God is for Philo analogous and serves the instruction and benefit of humans, having no bearing on the actual nature of the divine (*On the Unchangeableness of God* 57–64). The description of God in these terms here functions to reassure the readers that God's purpose and intentions can be counted on.

he guaranteed it by an oath: The verb "mediate," *mesiteuein*, can also mean "act as a guarantor" (BDAG, 634; MM, 399; Albrecht Oepke, *mesitēs, mesiteuō, TDNT* 4:598–624). Josephus uses the noun *mesitēs*, "mediator," in the sense of a "guarantor" (*Antiquities* 4.133; 20.62). In the latter reference Izates, the Mesopotamian king, offered his mediation (*mesiteia*) and oaths (*orkous*) as a guarantee that Artabanus would not take revenge on the Parthians. The author employs standard legal terminology here in speaking of divine surety (Attridge, 181; Koester, 327–28; Weiss, 362 n. 16).

18. *so that through two unchangeable things, in which it is impossible that God would prove false:* The two things referred to are God's word and God's oath. Philo notes that God's word is so trustworthy that it does not differ from an oath (*Allegorical Interpretation* 3.204; *Sacrifices of Cain and Abel* 93; *On Abraham* 273). Whereas it is possible for humans to swear falsely, God cannot. The argument is somewhat circular. When humans swear an oath they call on God as witness. God swears by himself, having no greater to call on. Even if humans call on God, they may swear falsely; but since God assures his oath by swearing it by himself, the greatest who is, there can be no falsehood. The absolute veracity of God is mentioned in a document of the Roman Church that shows dependence on Hebrews. *First Clement* 27:2 proclaims that "nothing is impossible for God except lying."

we who have taken refuge might have strong encouragement to seize the hope set out as a goal: The hortatory value of God's swearing an oath by himself is now made explicit. The readers are described as people who have fled. In 11:13-16 the Israelite ancestral generation will be described as wandering exiles in search of a homeland, a metaphor for anyone on the journey of faith. The author seems to include his audience in that image. If they are capable of any strong encouragement it is because of the assurance they have received from the word of God. The word for "encouragement," *paraklēsis*, is the same one the author uses to describe his whole work, "a word of encouragement," in 13:22. Such encouragement is at the very heart of his purpose. The purpose of encouragement is to seize the hope the author is talking about. The verb *prokeisthai* may point to something that is open or exposed, something that is present to someone, or something that is set out as a goal (BDAG, 871). The author uses it in this sense at 12:1-2. This sense of hope as something to attain is found elsewhere in the NT (Rom 8:24-25; Gal 5:5; Phil 1:20; Col 1:5; Titus 2:13).

19. *We have this hope, a sure and steadfast anchor of the soul:* Referring back to the hope mentioned in the previous verse, the author further qualifies it as a "sure and steadfast anchor." The only other place in the biblical tradition where these words occur together is in a series in Wis 7:23, but the combination is common in Hellenistic literature (Attridge, 183 n. 72; Koester, 329). Like "faith," "hope" for the author is an important virtue that facilitates access to God (7:19) and ensures that individuals will "hold on" and "persevere" (10:23).

that enters the interior place behind the curtain: Hope is personified and shown as a priest entering the Holy of Holies. The author now anticipates the next section of the sermon, which will speak of Jesus, the heavenly High Priest. "Hope" functions here as a transitional metaphor, doing what Christ does in 6:20; 9:12, 24-25. Like Christ, hope provides a way of access to God in the heavenly realm.

The instructions for building the Tabernacle in Exodus prescribe two curtains, one outer and one inner. The same arrangement was true of the Temple in Jerusalem, where the outer curtain separated the forecourt from the Temple proper and the inner curtain separated the Holy of Holies from the holy place. The word used here for curtain, *katapetasma*, often refers to the inner curtain (Exod 26:31; 36:35; 40:3) but can also refer to the outer curtain (Exod 26:36; 36:37; 40:8, 28). The image of hope entering into the "inner shrine" indicates that the author has the second curtain in mind.

20. *where Jesus, a forerunner on our behalf, has entered:* In 2:10 the author referred to Jesus as the "leader," and now a second title, "forerunner," is invoked. *Prodromos* signifies one who "runs on ahead" or "goes before." In the LXX it refers to first-fruits like the "first ripe bunch of grapes" (Num 13:20) or the "first ripe fig" (Isa 28:4), precursors of what the harvest might be like. The term has military and athletic connotations (Wis 12:8; see Attridge, 185 n. 91; Koester, 330; Otto Bauernfeind, *prodromos, TDNT* 8:235). As with "leader," this title also indicates that Jesus goes before others, making a way into the heavenly sanctuary for his followers.

having become a high priest forever according to the order of Melchizedek: In preparation for what follows in the next chapter, the author concludes this section with a reference to Ps 110:4, earlier alluded to in 5:10. In the previous reference the eternal nature of Christ's priesthood was not explicit, but was implied in the reference to "eternal salvation" in 5:9. There it was enough for the author to show the similarity of their priesthoods. Now that a contrast between the two will follow, the author makes explicit that Jesus is a high priest "forever." The allusion is therefore closer to the actual wording of the psalm, although the author has rearranged the words to place "forever" in the final emphatic position (see Attridge, 185).

The exhortation of 5:11–6:12 ended with the author encouraging his readers not to be sluggish, but to imitate those who through faith and patience inherit the promises. At 6:13 he presents an example of faith and patience in the one to whom the promise was originally given, Abraham. The promise included a name, numerous descendants, land, and a blessing (Gen 12:1-3). At the heart of the great Yahwist epic of the Pentateuch, the theology of the promise stressed God's fidelity with Abraham, even when he himself placed the promise in jeopardy. Thus Abraham is a fitting example for those who are being warned to persevere and remain faithful so that they might receive the fulfillment of the promise they, too, hope for.

Just as God's steadfastness featured importantly in the story of Abraham, so it does in this exhortation. Almost as if it were enough simply to mention Abraham in this regard, the author shifts his focus to the one who made the promises and how trustworthy he is. God's word is itself assured by his veracity, but to solidify the point with an eye to further assuring the readers, the author offers a midrashic reflection on Gen 22:16-17. In order to reassure Abraham that the promise would be fulfilled, God swore an oath by himself.

The fact that God swore such an oath was a matter of interest and speculation in Hellenistic Judaism. Certainly the veracity of God's word alone was proof that it would not go unfulfilled. Yet the text of Gen 22:16 stands, and it prompted discussion about the propriety of such an oath. The issue caught the imagination of great Jewish thinkers like Philo of Alexandria, who devotes a significant amount of text to trying to understand the meaning of God's oath to Abraham (*Sacrifices of Cain an Abel* 91–94; *On Abraham* 273; *Allegorical Interpretation* 3.203-8). In the end he concluded that the oath was not given because a guarantee of God's word was needed. Since all time is one to God, God can foresee that the promise will be fulfilled. This is not the case for humans, because of their limitations, so God swears an oath as a further assurance to them. Thus the oath was really sworn for Abraham's sake.

As with Hellenistic Jewish authors, the author of Hebrews is also fascinated by the fact that God swore an oath. Coming to a conclusion similar to Philo's, he emphasizes that its purpose was to offer assurance to humans, in this case the readers. They now are the heirs of the promise made to Abraham, and like him they are unable to see into the future to know assuredly that God's word is eternally true. Therefore the author stresses God's oath, which God had to swear by himself since there is no greater person to swear by. The oath God swore is placed at center stage in this text, with a goal of convincing the heirs of the promise that they will indeed receive its benefits.

God's will to bring the promise to fulfillment has not changed. The legacy of Abraham is now within reach for all who are his descendants. The fact that God swore an oath guarantees that the readers will not be disappointed as long as they, like Abraham, are people of faith and perseverance. The oath God swore to Abraham was prompted by Abraham's fidelity in not withholding his son, Isaac (Gen 22:17). This example stands in contrast to the earlier reference to God's swearing an oath in 4:3, where in response to the infidelity of the wilderness generation God swore that they would not enter into his rest. As the readers are exhorted not to imitate the wilderness generation, so as to be able to enter into God's rest, they are exhorted here to follow the example of Abraham by being faithful and by persevering. God's oath functions not only to guarantee the veracity of God's word, but also to engender hope in the readers. The transition to hope is facilitated by the reminder that the unchangeableness of God's will is assured by two unchangeable things: the word of God itself and the oath God swore to Abraham.

Hope emerges as the important theme at the end of the exhortation as the author makes a transition to the next section of his sermon. The image of hope as an anchor conflicts with its movement into the sanctuary. Anchors are stationary and are used to prevent movement. Yet the anchor-like hope itself enters the Holy of Holies behind the second curtain of the Temple. Mixing the metaphors, however, achieves the author's desired effect of placing the readers' solid hope in Jesus Christ. At the end of an exhortation against wavering and in favor of persevering, where the example of Abraham underscores the steadfastness of God and his promises, the image of hope as an anchor supports the author's intended goal. The readers are to hold fast, as stressed in other key sections of Hebrews, by keeping their eyes on the prize. The reason hope can enter the Holy of Holies is because Jesus himself has gone there as the "forerunner" whose constancy is guaranteed by the fact that he is an eternal High Priest of the order of Melchizedek. This juxtaposition effectively makes Jesus the hope, since he is the one who enters into the Holy of Holies on behalf of believers. The final reference to Melchizedek recalls 5:10, which explains how Jesus became the "source of eternal salvation." It also looks forward to 7:1, which embarks on a fuller discussion of this mysterious figure from Gen 14:18-20.

As a good pastor, the author of Hebrews has sought in this section of his sermon to marshal all possible evidence to show how the promises of God are destined to be fulfilled. In previous warnings, which were sometimes harshly worded (3:7-13; 4:1-2, 11-13; 5:11-14; 6:4-8), attention to human failing, disobedience, the inability to hear the word of God, and apostasy called that fulfillment into question by stressing the inadequacy of human response to God. A more hopeful note of encouragement ended with an exhortation to faithfulness and perseverance in order to inherit God's promises (6:12).

In this section of the sermon the author extends that encouragement with an exposition of why faithfulness and perseverance will benefit the readers.

Abraham was presented as a counterexample to the wilderness generation, as someone who through his own fidelity and patient endurance made the proper response to God. By placing his trust in God and not merely in himself, Abraham obtained the promise. Whereas the wilderness generation was tested, so also was Abraham. Where they failed, however, through disobedience, he succeeded through obedience. God swore an oath to each: the wilderness generation would never enter God's rest, and Abraham would be blessed and multiplied.

Like Abraham and the wilderness generation, the readers are faced with a similar choice of how to respond to God's word. The author wants them to know that they, like Abraham, can count on the surety of God's promise and can obtain it if they respond as he did, with faithfulness and patient endurance. But the author does not leave the matter there, for the readers have something Abraham did not have: "a sure and steadfast anchor" in the hope they place in Christ as their High Priest. This "hope" has entered the inner sanctuary with him for all time when he opened up a way to God, which for the readers is the final destination (12:22-24; 13:14). So the author's purpose in this part of the sermon is to reassure his readers that the fulfillment of God's promises rests on the surety of God's oath. In light of that fact they, like Abraham, will obtain the promises if they remain faithful and persevere to the end.

FOR REFERENCE AND FURTHER STUDY

Davidson, Richard M. "Christ's Entry 'Within the Veil' in Hebrews 6:19-20: The Old Testament Background," *AUSS* 39 (2001) 175–90.

Koester, Helmut. "Die Auslegung der Abraham-Verheissung in Hebr 6," in Rolf Rendtorff and Klaus Koch, eds., *Studien zur Theologie der alttestamentlichen Überlieferungen*. Neukirchen: Neukirchener Verlag, 1961, 95–109.

Spicq, Ceslas. "*Angkyra et prodromos* dans L'Hébr. VI 19-20," *ST* 3 (1949) 185–87.

Young, Norman H. "'Where Jesus Has Gone as a Forerunner on Our Behalf' (Hebrews 6:20)," *AUSS* 39 (2001) 165–73.

_____. "The Day of Dedication or the Day of Atonement? The Old Testament Background to Hebrews 6:19-20 Revisited," *AUSS* 40 (2002) 61–68.

III. The Message for the Mature:
Another Priest Like Melchizedek (7:1–10:39)

13. *Melchizedek and Abraham* (7:1-10)

1. This "Melchizedek, King of Salem, priest of the Most High God, met Abraham as he was returning from defeating the kings and blessed him," 2. and Abraham gave to him "one-tenth of everything." His name, first, means "king of righteousness"; then he is also king of Salem, which means "king of peace." 3. Without father, without mother, without genealogy, having neither beginning of days nor end of life, but resembling the Son of God, he remains a priest forever.

4. See how great he is! Even Abraham the patriarch gave him a tenth of the spoils. 5. And those descendants of Levi who receive the priestly office have a commandment in the law to collect tithes from the people, that is, from their kindred, though these also are descended from Abraham. 6. But he, who does not belong to their ancestry, collected a tithe from Abraham and blessed him who had received the promises. 7. It is beyond dispute that the lesser is blessed by the greater. 8. Here, tithes are received by those who are mortal; there, by one of whom it is testified that he lives. 9. One might even say that Levi himself, who receives tithes, paid tithes through Abraham, 10. for he was still in the loins of his ancestor when Melchizedek met him.

Notes

1. *This "Melchizedek, King of Salem, priest of the Most High God, met Abraham as he was returning from defeating the kings and blessed him":* Having ended the previous exhortation with an allusion to the description of Melchizedek taken from Ps 110:4, the author now draws on the only other text of the lxx that mentions this mysterious king. Hebrews condenses Gen 14:17-19, using some of the words that actually appear in the lxx version. The lxx account begins with Abraham's meeting with the king of Sodom after the former had defeated the Elamite king Chedorlaomer and the other kings who fought with him. They are listed in Gen 14:9 as Tidal of Goiim, Amraphel of Shinar, and Arioch of Ellasar. The author picks up the story after Abraham's victory over the kings by merely referring to his return from "defeating the kings." The Greek noun *kopē* can mean "cutting down" or "slaughter," to describe what Abraham had done. The fact that Melchizedek blesses Abraham anticipates the argument developed throughout the midrashic exposition of Melchizedek, that he is indeed superior to Abraham as the order of his priesthood is superior to Levitical order.

Melchizedek is identified as king of Salem, a priest of the Most High God, reflecting a common Hellenistic interpretation of him (see Philo, *Allegorical Interpretation* 3.79, 82 and Josephus, *War* 6.438; *Antiquities* 1.181; Joseph A. Fitzmyer, *The Genesis Apocryphon of Qumran Cave 1 (1Q20): A Commentary*. Biblica et Orientalia 18B [Rome: Editrice Pontificio Istituto Biblico, 2004] 245). Unlike other first-century authors, this one does not identify Salem with Jerusalem (Josephus, *War* 6.438; *Antiquities* 1.181).

2. *Abraham gave to him "one-tenth of everything":* One-tenth of everything means a tithe from the spoils Abraham gained from the battle with the kings. According to Deuteronomic practice none of the spoils were to be spared (Deut 7:2, 24-26; 20:16-18; Josh 6:21; cf. 7:1; 8:24-25; 10:39; 11:9, 11; Judg 1:17; 1 Sam 15:3).

His name, first, means "king of righteousness"; then he is also king of Salem, which means "king of peace": Hebrews explains Melchizedek's name in two ways. The first has to do with the etymology of the name itself, and the second is based on his office as king of Salem, followed by yet another etymology of that title. The Hebrew word for "king" is *melek* and the word for "right," "just," or "righteous" is *ṣedek*. Because the Hebrew *malkiᵓ* includes a pronominal suffix in the first person singular, the name literally means "my king is righteous," or if the latter part of the name referred to a Canaanite God, "my king is Zedek." An oft cited parallel is the name of another Jerusalemite king, Adonizedek in Josh 10:1, "my lord is Zedek" or "my lord is righteous." In Hellenistic Judaism Melchizedek's name was interpreted to mean "righteous king" (Philo, *Allegorical Interpretation* 3.79; Josephus, *Antiquities* 1.181), a tradition that Hebrews follows.

3. *Without father, without mother, without genealogy, having neither beginning of days nor end of life:* Adding to the mystery of Melchizedek is his obscure origin. At Qumran he was thought of as a heavenly being (Fitzmyer, *Genesis Apocryphon*, 247). Philo claims that Melchizedek's priesthood originated with himself, as he was a self-taught individual (*Preliminary Studies* 99). Here Hebrews goes beyond what can be known about Melchizedek from the LXX, whose silence may have allowed the author some freedom to cast him as the kind of figure that could support his christological claims. This description of Melchizedek's unusual pedigree favors a distinction between his priesthood and the Levitical priesthood, whose lineage was known. Hebrews presents Melchizedek as the type of a priesthood that is superior to the Levitical priesthood in order to establish a basis for the high priesthood of Christ.

But resembling the Son of God, he remains a priest forever: The verb "resemble," *aphomoioun*, is *hapax* in the NT. Earlier Hebrews used the more common verb "make like," *homoioun*, in 2:17, when explaining how the Son had to be made like his brothers and sisters. The LXX uses *aphomoioun* to describe an idol likened to an animal (Wis 13:14) to warn against assimilation to foreigners (Ep Jer 5) and to compare idols to natural phenomena (Ep Jer 63, 71). These negative contexts did not deter the author of Hebrews from adopting the word as a tool for comparing Melchizedek to the Son of God. The strength of the comparison lies in the notion of eternity attributed to each. Whereas the expression "a priest forever" may sound like an echo of Ps 110:4, the Greek of Hebrews is not an exact quotation of the psalm, as the author uses another word to signify the unending nature of Melchizedek's priesthood, *diēnekes*. This description anticipates that of the priesthood of Christ in 7:15-16. Interestingly, here Melchizedek resembles the Son of God, whereas in 7:15 Christ resembles Melchizedek, showing how each is identified with the other in the nature of their priesthoods. Melchizedek represents an alternative to the Levitical priesthood, which grounds a critical stage in the author's argument about the high priesthood of Christ.

4. *See how great he is! Even Abraham the patriarch gave him a tenth of the spoils:* The author continues to emphasize Melchizedek's stature by advancing the next stage of the argument. According to Gen 14:20 Abraham gave Melchizedek one-tenth of the spoils he had gained from his victory over the kings. The LXX is ambiguous because the subject of the verb "give," *didonai*, is not expressed. Following upon the blessing Melchizedek gave to Abraham, the text merely says "and he gave him one-tenth of everything." It is not clear if it is Abraham or Melchizedek who tithes. Hellenistic Judaism understood Abraham to have given the tithe (see Fitzmyer, *Genesis Apocryphon*, 250), as does the author of Hebrews. For Hebrews the fact that Abraham gave Melchizedek a tithe argues for the latter's greatness. The readers are invited to imagine this greatness as the author allows his argument to unfold. Abraham is referred to as "the Patriarch." The LXX speaks of the office of patriarch as a leadership role among the tribes or families of Israel (1 Chr 24:31; 27:22; 2 Chr 19:8; 23:20; 26:12), but only 4 Macc 7:19 and 16:25 use the title for Abraham, along with Isaac and Jacob. It is only here in the NT that Abraham is called a patriarch (cf. Acts 2:29; 7:8-9).

5. *And those descendants of Levi who receive the priestly office have a commandment in the law to collect tithes from the people, that is, from their kindred, though these also are descended from Abraham:* Hebrews mentions the Levitical priesthood explicitly as the comparison between it and Melchizedek is drawn further. The author makes clear that he has in mind the descendants of Levi who were priests, and who, on the basis of their office, had received tithes. There were some Levites who were not priests (Num 3:5-10; Neh 10:35-39). According to Num 18:21-32 the Levites were allowed to receive tithes from Israel because they had not been given an allotment of the land. They were, however, supposed to give an offering from what they received to the priests, represented by Aaron in Num 18:28. It is not clear whether the author of Hebrews knew of the distinction between Levites and priests. When the author specifies that the Levitical priests received tithes from the people, their kindred, he knows that all of Israel was bound by the Law to tithe to the Levites. This fact is important because it helps to construct an argument for the superiority of Melchizedek over Abraham. If the Levites, who are descendants of Abraham, like their kindred, may receive tithes from other Israelites, how much greater must Melchizedek be, who received a tithe from Abraham himself. The parity of the Levites and their kindred suggests that their reception of tithes is something less than Melchizedek's receiving from Abraham, thus implying the superiority of Melchizedek over Abraham. The point will be made even more explicit in vv. 9-10.

6. *But he, who does not belong to their ancestry, collected a tithe from Abraham:* The author continues the thought from the previous verse, making explicit the importance of Melchizedek's non-genealogical origin. Whereas the Levites received tithes from their kindred, those who shared their human origins, Melchizedek, who was without human genealogy, received a tithe from Abraham. The verb "collect tithes," *dekatoun*, occurs only here in the NT. The LXX uses it in 2 Esdr 20:38 in relation to the Levites' reception of tithes.

   and blessed him who had received the promises: The elegantly structured sentence concludes by contrasting what Melchizedek lacked, a genealogy, with what

Abraham had, the promises. The importance of the promises was already stressed in 6:13-15. In 8:6 the author will make the claim that the ministry of Christ is founded on better promises than was the old covenant. Following the text of Gen 14:19-20, Hebrews notes that Abraham was blessed by Melchizedek, resuming the mention of the blessing in 7:1. The majority of the references to blessing in Hebrews are tied to the blessing Abraham received from God (6:14), which was passed on to his descendants (11:20-21; 12:17). Thus it is striking that Melchizedek should bless Abraham.

7. *It is beyond dispute that the lesser is blessed by the greater:* The author is not laying down a general rule, as there are biblical examples of greater individuals being blessed by lesser ones (2 Sam 8:10; 14:22; 1 Kgs 1:47; 8:66; Ruth 2:4, 19). He is merely referring to the case at hand, namely that Abraham in this instance is the lesser and Melchizedek the greater, since the former paid a tithe to the latter.

8. *Here, tithes are received by those who are mortal; there, by one of whom it is testified that he lives:* Further evidence for the superiority of Melchizedek is adduced by the contrast between him and the Levitical priests. They are the ones referred to in the first instance, since they received tithes as mortals. Melchizedek, on the other hand, lives. The author uses the correlative adverbs "here" and "there" (*hōde men . . . ekei de*) to draw the contrast. Normally adverbs of place, they can also refer to the matter at hand with the force of "in this case . . . in that case" (BDAG, 1101). How exactly the author understood Melchizedek to be alive, and who is actually testifying to this fact, is not stated. In 7:17 it is Ps 110:4, where the mention of his eternal priesthood implies that he is immortal, as does the earlier reference to his origin and destiny, that he has "neither beginning of days nor end of life" (7:3). Elsewhere in Hebrews the Holy Spirit testifies through Scripture in 10:15, as does God in 11:2, 4, 5. In 11:39 the faith of the scriptural heroes attests to their greatness. The emphasis on Melchizedek as alive also looks ahead to 7:23-25, where the eternal priesthood of Christ is contrasted with the Levitical priesthood. Whereas Jesus continues as a priest forever, the mortality of the Levitical priests prevented them from remaining in office.

9. *One might even say that Levi himself, who receives tithes, paid tithes through Abraham,* 10. *for he was still in the loins of his ancestor when Melchizedek met him:* This part of the argument is a bit of a stretch, since Abraham is such a distant relative of Levi, and the author seems to know this. The expression "one might even say" was used in Greek to speculate about something for which there was no clear evidence (Attridge, 197; Koester, 345; Lane 1:158; Weiss, 392 n. 79). The reference to Abraham's loins as the place of his descendants is figurative (Gen 35:11; 2 Chr 6:9). These descendants have already been mentioned in relation to Levi in v. 5.

INTERPRETATION

Chapter 7 divides into three distinct parts, vv. 1-10, 11-19, and 20-28. The first part picks up on the mention of Melchizedek in 6:20 and launches into an exposition of his importance in the author's presentation of the priesthood of Jesus. Hebrews alone, in the NT, develops this aspect of Christology.

The author uses a historical point of departure by recalling the encounter between Melchizedek and Abraham in Gen 14:17-20. Details of the biblical account are replicated in Hebrews. First, there is the encounter itself (Gen 14:18). Second, Melchizedek is described as King of Salem and a priest of the Most High God (Gen 14:18). Third, comes the mention that Melchizedek blessed Abraham (Gen 14:19-20). Finally, the author recalls that Abraham paid a tithe to Melchizedek (Gen 14:20). Striking is the absence of the detail in Gen 14:18 that Melchizedek brought out bread and wine to Abraham. The *Genesis Apocryphon* changed the reference to "food and drink" in 1Q20, col. 22.15. The LXX and Hellenistic Judaism simply portray Melchizedek as offering hospitality to Abraham after the latter's victory, whereas later Christian tradition will interpret the detail as eucharistic (see Fitzmyer, *Genesis Apocryphon*, 248; Attridge, 188).

Apart from the scriptural witness, the author also drew on the tradition of Melchizedek in Hellenistic Judaism for the interpretation of his name as the king of righteousness, which one finds also in Josephus and Philo. Whereas Hebrews shares a common background with the presentation of Melchizedek in 1Q20, it diverges from the presentation of Melchizedek as a heavenly figure in 11QMelch and 4Q'Amram. Hebrews also omits the Hellenistic Jewish identification of Salem with Jerusalem.

The author's interest in Melchizedek was already shown earlier in 5:6 and 6:20, where he quoted Ps 110:4 in the characterization of Jesus' priesthood as being of the order of Melchizedek. In chapter 7 he expounds on the distinctiveness of Melchizedek's priesthood by comparing it to the more usual form of Israelite priesthood shared by Aaron and those Levites who were also priests.

A critical element of the argument in the first ten verses of the chapter comes in v. 3, where Melchizedek's origins are mentioned. Being without father or mother, without beginning of days or end of life, Melchizedek is likened to the Son of God in that he is a priest forever. The allusion to Ps 110:4 links the chapter to the previous citations of the psalm, anticipating the larger argument the author wishes to make in relation to the eternal priesthood of Christ. More immediately, in the present context, the ethereal origin of Melchizedek and his own eternal priesthood establish points of contrast with the Levitical priesthood. His priesthood is not limited by time as theirs is.

Furthermore, the role of Abraham in Genesis 14 anchors the argument for the Levitical priesthood as being something less than the priesthood of Melchizedek. Hebrews cleverly exploits the fact that even though Melchizedek came out to meet Abraham, the patriarch paid a tithe to the king. This simple customary act is transformed in the imagination of the author into a sign that Melchizedek was greater than Abraham (Heb 7:7; cf. John 8:53). Thus it has a christological significance.

In a way, the author of Hebrews has "re-scriptured" the story of Melchizedek for his own purpose by taking advantage of the omission of Melchizedek's genealogy and familial ties as well as the lack of detail about his life and death. Curiously, by filling that vacuum with a description of Melchizedek's origin, expressed in the form of a *via negativa* (7:3), he has expanded the biblical and Hellenistic Jewish tradition to create a figure even more mysterious than the one he had found there.

The substance of the author's comparison of Melchizedek to Abraham is presented in two parallel constructions. The contrast of Melchizedek, who received a tithe from Abraham before there was a Law, with the Levites, who were entitled to receive tithes under the Law, is facilitated by a typical Greek construction, *ho men* (7:5) . . . *ho de* (7:6). Then the contrast of Melchizedek, who lives, with the Levites, who are limited by their mortality, is accomplished by the Greek construction *hōde men . . . ekei de* (7:8). Each of the comparisons contains notice of the earthly nature of the Levites, descended through Abraham, and Melchizedek's ethereal nature, which transcends the earthly.

The final stage of the author's argument for the superiority of Melchizedek over the Levites and Abraham suggests that Levi paid tithes to Melchizedek through Abraham, since as a descendant of Abraham he, like all Israel, was in the loins of his ancestor. Although it may seem a farfetched suggestion, this is essential for the author's argument if he is to show the superiority of Melchizedek over the Levites, since they had not yet come into existence when Melchizedek met Abraham. One can only wonder how the case would have been made had the author of Genesis not portrayed Abraham as tithing to Melchizedek.

Drawing closer to the central argument of the sermon (8:1–10:18), the author inserts information that is important for the exposition of his christology. Taking the novel approach of presenting Jesus as a High Priest, he breaks new ground in the exposition of Jesus' person and work, the two main prongs of any christological endeavor. Certainly a serious challenge facing the author is the absence of any tradition that Jesus came from a line of priests (7:13). What complicates the picture still more is the author's desire to show that, as a High Priest, Jesus is superior to the Levitical priests (7:11). Enter Melchizedek.

The image of Abraham paying tithes to Melchizedek, and by association the Levitical priests still in Abraham's loins, captured the author's imagination. This act of submission on Abraham's part might contribute to the demonstration that Melchizedek's priesthood was recognized, even by Abraham, as superior to any that would follow. The speculation in Hellenistic Judaism over Melchizedek's mysterious origins, along with the oracle of Ps 110:4, might establish a line of priests not tied to any earthly temporal limits. The resultant notion of Melchizedek's priesthood as eternal and superior to the Levitical priesthood, and an oracle still standing, combined in the author's imagination to provide evidence enough for a christological portrait unique in early Christianity of Jesus as a High Priest. What the author has produced, however, should not be seen as the victory of a hyperactive imagination alone, for it is born of an extraordinary knowledge of Scripture and tradition and the ability to think "outside the box."

FOR REFERENCE AND FURTHER STUDY

Cothenet, Édouard. "Prêtre selon l'ordre de Melchisédech d'après l'épître aux Hébreux," *EspV* 110 (2000) 13–17.

Fitzmyer, Joseph A. "Melchizedek in the MT, LXX, and the NT," *Bib* 81 (2000) 63–69.

Kobelski, Paul J. *Melchizedek and Melchireša'*. CBQMS 10. Washington, DC: The Catholic Biblical Association of America, 1981.

Manzi, Franco. "Interrogativi, discusión e conferme. Sul binomio Melchisedek ed angelologia nell'epistola agli Ebrei e a Qumran," *ScC* 129 (2001) 683–729.

McNamara, Martin. "Melchizedek: Gen 14,17-20 in the Targums, in Rabbinic and Early Christian Literature," *Bib* 81 (2000) 1–31.

Nel, Philip J. "Psalm 110 and the Melchizedek Tradition," *JNSL* 22 (1996) 1–14.

Rooke, Deborah W. "Jesus as Royal Priest: Reflections on the Interpretation of the Melchizedek Tradition in Heb 7," *Bib* 81 (2000) 81–94.

Steyn, Gert J. "The *Vorlage* of the Melchizedek Phrases in Heb 7.1-4," *Acta Patristica et Byzantina* 13 (2002) 207–23.

Thomas, T. K. "Melchizedek, King and Priest. An Ecumenical Paradigm?" *EcumRev* 52 (2000) 403–409.

14. *A Priest in the Likeness of Melchizedek* (7:11-19)

11. Now if perfection had been attainable through the Levitical priesthood—for the people received the law on the basis of it—what further need would there have been for a different priest to be raised up according to the order of Melchizedek, rather than one to be named to the order of Aaron? 12. For when there is a change in the priesthood, there is necessarily a change in the law as well. 13. Now the one of whom these things are spoken belonged to a different tribe, from which no one has ever served at the altar. 14. For it is evident that our Lord was descended from Judah, and in connection with that tribe Moses said nothing about priests. 15. It is even more obvious when a different priest arises, resembling Melchizedek,

16. one who has become a priest not through a legal requirement concerning physical descent, but through the power of an indestructible life. 17. For it is attested of him, "You are a priest forever, according to the order of Melchizedek." 18. There is, on the one hand, the abrogation of an earlier commandment because it was weak and ineffectual 19. (for the law made nothing perfect); there is, on the other hand, the introduction of a better hope, through which we approach God.

NOTES

11. *Now if perfection had been attainable through the Levitical priesthood:* The author continues the argument begun in the previous section by linking vv. 11-19 to it by the Greek particle *oun*, "therefore." This section begins with a hypothetical question indicating that the author does not believe that perfection was attainable through the Levitical priesthood. The noun for "perfection," *teleiōsis*, occurs only here and in Luke 1:45 ("fulfillment") in the NT. The author prefers the verb "make perfect" (see 2:10; 5:9; 7:19, 28; 9:9; 10:1, 14; 11:40; 12:23). *Teleiōsis* is often associated with sacrifices offered during the consecration of priests in the LXX (Exod 29:22, 26, 27, 31, 34; Lev 7:37; 8:22, 26, 28, 31, 33; cf. 2 Chron 29:35), but it does refer to "fulfillment" or "completion" in Sir 31:10 and Jer 2:2. The issue in this verse is whether Israel had a "consecrating sacrifice," a *teleiōsis* that was more than an external act. Hebrews believes it did not, and so there was need for the kind of *teleiōsis* that would go beyond the external to the internal purification of the one so consecrated (Vanhoye, *Old Testament Priests*, 165–67). For this reason the cultic meaning of "perfection" in this context connotes the purification of the conscience (9:9, 14; 10:1, 14, 22).

for the people received the law on the basis of it: The parenthetical remark intends to show the link between the Law and the priesthood, and may imply a correlative weakness for the Law. Usually in Greek the construction for "on the basis of it" (*ep' autēs*) has a temporal dimension with the meaning of "upon" or "during," but here the sense is that the priesthood substantiates the Law (BDF §234.[8]).

what further need would there have been for a different priest to be raised up according to the order of Melchizedek, rather than one to be named to the order of Aaron?: This rhetorical question forms the apodosis ("then" clause) of the conditional sentence. At the heart of the question lies an allusion to Ps 110:4, "according to the order of Melchizedek," now explicitly distinguished from the "order of Aaron." If perfection were attainable under the Levitical priesthood, the psalm would not have referred to a different order of priests in the line of Melchizedek. The author interprets the psalm as prophetic and referring to Christ and his priesthood (5:5-6). Here the "different" priest is not just another in the priestly line, in the sense of "another." The adjective *heteros* can mean "other," or "different," which fits the context better (Attridge, 200; Koester, 353). By using the verb "raise up," *anistanai*, the author may simply mean "appoint" (BDAG, 83). An interesting parallel usage occurs in 1 Macc 14:41, where it refers to a prophet who will be raised up to succeed Simon Maccabeus, who was already selected by the people to be high priest forever (cf. de Silva, *Perseverance*, 271). New Testament authors sometimes use the same verb to refer to the resurrection of Jesus (see Matt 17:9, 23; 20:19; Mark 9:9, 31; 10:34; Luke 9:22; 18:33; 1 Thess 4:14). Since Jesus' priesthood is not one of physical descent (7:16) and is permanent, because he continues forever (7:24), an allusion to his resurrection here is not unlikely (Koester, 353).

When the author refers to the "order of Aaron" he must be thinking of it as part of the Levitical line, since the comparison with Melchizedek in this chapter has focused on the Levites. The Greek verb *legein* often means "say," but it can also mean "name" or "call" (BDAG, 390). Hebrews uses it in this last sense in 9:3 and 11:24.

12. *For when there is a change in the priesthood, there is necessarily a change in the law as well:* The author understands the priesthood to be so linked to the Law that a change in one necessarily produces a change in the other. The genitive absolute, *metatithemenēs gar tēs hierōsynēs*, may be translated temporally, "when there is a change in the priesthood," or conditionally, "if there is a change in the priesthood" (Lane 1:174; see Attridge, 200, on the conditional). Josephus uses the verb to indicate the transferance of the priesthood from one house to another (*Antiquities* 12.387) and the noun (*Against Apion* 1.286; cf. Philo, *On the Giants* 66) to indicate a "replacement." For Hebrews the change is not that simple. Verse 18 indicates that the change in question is an abrogation of the Law. The author uses the noun "change" in two other places, once to indicate how God took Enoch (11:5; see Philo, *On Rewards and Punishments* 16–17) and again to speak of the removal of the earthly order (12:27).

13. *Now the one of whom these things are spoken belonged to a different tribe, from which no one has ever served at the altar:* The identity of the different priest is now expressed, indirectly at first. He belongs to a tribe that has no priestly pedigree. The expression "a different tribe" recalls a "different priest" of v. 11. The next verse will name the tribe, Judah. The verb "belong to," *metechein*, also occurs in 2:14 and 5:13 to indicate how the Son shared in human nature. On its meaning see the Notes at 2:14. Here it is used again to speak about another way the earthly Jesus was related to his fellow humans, through his familial ties.

In making the claim that no one from the tribe of Judah served at the altar, the author seems to rely primarily on the Law's prescriptions for the priesthood and does not appear to be interested in Israel's tradition of sacral kingship. According to 2 Sam 8:18, David's sons may have been priests. Also, kings of Judah are certainly depicted at an altar in the Hebrew Bible (2 Sam 6:12, 17-18; 1 Kings 3:4; 8:5, 62-63). The verb *prosechein* followed by a dative means "occupy oneself with," "devote oneself to," or "apply oneself to" (BDAG, 880). Here the meaning "serve at" describes the priest's sacrificial function before the altar (*thysiastērion*). The author uses the common word for altar in the LXX, which occurs there 257 times.

14. *For it is evident that our Lord was descended from Judah:* The author clarifies the previous verse. The adjective "evident," *prodēlon*, occurs here and in 1 Tim 5:24 in the NT to refer to something that is plain to see. It is used four times in

1 Clement (11:1; 12:7; 40:1; 51:3), a document that depends on Hebrews (William L. Lane, "Social Perspectives on Roman Christianity during the Formative Years from Nero to Nerva: Romans, Hebrews, *1 Clement*," in Karl P. Donfried and Peter Richardson, eds., *Judaism and Christianity in First-Century Rome* [Grand Rapids: Eerdmans, 1998] 216). The descent of Jesus from the Davidic line is traditional in the NT (Matt 1:1, 6; 9:27; 15:22; Mark 10:47; Luke 1:27, 32; 2:4; 18:38; John 7:42; Rom 1:3; 2 Tim 2:8; Rev 22:16). The verb "descend from," *anatellein*, has this meaning only here in the NT. The noun, *anatolē*, refers to a Davidic descendant in Jer 23:5 and Zech 6:12. But one need not read messianic overtones into this part of the verse (Attridge, 201).

and in connection with that tribe Moses said nothing about priests: The conclusion of the verse adds nothing more than was stated in the previous one, that no one from the tribe of Judah served at the altar. The reference to Moses may be an allusion to his final blessing over the tribes of Israel, where he characterizes each of the tribes individually. For Judah he asks the help of other tribes (Deut 33:7), and for Levi the priesthood (33:8-11) (Koester, 355). Then again, the mention of his name may simply allude to the Torah, as it does in Luke 16:29.

15. *It is even more obvious when a different priest arises, resembling Melchizedek:* What was already evident becomes even more so (*perissoteron eti katadēlon*) when Melchizedek is factored into the argument. The author repeats the language of v. 11 to speak of this priest arising, changing the word found there for the line of priests from Melchizedek, "order," to "resembling," i.e., a priest in the likeness of Melchizedek. The likeness has already been anticipated in 7:3 in the mention that Melchizedek continues in his priesthood forever. On that basis Melchizedek resembled the Son of God. Here Christ's priesthood is likened to Melchizedek's because of its eternal character. The author brings the whole argument he has been making in this chapter to a focal point. Like Melchizedek's priesthood, the priesthood of Christ does not rest on priestly lineage, for neither of them can claim to have had that. Melchizedek is without genealogy (7:3) and Jesus, a descendant of Abraham, came from the tribe of Judah, which according to the Law had no claim to priesthood. Melchizedek's superiority over Abraham was grounded in the fact that, unlike the mortal Abraham and his Levitical descendants, he lives (7:8), having no end of life (7:3). Both Jesus and Melchizedek share an eternal priesthood, something that will be confirmed in the next verse.

16. *one who has become a priest not through a legal requirement concerning physical descent:* Literally the text reads "not according to a law of a fleshy commandment (*entolēs sarkinēs*). The adjective "fleshy," *sarkinos*, connotes what is physical or human (BDAG, 914), like its synonym *sarkikos*, found in a variant reading of this verse in some manuscripts of Hebrews (C³ D² Ψ 𝔐). Both adjectives appear in Paul, where they can mean simply what is material, physical, or human (*sarkikos:* Rom 15:27; 1 Cor 9:11; *sarkinos:* 1 Cor 3:1; 2 Cor 3:3) or, more pejoratively, what is due to the weakness of human nature (*sarkikos:* Rom 7:14; 1 Cor 3:3; 3:4 *v.l.*; 2 Cor 1:12; 10:4; *sarkinos:* Rom 7:14 *v.l.*; 2 Cor 1:12) (BDAG, 914). Elsewhere in the NT there is one occurrence of the pejorative *sarkikos* in 1 Pet 2:11. In the immediate context this characterization of the Law anticipates v. 18, while helping to develop the author's contrast between the material and the eternal throughout

chapter 7. It looks ahead, as well, to 9:9-10 where the author speaks of the inability of the Law to purify the conscience of the worshiper by means of gifts and sacrifices (cf. 9:13).

but through the power of an indestructible life: The adjective "indestructible," *akatalytos*, occurs only here in the NT (see Friedrich Büchsel, *akatalytos*, *TDNT* 4:338–39). The one instance of it in the LXX has the meaning of "unceasing" (4 Macc 10:11). The construction parallels the first part of the verse, saying literally "but according to the power of an indestructible life," thus opposing the earlier mention of a "law" with the "power of life." How exactly the author understands "indestructible life" is not immediately clear. He seems not to intend it literally to mean that Jesus' earthly life was indestructible, since earlier he alluded to the real suffering and death he had to undergo in order to become "a merciful and faithful high priest" (2:10-18; 5:7-10). Ultimately the power of his life is indestructible because he is the exalted Son who had passed through the heavens (4:14). The linking of Pss 2:7 and 110:4 in 5:5-6 helps the author to establish this claim.

17. *For it is attested of him, "You are a priest forever, according to the order of Melchizedek":* In v. 8 the author said of Melchizedek that Scripture "testified" that he lives (see the Notes at 7:8). Now the author provides the actual attestation by quoting once again Ps 110:4. The connection between the verses is facilitated by the use of the same verb, "testify to," *martyrein*. This is the seventh and penultimate time the author cites directly or alludes to the psalm verse (see 5:6, 10; 6:20; 7:3, 11, 15, 21), adding to its prominence in this part of the sermon.

18. *There is, on the one hand, the abrogation of an earlier commandment because it was weak and ineffectual:* This section of the chapter concludes with an *inclusio*, summarizing the author's thought. With the fulfillment of the above cited psalm verse, Jesus' priesthood abrogates the Levitical priesthood, which at the beginning of the section was shown to be unable to bring about perfection. The noun "abrogation," *athetēsis*, is a technical legal term for the annulment or cancellation of a decree or contract (MM, 12). The author uses it again in 9:26 for atonement for sin. Its verbal form (*athetein*) occurs in 10:28. The abrogation here is clearly different since it is not done by a human. Earlier the author referred to a change in the Law brought about by a change in the priesthood (7:12). Now it becomes clear that there was not a mere change, but that the Law was actually set aside because of its weakness and ineffectiveness. The words "weak," *asthenes*, and "ineffectual," *anōpheles*, add force to the opening hypothetical question. Attridge correctly ties the weakness of the Law to the fact that it governed the material and the fleshly (Attridge, 203). In this way the perfection spoken about in v. 11 was unattainable under the Levitical priesthood.

19. *for the Law made nothing perfect:* Another parenthetical remark begins the conclusion of this section by recalling its initial verse, questioning the ability of the Law to bring perfection.

the introduction of a better hope, through which we approach God: By contrasting the priesthood of Christ with the Levitical priesthood, the author shows a newness that comes from the introduction of a better hope. The noun "introduction," *epeisagōgē*, means something that is present in a way it was not before (BDAG, 361). It occurs only here in the NT. The "better hope" is predicated on the fact that the priesthood of Christ facilitates access to God. Of the eighteen times the comparative adjective "better" occurs in the NT, twelve of them are in Hebrews, often referring to Christ or things brought about by his priestly work. "Hope" is a constant virtue in the hortatory sections of Hebrews (3:6; 6:11, 18; 10:23). The verb "approach," *engizein*, means "get near to." The author uses it in 10:25 for the drawing near of the Day of the Lord, where the eschatological meaning is similar to what is found in other NT texts (Matt 3:2; 4:17; 10:7; Mark 1:5; Luke 10:9, 11; 21:8, 20, 28; Rom 13:12; Jas 5:8; 1 Pet 4:7).

Interpretation

Having relied on Scripture to introduce the priesthood of Melchizedek, and having shown how that foreshadows the priesthood of Christ, Hebrews now turns to the question of the adequacy of the Levitical priesthood in relation to the Law. In this section of the chapter the author leads his readers to consider the possibility of another priest from the order of Melchizedek, and the effect his priesthood has on the Law.

These nine verses are structured in three parts. First, a rhetorical question about the adequacy of the Law introduces the author's conviction that the Levitical priesthood was unable to fulfill the purpose for which it was instituted (7:11). Second, the author tries to show how a new priest in the likeness of Melchizedek brings about a change not only in that institution but in the Law as well (7:12-17). Third, he shows how this new priesthood has wider consequences because it effects an abrogation of the Law itself (7:18-19). Consequently the new priesthood brings a greater hope because it offers a new way to approach God.

The logic of this section of Hebrews builds from an initial observation the author makes in v. 11. Other NT authors relied on an interpretation of Psalm 110 that focused, for the most part, on its value for interpreting the exaltation of Christ to the right hand of God (Hay, *Glory at the Right Hand*, 155). The psalm's first verse had caught their attention as they sought validation for their belief that upon his resurrection Jesus made a return to the heavenly realm, where he was enthroned with God. The author of Hebrews draws on that tradition of the psalm's interpretation also (1:13; 2:9) but, unlike other NT authors, he has understood the psalm to have additional value in talking about another dimension of christology, Christ's sacrificial death (5:5-10). The fourth verse of Psalm 110 captured his imagination in a way it did not for other NT authors. Later in the sermon the once for all sacrifice of this new priest will be discussed, but for now it is enough to establish that he is indeed a priest according to the order of Melchizedek. That itself, of course, is not without its problems.

The fact that the verse begins with the mention of an oath sworn by God that the Lord, of whom the psalm speaks, is a priest forever according to the order of Melchizedek brought the author to conclude that the psalmist was not making just a simple declaration. Rather, he was handing on a divine oath as if it were a prophetic statement. He is a bit like Luke, who understood that David, as the author of the psalms, was a prophet who prophesied the resurrection of Christ in Ps 16:10 and his exaltation in Ps 110:1 (Acts 2:30-36). Presupposing the oracular nature of the psalms, it was only natural for the author to frame the question of why it was necessary for God to swear an oath regarding another order of priests since there was already a legitimate order provided for in the Law. He answers his question in 7:11: the Levitical priesthood was unable to attain perfection, by which he means it was finally unable to purify the consciences of those living under the Law, who had sinned. Thus, the author offers a global reason for the necessity of a change in the priesthood that then, in turn, produced a change in the Law itself. Having established this basic point, he will go on to show specific instances in which the inadequacies of the former priesthood have been surmounted in the priesthood of Christ.

The obvious problem with the argument thus far is that there is no attestation in the tradition that Jesus was descended from a priestly family. The author admits the difficulty openly in 7:13-14, perhaps anticipating a challenge to his reasoning. The force of his admission, however, is not really defensive. Rather, he sees the lack of Jesus' priestly lineage as a confirmation that there indeed has been a change in the priesthood. As the lack of a genealogy rendered Melchizedek greater than Abraham (7:7), the lack of physical descent from a priestly line renders Jesus greater than the Levitical priests. Priests like Melchizedek transcend physical descent because their priesthood is not tied to the Law, but is rather based on the power of an indestructible life. Since Jesus' resurrection and exaltation provide the evidence for such a life, his priesthood belongs to the order of the one who lives (7:8), and in him the psalm verse is fulfilled. It is important to note that the author is not arguing for a new line of priests according to the order of Melchizedek since the only priest he is interested in, Christ, exhausts that line. Rather, for Hebrews, Ps 110:4 makes possible the appearance of a non-Levitical priest who accomplishes what the Levitical priesthood was unable to attain.

The last two verses of this section solidify the author's argument. When he says that a former commandment has been abrogated he is speaking about the Law, which brought the Levitical priesthood into being and governed it. The reason for the abrogation is the Law's weakness and ineffectiveness, made obvious by the parenthetical remark of v. 19, echoing the question that began the argument (7:11). The weakness of the Law is the cause for the appearance of another priest, not from the line of Aaron (7:11).

With the appearance of this priest there came a change in the Law (7:12) as well as hope for what his priesthood could accomplish. In contrast to the Law, which cannot make perfect, the hope that resulted from the appearance of this new priest demonstrates that as a priest he accomplished what the Levitical priesthood could not do, i.e., provide adequate and permanent access to God (7:19).

A further consequence of this abrogation of the Law is the expansiveness of the access to God provided by Christ. Despite the fact that he descended from a tribe that never served at the altar, the advent of his priesthood brought about a broader means of access to God. In 13:10 the author proclaims "we have an altar from which those who served at the tent have no right to eat." Through the abrogation of the Law earthly priesthood ceases to be able to claim a premium on providing access to God. For Hebrews, priesthood is no longer tied to any tribal prerogative, and whatever rights to it that had previously existed no longer stand.

In answer to the question posed in 7:11, the author has shown that the inadequacy of the Levitical priesthood created the need for a new priest, Jesus Christ, whom Hebrews proclaims as the fulfillment of Ps 110:4. His priesthood can bring about the perfection, the purification of the conscience the Law could not attain. Consequently, those he serves have a better hope than they could have had under the Levitical priests, since they are able to approach God in a way that previously was not possible.

Approaching God with hope is a pivotal concern of this passage, which speaks to ancient and modern readers of Hebrews alike. Even though this text refers to an abrogation of the Law in relation to priesthood, its final message is that there has been a transformation of priesthood in Christ, making access to God possible for all people. The message of Hebrews on this point is one of expansiveness and inclusiveness.

FOR REFERENCE AND FURTHER STUDY

Cominskey, J. P. "The Order of Melchizedek," *TBT* 27 (1966) 1913–18.

Gédéon, M. N. "Prééminence de la prêtrise du Christ sur celle des Aaronides dans l'écrit addressé aux Hébreux," *Analecta Bruxellensia* 5 (2000) 81–96.

Horbury, William. "The Aaronic Priesthood in the Epistle to the Hebrews," *JSNT* 19 (1983) 43–71.

Marshall, J. L. "Melchizedek in Hebrews, Philo and Justin Martyr," *SE* 7 (1982) 339–42.

15. *A Priest Forever* (7:20-28)

20. And to the extent that this happened not without oath-taking—for others who became priests took their office without oath-taking, 21. but this one became a priest with oath-taking, by means of the one who said to him, "The Lord has sworn and will not change his mind, 'You are a priest forever'"—22. so also has Jesus become the guarantee of a better covenant. 23. Furthermore, the former priests were many in number because they were prevented by death from continuing in office; 24. but he holds his priesthood permanently, because he continues forever. 25. For which reason he is able for all time to save those who approach God through him, since he always lives to make intercession for them.

26. For it was fitting that we should have such a high priest, holy, blameless, undefiled, separated from sinners, and exalted above the heavens. 27. Unlike the other high priests, he has no need to offer sacrifices day after day, first for his own sins, and then for those of the people; this he did once for all when he offered himself. 28. For the law appoints as high priests those who are subject to weakness, but the word of the oath, which came later than the law, appoints a Son who has been made perfect forever.

NOTES

20. *And to the extent that this happened not without oath-taking:* The verse begins with a correlative construction that is separated from its completion in v. 22 by a parenthetical remark. The author has already used the correlative *kath' hoson*, "to the extent that" (BDAG, 729), in 3:3 where he compares Jesus with Moses. He will use it again in 9:27. Literally the verse begins "and to the extent that not without oath-taking." Something like "this happened" or "this took place" has to be supplied to complete the thought. Elsewhere the author employs correlative constructions at 1:4; 8:6; and 10:25.

for others who became priests took their office without oath-taking: According to the ordination ritual for priests in the Hebrew Bible no oath was required. Exodus 29 and Leviticus 8 specify an elaborate seven-day-long ordination, to be conducted with bathings, investitures, anointings, and sacrifices. There is no mention of oath-taking, although curiously Exod 29:9 does say that the priesthood shall belong to Aaron "forever," in the exact phrase of Ps 110:4, *eis tōn aiōna*.

21. *but this one became a priest with oath-taking, by means of the one who said to him, "The Lord has sworn and will not change his mind, 'You are a priest forever'":* The particle *de*, "but," resumes the comparison begun in the parenthetical remark. "This one" refers to Jesus. The oath-taking, however, was not on his part, as the instrumental clause demonstrates. In this case God was the one who swore the oath, something reminiscent of 6:17 where God swore an oath to confirm the unchangeableness of his purpose. The final time Ps 110:4 is cited now includes a fuller quotation, noting specifically that God swore. As in 6:17 the oath guarantees something that cannot change. At this point the author's interest becomes

clear. The mention of the fact that there was no oath sworn at the ordination of Levitical priests was intended to show the transient nature of their priesthood. The priesthood of Jesus is guaranteed by God's oath, that he is a priest forever. So that there can be no mistake about it the author omits the part of the verse referring to Melchizedek. He has served his purpose in the argument in chapter 7. To mention him here might have confused the issue and led the readers to wonder if the oath God swore applied also to him. The one who is a priest in his likeness is the one who received the guarantee of God's oath.

22. *so also has Jesus become the guarantee of a better covenant:* Now the author completes the correlation begun in v. 20. To the extent that his priesthood was established by an oath, Jesus became the guarantee of a better covenant. Hebrews makes yet another link between priesthood and Law. Earlier the author showed how the inadequacy of the Law brought about a necessary change in the priesthood (7:11-19). Now Jesus can ensure a better covenant because the adequacy of his priesthood to perfect what the Law could not perfect is guaranteed by God's oath. Consequently he becomes the "guarantee" of a better covenant. The noun for "guarantee," *engyos*, may derive from an older word for "hand" and comes to mean "something that is put in the hand" (Herbert Preisker, *engyos, TDNT* 2:329). It is a technical legal term for "collateral" or "security" or for someone who pledges to pay another's debt on default (MM, 179), and is sometimes translated "surety" (KJV, RSV; Hughes, 266). Other translations prefer "guarantee" (NAB, NRSV, NASB, NIV). Since, however, the surety was sometimes a person who covered for another's debts, or a family member (Prov 17:18; 22:26; Sir 29:14-20; cf. 2 Macc 10:28) the translation "guarantor" may also be appropriate (see NEB; Attridge, 208; Bruce, 170; Koester, 363; Montefiore, 127). In addition to being the guarantee of a better covenant, Jesus is the mediator of that covenant as well (8:6; 9:15; 12:24).

The noun "covenant," *diathēkē*, is used in the LXX to translate the Hebrew word *bᵉrîth*, which means an "agreement," an "arrangement," a "contract," or a "covenant" between two parties (HAL, 150–52). Covenant making in Israel had its origins in the custom of treaty making in the Ancient Near East. In the Hebrew Bible the word "covenant" is commonly used to describe a relationship with God, either of an individual or of Israel as a people. The Pentateuch records covenants made with Noah (Gen 9:8-15), Abraham (Gen 15:18-21; 17:1-14), and with Israel at Sinai through Moses (Exod 34:27; cf. 20:1-26). Although the oracle of Nathan, promising perpetuity to the Davidic dynasty, does not use the word covenant, the tradition understood that God had made a covenant with David (2 Sam 23:5; Ps. 89:28, 34). In later times the covenant was reformed under King Josiah (2 Kgs 23:1-3) and Ezra (Ezra 10:3; Neh 9–10). Jeremiah talks of a "new covenant" (31:31-34).

In secular Greek the word *diathēkē* signifies a "testament" or a "will." It almost always has this meaning in papyri and inscriptions (MM, 148). The NT associates the word with the death of Christ (Matt 26:28; Mark 14:24; Luke 22:20; 1 Cor 11:25). Hebrews will develop this tradition in 9:15-22; 10:29; 12:24; 13:20.

23. *Furthermore, the former priests were many in number because they were prevented by death from continuing in office:* The verse begins literally "those who have become

priests," to refer to the Levitical priesthood, hence the "former" priests. The liability of the Levitical priests' mortality was introduced in 7:8 and alluded to again in 7:16. Here the biological fact of their death is exploited to show the inferiority of their priesthood to Christ's. The verb *paramenein* can mean "stay" or "remain by," as in Phil 1:25 and 1 Cor 16:6. It can also mean "continue in an office" or an occupation (BDAG, 769; MM, 487–88). A related noun, *paramonē*, was a legal term for a contract binding someone to remain in service (*paramenein*), such as a slave whose manumission was deferred (LSJ, 1318; S. R. Llewelyn, *New Documents Illustrating Early Christianity*, vol. 6 [North Ryde, N.S.W.: Ancient History Document Research Centre, Macquarie University, 1992] 60–63).

24. *but he holds his priesthood permanently, because he continues forever:* The parallel construction to v. 23 draws the important contrast, which the author wishes to underscore. The adjective "permanent," *aparabatos*, is a legal term meaning "inviolate" or "unchangeable" (MM, 53). The verb "continue," *menein*, parallels *paramenein* of the previous verse. On the chiastic structure of this antithesis see Attridge, 211. "Forever" echoes the previous uses of the expression *eis ton aiōna* in reference to Melchizedek and Jesus in 5:6; 6:20; 7:17, 21.

25. *For which reason he is able for all time to save those who approach God through him, since he always lives to make intercession for them:* The adverb *hothen* draws the inference from the argument of the previous two verses in the sense of "therefore" (BDAG 693). It is a common element in the author's deliberative style (2:17; 3:1; 8:3; 9:18; 11:19).

    The description of Jesus as "able to save" contrasts with the description of the old cult in 10:4, namely, that the blood of bulls and goats is unable (*adynatos*) to take away sins. The adverbial expression "for all time" (*eis to panteles*) carries both a temporal sense (forever) and a modal sense (completely). Whereas in the past commentators may have been split over which to choose, more recent interpreters prefer to retain the ambiguity of the term by including both meanings (Michel, 276; Hughes, 269; Attridge, 210; Lane 1:176; Koester, 365; Long, 88). Thus Jesus saves both "completely" and "for all time."

    Those who are saved are the ones "who approach God through him." Gaining access to God is an important concept for Hebrews. The verb *proserchesthai* has cultic connotations and can mean "come into the presence of a deity" (BDAG, 878; MM, 547). Hebrews certainly uses it this way (4:16; 10:1, 22; 11:6; 12:18, 22). Jesus mediates this access by virtue of his eternal priesthood. The mention that "he always lives" echoes what was said of Melchizedek in 7:8, while affirming the ground of Jesus' priesthood, "the power of an indestructible life," in 7:16. His role as priest is here underscored by the fact that he "intercedes" on behalf of others. The verb *entynchanein* means "appeal to someone" (BDAG, 341). The LXX uses it in this way in Wis 8:21; Dan 6:12; 3 Macc 6:37. The word also means to appeal for or against someone when it is used with the appropriate preposition (1 Macc 8:32; 11:25; *T. Job* 17:5; Rom 8:27; 11:2). Paul uses it in Rom 8:34 for the intercession of the exalted Christ, which is how Hebrews employs it here. Paul, of course, does not relate the intercession to Christ's priesthood (cf. James C. Miller, "Paul and Hebrews: A Comparison of Narrative Worlds," in Gabriela Gelardini, ed., *Hebrews: Contemporary Methods—New Insights.* BINS 75 [Leiden and Boston: Brill, 2005] 260–61). Curiously, Pelagius imported the idea from Hebrews into his interpretation of Rom 8:34 when he wrote that Christ "as true and eternal high priest intercedes as he continually shows and offers that human nature which he assumed as a pledge to his Father" (*Expositio in Romanos*, quoted by Joseph A. Fitzmyer, *Romans: A New Translation with Introduction and Commentary*. AB 33 [New York: Doubleday, 1993] 533). Since Hebrews is a Roman document it is not implausible that Paul's thought in Rom 8:34 was a source for this aspect of the author's christology (Dieter Georgi, "Hebrews and the Heritage of Paul," in Gabriela Gelardini, ed., *Hebrews: Contemporary Methods—New Insights*, 239–44). In 9:24 the author's meaning about Christ's priestly intercession in heaven will be made clear.

26. *For it was fitting that we should have such a high priest:* In 2:10 the author described as "fitting to God" the perfection of the Son through suffering (see the Interpretation at 2:10-18); now he attributes the propriety of the Son's priesthood to his readers. The appropriateness of such a priest is predicated on the nature of his priesthood as described here and in vv. 27-28, where its propriety is based on his once for all sacrifice that completes his perfection.

holy, blameless, undefiled, separated from sinners, and exalted above the heavens: The nature of Christ's priesthood is described by a series of terms that one might expect to characterize a priest. In the LXX "holy," *hosios*, often translates the Hebrew adjective *ḥasîd*, where it can be applied to a person who practices *ḥesed*, "solidarity" or "loyalty" to God under the covenant (Deut 33:8; Pss 11:2; 17:26; 29:5; 36:28; 49:5; 85:2; 149:1; Wis 4:15). The adjective occurs only here in Hebrews, which like the NT in general prefers *hagios* (2:4; 3:1, 7; 6:4, 10; 8:2; 9:1, 2, 3, 8, 12, 24, 25; 10:15, 19; 13:11, 24). Josephus (*Antiquities* 19.332) tells an interesting story of a certain Simon from Jerusalem who denounced King Agrippa as "unholy," *ouch hosios*, and said that on that basis he should be prevented from entering the Temple, because entrance was forbidden to anyone who was ritually unclean (*euages*).

"Blameless," *akakos*, carries the sense of "innocent" and occurs only here and in Rom 16:18 in the NT. "Undefiled," *amiantos*, is also a rare word in the NT. James 1:27 applies it to "religion" and 1 Pet 1:4 refers it to a heavenly inheritance. It is almost as rare in the LXX (Wis 3:13; 4:2; 8:20; 2 Macc 14:36; 15:34), where it is related to ethical or ritual purity. The concept is well represented among the prescriptions of the Law in the LXX by prohibitions against defilement or pollution, often of a ritual nature and sometimes pertaining to priests (*miansis:* Lev 13:44; *miainein:* Lev 11:24, 44; 13:3, 8, 11, 14, 15, 20, 44, 59; 15:31, 32; 18:24, 25, 27, 28, 30; 21:1, 3, 4; 22:5, 8; Num 5:3, 13, 14, 19, 27, 28, 29; 6:7, 9, 12; 19:13, 20; 35:34; Deut 21:23; 24:4; cf. *miasmos:* Wis 14:26).

The placement of the expression "separated from sinners" makes its interpretation difficult. The primary meaning of the verb *chōrizein* is "be separated by space." In that sense the expression looks to the next qualification of Jesus' priesthood and means that he is separated from sinners by virtue of his heavenly exaltation. If, however, one reads the expression in relation to what precedes it, then it means that Jesus is different from sinners, something already stated in 4:15. Both meanings were probably intended by the author (BDAG, 1095; Attridge, 213; Koester, 363; Lane 1:176). The Mishnah tells of the separation of the high priest from his house seven days before the Day of Atonement (*m. Yoma* 1,1). The priest who was to burn the red heifer was separated from his house seven days before, during which time he underwent daily purifications (*m. Parah* 3,1). In both instances the object of the separation was to prevent ritual defilement (Str-B 3:696).

"Exalted above the heavens" literally means "higher than the heavens" (*hypsēloteros tōn ouranōn*). The place of his exaltation is described in 1:3 as "on high" (*en hypsēlois*). The process of exaltation required that he "pass through the heavens" in 4:14. In 8:1 Jesus is in heaven seated next to the throne of God, and in 9:24 he has entered into heaven itself.

27. *Unlike the other high priests, he has no need to offer sacrifices day after day, first for his own sins, and then for those of the people:* The daily sacrifices were made in the morning and the evening (Exod 29:38-42; Num 28:3-8), but the double sacrifice was required only for the Day of Atonement. On the necessity of many sacrifices see Philo, *Moses* 2.159. The author correctly notes this in 9:6, but here he has confused it with the daily sacrifices. Since Jesus is sinless (4:15), he has no need to offer sacrifice for his sins. Also, the author seems interested only in sin offerings and does not include the other types of sacrifices prescribed, i.e., grain and drink offerings. The priests' sin offering was not done daily, according to Lev 4:3. Strack-Billerbeck cautions that the expression "day after day" should be understood more loosely to mean that the priest offered the sacrifice on the day he had to offer it (3:698). That interpretation goes against the usual meaning of *kath' hēmeran*, "daily." Commentators who see a conflation of the daily sacrifices with those made for the Day of Atonement are on firmer ground (Attridge, 213; Koester, 368; Lane 1:194; Weiss, 424).

this he did once for all when he offered himself: The difference between the priesthood of Jesus and the Levitical priests lies in the "once for all" nature of his sacrifice (9:12, 26). Earlier he differed from them in their mortality, which required a succession of priests. He remains forever, and is singular. This was an argument for the superiority of his priesthood over theirs. Now that superiority is solidified by the quality of his sacrifice. "Once for all" encompasses both temporal (non-repeated) and modal (thorough) senses, as it does in 10:10. There was no need to repeat the sacrifice, not only because his death only occurred once but also because his sacrifice was so effective that it did not need to be repeated. He did what the Levitical priests could not do, namely, free people from the consciousness of sin (7:11; 10:2-4), by which the author means freedom from the guilt of one's past sins, which was gained in baptism (10:2, 14, 17-18, 22; see the Introduction, 7. *Conscience/Consciousness of Sin in Hebrews*). The contrast between the two priesthoods will be drawn again in 9:24-28.

The verb "offer," *anapherein*, is a synonym for *prospherein*. The latter is more common in Hebrews (20x), whereas the former occurs only here and in 9:28 and 13:15. Both verbs are used frequently in the LXX. Whereas the image of Jesus as a High Priest offering himself as a sacrifice is unique to Hebrews, the concept that he sacrificed himself for others is not (Mark 10:45; Luke 1:68; 24:21; Rom 3:24; 1 Cor 1:30; Eph 1:7; Col 1:14; Titus 2:14; 1 Pet 1:18-19).

28. *For the law appoints as high priests those who are subject to weakness, but the word of the oath, which came later than the law, appoints a Son who has been made perfect for-*

ever: The weakness of the Law has already been alluded to in 7:18. The fact that priests have weaknesses has provided two important elements that contrast with the priesthood of Christ. First, they sin (7:27), whereas he is sinless (4:15); and then they are mortal (7:23), whereas he lives forever (7:24-25).

Placing the oath (Ps 110:4) chronologically later than the Law, the author believes (like other NT authors) that David authored the Psalms (Luke 20:42-43; Acts 2:25-28, 34-35; Rom 4:6; 11:9-10).

INTERPRETATION

The previous section (7:11-19) established a link between the priesthood and the Law, with an eye to positing an inherent weakness in both, which required a new priesthood. This new priesthood could accomplish its purpose in a way other than the Levitical priesthood could, because it was able to purify the conscience. Thus there was a change in the priesthood that required a change in the Law (7:12). That change in Law was an abrogation (7:18) bringing about something greater, a better hope for greater access to God (7:19).

This section continues the argument for the superiority of Jesus' priesthood by focusing on two things. First, it is assured by an oath sworn by God; and second, the priest so appointed, Jesus, is the guarantee of a better covenant. There is a further expansion on the relationship of priesthood and Law. The section is structured in four parts: the importance of the oath (vv. 20-22); the permanence of Jesus' priesthood (vv. 23-25); the effectiveness of his priesthood (vv. 26-27); and a conclusion (v. 28).

The author invokes the power of an oath to offer his readers assurance. In 6:16 an oath is characterized as final, putting an end to all dispute. There God's oath ensures the promise made to Abraham which, for the readers of Hebrews, means that they can be confident of the hope that is set before them (6:18). In 6:19-20 that hope is described as a sure and steadfast anchor that reaches even into the inner shrine where Jesus has gone as a High Priest according to the order of Melchizedek. Those verses provided the transition to the discussion of the priesthood of Melchizedek and the priesthood of Jesus. In yet another effort to assure his readers that this priesthood is valid and permanent, the author returns to the power of the oath. Here the oath sworn in Ps 110:4 establishes the ground for a new priesthood according to the order of Melchizedek. If the Levitical priesthood was linked to the Law, the priesthood of Jesus has no such link, since the Law had to be abrogated for him to be a priest (7:13-14). The legitimation of Jesus' priesthood was the power of an indestructible life, his resurrection and exaltation. Now the author turns to a discussion of what guarantees that he is a legitimate priest: an oath sworn by God.

The previous section (vv.11-19) argued also for another priesthood on the basis of the inability of the Levitical priesthood to attain perfection. Here that perfection is guaranteed because Christ's priesthood was assured by God's oath. The author avers that the Levitical priests became priests without taking an oath, but the real point is that in relation to the Levitical priests God swore no oath that would guarantee their continuance in office.

As in 6:18-20, God's oath functions to assure the readers that their hope is anchored by the promise of a better covenant. Since the Law was abrogated, the readers may wonder about the status of the covenant. Hebrews is clear that there will be a new covenant (8:1-13). Within that discussion Jesus, as priest, will be described as a mediator of a better covenant. Here the author anticipates that point by showing how a better covenant is assured by the oath God swore in relation to Jesus' priesthood.

Even though the Law is not the ground of Jesus' priesthood and the old relationship between the priesthood and the Law has been severed, the author wants to show that in relation to a better covenant there is a better priesthood. One substantial difference between the Levitical priesthood and Jesus' is that his is permanent. The most obvious reason for this is that the Levitical priests were mortal (7:8) and were prevented from continuing in office (7:23). Since the oath sworn by God proclaims Jesus a priest forever, it stands to reason that he is a better mediator. Permanence has the advantage of continual and complete intercession (7:25). Here the question of the mediation of the priests is engaged. Since the Levitical priesthood was unable to purify the consciences of sinners, it rather made them conscious of sin (7:11; 10:2-4). The author ties that weakness to the mortality of the Levitical priests, which required that they replace one another. Jesus, on the other hand, makes it possible for those who approach God to be perfected (10:14) because he continues forever in his role as priest.

The eternal nature of Jesus' priesthood is supported in v. 28 by the title "Son." Reverting to "Son" (v. 28) echoes 5:5-6, where Ps 2:7 is joined to Ps 110:4. It may also recall for the reader the opening chapters of the letter, which established the superiority of the Son over the angels (2:5-14) and over Moses (3:1-6). The link between Jesus as Son and High Priest was first established in 1:3. Thus it is appropriate here to show that the better High Priest is the Son as well.

In this passage the author provides his readers with important information about the nature of Jesus' priesthood. In many ways it is superior to the priesthood of the old covenant: First, because he is Son, Jesus is a better priest and a better mediator. Second, because he is holy and blameless he does not need to offer sacrifices for his own sins. His was a once for all offering. Third, his priesthood is eternal. He has been perfected forever and appointed by God rather than by the Law. Fourth, his priesthood is guaranteed by an oath. If the readers need assurance that Jesus is a better High Priest and mediator of a better covenant, the author has met their need. In the actualization of Ps 110:4 Hebrews grounds Jesus' status as High Priest on a principle that confirms God's trustworthiness. The readers can have no better assurance than what they receive in a divine oath (6:17-18).

For Reference and Further Study

Brooks, Walter E. "The Perpetuity of Christ's Sacrifice in the Epistle to the Hebrews," *JBL* 89 (1970) 205–14.
Lorimer, W. L. "Hebrews VII 23f.," *NTS* 13 (1966–67) 386–87.
Martin, François. "Le Christ médiateur dans l'Épître aux Hébreux," *Sémiotique et Bible* 97 (2000) 37–45.
März, Claus-Peter. "'Wir haben einen Hohenpriester. . . .' Anmerkungen zur kulttheologischen Argumentation des Hebräerbriefes," in Marlis Gielen and Joachim Kügler, eds., *Liebe, Macht und Religion*. Stuttgart: Katholisches Bibelwerk, 2003, 237–52.
Vanhoye, Albert. *La Lettre aux Hébreux: Jesús-Christ, médiateur d'une nouvelle alliance*. Jésus et Jésus-Christ 84. Paris: Desclée, 2002.

16. *Jesus, the High Priest* (8:1-6)

1. Now the main point in what we are saying is this: we have such a high priest, one who is seated at the right hand of the throne of the Majesty in the heavens, 2. a minister in the sanctuary and the true tent that the Lord, and not any human, has set up. 3. For every high priest is appointed to offer gifts and sacrifices; hence it is necessary for this priest also to have something to offer. 4. Now if he were on earth, he would not be a priest at all, since there are priests who offer gifts according to the law. 5. They serve in a sanctuary that is an example and a shadow of the heavenly one; for Moses, when he was about to erect the tent, was warned, "See that you make everything according to the pattern that was shown you on the mountain." 6. As a matter of fact, he has now obtained a more excellent ministry, to the degree that he is the mediator of a better covenant, which has been enacted through better promises.

Notes

1. *Now the main point in what we are saying is this:* The "main point," *kephalaion*, is related to the Greek noun for head (*kephalē*). Thus it comes to mean "chief" or

"main point" (Epictetus, *Dissertations* 1.24.20; Isocrates, *Orations* 3.62; Josephus, *Antiquities* 17.93; *Against Apion* 1.219; Philo, *On Dreams*, 1.235; *Allegorical Interpretation* 2.102; *Special Laws* 2.39; Plato, *Gorgias* 453A; *Timaeus* 26C; BDAG, 541; LSJ, 944–45; MM, 342). It can also mean something that has been counted, such as a sum of money, a census, or an inventory of things, a usage reflected in the LXX (Lev 5:24; Num 4:2; 31:26, 49) and in Acts 22:28.

we have such a high priest: The adjectival phrase "such a high priest," *toiouton archierea*, recalls the assertion of 7:26 and looks ahead to the development of the argument in this section of the sermon (Attridge, 217).

seated at the right hand of the throne of the Majesty in the heavens: This allusion to Ps 110:1 echoes a similar allusion in 1:3. The expression "seated at the right hand of the throne" has two aspects in Hebrews. First, it locates the exalted Lord (12:2), and second, it signifies the completion of his priestly work (1:3; 10:12). Whereas the LXX speaks of God's throne (Isa 6:1; 66:1; Jer 14:21; Ezek 1:26; 43:7; Pss 9:4, 8; 10:4 [in heaven]; 44:7 [eternal]; 46:8 [holy]; 92:2; 96:2; 103:19 [established in the heavens]; Prov 8:27; Wis 9:4, 10 [throne of your glory]; Sir 1:8) and of God's majesty (Deut 32:3; Tob 12:6; 13:4; Pss 78:11; 92:1; 145:3; 150:2; Prov 18:10; Wis 18:24; Sir 2:18; 18:5; 39:15; 44:2), it does not speak of the "throne of the Majesty."

2. *a minister in the sanctuary and the true tent that the Lord, and not any human, has set up:* The noun for "minister," *leitourgos*, in the LXX commonly refers to a servant, a minister, an attendant, or an assistant (Josh 1:1[A]; 2 Kgdms 13:18; 3 Kgdms 10:5; 4 Kgdms 4:43; 6:15; 2 Chr 9:4; Pss 102:21; 103:4; Sir 10:2). It can also refer to priests (Isa 61:6; Sir 7:30; 2 Esdr 20:40). Normally the word for a "temple" or "sanctuary" in the LXX is *naos* or *hieron*. Hebrews calls it a *hagion*, which simply means a "holy thing," but which the author takes to mean a "holy place." Despite the ambiguity of the term *hagion*, the frequent use of it in Hebrews for the "sanctuary" suggests that meaning here (9:2, 3, 12, 24, 25; 10:19; 13:11). So Jesus is not a "minister of holy things" (Philo, *Allegorical Interpretation* 3.135) but is rather a "minister of the sanctuary" (Philo, *Flight and Finding* 93; MM, 4).

How both entities relate to one another in this verse is not clear, and the matter is not helped by Lev 16:16, which uses *hagion* to refer to the inner sanctuary, the Holy of Holies, and *skēnē* for the tent of meeting (see also Lev 16:20, 23; Num 3:38). In Lev 10:4 *hagion* seems to refer to the entire entity encompassing both the tent and the sanctuary. The LXX of Exod 29:30 prescribes that one of Aaron's sons go into the tent of meeting (*skēnē*) to minister (*leitourgein*) by means of holy things (*en tois hagiois*). The Hebrew has the singular "in the sanctuary" (*baqodesh*). Another curious example is Lev 21:23, dealing with the case of an ineligible priest: "But he shall not come near the curtain or approach the altar, because he has a blemish, that he may not profane my sanctuaries (*haq^edashîm*); for I am the Lord; I sanctify them." The LXX changes the plural to a singular (*hagion*) but retains the plural at the end of the verse, "them." Given the blurring of the distinction between "sanctuary" and "tent" in the LXX, perhaps one ought not to expect from the author of Hebrews greater clarity on their relationship. In 9:11-12 he seems to make a distinction between the tent and the sanctuary, and so it is likely that he intends the same here. The two terms should not be taken as synonyms.

That the tent was set up by God affirms its heavenly nature. The verb "pitch," *pegnynai*, is the usual term for pitching an actual tent. There is one OT text, Num 24:6, that portrays God as pitching tents, but the image is somewhat accidental. The translator of the LXX understood the Hebrew *ka²ªhalîm*, "like aloes," in Num 24:6 as *ka²ohalîm*, "like tents," thus changing the Hebrew text from "like aloes that the Lord has planted" to "like tents that the Lord has pitched." References to the Lord's "tent" are found in LXX Pss 26:5-6; 30:21; 77:60. The tent is not pitched by human hands, in contrast to what is said in 9:24 about the earthly sanctuary. For the understanding of the heavenly Temple in Judaism see Attridge, 222–24, and Cody, *Heavenly Sanctuary*, 9–46.

3. *For every high priest is appointed to offer gifts and sacrifices; hence it is necessary for this priest also to have something to offer:* The author repeats what he said in 5:1. The difference is that there the idea introduced a discussion of how the high priest is chosen and what are his qualifications to mediate between humans and God. Here the author is interested in showing that Christ is the true high priest, who also of necessity must have something to offer. His offering has already been mentioned in 7:27 ("himself"), something the author will elaborate on in 10:5-10.

4. *Now if he were on earth, he would not be a priest at all, since there are priests who offer gifts according to the law:* The previous chapter played the mortality of the Levitical priests off the eternity of Jesus' priesthood. The author showed there that Jesus had no claim to earthly priestly office (7:13-14). Here his intention is not to invalidate the high priesthood of Jesus, but to place it in a different context. Jesus was not entitled under the "fleshy law" (7:16) to be a priest, since he is not a priest "according to the law" (*kata nomon*) (7:16, 18) but according to the power of an indestructible life (7:16).

5. *They serve in a sanctuary that is an example and shadow of the heavenly one:* "Serve," *latreuein*, is sometimes synonymous with "minister," *leitourgein*. Both are common in the LXX (*latreuein:* Num 16:9; 1 Esdr 4:54; Sir 4:14; *leitourgein:* Exod 28:35, 43; Num 3:6, 31; 1 Kgdms 2:11). The noun for "copy," *hypodeigma*, was used in 4:11 with the meaning "example." This is its meaning in Sir 44:16 and 2 Macc 6:28. An example need not only be a moral one, and so the translation seems appropriate here.

   According to the author, the earthly sanctuary is an "example," *hypodeigma*, and a "shadow," *skia*, of the heavenly sanctuary. God had shown Moses the pattern of the sanctuary while he was on the mountain. The author of Hebrews believes that the earthly construction was not an exact copy of that. How could it be, since it was material? Rather, it was an example, something patterned on the heavenly prototype. That is why Hebrews uses the Greek noun *hypodeigma*, a cognate of *paradeigma*, a pattern or a model. If the author had been thinking in Platonic terms he would have referred to the earthly counterpart as a *mimēma*, a copy. The heavenly reality the author envisioned was probably like the heavenly sanctuary as described in Hellenistic Judaism. *Testament of Levi* 3:4-8 is helpful: "In the uppermost heaven of all dwells the Great Glory in the Holy of Holies superior to all holiness. There with him are the archangels, who serve and offer propitiatory sacrifices to the Lord in behalf of all the sins of ignorance of the righteous ones. They present to the Lord a pleasing odor, a rational and bloodless oblation. In the heaven below them are the messengers who carry the responses to the angels in the Lord's presence. There with him are the thrones and authorities; their praises to God are offered eternally" (translation by Howard Clark Kee in Charlesworth 1:789). Two chapters later it is described again in 5:1: "And an angel opened the gates of heaven for me and I saw the holy temple (*ton naon ton hagion*), and the Most High on the throne of glory" (ibid. 1:789). See also 2 Bar 4:3-6 (Cody, *Heavenly Sanctuary*, 9–46). God's throne is in a heavenly sanctuary.

Whether the author of Hebrews has been influenced by the dichotomy between the real world and the shadow world of Platonism is difficult to ascertain. It is likely that he is simply making a distinction between the earthly and the heavenly, so as to contrast the priesthood of Christ with the Levitical priesthood. On the problems with likening the thought of Hebrews to Platonism see Koester, 97–100.

when he was about to erect the tent, was warned, "See that you make everything according to the pattern that was shown you on the mountain": The author seems to assume that when Moses was on the mountain he had seen the pattern of the heavenly sanctuary, on which the earthly was to be modeled. The citation is a composite taken mainly from Exod 25:40 with the addition of "everything" from Exod 25:9. Faithful to the LXX with minor variations, Hebrews adds "everything," *panta*, because of the reference to "all" in Exod 25:9, which encompasses the sanctuary and its furnishings. Exodus 25:40 refers only to the lampstand and the utensils described in vv. 31-38. Hebrews may have been influenced by the final words of Wis 9:8, "You have commanded me to build a temple (*naon*) on your holy mountain and an altar (*thysiasterion*) in the city of your habitation, a copy (*mimēma*) of the holy tent (*skēnēs hagias*) that you prepared from the beginning." Wisdom's choice of *mimēma* for "copy" shows the influence of Platonism. In this text "holy tent" does not refer to the tent in the wilderness but to a heavenly archetype (see David Winston, *The Wisdom of Solomon: A New Translation with Introduction and Commentary*. AB 43 [New York: Doubleday, 1979] 203–205). The verb "warn," *chrematizein*, refers to oracular speech (LXX: Job 40:3; Jer 32:30 [bis]; 33:2 [bis]; 36:23; 37:2; 43:2, 4; NT: Matt 2:12, 22; Luke 2:26; Acts 10:22). Plutarch employs the verb in relation to the functioning of the Oracle at Delphi (*Moralia* 435C). In certain papyri *chrematizein* has the meaning of requesting or receiving an answer from a god (MM, 692; cf. Philo, *Moses* 2.238; Josephus, *Antiquities* 3.212).

6. *As a matter of fact, he has now obtained a more excellent ministry:* The temporal adverb *nuni* introduces a real condition after one that is contrary to fact; thus the translation "as a matter of fact" (BDAG, 682). In 1:4 the Son was described as having a "more excellent name." Here the comparative *diaphorōteras* is used again, now to modify "ministry." "Ministry," *leitourgia*, is from the LXX, where it occurs 45 times (see, e.g., Num 18:6, 7, 21, 23, 31).

to the degree that he is the mediator of a better covenant: Hebrews introduced the notion of a "better covenant" in 7:22, where Jesus was described as its guarantee. Here it is repeated in relation to the more excellent ministry he exercises as priest. "Mediator," *mesitēs*, is a common legal term in secular Greek, where it means "arbiter" (see Job 9:33), although in one papyrus (P. Lond. 370) it means "surety" (MM, 399). Philo refers to Moses as a *mesitēs* who reconciles the people to God at Sinai (*Moses* 2.166), and Paul thinks of him as a mediator of the Law in Gal 3:19. The Son had already been presented as superior to Moses in 3:1-6, where he is also referred to as the "apostle and high priest of our confession." It is logical that if Jesus is the mediator of another covenant it will be a better one, since the mediator is also better.

which has been enacted through better promises: Completing the trilogy of comparatives is the notion of "better promises," which are the ground of the better covenant's promulgation. In the LXX, the verb "enact," *nomothetein*, refers to legislating (Exod 24:12; Deut 17:10; 2 Macc 3:15; 4 Macc 5:25) or "teaching legal or ritual matters" (Ps 118:33), or "moral instruction in the ways of God" (Ps 24:8, 12; 26:11). Josephus uses it of Moses in *Against Apion* 1.284 and *Antiquities* 1.19. Philo uses it of God (*Allegorical Interpretation* 3.142; *Posterity and Exile of Cain* 143; *Unchangeableness of God* 61; *Moses* 2.192; *Special Laws* 1.161, 234), of Moses (*On Agriculture* 2; *Moses* 2.9; *On the Decalogue* 9), and of legislators in general (*On Drunkenness* 64; *On Sobriety* 46). In *Special Laws* 1.82 Philo uses the verb to describe what is legislated for the vestments of priests and the schedule of their ministry (see 1.140; 1.198) as well as the "enactments" of other laws (*Special Laws* 2.35, 39, 110, 120, 239; 3.80, 136; 4.11, 105).

"Promise," *epangelia*, is an important word for the author (4:1; 6:12, 15, 17; 7:6; 8:6; 9:15; 10:36; 11:9 [bis], 13, 17, 33, 39). He has assured his readers that, as heirs of the promise, they will receive an eternal inheritance (9:15; 10:36; 11:39-40; cf. 6:12) that contrasts with the earthly inheritance promised to Abraham (6:13-20; 11:9-12). The author notes ultimately that neither he nor his descendants received the eternal inheritance (11:13, 39). Only here are the promises referred to as "better," doubtless because they are the foundation of a "better covenant" but also because the inheritance, which is their object, is "better" than the homeland Abraham desired, since it is a heavenly one (11:16).

INTERPRETATION

As the first verse of this section indicates, the author is presenting his main point. The central argument of Hebrews runs from 8:1–10:18, and is the exposition of Christ as High Priest. The entire argument comprises a series of smaller sections, each providing a window into how the author understood the person and work of Christ in the process of salvation. This first section, 8:1-6, begins by drawing on the exaltation theme of 1:5-14, thus placing Christ, the High Priest, in the heavenly realm, the sphere of his cultic activity. This heavenly sanctuary is contrasted with the earthly Tabernacle before the section closes with the observation that as a priest Christ mediates a better covenant. The second section, 8:7-13, reflects on the nature of that better covenant, highlighting how it differs from the first covenant, with the help of the citation from Jer 31:31-34. The third section, 9:1-10, takes a closer look at the ritual of the old covenant and how, by design, it was unable to perfect the conscience of the worshiper. The fourth section, 9:11-14, presents the ritual of the new covenant in order to contrast the once for all sacrifice of Christ with the once-a-year service of the earthly high priest. The a fortiori argument of 9:11-14 reaches the conclusion that the ritual of the new covenant accomplished what the ritual of the former covenant could not, i.e., the purification of the conscience of the worshiper. The fifth section, 9:15-22, addresses the necessary death of the mediator. The sixth section, 9:23-28, focuses more specifically on the heavenly sanctuary as the locus of Christ's purifying ritual. The seventh and final section, 10:1-18, draws the logical conclusion of previous comparisons between the old and the new, i.e., the blood of goats and bulls cannot purify the conscience of sin. Therefore sacrifices are replaced by the will of God to sanctify worshipers through the self-offering of Jesus Christ, which brings about the perfection that the first covenant was unable to effect. The ultimate proof of that fact is that, unlike the priests of old, Christ, having once offered his service, was exalted and took his place at the right hand of God. These last verses conclude with a summary excerpt from Jer 31:33-34.

The opening verse of the passage under discussion here, 8:1-6, depicts the exalted Christ seated at the right hand of the throne of the Majesty in the heavens, an allusion to Ps 110 (109):1. Here Christ is not merely seated at the right hand of God, but is placed at the right of the throne of the Majesty; he is in a position of honor. The author is probably thinking back to 1:5-14, where he developed the superiority of the Son over the angels. There he included in the catena of scriptural citations one from Ps 45:6 (LXX: 45:7) and directed it specifically to the Son: "Your throne, O God, is forever and ever. . . ." Thus he imagines Christ seated on a throne alongside the throne of the Majesty.

Having identified Christ as a High Priest (v. 1) and a minister (v. 2), the author begins to compare him with the former priests who served at the Tabernacle. First, the nature of the place of their respective ministry is different, for the former priests served in a sanctuary made by humans, but the heavens are the works of God's hands (1:10; 9:11). Hence this space is referred to as the true tent (cf. 9:24). The heavenly sanctuary as described in Hebrews need not reflect direct Platonic influence in the author's thought, as the idea was already represented in Hellenistic Judaism (see the Notes at v. 2 above; Attridge, 222–24; Koester, 380; Weiss, 436–38). The author envisions here the transcendent reality of the sanctuary, where he imagines the exalted Christ now to be, having completed his self-offering. The argument was made earlier in the comparison with Melchizedek that Christ did not cease to be a priest once his offering was made (7:3, 21, 24). In his present capacity, and in proximity to the throne of God, he still intercedes on behalf of worshipers (7:25). Space and time have converged for the author at this point.

Nevertheless the comparison continues now to help his readers grasp a difficult claim. The subject of v. 3 is the matter of the offerings. As with every high priest, Jesus had to have something to offer. But just as has already been said in 7:27, there is a real difference. The former priests were obligated to offer sacrifices daily and repeatedly. Christ, on the other hand, made a once for all offering of himself. Furthermore, he could do this only because he was the eternal Son, for were he on earth he would not be a priest at all.

Hebrews proposes a novel idea in portraying Christ as the High Priest. The traditions handed down about the earthly Jesus never claimed that he descended from a priestly line. This had already been acknowledged in 7:13-14. So the author has to rely on his belief that there has been a real change in the priesthood (7:12) in order develop his thought on the priesthood of Christ. The one-time self-offering of Jesus on the cross shows a real difference between his priestly service and the service of Levitical priests. The fact that his sacrifice cannot be repeated serves as a basis for a real comparison between the two priesthoods, to the disadvantage of the Levitical priesthood.

According to the author's working definition of priesthood, lineage is not an important factor. Rather, a priest is someone who offers gifts and sacrifices (v. 3), an echo of 5:1. Already established, too, was the fact that like any high priest Jesus was called and had not appointed himself (5:5). Call is stressed over descent. In chapter 5 the author took pains to show how Jesus met the requirements for the priesthood, from divine appointment to sacrificial offering. Under his working definition he implicitly affirms everything said in 5:1-10 by examining the way Christ is and continues to be a priest, even after the sacrificial work had been completed. He establishes a link between this central part of the sermon and what has preceded it, helping to unify the whole.

The final verse of this section establishes that Jesus' ministry was in fact a better one than that exercised by those who were priests by lineage, and so the fact that on earth Jesus would not have been a priest seems not to be that important to the author after all. How he arrives at that conclusion is a bit complicated, and he does it sequentially. First he claims that Jesus was the mediator of a better covenant. Earlier, in 7:22, this same claim was made and was backed up by the fact that God had sworn an oath, "You are a priest forever." As an eternal mediator, then, Jesus was the mediator of a better covenant. In 9:15 the idea will be developed further, with the rationale that his death was redemptive. Finally, he will be part of the heavenly Jerusalem, where the readers will look to him precisely as a mediator of a new covenant because his blood speaks more graciously than Abel's (12:24).

The first covenant was certainly mediated by Moses. In Hellenistic Judaism it was also believed that it was mediated by angels, due to the LXX translation of Deut 33:2, where the Hebrew word *ešdat*, translated "host" in the NRSV, became *angeloi*, "angels." The tradition of the role of angels in mediating the Law is represented in texts such as *Jub* 1:29 and Josephus, *Antiquities* 15.136. The New Testament knows of the tradition as well (Acts 7:38, 53; Gal 3:19; see Str-B 3:554–56). Christ's superiority to the angels, then, would not only make him a mediator of a better covenant, but a better mediator than the angels were.

These first six verses present key elements of the argument of the subsequent chapters, and they anticipate the final segment of this entire argument (10:11-18). There the liturgical movement of Christ from sacrifice to session is summarized by emphasizing yet again the comparison of the two priesthoods, old and new. Earthly priests stand in their service, repeating sacrifices that are unable to remove sin. Christ, on the other hand, offered the single sacrifice for the removal of sin and then sat down at the right hand of God. From that point on there was no need to offer further sacrifices, as was confirmed by the text of Jer 31:33-34.

As a good preacher, the author of Hebrews makes clear what his main point is. Effective preaching requires that the preacher not attempt to make too many points, which might confuse and distract the listeners from what his or her real message is. In a sermon as long as Hebrews it is especially helpful at the beginning of the sermon's central argument for the author to call attention to the heart of his message. That the readers are not without a high priest of their own is the core idea of Hebrews. The expression "we have" not only reminds the readers that Christ is their High Priest but ties this central idea to what had preceded in the sermon and to what will follow. In fact, if one considers the objects of the expression "we have" in Hebrews one will find how the central idea of Christ as High Priest brings additional benefits that the readers "have." In 4:14-15 they have a great high priest who has been tested as they were. At 6:19 they have a "hope" that enters the sanctuary with him. Here in 8:1 they have an exalted High Priest. In 10:19 they themselves have "confidence" to enter the sanctuary. At 10:21 they have a great high priest over the house of God. In 13:10 they have an "altar" of their own. Finally, in 13:14 they have "no lasting city" here on earth. "We have" points to the sermon's central contention that Jesus is a great High Priest and to many of the most important consequences the author understands to derive from Christ in that role. Even though the tense of "we have" is present, the expression points to the future as well, showing how the readers already possess their final destiny.

For Reference and Further Study

Attridge, Harold W. "The Uses of Antithesis in Hebrews 8–10," *HTR* 79 (1986) 1–9.
Lee, Edwin K. "Words Denoting 'Pattern' in the New Testament," *NTS* 8 (1961–62) 166–73.

Moule, C. F. D. "Sanctuary and Sacrifice in the Church of the New Testament," *JTS* n.s. 1 (1950) 29–41.

Sabourin, Léopold. "Liturgie sanctuaire et de la tente véritable (Hébr. VIII.2)," *NTS* 18 (1971–72) 87–90.

Vanhoye, Albert. "La structure centrale de l'Épître Hébreux (Héb. 8/1-9/28)," *RSR* 47 (1949) 44–60.

17. *The New Covenant* (8:7-13)

7. For if that first one had been faultless, a place would not be sought for a second. 8. God finds fault with them when he says: "The days are surely coming, says the Lord, when I will complete a new covenant with the house of Israel and with the house of Judah; 9. not like the covenant that I made with their ancestors, on the day when I took them by the hand to lead them out of the land of Egypt; for they did not remain in my covenant, and so I had no concern for them, says the Lord. 10. This is the covenant that I will make with the house of Israel after those days, says the Lord: I will put my laws in their minds, and write them on their hearts, and I will be their God, and they shall be my people. 11. And they shall not teach one another or say to each other, 'Know the Lord,' for they shall all know me, from the least of them to the greatest. 12. For I will be merciful toward their iniquities, and I will remember their sins no more." 13. In speaking of "a new covenant," he has made the first one obsolete. And what is obsolete and growing old will soon disappear.

NOTES

7. *For if that first one had been faultless, a place would not be sought for a second:* As in 7:11 the author makes his point by means of a contrary-to-fact conditional sentence (see 8:4). There is some ambiguity in the absence of a noun qualified by the adjective "first." Two feminine singular nouns precede it, "ministry" and "covenant" (8:6). In view of the repetition of the adjective "first" in v. 13, the author must be referring to the first or earlier covenant. "Faultless," *amemptos*, is a standard biblical term for being "blameless" or "righteous," referring to individuals or to Israel as a whole (Gen 17:1; Job 1:1, 8; 2:3; 4:17; 9:20; 11:4; 12:4; 15:14; 22:3; 22:19; 33:9; Wis 10:5, 15; 18:21; Luke 1:6; Phil 2:15; 3:6; 1 Thess 3:13). "Place," *topos*, is used idiomatically here in the sense of "occasion," "reason," or "opportunity" (see LXX: Sir 4:5; 13:22; 19:17; 38:12; NT: Acts 25:16; Rom 12:19; Eph 4:27; Plutarch, *On the Control of Anger* 462B; Josephus, *Antiquities* 16.190, 258).

8. *God finds fault with them when he says:* The sense of "find fault," *memphesthai*, in the LXX is "assign blame" (Sir 11:7; 41:7). Paul uses it in Rom 9:19 and a variant

reading of Mark 7:2 employs it in relation to the Pharisees' criticism of Jesus' disciples for breaking the Law (K N W Q 0278 *f*¹·¹³ 28. (33). 565. 700. 2542 *pm* lat co).

the days are surely coming, says the Lord: The introductory formula "says the Lord" occurs often in the LXX, always spoken by a prophet, with most occasions in Jeremiah (1 Kgdms 2:31; 4 Kgdms 20:17; Amos 4:2; 8:11; 9:13; Zech 14:1; Isa 39:6; Jer 7:32; 9:24; 16:14; 19:6; 23:5; 28:52; 30:18; 31:12; 37:3; 38:27, 31, 38). The author prefers to use *legein* or one of its compounds to introduce scriptural citations (2:6, 12; 3:7, 15; 4:3, 7; 5:6; 6:14; 7:21; 9:20; 10:5, 8, 15; 12:5, 26; 13:6) as the change from *phanai* of the LXX (Jer 38:31) reflects. The Codices Alexandrinus and Sinaiticus have *legein*, so the change may be due to the author's use of a variant manuscript tradition (Attridge, 227).

I will establish: The LXX has *diatithenai*, "establish," while Hebrews has *syntelein*, "complete." The author's interest in the concept of "perfection" may be responsible for this change, since *syntelein* is similar in concept to *teleioun*, "to perfect," which also has the connotation of completion (2:10; 5:9; 7:19, 28; 9:9; 10:1, 14; 11:40; 12:23).

a new covenant: A better covenant was introduced in 7:22 and authorized in 8:6. Its goal will be explained in 10:12-18. Here and in 9:15 it is called "new." The author relies on Jeremiah for the idea of newness. Doubtless what had appealed to him in Jer 31:31-34 is the mention of the wilderness generation, who did not observe the covenant. Hebrews has already used their example in 3:7–4:11 to exhort its readers to obedience and fidelity. The fact that the new covenant is put in the mind and heart (8:10) and not on tablets removes it from the realm of the external, which is weak and ineffectual. Finally, the stress on the mercy of God and the forgiveness of sins (8:12) supports the author's understanding of the effective self-sacrifice of Christ, who accomplished what the earlier covenant could not (10:11-18).

9. *not like the covenant that I made with their ancestors:* Another modification of the LXX citation is introduced by the author in the change from *diatithenai*, "establish," to *poiein*, "make." Since the Jeremiah text stresses the divine initiative in the first covenant, Hebrews may have preferred the more concrete verb that also recalls the creation imagery of 1:2.

    on the day when I took them by the hand to lead them out of the land of Egypt: The historical prologue to the Decalogue in Exod 20:2 accomplishes its function by identifying who the covenanting God is: "I am the LORD your God, who brought you out of the land of Egypt."

    for they did not remain in my covenant, and so I had no concern for them, says the Lord: The operative word here for the author has to be "remain," a change introduced by the LXX translator. The author uses the same verb, *menein*, to describe the permanence of Jesus' priesthood (7:24) and to describe the lasting possession the readers have (10:34). In 12:27 the verb describes the "unshakeable kingdom" and in 13:14 the "lasting city." Each instance advances Hebrews' claim that through Christ something better has been introduced.

10. *This is the covenant that I will make with the house of Israel after those days, says the Lord: I will put my laws in their minds, and write them on their hearts, and I will be*

their God, and they shall be my people: The placement of the Law in the minds and hearts of the people rather than on stone tablets shows a concern for the internal over the external. The injunction to interiorize the covenant is found elsewhere in the Hebrew Bible (e.g., Prov 3:3; 7:3), as is the violation of the covenant (Jer 17:1). The phrase "I will be their God, and they shall be my people" defines the covenant relationship between one God and one people in Israel (Gen 17:8; Exod 29:45; Jer 24:7; 32:38; Ezek 11:20; 14:11; 37:23, 27; Zech 8:8).

11. *And they shall not teach one another or say to each other, 'Know the Lord,' for they shall all know me, from the least of them to the greatest:* The full effect of the covenant written on the heart will be the absence of instruction from outside, i.e., one another. Rather, those in covenant with God will inherently know who God is. Hosea called attention to the lack of knowledge of God as the source of Israel's covenant violation in his day (Hos 4:1).

12. *For I will be merciful toward their iniquities, and I will remember their sins no more":* Israel's God was known as a God of mercy (2 Sam 24:14; Isa 30:18; 55:7; 63:7; Ezek 39:25; Hos 2:19; Neh 1:11; Wis 15:1; Sir 2:7, 9, 17; Job 9:15; Pss 23:6; 25:6; 40:11; 51:1; 69:16; 103:4; 119:7, 156; 123:2), but the awareness of God's mercy did not preclude the possibility of punishment (Sir 5:6; 16:11, 12, 14). The author alludes to punishment without mercy for violations under the first covenant (10:28). The old covenant was not able to purify the conscience of guilt from sin, and so the fact that God will not "remember" Israel's sins (in the sense of continuing to hold them against God's people) is a decisive element in the new covenant. The verse appealed to the author of Hebrews precisely because he understood the sacrifice of Christ to reflect the spirit of the new covenant in its ability to purify the conscience of sin (9:14, 26, 28; 10:10).

13. *In speaking of "a new covenant," he has made the first one obsolete. And what is obsolete and growing old will soon disappear:* Just as a change in the priesthood abrogated the law on which it was based (7:12, 18), so a new covenant renders the first one obsolete. Obsolete things go the way of destruction. Here the noun *aphanismos* connotes the effect of destruction, its frequent meaning in the LXX (e.g., Deut 7:2; 3 Kgdms 9:7; 13:14; 4 Kgdms 22:19; Jdt 2:27; 4:1, 12), which is to "disappear" (BDAG, 155).

INTERPRETATION

The first six verses of this chapter ended on the affirmation that Jesus is the mediator of a better covenant. The author now turns his attention to explaining what he meant by that. This section (vv. 7-13) is framed by two verses containing the word "first" (vv. 7, 13) with a long citation from Jer 31:31-34 (LXX: Jer 38:31-34) between them. As the form of the text is largely dependent on the LXX citation, it may be broken down further into two additional sections: vv. 8-9 and vv. 9-12. The first addresses the failure of Israel to keep the old covenant, thus establishing the need for a new one. The second then spells out the content of the new covenant. This text is cited only in Hebrews among NT books, although Paul may allude to it in 1 Cor 11:25.

Analogous to the argument made in 7:11 concerning the Levitical priesthood, the author claims that if there were nothing wrong with the first covenant God would not have looked for an opportunity to redo it. Interestingly, he does not then say in the next verse that God found fault with *it*, but rather with *them*. Initially the text indicates that the inadequacy of the first covenant was a "people-problem." Presumably the author believes that the divine impulse to make a covenant in the first place was not misdirected. So also, the recognition that the people were not able to abide by the first covenant facilitates the divine impulse again, to renew the opportunity for the covenant relationship. On the surface it appears, however, that the author turns away from the fault of the people alone to focus on institutional problems of the covenant itself as well (Attridge, 227). Still, the change in the nature of the covenant would have to bring about a change in the people, which may have been the point of Jeremiah's original oracle.

To talk about a covenant in which the stipulations are placed in people's minds and hearts indeed redirects attention away from external ritual and toward the role of the individual in covenant observance. In essence, the Law did not change in Jeremiah's view, but the people had to. Therein lay the newness of the covenant. To that extent one might talk more about renewal than replacement, a renewal along the lines of the Deuteronomic reform in Israel that placed emphasis on the total devotion of one's heart to God (Deut 10:12-22). To a very real extent, under Jeremiah's oracle the "institution" of covenant was not altered that much. What he seems to have intended was to change the way people actualized the covenant in an effort to ensure that they would keep it, unlike their ancestors who broke it repeatedly. Since God always takes the initiative in making a covenant, the language of the text had to accommodate that reality.

Other prophetic texts are instructive for understanding changes in the covenantal relationship between God and Israel that do not require the abolition of the covenant. Ezekiel 16:59-63 chastises the people for their violations of the covenant, but then the oracle continues, "yet I will remember my covenant with you in the days of your youth, and I will establish an eternal covenant" (v. 60). Awareness of God's intention will produce shame in them, and when they come to know God they will be reduced to silence, but God will forgive them (vv. 61-63). So it is not the broken covenant that God remembers, but the covenant at its inception, when it was still pristine. Ezekiel does not call it a new covenant, but rather an eternal covenant, a term that is not isolated to his prophecy (LXX: Ps 104:10; Isa 24:5; 55:3; 61:8; Jer 32:3; 50:5; Ezek 37:26; Sir 45:7, 15; Bar 2:35; 2 Esdr 3:15).

How much the author of Hebrews knew about the original context of the Jeremiah citation cannot be ascertained. The elements of discontinuity and continuity in the text, however, seem to have caught his eye. Thus he deemed it appropriate to place this text at the outset of his sermon's central argument, and indeed to frame the argument with Jeremiah's very words (8:8-12; 10:16-17). Like Jeremiah, he was preaching to a people who needed a change of heart (3:13-15; 4:1-2, 11; 5:11-14; 6:1-8).

As the reprise of the oracle at the end of the larger argument shows, two things in particular caught his imagination. The first is that the Law would be placed in the people's minds and hearts. The second is that God will no longer remember sins. Together these two aspects render the observance of the covenant more viable. People who are invited to it may actually observe it more faithfully, as it is a different kind of covenant.

The next chapter will develop the argument that the blood of goats and bulls only sanctifies partially, by targeting the flesh of those who have been defiled (9:13). No matter what was purified with blood, whether the people, the tent, or the vessels of worship, the pardon of sin that resulted (9:22) remained external. This is one reason why the rituals had to be repeated year after year (10:1). A covenant based on a law written on hearts and minds, on the other hand, has power to penetrate beyond the flesh to the conscience in effecting purification (9:14).

Because the rituals had to be repeated year after year, the awareness of guilt from sin was never effectively dealt with under the first covenant (10:2). In fact, the sacrifices and their necessary repetition had the opposite effect, in the author's view, because they were a constant reminder of sin. Only a covenant in which God declares that God will no longer be cognizant of sin can bring about the desired purification of conscience, because of the freedom it brings the individual, who need no longer expiate sin yearly, thus being continually reminded of it.

According to Jeremiah the byproduct of the new covenant will be a people who will know God in their hearts. There will be no need for external instruction because they will have learned from the heart (v. 11). It sounds a bit like what Paul wrote in 1 Thess 4:9: "Now concerning love of the brothers and sisters, you do not need to have anyone write to you, for you yourselves have been taught by God to love one another." The Thessalonians were "taught by God," *theodidaktoi.* The author knows that his readers have been instructed (2:3; 6:1-3; 13:7) and that someone may try to instruct them further (13:9). But he also knows that it is well for the heart to be strengthened by grace (13:9), which can happen under a covenant by which law is written in minds and on hearts. Under the new covenant the heart directs people's actions and their responses to God.

This section closes on a note that highlights the sense of "newness" in the covenant described. The first covenant, by comparison, has to become "old." There cannot be a new covenant without an old one, and the author believes that once the new one is established the old one is already obsolete. The idea of removing something old to make way for the new is not alien to Judaism. The language of Lev 26:9-12 has affinity with the Jeremiah citation and with the contrast between old and new in relation to the covenant in v. 13, "I will look upon you with respect and I will make you fruitful and multiply you; and I will maintain my covenant with you. You will eat what is old (*palaia*) of the old things stored up (*palaia palaiōn*) and clear out the old (*palaia*) to make room for the new (*ek prosōpou neōn*). And I will put my covenant in you and I shall not abhor you. I will walk among you and will be your God and you shall be my people." The LXX translation is instructive for the way the MT's "I will place my dwelling in your midst" is changed to "I will put my covenant in you." The metaphor of clearing out the old for the new is associated in this text with the renewal of the covenant. The sentiment is similar to what both Jeremiah and the author of Hebrews knew: that is, renewal requires replacing old things with new things. The location of the covenant may have changed, but the formula of covenant identification remains the same: "I will be your God and you shall be my people." Discontinuity and continuity are elements inherent in renewal.

For Reference and Further Study

Daniels, Richard. "How Does the Church Relate to the New Covenant? or, Whose New Covenant Is It Anyway?" *Faith & Mission* 16 (1999) 64–98.

Lehne, Susanne. *The New Covenant in Hebrews.* JSNTSup 44. Sheffield: JSOT Press, 1990.

Murray, Scott R. "The Concept of *diathēkē* in the Letter to the Hebrews," *CTQ* 66 (2002) 41–60.

Peterson, D. G. "The Prophecy of the New Covenant in the Argument of Hebrews," *RTR* 38 (1979) 74–81.

18. *The Ritual of the First Covenant* (9:1-10)

1. Now even the first had regulations for worship and an earthly sanctuary. 2. For the first tent was constructed, in which were the lampstand, the table, and the presentation of the breads; which is called the Holy Place. 3. Behind the second curtain was a Tabernacle called the Holy of Holies. 4. In it stood the golden altar of incense and the ark of the covenant overlaid on all sides with gold, in which there were a golden urn holding the manna, and Aaron's rod that budded, and the tablets of the covenant; 5. above it were the cherubim of glory overshadowing the mercy seat. Of these things we cannot speak now in detail.

6. Such preparations having been made, the priests go continually into the first tent to carry out their ritual duties; 7. but only the high priest goes into the second, and he but once a year, and not without taking the blood he offers for himself and for the sins committed unintentionally by the people. 8. By this the Holy Spirit indicates that the way into the sanctuary has not yet been disclosed as long as the first tent is still standing. 9. This is a symbol of the present time, according to which gifts and sacrifices are offered that cannot perfect the conscience of the worshiper, 10. but deal only with food and drink and various baptisms, regulations for the body imposed until the time comes to set things right.

Notes

1. *Now even the first:* The verse begins with a consideration of the ritual requirements of the first covenant. The noun "covenant," *diathēkē*, is missing, as the verse is elliptical in Greek. The new and first covenants were mentioned, however, in 8:13, so it was not necessary to repeat the noun here.

   had regulations for worship: "Regulations," *dikaiōmata*, is the standard LXX term for the prescriptions governing the covenant (e.g., Lev 25:18; Num 15:16; 27:11; 30:17; 31:21; 35:29; 36:13; Deut 4:1, 5, 6, 8, 40, 45; 4 Kdgms 17:13, 37). *Latreia*, "worship," is used only here and in 9:6. The author used the verb *latruein* in 8:5 and will use it again in 9:9, 14; 10:2; 12:28; 13:10. The usage of *latreia* here approximates the sense found in the LXX for "ritual duties" (Exod 12:25-26; 13:5; Josh 22:27; 1 Chr 28:13[B]).

   and an earthly sanctuary: The adjective "earthly" is meant to contrast with "heavenly." The "sanctuary" was introduced in relation to the "true tent" in 8:2, referring to the heavenly sanctuary. Here the contrast is clear and the use of "earthly" makes the author's point. The only other place the adjective occurs in the NT is at Titus 2:12 in reference to "worldly passions."

2. *For the first tent was constructed, in which were the lampstand, the table, and presentation of the breads:* "Tent," *skēnē*, indicates that the author has the tent in the wilderness in mind and not the Temple in Jerusalem. Although the use of *prōtē*, "first," suggests that the author has more than one tent in mind, it will become clear in the next verse that he understands the sanctuary to be divided into two spaces. This understanding is drawn from the account in Exodus 25–27 of the building of the sanctuary in the wilderness, where the structure is so divided (see Exod 26:33). The verb "construct," *kataskeuazein*, is not used in the Exodus account of the building of the sanctuary, but rather *poiein*, "make" (see Philo, *Who Is the Heir* 112, where the object of the verb *kataskeuazein* is the Tabernacle, *skēnē*). Hebrews uses the participle of *kataskeuazein* in 3:3-4 to refer to the "builder" of the house. The same verb will describe Noah's response to God's command to build an ark in 11:7. Here it has the sense of "furnish" (see the Notes at 3:4). For the description of the lampstand see Exod 25:31-39, and for the table see Exod 25:23-30. The breads of the Presence were to be placed on the table (Exod 25:30). Why the author singles them out as though they were

not on the table is not clear. Hebrews uses *prothesis*, "presentation," for *enōpion*, "presence" as in the LXX account. The expression is part of the later tradition and is found at 2 Chr 13:11.

the Holy Place: The relative clause, "which is called the Holy Place," presents a number of problems, as reflected in the variant readings in some manuscripts. The feminine adjective "holy" and the neuter noun "sanctuary," *hagia*, differ only in the way they are accented in Greek. Some of the best manuscripts read simply *hagia* as a neuter plural (ℵ D¹ D² I P 0278. 33. 1739. 1881. 𝔐). Normally, the author uses the neuter plural for the inner part of the sanctuary (8:2; 9:8, 12, 24, 25; 10:19; 13:11), but here it refers to the outer part. Some miniscule manuscripts show the feminine singular (365, 629 *al* b), probably indicating a scribal attempt to avoid the anomaly of referring to the outer tent as though it were the inner. The reading "holy of holies" appears in 𝔓⁴⁶ A D. Attridge thinks this is the original reading, as it occurs in the oldest witness to Hebrews, 𝔓⁴⁶. In his view it would be more likely that a scribe would change "holy of holies" to "sanctuary" or "Holy Place" than vice versa (Attridge, 233). Still, one has to reckon with the text of Exod 26:33, where a distinction is made between the "Holy Place" and the "Holy of Holies." Perhaps the author is thinking of this distinction, especially since the second curtain in the next verse seems to be the one separating the two spaces in Exod 26:33.

3. *Behind the second curtain was a tabernacle called the Holy of Holies:* This curtain separated the most holy part of the sanctuary from the anterior portion (Exod 26:31-33; 36:35; 40:3). This part is designated by the word for "tent," *skēnē*, which means a "Tabernacle" as it does in Exod 25:9 and 26:1. As in the previous verse there are variants for the name of this Tabernacle, Holy of Holies. The best manuscript witnesses read "Holy of Holies" (ℵ* A D* I^vid 33, 1881 𝔐). Still others use the more definite "the Holy of Holies" (ℵ² B D² K L 0278. 1241. 1505 *al*). The oldest extant manuscript of Hebrews, 𝔓⁴⁶, has *ana*, but as the apparatus indicates, it is a scribal error for *hagia*.

4. *the golden altar of incense:* The noun *thymiatērion* refers to the altar of incense described in Exod 30:1-10; 40:5, 26 in the LXX where it is called a *thysiastērion*. It is also used for the censer in 2 Chr 26:19; 4 Macc 7:11; Ezek 8:11. Since the censer is not mentioned among the furnishings of the Tabernacle in Exodus 25–26, the author probably has the altar in mind. The placement of the altar is not entirely clear in the Exodus accounts. In Exod 30:6 it is supposed to be placed "in front of the curtain that is above the ark of the covenant in front of the mercy seat that is over the covenant." If "in front of the curtain" means that the ark of the covenant is on one side of the curtain and the altar of incense is on the other, then it should stand in the outer part of the tent and not in the Holy of Holies. Exodus 40:26 has Moses placing the altar of incense "in the tent of meeting before the curtain," which supports this interpretation. If, however, "in front of the curtain" means on the same side of the curtain as the ark of the covenant, then the author of Hebrews has placed it correctly. In support of this interpretation, Exod 40:5 places the altar before the ark of the covenant, and Philo (*Moses* 2.101) and Josephus (*Antiquities* 3.147) place the altar of incense in the outer tent.

the ark of the covenant overlaid on all sides with gold, in which there were a golden urn holding the manna: Along with the altar of incense the author places the ark of the covenant inside the Holy of Holies. The placement is correct according to the Exodus accounts. The construction of the ark itself is described in Exod 25:10-16; 37:1-5. Its placement in the Tabernacle is prescribed in Exod 40:1-3. Aaron supposedly placed the jar of manna "before the covenant" (Exod 16:33-34), which suggests that it was not in the ark itself. The MT does not describe the jar as golden, although the LXX does (Exod 16:33; see Philo, *Preliminary Studies* 100).

and Aaron's rod that budded: The budding rod of Aaron, according to Num 17:16-24 (LXX), was placed by Moses in the Holy of Holies. Twelve staffs with the names of the heads of the tribes were to be placed in the sanctuary, before the Lord. Aaron's name was to be inscribed on the staff of Levi. When Moses returned the next day he saw that Aaron's rod had sprouted a flower. This indicated that he was chosen by God for the priesthood, which was supposed to be a warning to rebels and to put an end to complaints. God instructed Moses to place his rod in the sanctuary before the covenant, but not in the ark itself.

the tablets of the covenant: The traditional understanding held that the ark of the covenant contained the second version of the tablets of the covenant (Deut 10:2; 1 Kgs 8:9; 2 Chr 5:10). The last two references claim that they were the only things in the ark.

5. *above it were the cherubim of glory overshadowing the mercy seat:* Exodus 25:18-22 describes two cherubim of hammered gold that faced each other with their wings spread. They were placed on each side of the mercy seat that was on the ark itself. The "mercy seat," *hilastērion* (Heb. *kappōret*) was a covering placed over the ark. It was the place where God would meet Moses and convey to him the commands he was to pass on to the Israelites (Exod 25:22). On the Day of Atonement the high priest sprinkled the blood of a bull and a goat on it and before it in order to make atonement for the sanctuary.

Of these things we cannot speak now in detail: Given the amount of material in the Pentateuch dealing with the construction of the tent and Tabernacle and how they were to be outfitted, it comes as no surprise that the author wishes to be selective about what he will include in his discussion. His purpose is to compare two covenants, not to give a detailed exegesis of relevant texts dealing with the subject matter. As is seen in the following verses, he thinks of the construction of the tent and Tabernacle and the placement of their furnishings as preparatory for the material he wishes to emphasize, the priestly ritual under the old dispensation.

6. *Such preparations having been made, the priests go continually into the first tent to carry out their ritual duties:* Here the participle of the verb *kataskeuazein*, used above in v. 2, has the same sense of "preparing" (see the Notes at 3:4). Hebrews does not focus on the ritual dimension of the tent and Tabernacle. The sphere of the priests is the outer tent. The fact that the author mentions that they enter the first tent continually (*dia pantos*) indicates that their ritual duties (*latreias*) must be repeated. Such service is described in Exod 27:21 as a "perpetual ordinance to be observed throughout the generations of Israelites" (cf. Lev 24:1-4). Maintaining the fire at the altar of sacrifice and offering the sacrifices prescribed was also a continual part of the rituals performed by priests (Lev 6:8-30; Num 28:1-10). In addition to those duties, the bread of the presentation had to be replaced and arranged on the table every Sabbath (Lev 24:5-9).

7. *but only the high priest goes into the second, and he but once a year:* Contrasted with the ordinary priests is the high priest, who alone may enter the inner Tabernacle, the Holy of Holies, and then only on the Day of Atonement (Lev 16:29-34: *hapax tou eniautou*; Josephus, *War* 5.236: *hapax kat' eniauton*). The expression "once a year" (*hapax tou eniautou*) anticipates the designation of Christ's eschatological self-offering in 9:12, 25 and 10:10, which is made "once for all." The issue here is the need to repeat the sacrifice yearly, which makes it like the rituals of the ordinary priests, which must of necessity be repeated.

and not without taking the blood he offers for himself and for the sins committed un-intentionally by the people: Leviticus 16:14-15 prescribes that the high priest carry the blood of the sacrificed bull and goat into the Holy of Holies to sprinkle it on and before the mercy seat, covering the ark. In this way he atones first for himself and his family (Lev 16:6) and then for the sanctuary and for the trans-gressions of the people (Lev 16:16). The detail is selected to contrast with the sacrifice of Christ mentioned later in 9:12; he did not need to carry the blood of goats and calves into the sanctuary since it was his own blood that made atone-ment. Earlier, in 5:3 and 7:27, the author mentioned the need for the high priest to make atonement for himself and for others in order to highlight the difference between his sacrifice and Christ's. The observation that the atonement is made for the "unintentional" sins of the people reflects Israel's ritual practice in general (Lev 4:2, 13, 22, 27; 5:18; 22:14). On the Day of Atonement, however, all sins were included (Lev 16:16, 30).

8. *By this the Holy Spirit indicates that the way into the sanctuary has not yet been dis-closed as long as the first tent is still standing:* The author takes the need for continual rituals and sacrifices to indicate that under the old covenant the priesthood was unable ultimately to fulfill its purpose (7:11). In 3:7-11 the author has the Holy Spirit speak through Scripture, as he does later in 10:15-17. Here no scriptural citation is attached, so how the Holy Spirit "indicates" the lack of access to God is unclear. The verb *dēloun* can mean "explain something further" or "make something known that was previously unknown" (BDAG, 222). The latter sense is evident here because the author understands the Holy Spirit to show the significance of the rituals associated with the old covenant, i.e., that they were unable to grant people access to God in the inner sanctuary. Entry into that sanctuary is available through the sacrifice of Christ, which grants unprece-dented access to God (6:20; 7:25; 9:11). Indeed, the author suggests that such access was prevented by the nature of the old covenant itself, here symbolized by the "first tent." The simple meaning is that only the high priest was able to enter the inner sanctuary (Lev 16:29-34; Philo, *Special Laws* 1.72; *Embassy to Gaius* 307; Josephus, *War* 5.236). Beyond that, the deeper meaning is that the rituals of the old covenant were powerless to grant such access to God, as for the most part they were restricted to the first tent (Attridge, 241; Lane 2:223). The mention of the first tent as "standing" does not refer to the existing ritual of Judaism in the author's day, but rather to the validity of the old covenant. The author's argu-ments about the tent, Tabernacle, and rituals are all drawn from Scripture and exegetical tradition rather than from contemporaneous Jewish ritual practice.

9. *This is a symbol of the present time, according to which gifts and sacrifices are offered that cannot perfect the conscience of the worshiper:* The antecedent of "this" is am-

biguous, and commentators are divided over whether the relative pronoun looks back to the first tent (9:8) or to both the first and second tents (9:7-8). The immediate antecedent is the first tent in the previous verse. Its symbolic value lies in the fact that the rituals that must be continually performed in it do not grant access to God in the way the sacrifice of Christ does. The expression "the present time," of which the first tent is a symbol, presents difficulties. It must be seen in relation to the "time that sets things right" in 9:10. It functions to draw a contrast between the time of the old covenant and the time of the new covenant. Some have taken it to refer to an unfulfilled old covenant that is still in effect at the time the author is writing Hebrews (Montefiore, 149; Franz Josef Schierse, *Verheissung und Heilsvollendung: Zur theologische Grundfrage des Hebräerbriefes* [Munich: Zink, 1955] 31; Otfried Hofius, *Der Vorhang vor dem Thron Gottes: Eine exegetisch-religionsgeschichtliche Untersuchung zu Hebräer 6,19f. und 10,19f.* WUNT 14 [Tübingen: Mohr Siebeck, 1972] 64). Others see it as synonymous with the "time that sets things right" in the next verse (Weiss, 459; Attridge, 241; Ellingworth, 441). Still others see both times overlapping (Koester, 398; Braun, 261; Grässer 2:134–35). That the two times are simultaneous seems preferable, given the author's understanding of the once for all sacrifice of Christ. Thus the first tent is a "symbol" in the way it points to the heavenly sanctuary, where the self-offering of Christ has already taken place. The antecedent of the relative clause, "according to which," is best understood as *parabolē*, "symbol." "Gifts and sacrifices" refers to the offerings used in the ritual under discussion (see the Note at 5:3). The terms were first introduced in 5:1 and were repeated in 8:3. Now we learn that these were ineffective in accomplishing their purpose. In 7:11 the author had already noted that perfection could not be attained through the Levitical priesthood. The inadequacy of the old ritual is specified here as not being able to perfect the conscience of the worshiper, in contrast to the sacrifice of Christ, which does precisely that (9:14; 10:10, 14). "To perfect" means to cleanse the conscience from guilt resulting from sin (cf. 10:2).

10. *but deal only with food and drink and various baptisms, regulations for the body:* The author concludes his point by stressing the limitations of the old ritual in its concern with food, drink, and various baptisms, which belong to the realm of the flesh (*dikaiōmata sarkos*). The last term recalls the weakness of the former priesthood, which was based on a "fleshly command" (*entolēs sarkinēs*) (7:16). "Regulations" forms an inclusion with 9:1. In the LXX the term "food," *brōma*, is used to refer to things that may be eaten, i.e., what is clean as opposed to unclean (Lev 11:34; 25:6; 1 Macc 1:63; 4 Macc 1:34). In Lev 25:37 and Deut 23:20 it is food sold for a profit. In Deut 2:6 and 28 it refers to what edibles may be purchased from non-Israelites. The noun is used frequently in the LXX for food in general. *Poma*, "drink," occurs only five times in the LXX, and only in 4 Macc 3:16 does it have the ritual meaning of a libation. Regulations for food and drink are mentioned in *Ep. Aristeas* (128, 142, 158, 162). "Various baptisms" refers to the ritual washings prescribed in the Law for priests (Exod 29:4; 40:12; Lev 8:6; 16:4, 24) and non-priests alike (Leviticus 15; Numbers 19).

until the time comes to set things right: This is a reference to the new dispensation in Christ. The abrogation of the old law was already mentioned in 7:18 as the change that came about with the priesthood of Christ (7:12). As the mediator of a new covenant (7:22; 8:6, 13) he ushers in a new era in which the completion of the old covenant is accomplished. "Time to set things right" may also be translated as "time of correction," a term that can refer to the correction of a law (Attridge, 243; Koester, 400). The expression occurs only here in the NT. It appears to be a time when believers have access to God in a new way as a result of Christ's self-offering. If guilt from sin could not be permanently removed under the old dispensation, it has been under the new dispensation, which is a time "to set things right" (Cody, *Heavenly Sanctuary*, 133; de Silva, *Perseverence*, 302–303).

INTERPRETATION

The argument in this section picks up where the author left off in the previous one. The observation that even the first covenant had regulations for worship recalls the contrast of the two covenants developed on the basis of the interpretation of Jer 31:31-34 (see Heb 8:8-12). Here the author turns his attention more particularly to a consideration of the ritual of the first covenant, with the admission that even it had regulations for worship.

The ten verses of this section form a distinct unit marked off by the use of the noun "regulations," *dikaiōmata*, in vv. 1 and 10. The text as a whole divides into two parts, vv. 1-5 and vv. 6-10. In the first verse two aspects of the old covenant are singled out for consideration: its regulations for worship and the place where those regulations are enacted, the earthly sanctuary. The order of their treatment is reversed, however, since the sanctuary is discussed before the regulations. In the subsequent sections of the chapter both topics recur.

In 8:5 there was already a reference to the construction of the earthly sanctuary, which helped to advance the comparison of the ministry of Christ with that of earthly priests. A similar contrast is alluded to in this section (v. 8) and will be developed more fully in 9:11-14. The description here is drawn from Scripture, since the earthly sanctuary was not in use after 70 C.E.

For the most part the description follows the specifications for the division of the space and the furnishings in Exodus 25–27 and 30:1-10, although there is some confusion about the location of the altar of incense. This, however, may stem from the ambiguity of the Exodus text itself (see the Notes at v. 4 above). Otherwise, in the outer portion of the Tabernacle stood the lampstand and the table, on which the bread of the Presence was placed. Calling this space "the Holy Place" may reflect the distinction found in Exod 26:33: "the curtain shall separate for you the holy place from the most holy," thus a division between the outer and inner sanctuary. The designation, however, is not without problems (see the Note to v. 2).

The most sacred portion of the Tabernacle, the Holy of Holies, is on the other side of the separating curtain (v. 3). Its furnishings, according to Hebrews, included the golden altar of incense, the ark of the covenant containing a golden urn of manna, Aaron's rod, and the tablets of the covenant (v. 4). What exactly was in the ark of the covenant may not be accurately described. According to Exod 16:33-34 the jar of manna was supposed to be placed before the ark of the covenant rather than in it. Also Num 17:16-24 (LXX) has Moses placing Aaron's rod in the Holy of Holies itself. Finally, according to tradition the tablets of the covenant were supposed to be in the ark (Deut 10:2), and some texts claim they were the only things in the ark (1 Kings 8:9; 2 Chr 5:10).

The author ends the description of the sanctuary abruptly by saying that he will not go into any more detail, which is a common rhetorical device indicating that he does not want to engage in a fuller discussion of the symbolic meaning of the sanctuary and its furnishings (Attridge, 238; Koester, 396; Lane 2:221).

The next part of the passage (vv. 6-10) attends to the priests ministering within the Tabernacle. Just as the division between the outer and inner portions of the sanctuary was important for the author, so, too, is the distinction between the high priest and the ordinary priests who minister there. These priests had appointed tasks that preoccupied their priestly ministry, restricted to the outer tent. They had to maintain the fire at the altar of sacrifice and replace the breads of presentation. They had also to present the regular offerings. The high priest, on the other hand, was the only priest to enter the Holy of Holies, once a year on the Day of Atonement. As he entered he carried the blood of the sacrificial bull and goat, offered as atonement for his own sins and those of the people.

The ritual for the Day of Atonement was elaborate, but Hebrews does not describe it. According to Lev 16:1-34 the tenth day of the seventh month was set aside as a day of fasting on which no work could be done by anyone, including resident aliens. It was designated a day of rest for the cleansing of sin, to be observed forever. On that day the high priest was supposed to go into the Tabernacle with sacrificial offerings, a bull calf for a sin offering and a ram for a burnt offering. His vestments were made of linen, inner and outer, and he could not don them until he had undergone a ritual washing. He was also supposed to receive from the people two male goats for sin offerings and a ram for a burnt offering.

The first sacrifice was the bull calf, which made atonement for him and his household. Then from the two goats he selected one by lot. One was to be sacrificed and the other became the scapegoat to be driven out into the wilderness. After sacrificing the bull calf, the high priest was to light the censer and carry it through the curtain, into the Holy of Holies, so that smoke from it would cover the mercy seat over the ark of the covenant. The final rubric calls for him to sprinkle the blood of the bull calf on the front of the mercy seat and before it seven times. He then repeated the ritual with the goat to make atonement of the sins of the people. When that was completed he went out to the altar and sprinkled it seven times with the blood of the sacrificial victims, placing some of the blood on the horns of the altar, thereby cleansing it from any uncleanness. The scapegoat ritual followed the atonement rituals. Then came the procedures for ritual bathing of the high priest and the one who freed the scapegoat. Finally the carcasses of the sacrificial animals were disposed of, as they were burnt outside the camp.

Without having described the ritual for the Day of Atonement in detail, the author has parts of it in mind as he draws the contrast between the old and the new covenant. In v. 8 it becomes clear that the arrangement of the Tabernacle and the rituals performed there daily and on the Day of Atonement stand as signs that the goal of purification of conscience has not been accomplished. The Holy Spirit, responsible for the scriptural account of the building of the sanctuary and the rituals conducted within it, shows by the details of the account that the way into the inner sanctuary has not yet been disclosed. According to Leviticus that way is open only for the high priest, and the prescriptions and regulations governing the sanctuary prevent anyone else from having access to God through it. The sanctuary acts as a barrier, symbolized by the inner curtain, which prevents even ordinary priests from entering.

The last two verses of the section disclose the author's purpose in attending to the sanctuary and the rituals of the first covenant. As a symbol of the old order, the sanctuary and its ritual have the power to prevent people from gaining complete access to God. Since the sanctuary is not standing after 70 c.e., it represents in the present time a ritual system that no longer can grant access to God. Because the author believed that even when the sanctuary was standing this ritual system suffered from the same lack of completion, it is curious that he would phrase his thoughts on it in this manner. Like the first covenant itself, the old ritual order emphasized the external: food, drink, various baptisms (9:13). The way opened up by Christ is the way into the sanctuary under the new covenant, which stresses the interior over the external and is able to purify the conscience of guilt from sin (9:14). In the present time, then, the ritual of the new covenant accomplishes what the old covenant could not achieve. How this comes about is the subject for the next section of the chapter.

FOR REFERENCE AND FURTHER STUDY

Hofius, Otfried. "Das 'erste' und das 'zweite' Zelt: Ein Beitrag zur Auslegung von Hbr 9:1-10," *ZNW* (1970) 271–77.

Koester, Craig R. *The Dwelling of God: The Tabernacle in the Old Testament, Intertestamental Jewish Literature and the New Testament.* CBQMS 22. Washington, DC: Catholic Biblical Association, 1989.

Salom, A. P. "*Ta Hagia* in the Epistle to the Hebrews," *AUSS* 5 (1967) 59–70.

Stanley, Steve. "Hebrews 9:6-10: The 'Parable' of the Tabernacle," *NovT* 37 (1995) 385–99.

Swetnam, James. "Hebrews 9,2 and the Uses of Consistency," *CBQ* 32 (1970) 205–21.
_____."On the Imagery and Significance of Heb 9:9-10," *CBQ* 28 (1966) 115–73.

19. *The Ritual of the New Covenant* (9:11-14)

11. But when Christ arrived as a high priest of the good things that have come about, then through the greater and perfect tent (not made with hands, that is, not of this creation), 12. he entered once for all into the Holy Place, obtaining eternal redemption not by means of the blood of goats and calves, but by means of his own blood. 13. For if the blood of goats and bulls, with the sprinkling of the ashes of a heifer, sanctifies those who have been defiled so that their flesh is purified, 14. how much more will the blood of Christ, who through the eternal Spirit offered himself without blemish to God, purify our conscience from dead works to worship the living God!

Notes

11. *But when Christ arrived as a high priest:* The contrast with the previous section of this chapter is facilitated by the recollection that Christ, as High Priest, is the mediator of a new covenant (8:6) inaugurated by his resurrection and exaltation (7:16). The sentence, spanning vv. 11 and 12, is quite complex, as the main verb, "he entered," is placed in the next verse, separated by dependent clauses that describe the place of his arrival (v. 11) and how he performed his service (v. 12) (see Lane 2:237 and Koester, 407 for a clear presentation of the structure). The participle *paragenomenos* signifies his arrival as High Priest in the heavenly sanctuary.

of the good things that have come about: Referred to here are the consequences of Christ's priestly service. The author treats these things as though they are a present reality (see 6:5), as in the previous section he has identified the "present" with the coming "time to set things right." In the sermon's eschatology the tension between present and future is evident. In 10:1 the good things will be spoken of as future, awaiting completion of what is presently available upon the future arrival of Christ (9:28; cf. 13:14). One need not look any further than the present chapter to discover what these good things are: eternal redemption (vv. 12, 15), purification of conscience (v. 14), a promised eternal inheritance (v. 15), forgiveness of sins (v. 22), putting away of sins (v. 22), and salvation (v. 28). A variant reading "the good things to come," *tōn mellontōn tōn agathōn* (א A D[2] I[vid] 0278. 33. 1881 𝔐 lat sy[hmg] co) is likely to be a scribal error making the text conform to 10:1 (Metzger, *Textual Commentary*, 668).

through the greater and perfect tent: "Through," the preposition *dia* followed by a genitive, can indicate passage through, especially with verbs of motion (BDAG,

224). Otherwise the meanings may be temporal, instrumental, or causal (BDAG, 224–226; Attridge, 245; Hofius, *Vorhang*, 67 n. 110; Weiss, 465–66). Some commentators prefer the instrumental sense because two other uses of *dia* followed by a genitive in v. 12 are instrumental (Montefiore, 150–51; Koester, 408, et al.). The "greater and more perfect tent" according to this interpretation of the prepositional phrase has to refer to the outer portion of the heavenly tabernacle. In the next verse the author will refer to the inner portion, the "holy place." Some commentators find such an interpretation untenable on the grounds that the heavenly sanctuary seems not to be divided into parts in Hebrews, or that the adjectives "greater and more perfect" seem inappropriate to describe the outer portion of even a heavenly sanctuary (Koester, 409). It is not altogether clear that the author does not understand the heavenly sanctuary to be divided into two parts. In 8:5 he notes that the earthly is a "copy and a shadow" of the heavenly. Also, his christology focuses on the self-offering of Christ and the shedding of his blood, which must take place in the innermost part of the heavenly sanctuary. Hebrews does not dwell on the ritual of the outer portion of the sanctuary, even when referring to the earthly one. As for the second objection, the fact that the tent is described as greater and more perfect is a logical conclusion to the author's thought about any portion of the heavenly sanctuary, as he has consistently made this point throughout the comparison in this section of the sermon between the old and new covenants (7:22; 8:6). Furthermore, as Attridge argues so well, the author's point is to correlate the movement of an earthly high priest in the ritual of atonement with that of Christ in his self-offering. The means of atonement are treated in what follows (Attridge, 247–48).

not made with hands, that is, not of this creation: The author recalls his thought in 8:2, where he portrays Christ as a minister in the "sanctuary and the true tent," referring to the heavenly as opposed to the earthly. The expression "not made with hands" corresponds to the idea in 8:2 that the heavenly sanctuary was set up by God and not by a human. A form of this tradition is evident in Acts 7:48-50. The expression "not of this creation" is another way of saying that the tent spoken of is the heavenly realm, where God dwells.

12. *he entered once for all into the Holy Place:* As in v. 2, the inner sanctuary is designated only by one word, *hagia*. There is a variant reading that adds "of holies" (P) and is probably a scribal error. The once for all nature of Christ's sacrifice is an essential part of the comparison between the old and the new covenants in Hebrews (7:27; 9:26, 28; 10:10).

obtaining eternal redemption: The noun "redemption," *lytrōsis*, occurs only three times in the NT, twice in Luke (1:68; 2:38) and here. The more common word for redemption in the NT is the compound *apolytrōsis* (Luke 21:28; Rom 3:24; 8:23; 1 Cor 1:30; Eph 1:7, 14; 4:30; Col 1:14; Heb 9:15; 11:35). In this context the word means a freeing from the constraints of the old covenant and its demands, particularly the consciousness of sin and transgression. The eternal nature of redemption shows the full effect of Christ's once for all sacrifice.

not by means of the blood of goats and calves, but by means of his own blood: The means of atonement is now addressed with the two additional prepositional phrases employing *dia* with the genitive, describing agency. In the ritual within the Holy of Holies on the Day of Atonement the blood of the sacrificial animals was sprinkled on the front of the mercy seat located on top of the ark of the covenant, and before the mercy seat as well (Lev 16:14-15). Only goats and calves are mentioned here, whereas the actual ritual called for one bull offered as a sin offering, one ram as a burnt offering (Lev 16:3), and two male goats, one as a sin offering and the other as a scapegoat (Lev 16:7-10). The atonement brought about by Christ, acting as eternal High Priest, was obtained by means of his blood, i.e., his sacrificial death, which elsewhere in Hebrews is the means of his perfection, rendering him the "source of eternal salvation" (5:7-10). In 9:22 the author will claim that there can be no forgiveness of sins without the shedding of blood. The expression "by means of his own blood" is meant also to contrast with 9:25, where it is noted that on the Day of Atonement the high priest enters the sanctuary "with blood not his own."

13. *For if the blood of goats and bulls, with the sprinkling of the ashes of a heifer, sanctifies those who have been defiled so that their flesh is purified:* The author draws his conclusion by means of a *qal wahomer* argument that proceeds from the lesser to the greater. Here the lesser side of the argument is articulated in an allusion to the Day of Atonement ritual that is combined with the ritual of the red heifer, described in Numbers 19. Distinct from the ritual of the Day of Atonement, this rite requires an unblemished red heifer to be sacrificed outside the tent of meeting. Its blood was sprinkled on the tent; then it was immolated and its ashes were gathered for use in the water purification rituals that were required when someone came into contact with a dead body. The water was supposed to be sprinkled on such individuals in order to purify them from the defilement (Num 19:10-20). Two things may have prompted the author to include this ritual. In the next verse he will call attention to the Christ who offered himself unblemished to God. Numbers 19 specifies that the red heifer be unblemished, whereas in Leviticus 16 that specification is not explicitly applied to the sacrificial animals. Also, since the object of the ritual was purification and not atonement per se, the author may have included it here because of his concern for purification at this point in his argument. Again the ritual facilitates the contrast between the purification of the flesh and the purification of the conscience in the next verse. On the verb "sanctify" see the Notes at 2:11.

14. *how much more will the blood of Christ:* The greater part of the argument is expressed through a forceful comparison introduced by the expression "how much more," *posǭ mallon.* The first element that makes the comparison effective is the recollection that Christ has entered the sanctuary with his own blood.

who through an eternal Spirit offered himself without blemish to God: Since his own blood was involved, he did not offer another sacrificial victim, but himself. The prepositional phrase "through an eternal spirit" is obscure. A variant modifies it to "Holy Spirit" in order to remove the difficulty (ℵ² D* P 81. 104. 326. 365. 629. 630. 2464. *al* a vg sa^mss bo). The more difficult reading, "eternal," is preferred. The expression should be understood in relation to "an indestructible life" in 7:16, which, as opposed to the "fleshly command," is the ground of Christ's priesthood. As the eternity of his priesthood is predicated of his "indestructible life," the means of his self-offering is enabled by the eternal Spirit (Ellingworth, 457). His blameless offering of himself contrasts with earthly high priests, who had to make atonement for their own sins (Lev 16:6, 11; Heb 7:27). Christ's priest-hood is likened to that of earthly priests in his ability to identify with human weakness, but without himself sinning (4:15).

purify our conscience from dead works to worship the living God: This section ends on an important note, that the high priestly ministry of Christ accomplished what the former priesthood was unable to do, "purify the conscience" (9:9). Purification was an essential part of the ritual of the old covenant and there were laws governing its practice (Leviticus 12–15). In the LXX it has to do with physical purification, and one does not find "conscience" as its object. Hebrews stresses the internal purification over the external, and the realm of the con-science or the awareness of one's guilt from sin features prominently in that purification (9:9, 22, 23; 10:2; 13:18). "Dead works" recalls the same expression in 6:1, which referred not to the "works of the Law" but rather to sins, which lead to death (see the Notes at 6:1). The goal of purification is to be able to wor-ship the living God. On the verb "worship," *latruein,* see the Note at 8:5. Since the self-offering of Christ has granted access to God in a way the old cult could not, purifying the conscience of guilt from sin enables one to approach and to worship the living God freely (10:21-22). As Attridge has rightly observed, however, "worship" in Hebrews is not restricted only to the Christian liturgy (Attridge, 252). "The living God" is a favorite epithet in Hebrews (3:12; 10:31).

INTERPRETATION

After discussing in the previous section the Tabernacle and its rituals, all prescribed under the old covenant, the author turns to the ritual of the new covenant. The argument is constructed in two parts, with the first two verses (11-12) presenting the contrast of Christ as High Priest with the high priest under the old covenant. The last two verses (13-14) form a *qal wahomer* (from the lesser to the greater) argument for the more effective self-offering of Christ and its ability to accomplish what could not be accomplished under the old dispensation: purification of the conscience.

The heart of the author's argument lies in the arrival of Christ as High Priest in the heavenly sanctuary, described as "the greater and more perfect tent." Calling him "high priest of the good things that have come about" celebrates a definitive moment in salvation history. It is clear in this opening verse that the author believes that the good things have happened. To a com-munity that has suffered as his readers have (10:32-39), this assertion may seem hollow. At 10:1 the author will make it seem as if the good things are still to come. As he says in 6:11, he desires his readers to show earnestness in realizing the full assurance of their hope, so it seems that everything has not been received, reached, or accomplished fully. Still, there has been much encouragement throughout the sermon to perseverance and endurance, because good things have already resulted from Christ's redemptive work (6:9-12). They have benefited from his self-offering to some extent even up to now. Within this chapter, then, the author will note a number of good things that may explain what he means in this verse: eternal redemption (vv. 12, 15), purification of conscience (v. 14), removal of sin (v. 22), and salvation (v. 28).

The contrast with the previous section first calls attention to the sanctuary he enters and then to the ritual means of his self-offering, corresponding to the two divisions of the previous section of text. The notice here that the tent was not made with hands recalls 9:2, where the first tent was "constructed." In case the reader has not grasped the point, the author makes it clear by adding "not of this creation." So there is no question that the author describes the heavenly sanctuary. He will return to the nature of this sanctuary in 10:1, as he refers to the "true form" of the "earthly shadows."

More comparison follows. The former priests had to enter the tent many times in the exercise of their ministry, and the high priest had to enter the Holy of Holies annually as long as he was in office. Christ, on the other hand, entered once for all. Whereas the former priests offered the blood of goats and bulls, Christ carried his own blood into the heavenly tent. As the last two verses of the section indicate, this is what made the real difference between the sacrifices of the old covenant and the one sacrifice of the new. Multiple sacrifices remind the worshiper of sin year after year (10:3). Since it is impossible for the blood of bulls and goats to remove sin (10:4), the worshipers never get to the point at which the consciousness of sin has ceased. That freedom comes only from the self-offering of Christ.

The author refers to the purification of the conscience from "dead works." The issue here is not like the one Paul addressed in Galatians, where faith was opposed to works of the Law. "Dead works" have already been mentioned in 6:1, as the works of sin. Purification from these works, then, brings about the kind of cleansing the author sees as definitive in the comparison of the old covenant with the new. It is purification from the consciousness of sin (10:2), or a permanent cleansing of one's guilt from past sins. Such a cleansing results in "hearts sprinkled clean from an evil conscience" (10:22). As the new covenant was written on the heart, it is not only the conscience that receives cleansing.

The work of Christ as High Priest in the heavenly sanctuary has opened up a way of access to God that was not possible before his "arrival." This new pathway is referred to in 10:19-20 as the "new and living way." By following that way Christians have access to God and confidence to enter the sanctuary by the blood of Jesus Christ (10:19). Thus the author believes that his audience should feel they are free and have unimpeded access to God. Anything that would stand in the way of that ability to approach God would have caused him serious concern.

As any preacher knows, comparison can be a helpful rhetorical tool when attempting to present ideas that are difficult for a congregation to grasp. This strategy is especially appropriate if one is trying to bolster the listeners' confidence in a matter of great importance to them. Often it is difficult to find the one image or idea that will capture an audience's imagination and solidify in its hearts and minds exactly what one wishes them to take away from what they have just heard. The author of Hebrews succeeds in this part of his sermon by offering hope for the future. He speaks of "good things to come" that are rooted in the effective priestly ministry of Christ. He then joins that notion to the idea of a complete removal of guilt for past sins, an important effect of Christ's priestly service that distinguishes it from the Levitical cult. Completing in this section of the sermon the comparison with the Levitical priests presented in the previous section, Hebrews leads its readers to see why the self-offering of Christ is able to purify their consciences and grant them access to God in a new way. In the end the author hopes that their confidence will be restored and their hope renewed.

Preoccupation with guilt over past sins can have a debilitating effect on a person. In extreme cases it may result in a scrupulosity that robs one of joy, confidence, and hope. As a good pastor, the author also knows that a troubled conscience may prevent one from entering into God's presence. Earlier, in 6:1-3, he had addressed the audience's need not to lay "again the foundation of repentance from dead works," that is, to repeat the rituals and instructions associated with their initial conversion. Guilt over past sins was preventing them from moving on toward maturity (6:1). The reference to the ability of Christ's death finally to purify their conscience from "dead works" in this passage recalls the earlier exhortation (6:1-3) and adds to it the reassurance that the readers are now able to approach God freely in worship. His careful attention to the situation of his readers shows how pastorally sensitive the author is to their needs, and how serious he is about restoring their confidence.

For Reference and Further Study

Brooks, Walter E. "The Perpetuity of Christ's Sacrifice in the Epistle to the Hebrews," *JBL* 89 (1970) 205–14.

Cosaert, Carl P. "The Use of *hagios* for Sanctuary in the Old Testament Pseudepigrapha, Philo, and Josephus," *AUSS* 42 (2004) 91–103.

Emmrich, Martin. "'Amtscharisma': Through the Eternal Spirit (Hebrews 9:14)," *BullBibRes* 12 (2002) 17–32.

Swetnam, James. "A Contribution to the Discussion of Hebrews 9,11," *Bib* 47 (1966) 91–106.

Thompson, James W. "Hebrews 9 and Hellenistic Concepts of Sacrifice," *JBL* 98 (1979) 576–78.

Vanhoye, Albert. "Esprit eternal et feu du sacrifice en Hb 9.14," *Bib* 64 (1983) 263–74.

20. *The Death of the Mediator* (9:15-22)

15. For this reason he is the mediator of a new covenant, so that when a death has occurred for the redemption of transgressions under the first covenant, those who have been called may receive the promised eternal inheritance. 16. Where a will is involved, the death of the one who made it must be established. 17. For a will is valid only for the dead, since it is not in force as long as the one who made it is alive. 18. Hence not even the first covenant was inaugurated without blood. 19. For when every commandment had been told to all the people by Moses in accordance with the law, he took the blood of calves and goats, with water and scarlet wool and hyssop, and sprinkled both the scroll itself and all the people, 20. saying, "This is the blood of the covenant that God has ordained for you." 21. And in the same way he sprinkled with the blood both the tent and all the vessels used in worship. 22. Indeed, according to the law almost everything is purified with blood, and without the shedding of blood there is no forgiveness [of sins].

Notes

15. *For this reason he is the mediator of a new covenant:* "For this reason," *dia touto,* connects this part of the argument with the previous section of the chapter (vv. 11-14). The *qal wahomer* argument that established the efficaciousness of Christ's sacrifice supplies for the author the essential qualification for Christ to act as mediator of the new covenant. The notion of Christ as mediator has already been introduced at 8:6 and the meaning here is the same as there (see 12:24). The "new covenant" recalls Jer 31:31-34 (LXX 38:31-34), which in 8:6-12 clarified exactly what Christ was mediating. By beginning this section of the chapter in this way the author now introduces further exposition of the significance of Christ's death in relation to the new covenant.

    so that when a death has occurred for the redemption of transgressions under the first covenant: "So that," *hopōs,* introduces the final clause. "Redemption," *apolytrōsis,* is a compound of the simple *lytrōsis* used in 9:12 (see the Note there). The link between redemption and the death of a sacrificial animal is established in the laws of redemption under the old covenant (Exod 13:11-15; 34:20), as it entailed the substitution of one victim for another. "Under the first covenant" employs the temporal use of the preposition *epi*, as in 9:26. Elsewhere in Hebrews it has the sense of "on the basis of" (8:6; 9:10). The noun "transgression," *parabasis*, occurred earlier in 2:2. The point is that the death of Christ brought about redemption from transgressions, which under the order of the first covenant could not be forgiven. This failure to perfect was already mentioned in 9:9 and will be revisited in 10:1-3.

those who have been called may receive the promised eternal inheritance: The author does not specify the object of the perfect passive participle, "those who have been called," *hoi keklēmenoi*. The only other clues in the sermon are found in 3:1, where the readers are referred to as those who have received a heavenly call, and in 11:8, referring to Abraham's call to receive an inheritance. As descendants of Abraham, now under the new covenant, the readers receive the promised eternal inheritance, which by its heavenly nature is distinct from what Abraham had received (11:16). They have already been referred to in 6:17 as the heirs of the promise. However, the category may include those called in faith prior to the advent of Christ, who had seen the promises from afar (11:13; Montefiore, 156; Hughes, 368). As commentators note, the idea of Christians as "called" is traditional in the NT (see Attridge, 255; Ellingworth, 462).

16. *Where a will is involved, the death of the one who made it must be established:* The word for "will" is *diathēkē*, the same word the author has been using for "covenant." Here he plays on it, but intends it to mean a will (LSJ, 394–95). It is a standard legal term in Greek. The simple sense here is that no will can be executed without first establishing that the person who made it has died. The verb "be established," *pheresthai*, has the sense of "announce" or "report" (LSJ, 1923; MM, 666). The verb *diatithenai*, here in its participial form *diethemenou*, "the one who made the will," is also a legal term occurring regularly in the papyri in formulas for wills (MM, 155–56). It is the same verb the LXX uses in Jer 38:31, 32, 33 to describe God's action in establishing a new covenant. The author either used a variant of the quotation in 8:8-12 or changed the first two instances of the verb to *syntelein* and *poiein*, retaining only the third.

17. *For a will is valid only for the dead:* The author appeals to the usual understanding of the execution of a will common in his day. *Bebaios*, "valid," is a legal term for guaranteeing the validity of something (BDAG, 172; MM, 107; see 2:3; 6:16). The noun "dead" is actually a dative plural. Some commentators believe the plural form anticipates the sacrifices to be discussed after this section (Attridge, 256; cf. Lane 2:243), but it can simply reflect the common legal practice of validating a will when people have died (Koester, 418).

18. *Hence not even the first covenant was inaugurated without blood:* The author shifts the focus back to the covenant. The verb *enkainizein*, "inaugurate," occurs only here and in 10:20 in the NT. In the LXX it has the meaning of "dedicate something new" or "inaugurate" in Deut 20:5; 3 Kgdms 8:63; 2 Chr 7:5; 1 Macc 4:36, 54, 57; 5:1; 2 Macc 2:29, and "renew" in 1 Kgdms 11:14; 2 Chr 15:8; Ps 50:12; Sir 36:5; Isa 41:1.

19. *For when every commandment had been told to all the people by Moses in accordance with the law:* The source of this verse is Exod 24:3-8. The text actually says that

Moses read the book of the covenant to the people, which may be what the author intends. He uses "told," *lalein*, perhaps because in Exod 24:3 it says that Moses "narrated" all the words of the Lord and the ordinances. The people then responded, "All the words that the LORD has spoken (*lalein*), we will do," something repeated in v. 7 as well. This custom was in accordance with the Law because God had prescribed a public reading of it.

he took the blood of calves and goats: Exodus 24:5 recounts that only "calves" were sacrificed and their blood alone was used in the ritual. The combination of "goats and calves" or "goats and bulls" occurred in Heb 9:12-13, and "bulls and goats" will appear in 10:4. The author has not been precise in recalling what kinds of animals were sacrificed in the various rituals he has already alluded to.

with water and scarlet wool and hyssop: This detail is missing in the account of Exod 24:3-8. Scarlet material, hyssop, and water are used in the ritual of the red heifer alluded to in 9:13 (see Num 19:6, 18, and 20) and in the cleansing of lepers in Lev 14:4-6.

and sprinkled both the scroll itself and all the people: That original account tells only of "dashing" (*prosechein* and *kataskedazein*) the blood against the altar and on the people, but not on the book of the covenant. The verb *rantizein*, "sprinkle," does occur in the LXX of Lev 6:20; 4 Kgdms 9:33; and Ps 50:9.

20. *saying, "This is the blood of the covenant that God has ordained for you":* Hebrews does not replicate exactly the LXX version of what Moses said to the people: "Behold the blood of the covenant, which the Lord has established with you, according to all these words." Perhaps the author had access to a different manuscript tradition that had already made these changes. It is likely, however, that he introduced the changes himself. The change from "behold" to "this" brings the citation in conformity with early Christian eucharistic tradition and the way the NT records the words Jesus spoke at the Last Supper (Matt 26:28; Mark 14:24; Luke 22:20; 1 Cor 11:24-25). The substitution of God for Lord is curious, since often in biblical citations the author allows the word "Lord" to stand (1:10; 7:21; 8:8, 9, 10, 11, 30; 12:5, 6; 13:6). The effect of this change is to direct the words away from Christ, thus rendering a eucharistic reference unlikely (Koester, 419). It is probable that the author is not making an explicit eucharistic reference here, but the change from "Lord" to "God" more probably intends to show that it was God who ordained the second covenant, and not Christ (Lane 2:245). Already in 5:5 the point was made that, like every high priest, Christ was appointed by God, and that he did not glorify himself in becoming a priest. Neither did he take it upon himself to inaugurate the new covenant (8:8-12). So the author may have wished to avoid the ambiguity of leaving "Lord" in the text at this point.

The change from "establish," *diatithenai*, to "ordain," *entellesthai*, may be in keeping with the author's practice (see the Note at 9:16). The verb "command," *entellesthai*, could allude to the "fleshly commandment," *entolē sarkinē*, of 7:16, which was the basis for the old priesthood. Thus the author may stress here the earthly nature of the Mosaic covenant. The verb *entellesthai* occurs again in 11:22 with its other meaning, "give instructions" (BDAG, 339). It is frequent in the LXX.

21. *And in the same way he sprinkled with the blood both the tent and all the vessels used in worship:* This detail is lacking in the Exod 24:3-8 account of the ratification of the Sinai covenant. Its inclusion here is anachronistic, since the tabernacle was not erected at the time the Sinai covenant was ratified. When it was built it was anointed with oil (Exod 40:9-11). The ritual of the Day of Atonement called for the use of blood in purifying the sanctuary (Lev 16:15-19), so the author may have this in mind. In fact, it appears that he has conflated the two traditions.

22. *Indeed, according to the law almost everything is purified with blood:* Blood was used in Jewish purification rituals (Exod 29:20-21; Lev 5:9; 8:15; 14:6, 14; 16:14-19), but other things like water (Lev 15:10, 13; 16:26, 28; 22:6; Num 19:7-9), fire (Num 31:21-24), and even flour were used when one could not afford other prescribed sacrificial animals (Lev 5:11). According to Lev 17:11, however, it was blood that made atonement. The use of the adverb "almost," *schedon,* inoculates the author from hyperbole, but his focus remains on the purifying aspect of blood. His interest is in contrasting the old and new covenants, where frequently he has alluded to the use of the blood of goats, calves, and bulls.

    and without the shedding of blood there is no forgiveness [of sins]: The noun "shedding of blood," *haimatekchysia,* occurs only in Christian authors (BDAG, 27) and was probably coined by the author. The noun "shedding" or "gushing," *ekchysis,* occurs in the LXX at 3 Kgdms 18:28 and Sir 27:15 with the accompanying genitive *haimatos,* "of blood." Although the noun "sin" does not occur in the verse, the use of "forgiveness," *aphesis,* in relation to sins is a frequent occurrence in the NT (Matt 26:28; Mark 1:4; Luke 1:77; 3:3; 24:47; Acts 2:38; 5:31; 10:43; 13:38; Eph 1:7; Col 1:14; Heb 10:18).

Interpretation

The previous section concluded that if the blood of sacrificial animals under the old covenant could sanctify those who had incurred defilement, then the blood of Christ would certainly be capable of purifying one's conscience from dead works (9:13-14). With that in mind, the author looks at the role of blood under the old covenant. He makes three points: first, blood is redemptive; second, blood is ratifying; third, blood is purifying. Part of the author's purpose here is to make a link between the role of blood under the first covenant and the role of Christ's blood in the establishment of the second covenant. His larger purpose is to show how the effects of Christ's death are constitutive of his role as the mediator of a better covenant.

The opening verse of this passage joins it to what had preceded by means of "for this reason." The immediate reason is that the blood of Christ is able to purify the conscience. This ability to cleanse the conscience of consciousness of sin (9:14) rendered him the mediator of a better covenant (9:15). The passage goes on to spell that out by calling attention to the effects of Christ's redemptive death.

Under the first covenant there could be no redemption from transgression without the death of a sacrificial animal. The same is true under the new covenant, but with a difference. In the case of Christ's death, the result was the fulfillment of the promise of an eternal inheritance. As with any inheritance, it cannot be received until the person bequeathing it has died. Here the author plays on the word *diathēkē* (vv. 16-17), which can mean "covenant" or "testament" (cf. Gal 3:15). The mention of the eternal inheritance recalls eternal redemption in 9:12, providing the link with the blood of Christ as redemptive. In the previous section the author noted that he entered the sanctuary "with his own blood, thus obtaining eternal redemption." Here that redemption is an inheritance that can now be claimed by the heirs, because he has died.

The observation that even the first covenant had to be inaugurated with blood implicitly claims that the second covenant was also inaugurated with blood, which constitutes the second effect of his death. Thus the author sees the blood of Christ as ratifying the new covenant in the way the blood of sacrificial animals ratified the old one. Consequently, the function of re-telling the story of Moses ratifying the covenant with the people in Exod 24:3-8 becomes evident. Even if the author does not get all the details correct, he makes his point by importing the water, wool, and hyssop and the sprinkling of the scroll. The covenant had to be ratified with blood, and the blood had to come from somewhere. It came from sacrificial animals.

Noting in v. 21 that Moses then sprinkled blood on the tent and the vessels to be used in worship, the author includes details missing from the account of the ratification of the covenant in Exod 24:3-8. These details seem to have been drawn from the ritual of the Day of Atonement (Lev 16:15-19). It would be misguided, however, to see here a simple mistake on the author's part. It is likely that he placed the details here as a transition to the next section, where he takes up the purification of the heavenly sanctuary.

The third effect of Christ's redemptive death is the forgiveness of sins. When the author recalled the citation from Jer 31:31-34 about the new covenant (8:8-12), he included the verse that says "for I will be merciful toward their iniquities and I will remember their sins no more" (8:12). The purifying effect of Christ's sacrificial blood fulfilled that part of Jeremiah's prophecy. In 2:17 Hebrews stressed that Christ was a merciful and faithful High Priest in his work of atonement. He had so understood the human condition that he could be so described. Here the full effect of his role as High Priest comes to the fore, i.e., sins are forgiven and they are no longer remembered by God. The new covenant is now in place.

In this part of the sermon the author stresses that Christ had to die in order for the promised eternal inheritance to be handed on to others. Once his death had occurred it became possible for the "heirs" to receive their inheritance, as in the case of any "will" or "testament" left behind by the one who made it. Unlike the case of a normal "will" or "testament," however, other effects accompanied his death. The ratification of the new covenant was brought about when he died (9:18), and there was also forgiveness of sins (9:22). The full meaning of his death, then, rendered Christ the mediator of a better covenant (9:15), in which the forgiveness of sins is a prominent feature (8:12).

The author has taken a deliberate and systematic approach in leading his readers to the realization that they have in Christ a mediator of a better covenant. He has used comparison well in highlighting the differences between the old covenant and the new and in explaining what changes had been brought about in the priesthood (7:12), which administered the new covenant. Key in the developing argument has been the author's emphasis on the purification of the conscience, i.e., the removal of the consciousness of guilt from sin. Those redeemed under the new covenant are freed from the need to dwell on sin (9:14). Likewise, God no longer remembers their sins (8:12). At this point in the sermon, then, the readers have been introduced to the meaning of redemption under the rubric of the new covenant and they can clearly see how different the meaning of that term is from what was formerly possible under the old covenant. The author has actualized for his readers the concept of atonement so that it informs their lives as "those called to receive the promised eternal inheritance" (9:15).

For Reference and Further Study

Berényi, Gabriella. "La portée de *dia touto* en Hé 9.15," *Bib* 69 (1988) 108–12.

Hughes, John J. "Hebrews ix.15ff. and Galatians iii.15ff.: A Study in Covenant Practice and Procedure," *NovT* 21 (1979) 27–96.

Lincoln, Lucy. "Translating Hebrews 9:15-22 in Its Hebraic Context," *JOTT* 12 (1999) 1–29.

Martin, François. "Le Christ médiateur dans l'épître aux Hébreux," *SémiotBib* 97 (2000) 37–45.

McCarthy, Dennis J. "Further Notes on the Symbolism of Blood and Sacrifice," *JBL* 92 (1973) 205–20.

Swetnam, James. "A Suggested Interpretation of Hebrews 9.15-18," *CBQ* 27 (1965) 373–90.

21. *Sacrifices of the New Covenant* (9:23-28)

23. Thus it was necessary for the examples of the heavenly things to be purified with these things, but the heavenly things themselves need better sacrifices than these. 24. For Christ did not enter a sanctuary made by human hands, a mere copy of the true one, but he entered into heaven itself, now to appear before the face of God on our behalf. 25. Nor was it to offer himself again and again, as the high priest enters the Holy Place year after year with the blood of another, 26. for then he would have had to suffer again and again from the foundation of the world. But as it is, he has appeared once more at the end of the ages for the removal of sin by the sacrifice of himself. 27. And just as it is appointed for mortals to die once, and after that the judgment, 28. so Christ, having been offered once to take away the sins of many, will appear a second time, apart from sin, to those who eagerly await him for salvation.

Notes

23. *Thus it was necessary for the examples of the heavenly things to be purified with these things:* Hebrews has argued from necessity for a change in the Law (7:12), for the once for all sacrifice of Christ (7:27), for the need of priestly offerings (8:3), and for the establishment of a person's death in the execution of a will (9:16). Now the author turns to the purification of the heavenly sanctuary and again uses the characteristic *anangkē* (cf. *anangkaion* at 8:3). The necessity derives from what has been articulated in the previous passage (9:15-22) and the purification rituals of the first covenant; hence the resumptive "therefore," *oun*, in the opening verse. "Examples" are *hypodeigmata*, a word already used to describe the earthly sanctuary in 8:5. Although the noun was singular there, it encompassed the sanctuary and its furnishings as indicated by God's command to Moses "to make everything according to the pattern" shown him. Here the plural refers more explicitly to whatever was to be purified by the sacrifices of the first covenant. "To be purified," *katharizesthai*, used in relation to the old covenant refers to blood purification (9:22). In relation to the new covenant it is the cleansing of the conscience (9:14; 10:2), which is the removal of the awareness of guilt due to sin; such cleansing is the work of Christ as High Priest (see 1:3 and Introduction, 8, *Conscience/Consciousness of Sin in Hebrews*). The elements of the old ritual are referred to only by the demonstrative "these things," *toutois*.

but the heavenly things themselves need better sacrifices than these: It is not clear why the heavenly things need to be purified. It may simply be the consequence of the author's understanding of the necessity of Christ's self-offering. Is it Hebrews' answer to the question, *Cur Deus homo?* (cf. Weiss, 479). Or does it follow from the logic of the comparisons the author has been drawing all along between the old and the new covenant? (That is, as the former covenant required the purification of the sanctuary by sacrificial blood, the new and better covenant [7:22], founded on better promises [8:6], requires better sacrifices [12:24] to purify the heavenly sanctuary.) Commentators have answered the question variously. Some have taken "heavenly things" to mean heaven itself, defiled by human sin (Dunnill, *Covenant and Sacrifice*, 232; Koester, 421; Lane 2:248; James Moffatt, *A Critical and Exegetical Commentary on the Epistle to the Hebrews* (ICC; New York: Scribner, 1924) 194; Westcott, 271). Others have suggested the earthly reality of the church or its members (Bruce, 219; Cody, *Heavenly Sanctuary*, 192–96, Vanhoye, *Old Testament Priests*, 205). Montefiore (160) and Attridge (262) take the object of purification to be the consciences of believers, which fits well with the notion of the purification of conscience in the sermon (9:14; 10:2). The interpretation that the author is referring to the expulsion of Satan from heaven (Bleek 2.2:588; Michel, 324) has received little support. Ellingworth (477) sees the rite of purification as inaugural, without inferring any need for actual purification. In the context this seems like the best option.

24. *For Christ did not enter a sanctuary made by human hands:* A humanly constructed sanctuary is a negative description in Hebrews, as was noted in 9:11. The same is true of other NT texts (Mark 14:58; Acts 7:48; 17:24).

   a mere copy of the true one: The author repeats the idea expressed in the opening verse that the earthly sanctuary is a "copy" of the true one in heaven. The noun for "copy" here, however, is *antitypos*, a term drawn from Platonic philosophy to refer to the earthly representation of what exists in the ideal world (BDAG, 91). The author expressed a similar idea about the true heavenly sanctuary in 8:2, 5.

   now to appear before the face of God on our behalf: The verb *emphanizein* means "show" or "manifest." In the LXX it has the meaning of "appear" in Wis 17:4 (see Diogenes Laertius, *Lives of Eminent Philosophers* 1.7; Philo, *Special Laws* 3.191; Josephus, *War*, 6.47; *Antiquities* 1.223). In the LXX people come "before the face of God" in a worship setting (Exod 23:15, 17; 34:20, 23; Deut 16:16; 1 Kgdms 1:22; Ps 42:2).

25. *Nor was it to offer himself again and again:* The repeated nature of the sacrifices of the old covenant is seen as a negative thing (9:6), which Hebrews contrasts with Christ's "once for all" sacrifice (9:12; 10:10; see the Notes at 9:6).

   as the high priest enters the Holy Place year after year with the blood of another: See the Notes at 8:7; 9:6; and 12.

26. *for then he would have had to suffer again and again:* The verb *dein* in the imperfect *edei* connotes the necessity of something that should have happened. Verbs of necessity used in the imperfect without the particle *an* indicate something that should have happened but did not actually take place (BDF §358). The argument draws the logical conclusion that if Christ were like an earthly high priest, who offered sacrifice annually in the sanctuary, he would have had to sacrifice himself over and over again.

   from the foundation of the world: The author means from the beginning of creation (see the Notes at 4:3).

   But as it is, he has appeared once more at the end of the ages: The adverb *nuni* is frequent in Paul, with almost half of the instances in Romans. The sense of it here is to introduce a real condition after an unreal one (BDAG, 682). The wording is similar to Rom 3:21, where righteousness "has appeared." The author has already used this adverb in 8:6. The appearance takes place at the "end of the ages," an apocalyptic term drawn from the LXX and Hellenistic Judaism (Dan 9:27; 12:13; 4 *Ezra* 6:25; *T. Levi* 10:2; *T. Zeb.* 9:9; *T. Benj.* 11:3; *T. Mos.* 12:4). Elsewhere in the NT the expression occurs in Matthew (13:39, 40, 49; 24:3; 28:20).

for the removal of sin by the sacrifice of himself: The noun "removal" is the same word used in 7:18 for the abrogation of the former commandment. The author may appeal to an element of Jewish apocalyptic here (Attridge, 265). The sense is eschatological, as the author knows that sin has not been completely eradicated (6:4-8; 12:1; 13:11-15).

27. *And just as it is appointed for mortals to die once and after that the judgment:* The author draws on common wisdom to bring the comparison to a close. In the LXX the verb "be appointed," *apokeisthai,* occurs in relation to death in 2 Macc 12:45 and 4 Macc 8:11. One need not see Hebrews advocating a particular judgment, which is rare in the NT (see Luke 16:22-23). Rather, judgment takes place at the end of the ages (Matt 25:31-34; John 5:28-29; 2 Thess 2:9-10; 1 Pet 4:5; Rev 20:12-13).

28. *so Christ, having been offered once to take away the sins of many:* The author returns to the "once for all" nature of Christ's death. The verb "offer," *prospherein,* is standard cultic terminology and has been used throughout the sermon (8:3; 9:7, 9; 10:1, 11, 12, 14). The contrast with the old ritual is enhanced by the choice of the aorist passive participle; whereas the former priest offered, Christ is offered. The author uses another compound of *pherein, anapherein,* for the "taking away" of sins effected by Christ's self-offering. There may be an echo here of Isa 53:12 "He bore (*anēnengken*) the sins of many and because of their sins he was handed over" (Attridge, 266; Lane 2:250). "The many" also recalls Mark 10:45; 14:24.

will appear a second time, apart from sin, to those who eagerly await him for salvation: The reference is to the *parousia,* Christ's second coming, perhaps prompted by the notion of judgment in the previous verse. The expression "apart from sin," *chōris hamartias,* recalls the author's stress on the sinlessness of Christ, since it can also be translated "without sin" (4:15; 7:26; 9:14). In this context it refers to the object of his return, which will be to bring salvation rather than to deal with sin. The taking away of sins was accomplished in Christ's self-offering, and so his return will not be accompanied by another atoning sacrifice. Rather, it will complete the salvation brought about by his death. "Salvation" in this context refers to the "eternal salvation" of 5:9, of which Christ is the pioneer (2:10) and source (see 7:25).

INTERPRETATION

Bringing the chapter to a close, this part of the comparison of the old and new covenants focuses on the definitive nature of Christ's ministry as High Priest. The author reiterates that Christ enters into the heavenly sanctuary (9:11) and stresses again that his sacrifice was not repeated (7:27). He also repeats the observation that Christ brought his own blood into the sanctuary (9:12). The repetition is necessary to remind the readers what exactly are the better sacrifices that can cleanse the heavenly sanctuary.

The need for the heavenly sanctuary to be purified rests on the comparison with the earthly sanctuary. Earlier, the description of the ritual for the Day of Atonement (9:6-10) did not specify the purification of the sanctuary or of the altar, which was actually prescribed in the ritual. According to Lev 16:16-19, 32-34 the tent and the altar had to be purified from the defilement of the people. In Hebrews this detail was introduced in 9:21, instead, in relation to the ratification of the old covenant. Thus the author has conflated the purification of the Tabernacle with the ratification of the covenant. The joining of the two traditions in 9:19-22 concluded with the observation that "almost everything under the law is purified with blood." The author may indicate by "almost" that he knows not all sacrifices are bloody (see the Notes at 9:22), but he is still clearly interested in the efficacy of blood for atonement and purification. Why he conflated the two traditions is a matter for speculation. The clue to his thinking may lie in 9:18, where he says: "not even the first covenant was inaugurated without blood." Like it, the new covenant had to be inaugurated with blood. As he understood that inauguration to have involved the sprinkling of blood on the tent and the vessels for worship, he believed that the new and better covenant also required a purification of the heavenly sanctuary by better sacrifices (see Ellingworth, 477).

That the sacrifices that purified the heavenly sanctuary were indeed better is confirmed by the fact that Christ actually entered heaven itself, where he came face-to-face with God (v. 24). The high priest, on the other hand, encountered only the presence of God symbolized by a cloud over the mercy seat (Lev 16:2). The purpose of his entrance into heaven is to intercede with God for others, a role the author called attention to earlier when discussing Christ's priesthood. In 6:20 he called him "the forerunner on our behalf" with language similar to what he uses in this section. Perhaps the best text, however, to illustrate the author's meaning here is 7:25, where Christ's role as eternal intercessor is introduced. As the eternal High Priest, who has entered heaven itself, "he is able for all time to save those who approach God through him, since he always lives to make intercession for them."

As yet another sign of the superiority of Christ's sacrifice, the author returns to the element of Christ's self-offering he deemed decisive in determining its superiority over the sacrifices under the old covenant: Christ offered himself only once (7:27; 9:12, 26, 28; 10:10). Were his sacrifice not unique, it would have had to be repeated, which means Christ would have had to suffer over and over again, from the beginning of time. At this point the author turns to another aspect of Christ's self-offering that distinguishes it from sacrifices under the old covenant: it has eternal consequences.

The expression "the foundation of the world" is paired in v. 26 with "the end of the ages." Recalling the opening of the sermon, where the Son's role in creation was highlighted (1:2) and his eternal status was stressed (1:8-12), the author makes a link between creation and redemption. The earthly Jesus made his once for all self-offering within the realm of time (5:7-8), which itself had been created by the preexistent Son (1:2). Once he was perfected (2:10; 5:9-10), however, he entered into heaven to take his place at the right hand of God (1:3; 10:13), outside the realm of the ages, within eternity itself. It is from there that he intercedes for all time and serves as the source of eternal salvation (5:9). As "source" he is both the point of origin and repository of eternal salvation. Thus he is able to help others (4:16). In the context here, that help comes in the removal of sin, by which the author means sin's ultimate abolition, as he employs the same noun he used in 7:18 to signal the abrogation of the law.

The concluding two verses elucidate the eschatological significance of Christ's death. From the commonplace that all mortals die, whereupon comes judgment, the author shifts to salvation. He notes that Christ will return a second time, apart from sin. His first appearance in time effectively dealt with sin, as the previous verse indicates; he took it away. Earlier it was established that Christ was prepared for his priestly ministry in his earthly existence. He became like his brothers and sisters in every respect, apart from sin, so that his own self-offering would be an effective atonement before God (2:16-18; 4:14-16). Having brought that atonement about through his death, upon his return he will bring the effect of his own self-offering to those who await him. He will bring them to the eternal salvation of which he is the source.

The expression "to those who await him" recalls 5:9, where Christ is described as the source of eternal salvation "for those who obey him." For the author, salvation is sure because of Christ's self-offering, validated in his exaltation, but he does not merely encourage his readers to wait for that salvation to arrive. The hortatory sections of Hebrews remind the readers that they will be subject to judgment (2:1-3; 3:12-13; 4:1-2, 11-13; 6:4-8; 10:26-31; 12:3-11), and like all those to whom God's word was sent, they must receive it accordingly (4:2). The author calls not only for endurance, but for obedience as well. The model is Christ himself, who was obedient to the one who could save him from death (5:7).

In this final passage of the chapter the author recapitulates his presentation of the heavenly sanctuary and the movement into it by Christ the High Priest. As usual, he plays on the analogy of the heavenly sanctuary with the earthly and then moves further to show where the analogy breaks down. His goal is achieved by recalling that Christ entered a sanctuary not made with hands, to intercede face-to-face with God for those whom he serves (v. 24) by means of a non-repeatable sacrifice marked by an offering of his own blood (v. 25), and so to put an end to sin (v. 26), so that when he returns he will not be preoccupied with sin, but will rather bring salvation

(v. 28). In this passage, then, he has offered a brief compendium of his understanding of how Christ's atoning self-offering differs from the offerings under the old covenant, in order to help his readers grasp the newness of the covenant Christ administers.

For Reference and Further Study

Dunnill, John. *Covenant and Sacrifice in the Letter to the Hebrews.* SNTSMS 75. Cambridge: Cambridge University Press, 1992.

Omanson, Roger L. "A Superior Covenant: Hebrews 8:1–10:18," *RevExp* 82 (1985) 361–73.

Swetnam, James. "Sacrifice and Revelation in the Epistle to the Hebrews: Observations and Surmises on Hebrews 9,26," *CBQ* 30 (1968) 227–34.

Vanhoye, Albert. "L'intervention decisive du Christ, He 9, 24-28," *AsSeign* 63 (1971) 47–52.

Young, Norman H. "The Gospel According to Hebrews 9," *NTS* 27 (1981) 198–210.

22. *The Once for All Sacrifice of the New Covenant* (10:1-18)

1. Since the law has only a shadow of the good things to come and not the same form of these realities, it can never make perfect those who approach, by the same sacrifices that they offer continuously year after year. 2. Otherwise, would they not have ceased being offered, since the worshipers, cleansed once for all, would no longer have any consciousness of sin? 3. But in these sacrifices there is a reminder of sin year after year. 4. For it is impossible for the blood of bulls and goats to take away sins. 5. Consequently, when Christ came into the world, he said, "Sacrifices and offerings you have not desired, but a body you have prepared for me; 6. in burnt offerings and sin offerings you have taken no pleasure. 7. Then I said, 'Behold I have come to do your will, O God,' (as it is written of me in the head of the book)."

8. When he said above, "You have neither desired nor taken pleasure in sacrifices and offerings and burnt offerings and sin offerings" (these are offered according to the law), 9. then he added, "Behold, I have come to do your will." He abolishes the first in order to establish the second. 10. And it is by God's will that we have been sanctified through the offering of the body of Jesus Christ once for all.

11. And every priest stands day after day serving and offering again and again the same sacrifices that can never take away sins. 12. But when Christ had offered for all time a single sacrifice for sins, "he sat down at the right hand of God," 13. and since then has been waiting "until his

enemies would be made a footstool for his feet." 14. For by a single offering he has perfected for all time those who are sanctified. 15. And the Holy Spirit also testifies to us, for after saying, 16. "This is the covenant that I will make with them after those days, says the Lord: I will put my laws in their hearts, and I will write them on their minds," 17. he also adds, "I will remember their sins and their lawless deeds no more." 18. Where there is forgiveness of these, there is no longer any offering for sin.

Notes

1. *Since the law has only a shadow of the good things to come:* This verse is connected to what precedes it by the particle *gar*, meaning "since" or "for." In 8:5 the earthly sanctuary was called a "copy" and a "shadow" of the heavenly one. At 9:24 the author described it as a "copy." Now he returns to "shadow." He does not mention the earthly sanctuary explicitly, but rather speaks of what the Law "has," *echein*; he implicitly has the sanctuary in mind as he concludes the argument contrasting the sacrifices of the old covenant with those of the new. In 9:11 the author spoke of the "good things that have come about" as though they were a present reality, based on the appearance of Christ as High Priest. Because he is speaking of the old ritual of the Mosaic covenant he places these things in the future, since that covenant predated Christ's appearance as High Priest (see the Notes at 9:11).

   not the same form of these realities: A variant reading in the oldest manuscript of Hebrews, $\mathfrak{P}^{46}$, complicates an already difficult verse by omitting the word "same." This variant assimilates the shadow to the image rather than contrasting the two. Many commentators find that reading doubtful (Attridge, 267; Braun, 288–89; Ellingworth, 491; Hughes, 390; Lane 2:254; Weiss, 501–502). Therefore this clarification stresses that the "shadow" is not exactly the same at the heavenly prototype. The noun *eikōn* means "image" and was used of representative depictions. Here the meaning is that the earthly sanctuary does not adequately reflect the heavenly. Philo, reflecting the Platonic understanding, sees "shadow" and "image" as synonyms (*Allegorical Interpretation* 3.96). Hebrews does not share that view. "Realities" are simply "things" in the plural because the author is thinking of the sanctuary and all its furnishings (see the Notes at 9:23).

   it can never make perfect those who approach: At 6:1 the author exhorted his readers to move toward perfection. Then in 7:11 he began an exposition of why perfection could not be attained by the Levitical priesthood. As he prepares to make the decisive argument about the effect of Christ's priesthood he recalls again that perfection, the purification of the conscience, i.e., the removal of guilt from sin, could never have been achieved by the sacrifices offered in the earthly sanctuary. Those who first approach are the priests who come before God in the sanctuary (see the Notes at 4:16). A variant reading in some good manuscript witnesses (ℵ A C D[1] P 0278. 33. 81. 104. 614. 1241. 1505. *pm* a b z* vg[ms] sy) has "they [i.e., the priests or the sacrifices] can never make perfect." It is likely that the reading is a result of harmonizing with the plural verb in the preceding relative clause, "they offer."

by the same sacrifices that they offer continuously year after year: Multiple priests (7:23) and multiple sacrifices (7:27; 8:4; 9:6, 25-26) are indications of the weakness of the old covenant.

2. *Otherwise, would they not have ceased being offered:* The verb *pauein*, "cease," accompanied by a participle, means to stop doing something. The construction is common in the LXX (Gen 11:8; 18:33; 24:19; 27:30; Num 16:31; Josh 8:24; Tob 14:1; Jdt 5:22; 14:9; Esth 15:1; Job 29:9; 37:19; Isa 38:20; 1 Macc 2:23; 3:23; 11:50) and occasional in the NT (Luke 5:4; Acts 5:42; 6:13; 13:10; 20:31; 21:32; Eph 1:16; Col 1:9). The fact that the sacrifices had to be offered continually indicates that they did not accomplish their purpose. Asking this question does not suggest that sacrifices were still going on when the author wrote, as some commentators have maintained (Bruce, 227; Hughes, 391; Vanhoye, *Situation*, 49–50). The author has been arguing solely from Scripture and not from Jewish ritual practice in his day (Attridge, 272; Braun, 291; Grässer 2:208–209; Weiss, 503 n. 22).

   since the worshipers, cleansed once for all, would no longer have any consciousness of sin: The language of this verse has been used throughout the argument in these chapters. The "worshipers," *latreuontas* (9:9), are those who offer "service," *latreia* (9:9). They continue to have "consciousness of sin," *syneidēsin hamartias*, because their "consciences," *syneidēsis*, cannot be perfected under the old covenant (9:9). Repeated atoning sacrifices demonstrated for the author of Hebrews that those who lived under the old covenant were always aware of guilt from sin. The need for these sacrifices served as a constant reminder of the power of sin in one's life. As the rhetorical force of "once for all" indicates, the intent here is to confirm what the author wrote in 9:14, that the blood of Christ is capable of finally cleansing the conscience. He has stressed that Christ's sacrifice is "once for all," unlike those of the old covenant (see the Notes at 7:27).

3. *But in these sacrifices there is a reminder of sin year after year:* "These," *autais*, refers back to the sacrifices mentioned in v. 1. Numbers 10:10 speaks of "sacrifices of well-being," *tais thysiais tōn soteriōn*, which will remind Israel of God. Numbers 5:15 mentions a particular kind of grain offering, the "sacrifice of remembrance," *thysia mnēmosynou*, that "recalls sin," *anamimnēskousa hamartian*. The author seems to mean here that the rites of the old covenant made people conscious of sin.

4. *For it is impossible for the blood of bulls and goats to take away sins:* Not only can the sacrifices mentioned here not purify the conscience or remove the awareness of guilt from sin, they cannot remove sin itself. The author echoes 9:22: the forgiveness of sins requires the shedding of blood. There he made reference to the ritual of the Day of Atonement and the sprinkling of blood. Here he is emphatic: that ritual was ineffective on the basis of the sacrificial blood that was used. He has already mentioned in 9:26 how sin is removed by the once for all sacrifice of Christ.

5. *Consequently, when Christ came into the world, he said:* The expression "came into the world" has a Johannine ring to it (John 1:9; 3:19; 6:14; 9:39; 11:27; 12:46; 16:21, 28; 18:37). John uses it mostly to refer to the coming of the preexistent Son into the world, although in 16:21 it refers to the birth of a human (see 1 Tim 6:7). The

author introduces the psalm citation with the formula "he said." Christ has spoken once before in Hebrews, at 2:12-13. In both instances what he says is not drawn from the Jesus tradition, but rather from the LXX. As the psalms that Christ quotes interpret important aspects of the author's christology, Hebrews employs them to explain the significance of the Christ event. Trying to pinpoint when the author imagined Christ to speak misses the point, for it is really the Scripture that is speaking about him.

5b-7. *"Sacrifices and offerings you have not desired, but a body you have prepared for me; 6. in burnt offerings and sin offerings you have taken no pleasure. 7. Then I said, 'Behold I have come to do your will, O God,' (as it is written of me in the head of the book)":* The citation from Ps 39:7-9 generally follows the text of the LXX with some significant variations, notably at the end. Where the LXX reads "'Behold I have come, (as it is written of me in the head of the book). I wish to do your will, O my God,'" Hebrews has "re-scriptured" the verse: "'Behold I have come to do your will, O God, (as it is written of me in the head of the book).'" The alteration renders Christ's intention to do the will of God more forcefully than the LXX, where that intention is construed as a wish rather than as a purpose. By rearranging the parenthetical remark the author makes the verse a fulfillment of Scripture.

Sacrifices and offerings you have not desired: "Sacrifices," *thysiai*, is more frequent in the LXX than "offerings," *prosphora* (3 Kgdms 7:48; 1 Esdr 5:51; Ps 39:7; Sir 14:11; 31:18, 19; 32:1, 6; 38:11; 46:16; 50:13, 14; Dan 3:38; 4:34). Elsewhere in Hebrews the author uses "sacrifice" at 5:1; 7:27; 8:3; 9:9, 23, 26; 10:1, 11, 12, 26; 11:4; 13:15, 16. *Prosphora* is used only in this chapter (10:5, 8, 10, 14, 18).

but a body you have prepared for me: The LXX has altered the MT in this verse, which reads "but ears you have dug for me" (Ps 40:7). This is the only instance in the LXX where the verb "prepare," *katartizein*, translates the Hebrew root *krh*, "hollow out." Some LXX manuscripts do read "but ears you have prepared for me," (La^G Ga), but the most reliable witnesses have "body." Hebrews depends on a LXX manuscript tradition that has already made the change (Gheorghita, *The Role of the Septuagint*, 48). The words refer to the incarnation of the Son (2:9, 14, 17).

in burnt offerings and sin offerings: The whole burnt offering is introduced in Lev 1:3, which specifies a male sacrificial animal without blemish. The animal may be a bull, sheep, goat, turtledove, or pigeon. It is an atonement offering (1:4) that is supposed to be pleasing to the Lord (1:9) and is included among the sin offerings in Lev 4:1–5:13. Whole burnt offerings were a form of sin offering, i.e., a sacrifice for atonement (Lev 4:35) in which the entire animal was consumed by fire. Sin offerings were a form of burnt offering in which the animal was not completely immolated. The difference between the two becomes clear in Lev 6:26, which prescribes that the priest must consume part of the sin offering.

you have taken no pleasure: The point of the psalm is that ritual sacrifice does not please the Lord as much as obedience. This would seem to contradict texts such as Lev 1:9, 13, 17; 2:2; 3:16; 23:18; Num 15:3, where sacrifices are declared to be pleasing to the Lord. In the Deuteronomic literature complete devotion to the Lord is the proper attitude governing all religious activity (Deut 6:5; 10:12; 11:13;

26:16; 30:2, 10; Josh 22:5; 1 Sam 7:3; 12:20, 24). God's displeasure at hollow ritual and sacrifice can at times be strongly expressed in the prophetic writings (Isa 1:11-15; Jer 6:20; 7:21-23; Amos 5:21-25; Hos 6:6; 8:4). This devotion includes sacrifice, but without complete obedience sacrifice is empty (1 Sam 13:11-14; 15:17-23; Philo, *On Noah as Planter* 108). Philo distinguishes between "ritual" and "holiness," where the former focuses only on externals (*The Worse Attacks the Better* 21). In this light obedience does not replace sacrifice, but it is more important.

7. *Then I said, 'Behold I have come to do your will, O God:* The words of the psalmist, now attributed to the Son, disclose his obedient service to God (see 5:8). Hebrews "re-scriptures" the LXX so that the Son does not merely intend to do the will of God, but actually does it.

   (as it is written of me in the head of the book)': The MT has "as it is written of me in the scroll of the book." The LXX changed that to "the head of the book," which in Ezek 2:9 is a circumlocution for the entire scroll (cf. Isa 34:4; Ezek 3:1-3; 2 Esdr 6:2). Exodus 24:7 refers to the "book of the covenant," which provides the author with the only other use of the word. In Deut 17:18 the noun "book," *biblion*, refers to the Law (see 31:9, 24, 26; Josh 24:26; 1 Esdr 9:45; Neh 8:1, 3; 1 Macc 1:56; 3:48). It can mean any kind of writ (Deut 24:1, 3; Josh 18:9; 2 Kgdms 11:14; 3 Kgdms 20:8; 4 Kgdms 5:5, 7; 10:1, 6, 7; Neh 7:5; Mal 3:16; Isa 29:12; 30:8; 37:14; 50:1; Jer 3:8).

8. *When he said above:* The adverb *anōteron* can mean "above" (Lev 11:21; Neh 3:28) or "higher" (Luke 14:10). The author comments on the words of Christ, not those of the psalmist.

   You have neither desired nor taken pleasure in sacrifices and offerings and burnt offerings and sin offerings: The author addresses the two parallel lines (v. 7) in the psalm governing sacrifices and God's response to them. The combination of the lines yields a multiplicity of sacrifices, which Hebrews sees as a negative thing.

   (these are offered according to the law): The author editorializes on the words of Christ with a parenthetical remark that hearkens back to earlier mention of things established or done according to the Law (7:5, 12, 16, 19, 28; 8:4; 9:19, 22; 10:1) and notes that despite that fact, the sacrifices in question were neither desired by nor pleasing to the Lord. The remark should not be construed as coming from Christ.

9. *then he added, "Behold, I have come to do your will":* The obedient Son is described at 5:8 (see the Notes). The gospel tradition portrays Jesus as accepting his death as the will of God (Matt 26:42; Luke 22:42; John 4:34; 5:30; 6:38-40; 19:30). Paul speaks of the obedience of Christ in Rom 5:19 and Phil 2:8.

   He abolishes the first in order to establish the second: The verb "abolish," *anairein*, normally means simply "take away" in the NT (BDAG, 64). Josephus uses it for "abolition of duties on sales" (*War* 2.4) and the "abolition of honorary rights of citizenship" (*Against Apion* 2.41). In *T. Gad* 5:3 humility abolishes envy. The verb *histanai* often means "validate," but it can also mean "establish" and is used with *diathēkē*, "covenant" (Gen 6:18; 9:11; 17:7, 19, 21; Exod 6:4; Lev 26:9; Deut 9:5; Sir 45:24; Bar 2:35). Philo uses the expression only when he is citing the LXX

(*On the Sacrifices of Cain and Abel* 57; *On the Change of Names* 57; *On Dreams* 2.223, 224).

10. *And it is by God's will that we have been sanctified through the offering of the body of Jesus Christ once for all:* On the identity of God's will with Christ's see the previous Note. The author has spoken of "sanctification" that comes from the death of Christ in 2:11. In 9:13 the "sanctification" that resulted from the ritual of the red heifer is associated with the "purification of the flesh," which is then contrasted with the "purification of the conscience" that results from Christ's self-offering in 9:14. At 10:14, 29, and 13:12 the author will refer to this sanctification again. "Sanctification" has to do with cleansing and purification of the conscience of guilt from sin, which the author sees as the effect of the once for all offering of Christ. This cleansing distinguishes his cultic act from the repeated sacrifices under the old covenant. On the verb "sanctify" see the Notes at 2:11.

11. *And every priest stands day after day serving and offering:* Some manuscripts read "every high priest" (A C P 0278. 104. 365. 614. 630. 1175. 2464. *al* sy^p.h** sa), but "every priest" is better attested ($\mathfrak{P}$^46.79vid $\aleph$ D Ψ 33. 1739. 1881. $\mathfrak{M}$ bo). The variant assimilates this verse to the beginning of 5:1 and 8:3, and is unnecessary, as the high priest is himself a priest. Whereas the verb *leitourgein*, "serve," is frequent in the LXX, it occurs only three times in the NT and only once in Hebrews, which prefers "offering," *prospherein* (5:1, 3, 7; 7:27; 8:3, 4; 9:7, 9, 14, 25, 28; 10:1, 2, 8, 11, 12; 11:4, 17; 12:7).

    the same sacrifices that can never take away sins: A reiteration of 10:4 and a restatement of the ineffectiveness of the daily and multiple sacrifices that priests offered under the old covenant. The stress on the inability of these sacrifices to take away sins recalls the inability of the old covenant to perfect the conscience of the worshiper (9:9; 10:1).

12. *But when Christ had offered for all time a single sacrifice for sins:* The once for all sacrifice of Christ is contrasted with the multiple sacrifices of the old covenant (see the Notes on 9:26-28). "For all time," *eis to diēnekes*, described the priesthood of Melchizedek in 7:3, where the author likened it to the priesthood of Christ. It was used at 10:1 to indicate the inadequacy of the Law, and it will occur in 10:14 to show the completion of Christ's sacrifice.

    "he sat down at the right hand of God": The author alludes to Ps 110:1 as well as to his own Exordium (1:3). The psalm also features prominently in the exposition of the superiority of the Son over the angels (1:13). Here the author links the work of Christ as Son with his work as High Priest. On the similarity of this formulation of the psalm allusion to Mark 16:19 see the Interpretation at 2:5-9.

13. *and since then has been waiting "until his enemies would be made a footstool for his feet":* Another citation of Ps 110:1 recalls Heb 1:13. The enemies are not specified there or here, as the psalm is being used as an image of exaltation and triumph. Paul alludes to the psalm verse in 1 Cor 15:25, where the enemies are "every ruler and every power" and the last enemy is "death." The durative sense of "until" is present in that verse as here, but it is not clear that Hebrews envisions the same end-of-time scenario as did Paul.

14. *For by a single offering he has perfected for all time those who are sanctified:* The "single offering," *prosphora*, echoes the noun in the psalm citation at vv. 5 and 8, but it has the interpretation of the noun in v. 10 in view, which is the same as the "one sacrifice" of v. 12 (Attridge, 280 n. 34), i.e., the offering of the body of Jesus Christ. That Christ's self-offering had done what the sacrifices of the old covenant could not do, that is, bring the worshipers to perfection, has been a staple of the author's comparison of the old and new covenants (7:11, 19; 10:1). So "those who are sanctified" are opposed to "those who approach" in 10:1. On the verb "sanctify" see the Notes at 2:11.

15-17. *And the Holy Spirit also testifies to us, for after saying,* 16. *"This is the covenant that I will make with them after those days, says the Lord: I will put my laws in their hearts, and I will write them on their minds,"* 17. *he also adds, "I will remember their sins and their lawless deeds no more":* The author concludes this section of the sermon by selecting for a focus two verses of the Jeremiah citation that helped form the beginning of the argument in 8:8-13. He recalls 8:10 in v. 16 and 8:12 in v. 17. The Holy Spirit is credited as the source of Scripture, as in 3:7, but the verses cited have been altered to make the author's intended meaning clear to his readers. In 8:10 the covenant is established with "the house of Israel," whereas here it is simply with "them," making possible a more general application of the text. Also, the order of "minds" and "hearts" from 8:12 has been reversed to place "hearts" first. This may anticipate the focus on the heart in the hortatory section that follows (10:22; Attridge, 281). It also recalls the Deuteronomic injunction to serve the Lord with one's whole heart. The Deuteronomic ideal informed Israel's cultic life to the extent that it understood how ritual and sacrifice were pleasing to God when accompanied by the proper interior disposition (see the Notes to v. 8 above). The last alteration of the Jeremiah citation (31:33, 34) comes in the addition of "their lawless deeds" in v. 17. This addition may look back to 1:9, where it is said that the Son hates "lawlessness" (Koester, 436).

18. *Where there is forgiveness of these, there is no longer any offering for sin:* The concluding verse further interprets v. 17, as "not remembering" is replaced with a more positive notion of "forgiveness." In the context of the argument the verse has another function: it highlights the significance of Christ's self-offering. In 9:22 the author observed that under the old covenant there could be no forgiveness of sins without the shedding of blood. Now there is an end to sin offerings because of the kind of forgiveness that has resulted from Christ's death (9:28).

INTERPRETATION

The central argument of Hebrews (8:1–10:18) now comes to a close in this lengthy summation of the author's chief points. The main focus, though, sounds the note the author has repeated variously over the last two chapters: the sacrifices of the old covenant were powerless to purify the conscience of the worshiper and to remove awareness of guilt from sin. Perfection of that order could only be accomplished by the once for all sacrifice of a high priest, which would overcome the limits of ritual under the first covenant.

These verses are structured in four parts: (1) vv. 1-4, the ineffectiveness of the old sacrifices; (2) vv. 5-10, Christ's effective sacrifice; (3) vv. 11-14, the proof that Christ's sacrifice was complete; and (4) vv. 15-18, sacrifice is not necessary under the new covenant. This conclusion looks back to the longer exposition of the differences between the old and new covenants developed in chapter 9.

The opening verses recall what was said about the Tabernacle in 8:3, now applied to the Law in general. Law here refers to the ritual prescriptions discussed earlier, particularly those governing the Day of Atonement. The author presents the Law as something that foreshadows the sacrifice of Christ, which is the effective sacrifice of atonement. The view of the Law as a shadow finds support in the initial verses of the previous section (9:23-24), where the author alluded to the purification of the "sketches of the heavenly things," i.e., the earthly Tabernacle and the belief that Christ entered into the "true tent."

The heart of v. 10 draws the readers' attention to a point to which the author has been carefully leading them throughout the sermon. Even outside the formal structure of the central argument he has consistently called into question the ability of the Law to bring individuals to perfection, i.e., the purification of their consciences. Earlier, in 7:11-14, the idea that the Law was inadequate in this regard was planted in a question concerning the ability of the Levitical priesthood to help people attain perfection. The question in 7:11, "what further need would there have been to speak of another priest arising . . .?" subverted any claim that might have been brought forth that the Levitical priesthood was a sufficient means for bringing about atonement. The parenthetical remark in that verse linked the priesthood and the Law together, and a similar subversion in 4:8 undermined the idea that the ancestral generation had attained what it had been promised, "For if Joshua had given them rest, God would not speak later about another day."

The most telling subversion, if not the most effective for the author's purpose, comes within the framework of the central argument in 8:7, "For if that first covenant had been faultless, there would have been no need to look for a second one." Contributing to the author's view that the first covenant was not faultless was the fact that its priests and sacrifices were multiple (7:23; 9:6, 25; 10:11). These many priests and repeated sacrifices stand over against the singular high priest, Christ, and his "once for all" self-offering (7:24; 9:12, 25; 10:12, 14).

The subversion continues in v. 2 with the question placed in the minds of the readers, "if the multiple sacrifices of the old covenant could bring worshipers to perfection, would they not have ceased to be offered?" The author's logic is straightforward; if these sacrifices had been effective, the worshipers would no longer have consciousness of sin. The fact that they are repeated year after year signifies that the needed cleansing of conscience has not occurred. It is not, however, only the repeated nature of the sacrifices that indicates their inadequacy to purify the conscience; it is also the nature of the rituals themselves. Since the author is talking about something that occurs "year after year" he must be thinking of the annual ritual for the Day of Atonement. The purpose of that ritual in the author's estimation was not only to atone for sin; it also acted as a reminder of sin, forcing the people to attend to their sinfulness. If anything, it promoted the consciousness of sin (cf. Philo, *Special Laws* 1.215).

At this point it may be well to bear in mind that the author's perception of the ritual for the Day of Atonement and the way Jews understood that ritual may not agree. Doubtless Jews believed that by acknowledging their sins in this annual ritual and performing the rites prescribed they had achieved the atonement they sought. The author is viewing the old covenant from outside, and his own concern to interpret Christ's self-offering, his role as High Priest, and his inauguration of a new covenant has forced him to bring forth the kinds of arguments he has used in these chapters of the sermon to make his claims persuasive. Furthermore, his conclusion in v. 4 that "it is impossible for the blood of goats and bulls to take away sins" could only apply to Judaism as long as the Temple stood. In his own day these sacrifices had ceased, and other forms of atonement were practiced. So his argument for Christ's role as High Priest is enhanced by the end of the old sacrificial Law. Interestingly, this makes his own claim at the end of this section (v. 18) that "there no longer is sacrifice for sins" multivalent. He means it in relation to the forgiveness brought through Christ, whereas Jews in his day would take it as a simple acknowledgment that indeed those sacrifices are no longer offered, since the Temple has been destroyed.

In this light it is all the more interesting that at this point in his conclusion the author elucidates the issue of the role of sacrifice by transposing a citation from the LXX version of Ps 39:7-9 to the lips of Jesus. The psalm itself fits within the tradition of the prophetic critique of sacrifices that are offered without the proper internal dispositions (see the Notes to vv. 5b-7 above). A more positive expression of the same comes in Sir 35:1-12, where those dispositions are named by the sacrifices themselves, e.g., "The one who keeps the law makes many offerings; one who heeds the commandments makes an offering of well-being" (v. 1). Hebrews, however, goes further than the prophetic critique in opposing sacrifices to obedience. Rather than a desire for sacrifice, the Son proclaims that God has prepared a body for him, an unmistakable reference to his incarnation. That body becomes the vehicle of his worship, declared in the remainder of the psalm citation, "Behold, I have come to do your will." It is also the vehicle of his obedient self-offering. The force of the author's thought is evident in vv. 9-10. In choosing obedience, Christ abolishes the need for sacrifices, meaning that his own self-offering has rendered them obsolete (8:13). The author elaborates here on the notice in v. 4 that "it is impossible for the blood of goats and bulls to take away sins." Sin is removed and the consciousness of sin taken away by the obedient sacrifice of Christ. The effect of that offering extends to all who are sanctified by it (10:10).

The third part of this section (vv. 11-14) recalls the session of Christ at the right hand of God, a scene that has been cited or alluded to before in the sermon (1:3, 13; 8:1). The image contrasts with the priests who stand, and who must stand, over and over again offering the sacrifices, which themselves must be repeated. Christ having sat down, his priestly work is finished in what the author calls "the single sacrifice for all." It is that single offering that perfects or completes for all time those who are sanctified. In 2:10 it is Christ himself who undergoes perfection through suffering, and there the point is that he is sanctified by it. So it is not only completion that binds Christ to those who benefit from his death. There is a shared "sanctification" as well. More importantly, however, the expression "those who are sanctified" contrasts with "those who approach" (10:1), since their approach is granted by means of the blood of goats and bulls, which cannot sanctify. It is not merely a matter of approach or offering under the old covenant, for sanctification connotes the completed work of Christ, granting access to God that was not possible before.

The final section of this passage (vv. 15-18) offers scriptural testimony to what the author claims here by repeating two verses from Jeremiah 31 that he had previously used to define the reality and difference of the new covenant from the old (8:8-12). Here the verses are used in a climactic way. Jeremiah 31:33-34 represents the author's sincere belief that God continues to want to be in a covenant relationship with God's people. As has already been elucidated in chapter 9, the new covenant does not stress external rituals but rather looks to internal dispositions of the heart, chief among which is obedience. Also, under the new covenant God does not recall sins. Unlike the sacrifices of the old covenant, whose rituals were a reminder of sin, the efficacious self-offering of Christ not only takes away sin but removes the guilt of past sins as well, making the repeated offerings of the old covenant obsolete (v. 18).

Why does the author of Hebrews argue so vigorously for this notion of the new over the old and for the fullness of forgiveness that takes the old Law's sacrifices out of the picture? It is tempting to think that the author is dealing with a group of individuals in the community who think otherwise, perhaps in a completely opposite direction. If that were true, it could be a position more easily maintained were the Temple still standing. Hebrews, however, gives no real indication that sacrifices are still being offered in

Jerusalem. For a document that was probably written after the destruction of Jerusalem and the Temple in 70 C.E., the focus on sacrifice is indeed puzzling.

However, the stress on the new covenant may offer a glimpse into what the issue may be that causes the author to argue in this way. The internal dispositions required in the new covenant can be practiced as easily in an environment where there no longer is sacrifice as in one where sacrifices are still being offered. There is always opportunity for individuals like the wilderness generation to "go astray in their hearts" and not to know God's ways (3:10). The comfort and security of repeating external ritual actions associated with the readers' initial conversion (6:1-3) makes true internal conversion and progress toward maturity difficult. One is reminded of the saying in 1 Sam 15:23, "rebellion is no less a sin than divination, and stubbornness is like iniquity and idolatry." There are not many clues in Hebrews that allow for an unencumbered description of the community's situation, but the few there are may show that there were some problems resulting from too much concern about external rites. The inability of the readers to move on to maturity seems to result from the fact that they were somehow stalled at the level of their initial conversion and unable to progress further (5:11–6:3). If they were engaging in repeated ritual cleansings that should have been confined to their first repentance, then one can see in this context how the stress on the "once for all" nature of Christ's sacrifice might help to free them to move further in their spiritual development.

In 4:12, the word of God exposes the thoughts and intentions of the heart. This description of the function of God's word is pursued in 5:11-14, where the readers are accused of being dull of hearing and where the ability to distinguish between good and evil is a matter for the heart (5:14). Then follows the exhortation to leave elementary things, including the focus on external acts: dead works, instructions about ablutions, and the laying on of hands. The concern for external ritual over internal disposition may also lie behind the apostasy that makes repentance impossible. The curious claim in 6:6 that those who apostasize "crucify (*anastaurein*) the Son of God on their own account" could actually be translated "crucify again." This may mean symbolically that by repeating external rituals aimed at removing guilt over sin and intended to be performed only at the time of their conversion these individuals were counterfeiting the "once for all" self-offering of Christ by trying to offer it over and over again. Key to this understanding is the expression in 10:18, "Where there is forgiveness of these (sc. sins), there is no longer any offering for sin." The author means here that under the new covenant Christ's death was so effective that there remained no consciousness of sin, not even on God's part: "I will remember their sin no more." A similar expression of the author's sentiment in 10:18 is found at 10:26, where the question of repentance after deliberate sin is taken up.

There the possibility of repentance is ruled out because "there no longer remains a sacrifice for sins." By this the author means people who try, through symbolic external rituals, to effect what was attempted under the old covenant are doomed to futility, since the once for all self-offering of Christ has rendered such acts obsolete for them. So in Hebrews the point of proclaiming the new over the old, the better sacrifices and better promises, indeed, the better covenant is not about individuals contemplating a return to Judaism (Barnabas Lindars, "The Rhetorical Structure of Hebrews," *NTS* 35 [1989] 382–406). Rather, the author seems to be concerned with Christians who feel the need to repeat the purification rituals they underwent at the time of their conversion because they are still plagued by guilt from past sins. This the author sees as unnecessary on the basis of his understanding of the effective self-offering of Christ. Therefore he can exhort his readers to approach God with sprinkled hearts (10:22), the locus of purification under the new covenant.

Hebrews invites its readers to take seriously the good news that the death of Christ was efficacious for the removal of sin for all time. He suffered once and need not suffer again. Since Christ's death inaugurated a new covenant that focuses not on the consciousness of sin but rather on an obedient response to God, there is no need for repeated "sacrifices" or external rituals of atonement. These are replaced by conforming one's heart, internally, to God's will. Christ is always the model for the readers in Hebrews, something that is no less evident at the end of the sermon's central argument. The readers know what he has done for them by means of his self-offering, which has purified their consciences of sin. When they imitate his obedient response to God they acknowledge that he has accomplished for them what they could never do for themselves.

For Reference and Further Study

Grelot, Pierre. "Le texte du Psaume 39,7 dans la Septante," *RB* 108 (2001) 210–13.

Jobes, Karen H. "Rhetorical Achievement in the Hebrews 10 'Misquote' of Psalm 40," *Bib* 72 (1991) 387–96.

Johnsson, William G. "The Cultus of Hebrews in Twentieth-Century Scholarship," *ExpTim* 89 (1977–78) 104–108.

Nelson, Richard D. "'He Offered Himself.' Sacrifice in Hebrews," *Int* 57 (2003) 251–65.

23. *The Call to Approach* (10:19-25)

19. Therefore, brothers and sisters, since we have confidence to enter the sanctuary by means of the blood of Jesus, 20. by the new and living way that he opened for us through the curtain (that is, by means of his flesh), 21. and since we have a great priest over the house of God, 22. let us approach with a true heart with fullness of faith, with our hearts sprinkled from an evil conscience and our bodies washed with pure water. 23. Let us hold fast to the confession of our hope without wavering, for he who has promised is faithful. 24. And let us consider how to provoke one another to love and good deeds, 25. not neglecting to meet together, as is the habit of some, but encouraging one another, and all the more as you see the Day approaching.

Notes

19. *Therefore, brothers and sisters, since we have confidence:* On "brothers and sisters" see the Notes at 3:1. On "confidence" see the Notes at 3:6.

    to enter the sanctuary by means of the blood of Jesus: "To enter" is literally "for an entrance into the sanctuary," where the noun *eisodos* signifies a portal for access. The noun can be used for an actual entrance (2 Pet 1:11) or for the act of entering (Acts 13:24; 1 Thess 1:9; 2:1). Philo uses it for the entrances to the Tabernacle (*On Moses* 2.78, 91, 93, 94) and the Temple (*Special Laws* 1.156) and also for the meaning "making an entry" (*On Abraham* 116; *On Joseph* 183; *Moses* 1.302; 2.62). Interestingly, Philo also uses this term for the orifices of an anthropomorphized God (*Sacrifices of Cain and Abel* 96; *Unchangeableness of God* 60; *On Dreams* 1.235) or symbolically as the way into the body (*On the Creation* 119). On "sanctuary" see the Notes at 9:2. The instrumental sense of the preposition *en* is operative here. Blood featured prominently in the preceding chapter, where it was most often the blood of sacrificial animals. At 9:14 the author appealed to the greater effect of the "blood of Christ" in purifying the reader's conscience, since he entered the sanctuary with his own blood (9:12), unlike the high priest who must enter it with blood not his own (9:25). The "blood of Jesus" occurs only here in the sermon, although the author uses his name twelve other times (2:9; 3:1; 4:8, 14; 6:20; 7:22; 10:10; 12:2, 24; 13:8; 12:20, 21). The twelve occurrences of "Christ" show an almost equal preference for that title (3:6, 14; 5:5; 6:1; 9:11, 14, 24, 28; 10:10; 11:26; 13:8, 21).

20. *by the new and living way that he opened for us:* The noun "way," *hodos*, confirms the interpretation of *eisodos* in the previous verse as an "entrance." The adjective "new" or "recent," *prosphatos*, occurs only here in the NT. The author has used the adjective "living" to refer to the word of God (4:12) and Christ himself (7:25), and will use it of God in 10:31. Both adjectives capture the full effect of the "way" opened up by Christ. The verb "open," *enkainizein*, was used in 9:18 to describe the inauguration of the first covenant with blood (see the Notes at 9:18). *Hodos* is a normal word for "way," "road," or "path." Figuratively, it is synonymous here with "entrance." Philo uses *hodos* to refer to the "way" or

"road" that leads to God (*On the Creation* 144; *Posterity and Exile of Cain* 31, 101; *Unchangeableness of God* 160; *Migration of Abraham* 195). "New" recalls the earlier description of Jesus as the "forerunner" in relation to his priesthood (6:20).

through the curtain (that is, by means of his flesh): This part of the verse is difficult to understand because of the preposition "through" and the position of the parenthetical remark. *Dia* can have a local (through) and an instrumental (by means of) sense. It is actually written only once, in relation to the curtain, but it also governs "flesh" since both are equated here. Other uses of the expression "that is" in Hebrews confirm this interpretation, as what follows "that is" stands in apposition to what precedes it (2:14; 7:5; 9:11; 11:16; 13:15). Construing both uses of "through" as local presents a difficulty in grasping the author's thought. If the way into the heavenly sanctuary inaugurated by Christ is through a metaphorical "curtain" on the analogy of the curtain separating the outer from the inner parts of the tabernacle, then how could he have passed through his own body? Some have gotten around this problem by proposing that "flesh" refers to the incarnation of Christ, and since his human body was "torn" at his death the access to the heavenly sanctuary was opened through it (e.g., Hughes, 410). But as Westcott observed, this renders Christ's flesh as much an obstacle to God as was the veil of the tabernacle (*Epistle to the Hebrews*, 320). Resolving this problem seems to preclude the local sense of "through" being applied both to "curtain" and to "flesh." Looking back to 10:19, where we find the instrumental sense of the preposition *en*, "by means of his blood," the parallel of "blood" and "flesh" in this verse suggests that the first instance of *dia* should be local and the second instrumental (Attridge, 285–87; Lane 2:275; Koester, 443–44; Ellingworth, 521). In that way Christ's flesh is not an obstacle to God but a means of access to God's presence. Thus "flesh" refers not to Christ's incarnation in general, but rather to his death, as is indicated by the mention of his blood in the previous verse.

21. *and since we have a great priest over the house of God:* Here we have an echo of earlier texts. In 4:14 the author introduced the exhortation "let us hold on to our confession" with the reminder that he and the recipients have "a great high priest." Also, in 3:6 Christ was described as faithful "over God's house" as a son, whereas Moses was faithful as a servant. The reminder functions in a similar way here.

22. *let us approach with a true heart with fullness of faith:* The first of three hortatory subjunctives in this section, "let us approach," recalls 4:16. The order of the subjunctives is reversed here, with "approach" coming before "hold fast." On the verb "approach" see the Notes at 4:16. The qualification of approaching with a "true heart" characterizes the desired interior disposition under the new covenant (8:10; 10:16). Similar expressions occur in the LXX at Isa 38:3; 2 Chr 25:2; Jdt 8:28; cf. Ps 14:2 where it connotes sincerity or honesty. "Fullness of faith" echoes "fullness of hope" in 6:11 and looks forward to the exposition of faith in chapter 11. It is likely that the author intends a connection between a "true heart" and "fullness of faith" (Attridge, 288).

with our hearts sprinkled from an evil conscience and our bodies washed with pure water: The image of hearts "sprinkled" contrasts with the earlier rituals involving the sprinkling of blood and ashes (9:13). Christ's sacrifice was able to purify the conscience in a way that the rituals of the old covenant were not (7:11; 10:1-2; see the Notes at 7:11). There may be an echo of Ezek 36:25-26 here. The author is probably recalling the readers' baptism (Attridge, 289; Ellingworth, 524; Koester, 444–45; Weiss, 530).

23. *Let us hold fast to the confession of our hope without wavering:* The second hortatory subjunctive echoes a similar injunction in 3:6 and 14. The object in the former is "confession," as here, and in the latter "confidence," mentioned in 10:19. The "confession of hope" is objective as opposed to a "hopeful confession" on the part of the readers. "Hope" is a prominent virtue in Hebrews (3:6; 6:11, 18, 19; 7:19; 11:1). That hope should be "without wavering" recalls the image of hope as an anchor that keeps the believer steadfast (6:19). It is also in that context that hope united the believer to Christ by entering into the inner sanctuary where Jesus as High Priest and forerunner had entered (6:20).

for he who has promised is faithful: The author refers to God the author of the promise to Abraham (6:13-15), who considered God faithful (11:11). In the LXX and in Hellenistic Jewish tradition the image of a faithful God is common (Deut 7:9; 32:4; Pss 18:7; 144:13; 3 Macc 1:9 [A]; 2:11; Philo, *Allegorical Interpretation* 3.204; *Sacrifices of Cain and Abel* 17; 93; *Who Is the Heir* 93); so also in the NT (1 Cor 1:9; 10:13; 2 Cor 1:18; 1 Thess 5:24; 2 Thess 3:3).

24. *And let us consider how to provoke one another to love and good deeds:* The third hortatory subjunctive, "let us consider," takes "one another" as its object, with the goal of provocation to love and good deeds. The verb was used in 3:1 in an exhortation to consider that Jesus was faithful to God (the one who appointed him). For its range of meaning see the Notes at 3:1. Its use here makes yet another link between this section of the sermon and 3:1-6. "Provocation," *paroxysmos*, is the same noun used for a convulsion in medical terminology (BDAG, 780). The verb *paroxynein* is more common in the LXX than the noun, which occurs only twice at Deut 29:27 and Jer 39:37, both pejoratively. The meaning "stimulate" is found in Josephus (*Antiquities* 16.125). The only other occurrence of the noun in the NT is in Acts 15:39, marking the cause of the separation of Barnabas from Paul. It is the equivalent of the English "paroxysm." The mention of love completes the series of virtues: faith (v. 22), hope (v. 23), and love (v. 24), in this passage. "Good works" are opposed to "dead works" in 6:1.

25. *not neglecting to meet together, as is the habit of some:* The noun *episynagōgē* is more vivid than the simpler *synagōgē*, and with the *epi* prefix it has a more specific local sense. It occurs only twice in the LXX in conjunction with the verb *synagein*, "to gather": in 2 Macc 2:7, where it refers to the "gathering" of God's people, and in the *Psalms of Solomon* 17:50. The verb *episynagein* is frequent in the LXX but infrequent in Josephus, Philo, and the Pseudepigrapha. The noun "habit," *ethos*, means some customary action or belief. The verb "neglect," *engkataleipein*, normally means to abandon or desert (BDAG, 273; MM, 179). It occurs frequently in the LXX and can refer to God's failure to abandon Israel (Deut 4:31; 31:6; Josh 1:5; 24:20), to Israel's abandonment of God (Deut 28:20; 31:16; 32:15, 18; Judg 2:12, 13, 20; 10:6, 10), or to Israel's abandonment of fellow Israelites (Josh 22:3). It has the sense of "neglect" in Deut 12:19.

but encouraging one another: The author wants his readers to replace their negative behavior with more positive deeds. Mutual exhortation was practiced in Pauline churches and was part of the practice of psychagogy in philosophic communities (see Malherbe, *Letters to the Thessalonians*, 322–27). The verb "encourage," *parakalein*, is a stock term in Christian exhortation (see Otto Schmitz and Gustav Stählin, *parakaleō* [NT], *TDNT* 5:779–93). The author has encouraged his readers toward mutual exhortation in 3:13 as here, something that echoes his purpose in writing Hebrews to offer a "word of encouragement" (13:22).

the Day approaching: This is most likely an eschatological reference to the judgment day or the Day of the Lord (see 1 Cor 1:8; 5:5; 2 Cor 1:14; 1 Thess 5:2; 2 Thess 2:2; 2 Pet 3:10).

INTERPRETATION

With the central argument of Hebrews completed, the author now returns to exhorting the community to embrace the truth of what he has just explained. Language used in the exposition is brought forth in this new context and given hortatory force. The spatial movement of this text is interesting, as readers and author together are encouraged to enter the sanctuary as Christ did and to approach, i.e., take advantage of the access that has been offered to them. The call to hold fast may seem like a request to stop moving, but it means to keep faith all the while they are moving in the direction of a Day that is approaching them from the other direction. This, in the author's estimation, is a cause for hope. The verses are structured in two sections: vv. 19-23, entrance into the sanctuary; and vv. 24-25, fellowship in the earthly sanctuary.

Again stressing what is new, the author invites the readers to enter into the inner sanctuary, where under the old covenant only the high priest could go, and then only once a year. According to Lev 16:2 even the high priest could not enter the Holy of Holies except on the Day of Atonement, under penalty of death, to which all Israelites were subject (Num 17:13). Thus it is remarkable that the readers are invited to enter the heavenly sanctuary. The difference, of course, is the access to God granted through the blood of Christ. In keeping with the theme of the new covenant this blood, which also ratified it, is called the new and living way. The way has been opened up through the curtain. Here the author speaks metaphorically, referring to the curtain that divided the outer portion of the Tabernacle from the inner. That curtain acted primarily as a barrier, keeping people from transgressing the sacred limit. Here the curtain is a portal, granting access to God.

The readers are encouraged to enter with confidence, which has both an objective and a subjective aspect. The objective aspect resides in the assurance that the way is indeed open. The subjective aspect resides in their interior boldness, which has its source in their faith in the assurance they have received (see the Notes and Interpretation at 3:1-6). Yet another characteristic of their approach echoes the interiority of the new covenant already proclaimed (8:8-12; 10:1-18). Not only are their hearts the repositories of the fullness of faith, but they have been sprinkled clean from an evil conscience. Thus they have received the purification of conscience that is the effect of Christ's atoning death (9:14).

Through baptism (v. 22) the readers have received the cleansing of conscience the author speaks of. This is the only ritual of purification he believes they need. Any additional rituals are seen to call into question the "once for all" nature of Christ's self-offering by returning one symbolically to life under the old covenant. The author has already addressed this issue in 6:1-2; 10:1-18, and will return to it in 10:26-27. For the readers, sacrifices for sin have been done away with through the atoning death of Christ, so that baptism is the only ritual that can ultimately purify the conscience of believers.

The second part of the passage takes the next logical step, encouraging the readers not to waver in their faith and hope. God is faithful, and so nothing less is asked of them. The concrete expressions of their faith are made in the community, where they share fellowship in an earthly sanctuary. The model in this regard is the Son, portrayed in 2:12 as proclaiming the words of Ps 22(21):23, "I will proclaim your name to my brothers and sisters; in the midst of the assembly I will praise you."

Two things are mentioned in particular regarding their communal life. The first is that they are to provoke one another to love and good works. This kind of communal exhortation was suggested in 3:13 and, despite the warning against apostasy, the author clearly affirmed the fact that they have already exercised the kind of love for one another he has in mind here (6:10-11). Beyond those general remarks he does not offer a concrete means to accomplish the goal. One might expect it to be the manifestation of love and care that was characteristic of early Christian communities.

The second request the author makes is that the recipients not neglect the communal assembly (10:25). Without any details of what form such neglect has taken, one can only speculate about the reasons why people would absent themselves from fellowship with others. The reference to the approaching Day need not lead one to conclude that there was lassitude among some community members stemming from the delay of the *parousia*, or a belief that it had already occurred. Were that the case it might have been expected that the author would launch into a more forceful exhortation on the end time like that found in 2 Thess 2:1-12. Given all the stress on the cleansing of the conscience in these chapters, perhaps the awareness of guilt from past sins prevented people from freely joining in the communal assembly. Here the function of calling them back together is in service of their realizing the benefits that have been brought about by Christ's redemptive work. What the author has written here should be seen in relation to 10:32-39. Any community that has endured the suffering this one has should not squander its inheritance by eroding the support they have offered to one another in the past. It is not only in difficult times that it is important for communities to meet and band together, but in all times and seasons they need to await the approaching Day as those who have been promised an eternal inheritance and who together will receive it (13:13).

FOR REFERENCE AND FURTHER STUDY

Dahl, Nils A. "A New and Living Way: The Approach to God according to Hebrews 10:19-25," *Int* 5 (1951) 401–12.

Leithart, Peter J. "Womb of the World: Baptism and the Priesthood of the New Covenant in Hebrews 10.19-22," *JSNT* 78 (2000) 49–65.

MacRae, George W. "Heavenly Temple and Eschatology in the Letter to the Hebrews," *Semeia* 12 (1978) 179–99.

Pelser, G.M.M. "A Translation Problem—Heb. 10:19-25," *Neot* 8 (1974) 43–53.

24. *A Warning of Judgment* (10:26-31)

26. For if we intentionally sin after having received the knowledge of the truth there no longer remains a sacrifice for sins, 27. but a fearful expectation of judgment, and a fiery zeal that will consume the adversaries. 28. Anyone who abrogates the law of Moses dies without mercy "on the testimony of two or three witnesses." 29. How much worse punishment do you think will be deserved by the one who has spurned the Son of God, profaned the blood of the covenant by which he [or she] was sanctified, and insulted the Spirit of grace? 30. For we know the one who said, "Vengeance is mine, I will repay." And again, "The Lord will judge his people." 31. It is a fearful thing to fall into the hands of the living God.

NOTES

26. *For if we intentionally sin after having received the knowledge of the truth:* It is likely that the author has in mind the distinction in the Law between unintentional and intentional sinning (Lev 4:2, 13, 22, 27; 5:15; Num 15:27, 28, 29; 35:11; Deut 19:4; Josh 20:3, 9). The adverb *akousiōs* in these LXX texts covers unintentional acts. Hebrews instead uses *ekousiōs*, "intentionally," which is not actually used to specify intentional sin in the LXX, most likely because unintentional sinning is the exception (cf. Num 15:30-31). There is, however, one curious textual situation

that illustrates the distinction between these adverbs in relation to sinning. The
LXX of Job 31:33 reads: "And if when sinning unintentionally (*akousiōs*) I cover
up my sin," where a variant reading in S¹ has "And if when sinning intentionally
(*ekousiōs*) I cover up my sin." Philo contrasts these adverbs in *The Worse Attacks
the Better* 96 (for the use of the adjectives *ekousiōs* and *akousiōs* in reference to
something voluntary or involuntary see *Allegorical Interpretation* 3.141; *Cherubim*
96; *Sacrifices* 48; *Posterity and Exile of Cain* 10, 11, 48; *Unchangeableness of God* 48,
75, 113, 128; *On Agriculture* 176; *On Drunkenness* 66, 95; *Confusion of Tongues* 179;
On Flight and Finding 53, 65, 76, 86, 102, 105, 108, 115; *On Dreams* 1.71; *Special
Laws* 1.227, 235, 238; 2.52; 3.128, 134; *Questions on Genesis* 4.64).

   "After having received the knowledge of the truth" refers in general to the
enlightenment of the readers spoken of in 6:4. By making "knowledge" the
object of "receiving" the author rules out invincible ignorance. His readers
should know better. Specifically, "truth" means the teaching about the efficacious "once for all" self-offering of Christ, that it alone can purify individuals
completely from guilt over past sins.

there no longer remains a sacrifice for sins: This recalls the requirements for the
forgiveness of sin under the old covenant in 9:22 and the observation that, forgiveness having been given through the self-offering of Jesus, no other offering
can be made to expiate it (10:18). There the author used *prosphora*, "offering."
Here the word is *thysia*, "sacrifice." Together they receive a special focus and
interpretation in 10:5 and 8, as they are placed into perspective by the obedient
self-offering of Christ. In this context it may mean that attempting any other
rites of purification is senseless, since that end has been accomplished by Christ's
death.

27. *but a fearful expectation of judgment and a fiery zeal that will consume the adversaries:*
   "Expectation," *ekdochē*, is *hapax*. The sense is similar to its verb *ekdechesthai*, used
   in 10:13 and 11:10, "await." The element of fear is coordinated with the final
   verse of the passage.
      The zealous God is a standard image in the LXX (Exod 20:5; 34:14; Num 25:11;
   Deut 4:24; 5:9; 6:15; 29:20; 4 Kgdms 19:31; Ps 79:5; Wis 5:17; Isa 63:15; Ezek 36:6;
   38:19; Nah 1:2). For the association of zeal with a consuming fire see Deut 4:24;
   Isa 26:11; Zeph 1:18.

28. *Anyone who abrogates the law of Moses dies without mercy:* The verb "abrogate,"
   athetein, means to "declare something invalid" or "reject" it (BDAG, 24; MM,
   12). Hebrews has used the noun in 7:18 for the "setting aside" of the old Law
   governing the priesthood and in 9:26 for the removal of sin. In the LXX the verb
   connotes a violation of the Law in general and not merely some specific commands (Ps 89:34; Isa 24:16; Ezek 22:26; 1 Macc 15:27). For the legal connotation
   of abrogating a will see Josephus, *War* 1.646. In the NT the verb occurs in Mark
   7:9 in relation to the Law. Death without mercy is prescribed for idolatry in
   Deut 13:6-11 and is designed to act as a deterrent by instilling fear. Showing no
   pity, however, was not restricted to cases of idolatry, as Deut 19:21 indicates.
"on the testimony of two or three witnesses": Deuteronomy 17:6 mandates that two
witnesses are required for the imposition of the death penalty for idolatry, but

the need for more than one witness was stipulated for the proof of any crime or wrongdoing (Deut 19:15).

29. *How much worse punishment do you think will be deserved:* The argument moves from the lesser to the greater. A similarly structured question occurs in 2:2-3, and on a more positive note in 9:13-14. See also the variation using "how much less" in 12:25. The "punishment" in question is *timōria*, which in secular Greek is a punishment inflicted by a god (BDAG, 1006; see, e.g., Plutarch, *Moral Essays* 566E). While this noun occurs only here in the NT, it is found in the LXX and Hellenistic Jewish literature (1 Esdr 8:24; Prov 19:29; 24:22; Wis 19:13; Jer 38:21; Dan 2:18; 2 Macc 6:12, 26; 3 Macc 2:6; 4:4, 13; 7:3; 4 Macc 4:24; 11:3; Philo, *On Creation* 169; *Allegorical Interpretation* 1.107; *Cherubim* 78; *The Worse Attacks the Better* 169, 176; *Giants* 47; *On Agriculture* 100; *Flight and Finding* 84; *Special Laws* 1.54, 55, 284, 316; 2.232, 242, 253, 255, 257; and passim). For the meaning of *dokein* as "think" see the Notes at 4:1.

by the one who has spurned the Son of God: The verb "spurn" really means to "trample under foot" (Matt 5:13; 7:6; Luke 8:5; 12:1) and figuratively comes to mean "spurn" or "scorn" (BDAG, 523). The author's thought is related to the "re-crucifying" of Christ referred to in 6:6, which is intended symbolically. Christ's crucifixion brought about a definitive purification of the consciousness of guilt from sin. Deliberate, persistent sin shows a lack of true knowledge, i.e., of the meaning of the once for all self-offering of Christ and its effects. One involved in such sinning, then, spurns the Son of God, and any attempt at additional repeated rituals of purification further complicates the matter, since his death has abolished these rituals for Christians (10:9).

profaned the blood of the covenant by which he [or she] was sanctified: Although "blood of the covenant" sounds like an echo of the words spoken by Jesus at the final meal with his disciples (Matt 26:28; Mark 14:24; Luke 22:20; 1 Cor 11:25), it should probably be taken here in a non-sacramental way to mean the blood of the new covenant as compared with that of the old (9:20). Some commentators do take it as a reference to the Eucharist (Hughes, 423; Montefiore, 179). To profane the blood of the covenant is actually to treat it as "common," *koinon* (see 1 Macc 1:62; Mark 7:2, 5; Acts 10:14, 28; 11:8; Rom 14:14; Rev 21:27). Standing in opposition to that profanation is the individual's sanctification (2:11; 10:10, 14; 13:12). On the verb "sanctify" see the Notes at 2:11. Here the profanation follows from the spurning, mentioned above. It was the blood of Christ, not the blood of goats and bulls, that brought about the definitive purification of conscience for the readers. Repeated deliberate sin calls into question the efficaciousness of the blood of the covenant for the purification of conscience.

insulted the Spirit of grace: "Insult," *enybrizein*, is *hapax* in the NT and occurs only once in the LXX in a variant reading of Lev 24:11 [A1]. For the meaning of "insult" see Josephus, *War* 6.128; *Antiquities* 1.47, 165; 2.129; 5.314; 11.194; 20.117. Philo uses this verb once (*Special Laws* 4.202). The author may be making an oblique reference to the sin against the Holy Spirit (Mark 3:29; Luke 12:10; Attridge, 295). Those who commit apostasy after having been enlightened are called partakers of the Holy Spirit in 6:4. They are such because the Holy Spirit is instrumental in Hebrews for the proclamation of the word (2:4; 3:7). Anyone involved in the activity mentioned earlier in this verse would necessarily insult the Holy Spirit by rejecting the grace that accompanied the word of God (2:1-4), now spoken through an eternal Son. Grace and sanctification were given to the readers by means of the blood of Christ, which was offered through the eternal Spirit (9:14). Any profaning of that blood is taken as an insult to the Spirit.

30. *For we know the one who said, "Vengeance is mine, I will repay"*: A standard element in exhortation is to remind the readers of what they already know (Malherbe, *Letters to the Thessalonians*, 84–86). The circumlocution for God affirms that God will act on God's word, i.e., the offenders should expect judgment. The LXX citation of Deut 32:35 reads, "In a day of vengeance, I will repay," which differs from the MT original, "Vengeance is mine and recompense." Luke alludes to the LXX reading in 21:22, "because these are days of vengeance, as is written." The only other place in the NT where there is an explicit citation of this text is Rom 12:19, where it is in exactly the same form as in Hebrews. It may be possible that both Paul and Hebrews know an alternate version of the LXX, but it may also be possible that Hebrews, written in Rome, knows the Pauline version. Reserving the execution of vengeance to God is biblical (Lev 19:18; Prov 20:22; 24:29; Sir 28:1).

And again, "The Lord will judge his people": Another citation, now from Deut 32:36, is more exact except for the omission of *hoti*, "for," which is in the LXX text. The phrase occurs in Ps 135(134):14. For the notion of God as judge in Judaism and early Christianity see the Notes at 12:23.

31. *It is a fearful thing to fall into the hands of the living God*: The context requires that *phoberos* be translated as "fearful," as the theme of judgment runs throughout this section. This verse recalls v. 27, where the prospect of judgment is fearful. Although the adjective can mean "awesome," that meaning is not attested in Hebrews (cf. Swetnam, "Hebrews 10:30-31"). To fall or be given into someone's hands means to be overtaken by that one (Judg 4:9; 6:13; 15:12, 18; 1 Sam 28:19; 2 Sam 21:9; Neh 9:27; Job 16:11; Jer 12:7; 21:7, 10; 22:25; 26:24; 32:4, 24, 25, 28, 43; Ezek 10:7; 23:9, 28; 2 Macc 12:24; 13:11; 14:42; Matt 26:45; Mark 14:41; Luke 10:30, 36). For a positive sense of falling into God's hands see Sir 2:18 (LXX). "The living God" is a standard epithet for Israel's God, who is distinguished from lifeless idols (Deut 5:26; 1 Kgdms 17:36; 3 Macc 6:28; Hos 2:1; 1 Thess 1:9). The living God is mentioned at Heb 3:12; 9:14; 12:22.

INTERPRETATION

In this passage the author introduces a warning that parallels the one given in 6:4-8. The shared topic between the two units is intentional sinning after having received "knowledge of the truth." The idea recalls 6:4 where the subject is "those who have once been enlightened." There the sinners "re-crucified" the Son of God (6:6); here they have spurned the Son of God (v. 29). There they have made him a spectacle (v. 6); here they have profaned the blood of the covenant (v. 29). The earlier warning ended on a note of judgment (v. 8), as it does here (v. 30). These parallels suggest that the author is repeating the warning now that the central argument of the sermon (8:1–10:18) has been presented. In the context, then, the warning might make more sense to the readers after the priestly work of Jesus has been explained. It is hard to know if these warnings are general and are part of an effort to prevent deliberate sinning, or if the author is actually address-ing a real situation in the community. The theoretical nature of the warning argues for the former, whereas the fact that the warning is repeated here suggests that the author is not merely engaging in theological speculation. If he addresses a real situation, he has interpreted it as the readers' failure to have full confidence in the once for all efficacious death of Christ to bring purification of conscience, i.e., the removal of guilt from sin, which is an essential element of the new covenant. The failure was perhaps accompa-nied by repetition of purification rituals and instructions that were sup-posed to be confined to the time of the readers' first repentance, i.e., their conversion or purification (6:1-2). These acts rendered counterfeit the claim that "there no longer remains a sacrifice for sins" (10:18, 26).

The warning opens with a reference to intentional sinning (v. 26), reflect-ing the distinction Judaism made between willful and inadvertent sinning (see the Notes at v. 26 above). However, the author does not specify what constitutes deliberate sin, or what conditions must be met for a sin to be considered deliberate. In the previous passage (10:19-25) he referred to some people neglecting to meet together with the community, but it is not clear whether this failure constitutes deliberate sin. The present participle of the verb "sin" shows that the act was not a one-time offense (Attridge, 292), and so perhaps the repeated nature of the sin demonstrated that it was willful. Presumably unintentional sinning would require no ritual of purification. The issue seems to be one of persistent deliberate sin, for which the author believes there can be no forgiveness, since after the death of Christ there can be no other offering for sin (10:18). Actually, in much stronger language the author has already affirmed in 10:9 that for the readers Christ has abolished the sacrifices associated with the old covenant in order to establish the new covenant. One reason for the abolition of those sacrifices is that the complete removal of guilt from sin accomplished by Christ's death made it possible for people to have free access to God and to know God in a new way (8:11). Proper knowledge of God made it possible for God to promise to be merciful toward the people's iniquities and remember their sins no more (8:8-12; 10:16-18).

Curiously, the force of the warning in this passage seems to contrast sharply with the image of a merciful God who does not look harshly on sin. Here God's judgment marked by fiery zeal, which is capable of con-suming the sinner, takes the place of a sacrifice for sins. The imagery drawn from the LXX (see the Notes at v. 27 above) will be revisited in the final verse.

The language of judgment here is strong and forceful because the author deems the issue of deliberate sinning so serious. This view is confirmed by the reference to anyone who abrogates the law of Moses, as the punishment prescribed for that offense was death without mercy.

The *qal wahomer* (from the lesser to the greater) argument that concludes the warning puts the issue in perspective. Anyone who spurns the Son of God profanes the blood of the covenant, and insults the Spirit of grace receives much worse than what was meted out under the Mosaic covenant. What constitutes spurning the Son of God is determined by the second element, profaning the blood of the covenant. At 9:18 the author reminded the readers that "not even the first covenant was inaugurated without blood." He then recounted the story of Moses inaugurating the covenant, including the pronouncement, "This is the blood of the covenant, that God has ordained for you." Just as the first covenant was inaugurated with blood, so also was the second, but this time with the blood of Christ. The addition of the line "by which he [or she] was sanctified" alludes to the sanctification that resulted from the "offering of the body of Jesus Christ once for all" (2:11; 10:10). Deliberate, persistent sin ignores the meaning of his once for all offering.

The author reinforces the prospect of judgment by adding the modified citation from Deut 32:35. In their original setting these words were applied to Israel's enemies, but now the author directs them at Christians who fail to accept the truth about Christ's death. Further support is added by another Scripture citation from Ps 135(134):14, "The Lord will judge his people." Originally the psalm proclaimed God's vindicating judgment for Israel against its enemies, whereas here it becomes a proclamation of damning judgment.

Concluding it all, the author uses one of his favorite epithets for God, "the living God." Falling into God's hands here refers to falling under God's judgment as described in v. 27. The prospect of that judgment is indeed "fearful"; the very mention of it is incentive enough to avoid that fate. Throughout the sermon the author uses fear as a motivating factor in exhortation (2:2-3; 3:12; 4:1, 12-13; 6:8). When this verse is seen in relation to 3:12, where apostasy is described as "falling away from the living God," the irony is that in so sinning one actually falls "into the hands of the living God."

In this passage the reader confronts one of the most difficult teachings of Hebrews, that deliberate, persistent sin cannot be forgiven and will be harshly judged. The matter is further complicated by the lack of a clear statement from the author about what constitutes this kind of sin. Since he seems to be referring to repeated sins of this nature, it appears that he is speaking of a "state" rather than an isolated act. If this is how the author understands "apostasy," he must have in mind an individual who has fallen away from God (3:12) and has remained in that state of alienation. Indeed, the sense of that condition in 6:4-8 is that the alienation is so serious that even if there were the possibility of a second repentance it would be of no avail: hence the impossibility of making an attempt at a second repentance.

In some ways this teaching is arrived at through the logic of the author's thought on the atoning death of Christ. Since "sacrifices for sin" have been abolished by his death, for his audience there can be no sacrificial means of atonement after one's first repentance. This understanding of the effects of Christ's death is consistent with the warning in 6:4-8, where apostasy is likened to crucifying Christ again (6:6), since the sin involved would require an atonement that cannot take place again. In the author's logic sin cannot be forgiven without the shedding of blood (9:22), and the blood of Christ cannot be shed more than once (9:26). Therefore under the new covenant, in which God's merciful forgiveness involves not recalling sins (8:12), "there is no longer any offering for sin" (10:18).

In 9:26 the author says that Christ "has appeared once for all at the end of the ages for the removal of sin by the sacrifice of himself." This is a statement about ultimate atonement, which is complete and final. By means of his entrance into the heavenly sanctuary, where he put away sin once for all, Christ has also inaugurated the new covenant. To the extent that this covenant stresses the interior over the exterior (8:10), the transformation of the human heart replaces the need for external sacrifices (10:22), another reason why there are no longer sacrifices for sin.

Surely the author knows what the transformation of the human heart involves, as something that can only take place over time. He has warned his readers about not hardening their hearts (3:7-11, 13) and against having an "unbelieving heart" (3:12), and has offered the possibility of mutual exhortation as a remedy for the condition (3:13). He also mitigated the harsh warning of 6:4-8 with softer words in 6:9-12, as he will do with this warning in 10:32-39. It would appear, then, that the warning here is harshly worded for rhetorical effect because the author deemed it necessary to get his readers to consider seriously what the consequences of deliberate, persistent sin may be.

FOR REFERENCE AND FURTHER STUDY

Gleason, Randall C. "The Eschatology of the Warning in Hebrews 10:26-31," *TynBul* 53 (2002) 97–120.

Katz, Peter. "The Quotations from Deuteronomy in Hebrews," *ZNW* 49 (1958) 68–85.

Mugridge, Alan. "Warnings in the Epistle to the Hebrews: An Exegetical and Theological Study," *RTR* 46 (1987) 74–82.

Oberholtzer, Thomas K. "The Danger of Willful Sin in Hebrews 10:26-39," *BSac* 145 (1988) 410–19.

Proctor, John. "Judgement or Vindication? Deuteronomy 32 in Hebrews 10:30," *TynBul* 55 (2004) 65–80.

25. *A Note of Hope* (10:32-39)

32. But recall those earlier days when, after you had been enlightened, you endured a hard struggle with sufferings, 33. sometimes being publicly exposed to reproaches and sufferings, and sometimes being partners with those so treated. 34. For you had compassion for those who were in prison, and you accepted the seizure of your possessions with joy, knowing that you yourselves possessed a better and more lasting possession. 35. Do not, therefore, abandon your confidence, which has a great reward. 36. For you need endurance, so that when you have done the will of God you may receive what was promised. 37. For yet "in a very little while, the one who is coming will come and will not delay, 38. but my righteous one will live by faith. My soul takes no pleasure in anyone who shrinks back." 39. But we are not of those shrinking back to destruction, but of those of faith for the preservation of the soul.

Notes

32. *But recall those earlier days when, after you had been enlightened:* Recollection is a standard part of Christian exhortation (1 Cor 4:17; 2 Tim 1:6; 2:14). In 2 Peter the author uses the device as a way of preventing his readers from slipping into complacency (3:1-2). On "enlightenment" see the Notes at 6:4.

    you endured a hard struggle with sufferings: "Endure," *hypomenein*, means basically to hold one's ground or to persevere. It is a stock term in Christian exhortation (Rom 12:12; 1 Cor 13:7; 2 Tim 2:12; Jas 1:12; 5:11; 1 Pet 2:20). The verb is used elsewhere in Hebrews at 12:2, 3, 7, and the need for endurance is counseled at 10:36. The noun for "struggle," *athlēsis*, occurs only here in the NT and is not attested at all in the LXX. When used in relation to athletes it connotes a "contest." Here the object is suffering. Athletic imagery is used in the NT metaphorically for the struggles of living the Christian life (Acts 20:24; 1 Cor 9:24-27; Gal 2:2; Phil 2:16; 3:13-14; 2 Tim 2:5; 4:7).

33. *sometimes being publicly exposed to reproaches and sufferings:* The root of the English "theatrical" is easily recognized in the verb "be publicly exposed," *theatrizein*. It occurs only here in the NT and is not attested in the LXX. It is even rare in secular Greek. What the exact nature of the public exposure was is not specified.

Since "reproach," *oneidismos,* involved insult, abuse, and revilement, the readers may have suffered some kind of verbal abuse. If the author has Psalm 69(68) in mind, which the Synoptic Passion narratives allude to, he may be referring to a reproach similar to what Christ suffered (Matt 27:34, 48; Mark 15:23; Luke 23:36). The noun *oneidismos* occurs five times in this psalm (vv. 8, 10, 11, 20, 21[LXX]), and it appears frequently elsewhere in the LXX. The noun "suffering," *pathēma,* is more frequent in the NT and connotes physical abuse (Rom 8:18; 2 Cor 1:5, 6, 7; Phil 3:10; Col 1:24; 2 Tim 3:11; 1 Pet 1:11; 4:13; 5:1, 9). As most of these references have something to do with the sufferings of Christ, and since the author uses this same noun at 2:9-10 in relation to Christ's sufferings, it is likely that he is trying to make a connection between the readers' sufferings and Christ's.

sometimes being partners with those so treated: "Partners," *koinōnoi,* occurs only here in the NT. The Greco-Roman friendship tradition stressed that everything among friends was common, which meant sharing in joys and sufferings. This tradition was appropriated *mutatis mutandis* by Christians (Acts 2:43-47; 4:32-37). Paul emphasized the sharing of sufferings especially (1 Cor 12:26; 2 Cor 1:7; Gal 6:2; Phil 4:14). One need only look to Heb 2:14-18 to find an example of such sharing within the sermon itself. The intense sharing exemplified in this verse stands in contrast to the fact that some members had ceased sharing fellowship with the whole community (10:25).

34. *For you had compassion for those who were in prison:* The same verb "have compassion," *sympathēsai,* is used in 4:15 of Jesus, who as High Priest is able to "sympathize" with weak humans. The recipients of the readers' compassion were prisoners. They are not identified but are probably their friends or family members. The general nature of the term "those who were in prison" makes it likely that not all of them were Christians, although some may have been.

you accepted the seizure of your possessions with joy: The verb "accept," *prosdechesthai,* is cognate to the verb used in 1 Thess 1:6 and 2:13 to describe the Thessalonians' reception of the word of God. In 1 Thess 1:6 it is even qualified with the same expression found here, "with joy," *meta charas,* used again by the author in 13:17 of the joy of their leaders. Joy is a factor in Jesus' endurance of suffering in 12:2, as well as in withstanding discipline in general (12:11). The seizure could have been official or unofficial (see Koester, 460 for the relevant non-biblical texts). "Possessions," *hyparchonta,* is a normal word for goods (BDAG, 1029).

knowing that you yourselves have a better and more lasting possession: This contrast was a staple of early Christian preaching: material goods ought not to prevent one from entering the reign of God (Matt 6:19-21; Mark 10:17-22; Luke 12:13-21, 33-34; 18:18-25). The noun *hyparxin* can mean a possession and is meant to contrast with the plural "possessions" above. The fact that it is better and more lasting suggests that it is immaterial, perhaps salvation (Attridge, 300). Hebrews stresses what abides over what perishes in 1:11-12; 12:27-28; 13:14.

35. *Do not, therefore, abandon your confidence:* On "confidence" see the Notes at 3:6. The author exhorts the readers not to "abandon," *apoballein,* which can mean to "throw away" as in Mark 10:50 (BDAG, 107). The sense is stronger here, where the readers might willfully stop cultivating confidence (3:6, 14).

which has a great reward: "Reward," *misthapodosian*, is the same noun as in 2:2, where it means a just punishment. For the etymology see the Notes at 2:2.

36. *For you need endurance:* The noun "endurance," *hypomonē*, recalls the opening verse of this passage, where the verb "endure" was used. In 5:12 the author chided the readers for "having need" for someone to teach them the basics. This noun is standard in early Christian exhortation (e.g., Rom 2:7; 5:3; 8:25; 15:4, 5; 2 Cor 1:6; Col 1:11; 1 Thess 1:3; 2 Thess 1:4; 3:5; 1 Tim 6:11; 2 Tim 3:10; Titus 2:2; Jas 1:3; 2 Pet 1:6).

    that when you have done the will of God you may receive what was promised: The author makes clear that if they endure they will have done the will of God. The expression "do the will of God" is biblical (1 Esdr 8:16; 9:9; Pss 1:2; 30(29):5, 7; 40(39):8; 103(102):21; 143(142):10; Isa 44:28; Matt 7:21; 12:50; 18:14; Mark 3:35; John 4:34; 6:38; Eph 6:6; 1 John 2:17). The author predicates the reception of God's promises on the readers' ability to endure, provided they are doing God's will. The verb "receive," *komizein*, occurs in eschatological contexts elsewhere in the NT (2 Cor 5:10; Eph 6:8; Col 3:25; 1 Pet 1:9; 5:4). A contrast is being drawn here between the readers and the ancestors and heroes of faith (ch. 11) of whom it is said that they did not receive the promises (11:39).

37. *For yet "in a very little while, the one who is coming will come and will not delay, 38. but my righteous one will live by faith. My soul takes no pleasure in anyone who shrinks back":* The Scripture citation is a composite of Isa 26:20 and Hab 2:3-4. The author is faithful to the wording of the LXX with some modifications, the greatest of which is structural. Where the LXX of Hab 2:3 has simply the participle *erchomenos*, "one who comes," Hebrews adds a definite article, *ho erchomenos*, "the one who comes." "The one who comes" is used of the Messiah in the NT (Matt 3:11; 11:3; 21:9; Mark 11:9; Luke 7:19; 19:38; John 1:15, 27; 11:27). It is also applied directly to Christ (Matt 24:50; Luke 12:46; 13:35; Rom 11:26; Rev 2:25; 3:3). Hebrews also changes the mood of the verb "delay" from the subjunctive, "he may not delay," to the future indicative, "he will not delay." The author then transposes and rearranges the LXX text to help accomplish his purpose. In the LXX of Hab 2:4 the clause "but the righteous one will live by my faith" follows "if he shrinks back, my soul will not be favorable to him." Hebrews "re-scriptures" the verse by placing "but my righteous one . . ." before "if he shrinks back." The author also puts the preposition "my" in front of "righteous one" instead of "faith." The effect of these changes is to interpret the Habakkuk citation christologically. The way the LXX text is structured makes the subject of "shrinks back" "one who is coming." This can hardly refer to Christ, so by moving the clauses around, the author makes the subject of "shrinks back" someone else, who becomes emblematic of the readers being exhorted not to shrink back (Gheorghita, *The Role of the Septuagint*, 170–79).

39. *But we are not of those shrinking back to destruction, but are of those of faith for the preservation of the soul:* The author concludes the exhortation in a way that capitalizes on his "re-scripturing" of the Habakkuk citation. The noun *hypostolēs*, "shrinking back," plays off the conditional clause "if he shrinks back" in the previous verse, in keeping with the sermon's exhortations to advance, approach,

and move toward the goal. It has the sense of being in a state of timidity (BDAG, 1041). "Destruction," *apōleia*, is an eschatological term in the NT (Matt 7:13; Acts 8:20; Rom 9:22; Phil 3:19; 1 Tim 6:9; 2 Pet 3:7; Rev 17:8, 11), which contrasts in this verse with "the preservation of the soul."

INTERPRETATION

As the author had done in chapter 6, he follows a stern warning with encouragement, here designed to shore up his readers' hope. Recalling the hardships and sufferings they have undergone, he once again exhorts them to confidence and endurance as he leads them to the next chapter, which will showcase his encomium on faith. This preparation is facilitated in no little way by the inclusion of a scriptural text bringing Isa 26:20 and Hab 2:3-4 together. The "re-scripturing" of these verses from the LXX orients the author's thought to eschatological fulfillment and the need to keep faith and to endure. The passage is structured in three parts: (1) vv. 32-34, the recollection of the suffering and compassion of the readers; (2) vv. 35-36, an exhortation to confidence and endurance in preparation for reception of the eschatological promises; and (3) vv. 37-39, a transitional witness of Scripture confirming the value of faith and endurance, in anticipation of chapter 11.

Drawing on the athletic imagery of the "contest," the opening verses follow a standard practice in Christian exhortation: reminding the readers of hardship already endured in order to affirm that they are capable of remaining steadfast in the face of tribulation. The sufferings referred to in this passage are past. How remote they may have been is difficult to ascertain. It is possible that the tribulation in view in this passage took place in the late 40s under the emperor Claudius or in the mid-60s under Nero (cf. Lane, "Roman Christianity," 215; Helmut Feld, "Der Hebräerbrief: Literarische Form, religionsgeschichtlicher Hintergrund, theologische Fragen," *ANRW* II.25.4, 3591). Although it is presumed that the latter of the two persecutions was more violent, one need not conclude that members of the community had actually died. Still, given the description of the suffering here, it is likely that it refers to the time of Nero. Later the author will refer to present suffering in the community (12:4), which is probably associated with the situation of Jews and Christians in Rome in the aftermath of the destruction of Jerusalem and the Temple in 70 C.E. (see Introduction, 3. *Date*).

These sufferings could have taken forms other than physical violence and execution. Indeed, the things mentioned in this text consist of public reproach and seizure of property. Some people had been imprisoned and members of the community showed them compassion. In the current context the author seems to be not so much interested in recounting with precision the circumstances of past tribulations as he is in reflecting with his readers on their endurance and mutual support for others in a time of suffering. The note that some had their possessions seized points ahead to the better and more lasting possession that is theirs.

The central part of the passage encourages the readers once again to hold on to their confidence, here joined to the promise of a reward. Earlier, in 4:16, that reward was mercy and grace in time of need. Here, since there is yet another time of need under discussion, it is reasonable to assume that the reward is the grace to endure. That reward is not the end of the story, however, since the next verse (v. 36) spells out more clearly why they ought to endure: in order to receive what was promised. Endurance, then, is required for both the short and the long term. In more immediate circumstances it may be a question of survival as well as remaining firm in the faith. In the long run it is oriented toward being able to see the fulfillment of what was promised. This theme will return in chapter 11 as the example of those who sustained themselves with faith, without receiving what was promised, functions to encourage the faith of those destined to receive what was promised (11:39-40).

The final verses of the section demonstrate the skill of the author in bringing forth the witness of Scripture in support of his teaching and exhortation. The creative rearrangement of Scripture shows that he values the tradition that has been handed on but he does not view that tradition as static. Transposing and juxtaposing verses, changing the mood, tense, and number of verbs, and substituting nouns and pronouns are just some of the ways the written tradition he has received is "re-scriptured" for the need of the audience it now addresses. Thus in his use of the LXX the author of Hebrews is as much a hermeneut as a tradent.

In this particular case the author has transformed the citation from Hab 2:3-4 into a messianic prophecy referring to Christ by simply placing a definite article in front of the participle "he who comes." The modification of Scripture is further facilitated by inserting the personal pronoun "my" before "righteous one," thereby identifying that individual as the righteous one of God, the individual who lives by faith. The author has moved this verse from where it is in the original, so that "the one who comes" would not appear to "shrink back." The effect is to present a situation in which a righteous individual can go forward in faith or shrink back, in the latter case not pleasing God. The overall effect of the verse shows an individual poised in expectation of the end time and anticipating its arrival in faith. This is the example the author wants to present to his readers, as the concluding verse shows. Now they are exhorted not to shrink back, but rather to exhibit the faith of the righteous. The author is not only skilled at "re-scripturing" the text; he can actualize it as well.

Suffering can isolate a person from other people and sometimes produce in the sufferer a sense of entitlement, or a feeling that no one really knows, or can know, what they have endured. The remarkable thing about this passage is that, because of their own sufferings and the way they endured them, the readers are able to show compassion to others. Their compassion toward prisoners and the acceptance of the seizure of their property is exemplary in this regard for the way they were able to accept their sufferings in view of their final eschatological goal. By recalling this experience of theirs the author presents a Christian perspective on suffering. He in no way trivializes or reduces the real suffering they had undergone. He simply situates it in relation to larger issues in their Christian lives that require their attention as well. The readers could just as easily have fallen victim to their own plight and turned in on themselves. Rather, they reached out to others in need, becoming model Christians who understand the role of suffering in their lives.

For Reference and Further Study

Cavallin, Hans C. C. "'The Righteous Shall Live By Faith,'" *ST* 32 (1978) 33–43.

Fitzmyer, Joseph A. "Habakkuk 2:3-4 and the New Testament," in idem, *To Advance the Gospel: New Testament Studies*. New York: Crossroad, 1981, 236–46.

Lewis, Thomas W. "'. . . And if he shrinks back' (Hebr X.38b)," *NTS* 22 (1975–76) 88–94.

Sanders, James A. "Habakkuk in Qumran, Paul and the New Testament," in Craig Evans and James A. Sanders, eds., *Paul and the Scriptures of Israel.* JSNTSup 83. Sheffield: Sheffield Academic Press, 1993, 98–118.

IV. Heroic Faith and the Discipline of Suffering (11:1–12:13)

26. *The Assurance of Faith* (11:1-7)

1. Now faith is the assurance of things hoped for, the proof of things not seen. 2. For by this our ancestors were approved. 3. By faith we understand that the worlds were prepared by the word of God, so that what is seen was made from things that are not visible.

4. By faith Abel offered to God a more acceptable sacrifice than Cain's. Through this he received approval as righteous, God himself giving approval to his gifts; he died, and through it he still speaks. 5. By faith Enoch was taken so that he did not experience death, and "he was not found, because God had taken him." For it was attested before he was taken away

that "he had pleased God." 6. And without faith it is impossible to please God, for whoever would approach him must believe that he exists and that he rewards those who seek him. 7. By faith Noah, warned by God concerning things not yet seen, respected the warning and built an ark to save his household; by this he condemned the world and became an heir to the righteousness that is in accordance with faith.

NOTES

1. *Now faith is the assurance of things hoped for:* On "assurance," *hypostasis*, see the Notes at 1:3. Commentators are divided over whether "assurance" is an objective or a subjective thing. Those favoring the objective (Spicq 2:236–38; Michel, 373) choose a translation that captures the sense of "substance" or "reality" (e.g., Attridge, 309–10; Braun, 337; Lane 2:328; Westcott, 352–53; Héring, 98). Support for that option rests largely on the philosophical background of the noun and the lack of evidence for the subjective sense in the usual sources. Those who favor a subjective sense (e.g., Bruce, 278; Montefiore, 186; Hughes, 439) look to the LXX, where some examples of *hypostasis* translate Hebrew words that connote "hope" (Ruth 1:12; Ps 38:8; Ezek 19:5). It is not out of the question that the author may intend both senses. One of his favorite words, for example, "confidence," *parrhēsia*, has both an objective and a subjective dimension (see the Note to 3:6). The substance of faith, then, is not something the believer can produce at will, because it rests on a reality that transcends the individual. Still, the experience of trust in that transcendent reality cannot be completely excluded from the believer's experience of faith (cf. Josephus, *Antiquities* 18.24). The translation "assurance" covers both these aspects, since an assurance can be a guarantee (MM, 596–60; Spicq 2:336–38; Helmut Koester, *hypostasis*, TDNT 8:572–89) coming from outside, as well as a feeling of confidence in what is assured (Ps 38:8[LXX]; Grässer 3:94–96; Koester, 472). "Things hoped for" parallels "things not seen" in the next part of the verse. In Hebrews these objects of hope are things yet to be realized, i.e., the final destination of the believers: salvation (1:14; 2:3; 6:9, 11; 7:19, 25; 9:28; 10:23), rest (4:1, 6, 9), perfection (6:1; 11:40), promises (4:1; 6:12, 17; 8:6; 9:15; 10:36), purification of conscience (9:14), eternal inheritance (1:14; 6:12, 17; 9:15), redemption (9:15), and an unshakeable kingdom (12:28).

the proof: The usual translation of *elenchos* as "conviction" cannot really be supported, since this noun in its normal sense means a "proof," a "demonstration" (LXX: Job 23:4, 7; Epictetus, *Dissertations* 3.10.11; Josephus, *War* 4.337; Philo, *On Abraham* 35, 135, 141; *On Joseph* 107, 127, 235; *Moses* 1.272; 2.177, 200; *On the Decalogue* 140, 151; *On Rewards and Punishments* 4; P. Oxy. 2. 237.7.17; Josephus, *War* 1.530, 540, 601, 605, 626; *Antiquities* 16.233, 258, 333, 354, 363; 17.99, 101, 127; 20.47; *Life* 91; *Against Apion* 2.17; BDAG, 315), or a "reproof" (LXX: Hos 5:9; Hab 2:1; Job 6:26; 16:21; Ps 72:14; Prov 1:23, 25, 30; 5:12; 6:23; 12:1; 13:18; 15:10; 27:5; 29:1; Wis 1:9; 2:14; Sir 16:12; 20:1; 21:6; NT: 2 Tim 3:16 [*v.l.*]; Philo, *On Creation* 128; *Allegorical Interpretation* 3.49, 50; *The Worse Attacks the Better* 146; BGU 4.1138.13; Josephus, *War* 1.593, 599; *Antiquities* 8.252). In the NT the verb *elenchein* supports the meaning of "proof," as it means to "convict someone of something" (John 8:46; Jas 2:9). One needs proof to do that convincingly.

things not seen: In 2 Cor 4:18 Paul uses the same verb, *blepein,* for things "seen and unseen," qualifying the latter by saying these are "eternal." In Rom 8:24 he links what is seen and unseen to hope, concluding that no one hopes for something seen, but rather for what is not seen. While there may not be a direct correspondence between Paul and Hebrews on this point (Attridge, 311), the author, writing to a Roman church, may be making a connection to a tradition of that church with which his readers may have been familiar. In 8:25 Paul goes on to say that "If we hope for what we do not see, we expect it through endurance (*hypomonē*)." The author of Hebrews could have agreed with that sentiment. The invisible will be distinguished from the visible in 11:3.

2. *For by this our ancestors were approved:* "By this" refers back to the first verse and anticipates what follows (see v. 4b). The faith of the ancestors is that by means of which they were approved. The verb *martyrein,* "approve," in the passive here probably indicates that it is God who did the approving. The "ancestors" are designated by a common term in the LXX and Hellenistic Judaism for the elders of Israel, *presbyteros* (LXX: Exod 17:5; 18:12; 19:7; Lev 4:15; Num 11:16, 24, 25, 30; Deut 31:9, 28; 32:7; etc.). Usually in the LXX the noun *patēr* is used for "ancestor."

3. *By faith we understand that the worlds were prepared by the word of God:* "The worlds," *tous aiōnas,* although plural, refers to the world or the universe. The noun *aiōn* has this meaning in the LXX (Ps 65:7; Tob 13:7; Wis 13:9; 14:6; 18:4; Sir 36:26). In Matt 13:22 it refers to this world. The verse refers to the process of creation by God's word (LXX: Gen 1:3, 6, 9; Ps 32:6; Wis 9:1; NT: John 1:3; Philo, *Sacrifices of Cain and Abel* 65). In 1:2 the world was created through the Son.

so that what is seen was made from things that are not visible: The result of the process of creation is that out of the invisible came the visible. This need not be construed as *creatio ex nihilo,* but rather intends that the origin of the world lay in what was not a visible entity (Hughes, 443–52). The realm of things that are not visible lies beyond the sensible world (Philo, *On Creation* 16). This notion is at home in Hebrews, where the heavenly serves as a prototype of the earthly (8:5; 9:23).

4. *By faith Abel offered to God a more acceptable sacrifice than Cain's:* One curiosity arising from the author's presentation of Abel as the first example of someone who embodies faith is the silence of the Genesis 4 account on the matter. This, of course, led to speculation about why one brother's offering was more acceptable than the other's. Philo wrote an entire treatise on it, *On the Sacrifices of Cain and Abel,* in which he contrasted the brothers' sacrifices. Abel's sacrifice was superior to Cain's for three reasons: (1) it was living; (2) it was of the firstborn; and (3) it was stronger (88).

Through this he received approval as righteous: "This" can refer to Abel's faith or to his sacrifice. The Genesis account says that God looked favorably on his sacrifice, so if sacrifice is the antecedent of "this," perhaps the author has Gen 4:4 in mind. It is more likely in this context, however, that faith is the antecedent, as the same relative construction occurs in 1:7 with the antecedent "faith" (Attridge, 316). Genesis 4, however, does not speak of Abel's faith. The verb *martyrein*, "he received approval," means "be attested to" (7:8, 17; 10:15; 11:2, 5, 39). The author believes that God attested to Abel's righteousness, another detail lacking in the original Genesis account. The author may know of the Hellenistic Jewish tradition about the righteous Abel (Attridge cites *1 Enoch* 22:7; *T. Abr* 13:2-3; Matt 23:35; and 1 John 3:12). If he did know this tradition, it is possible that the author reasoned that, because of his righteousness, Abel must have had exemplary faith. He could have arrived at this conclusion on the basis of Hab 2:4, which he had cited in the previous chapter: "my righteous one shall live by faith," since specific traditions about Abel's faith are lacking (cf. Attridge, 317).

God himself giving approval to his gifts: The author returns to the Genesis account and acknowledges that it was not only through his faith that Abel was approved by God, but also through his gifts, *dōra*. Hebrews uses the two terms synonymously in 5:1; 8:3, 4; and 9:9.

he died, and through it he still speaks: The antecedent of "it" is likely faith. Just how Abel speaks beyond the grave is not stated. The biblical account tells of the blood of Abel crying out to God from the ground (Gen 4:10). Koester (476) points out, however, that this is not exactly the same as "speaking," as it carries a sense of accusation and vengeance. Another possibility is that he speaks through the Scripture that keeps his story alive (Spicq 2:343).

5. *By faith Enoch was taken so that he did not experience death:* The mysterious figure of Enoch was a righteous individual, and as the Scripture says, "he walked with God" (Gen 5:24). The verb "be taken," *metatitesthai*, means "be translated from one place to another" (BDAG, 643; lxx). Literary accounts of great persons being taken up into heaven on the analogy with Elijah were popular in Hellenistic Judaism, and there is an entire Enoch literature that attests to interest in him. The tradition most likely developed from the curious reference to his disappearance when he was taken by God (Gen 5:24).

and he was not found, because God had taken him: This line of the verse is almost identical to the lxx of Gen 5:24.

For it was attested before he was taken away that "he had pleased God": The expression "it was attested" refers to scriptural witness (7:8, 17; 10:15; 11:2, 5, 39). "He had pleased God" is the lxx's translation of the Hebrew, which reads, "Enoch walked with God." The link between Enoch as someone who pleased God and someone who had faith is confirmed by the following verse. There are, however, references in Hellenistic Judaism that portray Enoch as righteous (*T. Levi* 10:5; *T. Dan* 5:6; *T. Benj* 9:1; *1 Enoch* 1:2; 12:1; *Jub* 10:17). As with Abel, he may be an example of the righteous one who lives by faith (Koester, 482).

6. *And without faith it is impossible to please God:* The beginning of this verse sounds like special pleading. Hebrews speaks about pleasing God in 13:16 and 21.

for whoever would approach him must believe that he exists and that he rewards those who seek him: On the verb "approach" see the Notes at 4:16. This verse sounds like a truism, for who would believe in a god that did not exist? It is not entirely out of place, however, in a discussion of faith that includes "proof of things not seen." God in Hebrews is invisible (11:27) but God is still the object of faith (10:22). God is presented in Hebrews as a God who rewards justly (2:2; 10:35; 11:35). Seeking God is a proper attitude in Jewish piety (LXX: Deut 4:29; 1 Esdr 7:13; 8:50; Pss 26:8; 104:4; Prov 16:8; Mal 3:1; Isa 55:6; Jer 50:4).

7. *By faith Noah, warned by God concerning things not yet seen:* Noah is said to have been warned by God. The verb "warn," *chrēmatizein,* was used earlier in relation to Moses (see the Notes to 8:5). "Things not yet seen" recalls v. 1, "proof of things not seen." Here, however, the expression refers not to heavenly realities and awaited fulfillments, but rather to the flood.

respected the warning and built an ark to save his household: "Respect," *eulabeisthai,* contains the root of the noun *eulabeia,* "awe" or "fear" (Heb 5:7; 12:28). The sense, then, is that Noah responded out of piety. Only Hebrews in the NT uses this verb, but it is plentiful in the LXX, where it often has the sense of fear alone, but sometimes carries the meaning of "fear of the holy" (e.g., Exod 3:6; Jer 5:22; Nah 1:7; Zeph 1:7; 3:12; Zech 2:13; Mal 3:16; Sir 7:29; Wis 7:29). It may be that the author has this meaning in mind. Genesis 6:22 simply says that "Noah did (*epoiēsen*) everything that the Lord God had commanded him." Hebrews notes that Noah built the ark to save his household (on the verb "build," see the Notes at 9:2).

by this he condemned the world: "By this" can refer to "faith" at the beginning of the verse or to "the ark"; given the context, "faith" is more probable (cf. Westcott, 356). The verb "condemn," *katakrinein,* is a legal term that means "pronounce judgment" (LXX: Esth 2:1; Sus 41, 48, 53; Wis 4:16; BDAG, 519; MM, 328). Genesis makes no mention of such a condemnation. The author may have in mind the tradition of Wis 2:12, where the righteous one, simply on the basis of his/her own righteousness, reproaches (*oneidizein*) those who transgress the Law (cf. Matt 12:41-42; Luke 11:31-32). So Noah's faith itself is the instrument of condemnation. Hellenistic Judaism's tradition about Noah portrays him as someone who proclaims righteousness (Josephus, *Antiquities* 1.74; *Sib Or* 1.125-36; *Jub* 7:20, cited by Koester, 476).

became an heir to the righteousness that is in accordance with faith: Genesis 6:9 and 7:1 leave the impression that Noah was the progenitor of righteousness and not an heir to it. The author is attempting to inspire the readers to endurance and steadfastness in faith. Noah and his family were saved because of his faith, and faith will serve as the basis for the inheritance promised to those who follow his example (1:14; 6:12, 17; 9:15). The last part of the verse shows how closely the author sees the relationship of righteousness and faith to be.

INTERPRETATION

One of the best known parts of Hebrews, chapter 11 presents the readers with a catalogue of heroes of faith for their consideration and edification. Faith plays a pivotal role in the sermon as the virtue that demonstrates obedience to the will of God. The premier example of faith is Christ himself

(2:13; 5:7), but the figures brought forth in this chapter attest to its perennial value. The lesson for the readers is that if such faith were possible before the coming of Christ, how much greater are the opportunities for faith now that he has come (Eisenbaum, *Jewish Heroes*, 186).

The chapter comprises six parts presenting groups of heroes from Israel's past. The first seven verses offer a brief definition of faith in three verses followed by the examples of Abel, Enoch, and Noah (11:1-7). In 11:8-12 the attention shifts to Abraham and Sarah. The catalogue of exemplars is interrupted by vv. 13-16, with a brief evaluation of those already presented. The catalogue resumes in vv. 17-22 with a return to Abraham and the binding of Isaac. In this section the descendants of Abraham, Jacob, Esau, and Joseph are included as well. The fifth subdivision, vv. 23-31, includes Moses, the walls of Jericho, and Rahab. In the final section, vv. 32-40, the author concludes with a cursory treatment of judges, kings, and prophets, as well as martyrs, who suffered all sorts of tribulations. The overall conclusion is that none of these individuals, even though they exhibited faith, received what was promised.

Hebrews is not unique in cataloguing heroes in this way; such catalogues are extant within the Bible and the literature of Hellenistic Judaism, as well as in Greek and Roman literature. Major studies have analyzed and compared the lists of heroes in these various literatures to the eleventh chapter of Hebrews (see Michael R. Cosby, *The Rhetorical Composition and Function of Hebrews 11 in Light of Example Lists in Antiquity* [Macon, GA: Mercer University Press, 1988]; Eisenbaum, *Jewish Heroes*; Hartwig Thyen, *Der Stil*). In general, these studies conclude that such lists of exemplars may show some formal similarities to one another, but each functions differently in the literature in which it is located. The same may be said of Hebrews 11.

Within the biblical tradition hero lists are found in Sirach 44–50; 1 Macc 2:51-60; Wisdom 10; 4 Maccabees 16:16-23; 18:11-19. Some include Acts 7 in the NT. In Hellenistic Jewish literature they are found in the Damascus Document at Qumran (CD); *4 Ezra* 7:105-111; Philo, *On Rewards and Punishments* 11–51; and *On the Virtues* 198–227 (see Eisenbaum, *Jewish Heroes*, 35–52).

The unit under consideration here is 11:1-7. The first three verses offer a working definition of faith (Attridge, 307). As such they determine the shape of the sections that follow, where the definition is applied to various figures, whom the author believes embody faith. These verses are held together by a consideration of the role of faith in relation to what is seen and unseen. To some extent placing faith in the unseen is an idea commonly held in faith-based religions, but in Hebrews the focus is sharper in light of the pilgrimage motif running throughout the sermon. The readers are invited to move toward the unseen in order to receive the fulfillment of God's promises. One need not conclude to a specific problem in the readers that the author was trying to address. There does not seem to be evidence in the sermon for a group of empiricists who refused to believe anything they could not see or demonstrate. Rather, the author employs the seen/ unseen duality for comparative purposes. The ancestors had faith in promises unseen and ultimately unrealized, and their example should inspire the readers to go beyond even the faith they had. The cause for confidence is, in part, what they see or what the author invites them to see. Indeed, there are things they are unable to see (2:8). They do, however, see Jesus (2:9) in the example of his own faith, as he endured suffering for the joy that lay ahead of him (12:2). It is to him that they are exhorted to look. So, as with the heroes, it is not the faith of Jesus per se that the readers are able to apprehend, but what faith led him to do. Faith then makes the intangible tangible in the actions that express faith in people's lives. That is the role of faith in relation to the seen and unseen.

That having been said, it is curious that the first heroes on the list are not known explicitly in the biblical tradition for their faith as much as for their righteousness (see the Notes above). The author, however, does not make a strict dichotomy between faith and righteousness, having been so strongly influenced by Hab 2:2-3.

In v. 2 the example of Abel and the notice that "he received approval as righteous" illustrate faith. So two things are operative. First, Abel was righteous, and the "righteous live by faith." Second, he was approved by God, which is yet another proof that he had faith. Abel is also an example of one whose faith extends beyond the grave. Despite the fact that the readers know that Abel did not simply die but was murdered, the author presents his death as unremarkable. The untimely death of the righteous is a part of biblical tradition (Wisdom 2), which the author might have exploited in the example of Abel but chose not to. Rather, he passes over that aspect of the biblical narrative in order to show that Abel's death did not put an end to his faith, as it still speaks. The reference is probably to that part of the Genesis account in which God proclaims that Abel's blood cries out from the ground, here taken as a witness to his faith. The fact that Abel leads the list of witnesses who attest to the power of faith is also a way in which his faith still speaks, for the author has himself given it a voice.

Enoch, too, was approved by God, since he was attested as "having pleased God." The author notes that Enoch did not see death; thus he lives. Some commentators see an echo of Hab 2:2-3 in this description. Since Enoch lives, he is not only righteous but an example of faith (Koester, 482). Braun (*An die Hebräer*, 348) looks to *3 Enoch* 6:3 for an important link between righteousness and faith, "And this one whom I have removed from them is the choicest of them all and worth them all in faith, righteousness, and fitting conduct" (trans. P. Alexander in Charlesworth 1:261). There is, however, no evidence in these verses that the author knows of the tradition of Enoch as righteous. Interestingly, Sir 44:16 places Enoch right before Noah, and the entry on him shares language with Hebrews: "Enoch pleased the Lord and was taken up, an example of repentance to all generations." Repentance rather than righteousness seems to be the thing for which Enoch is remembered. But even that seems not to have appealed to the author.

After the example of Enoch, the author expands a bit on the relationship between faith and pleasing God. The claims made here are self-evident. If a person did not believe that God existed, i.e., did not have faith, there would be no attempt to try to please God. This interlude follows on the observation that Enoch pleased God and represents the author's effort to make a closer connection between Enoch and faith. Doubtless he was aware of the tradition that presented Enoch as a model of repentance, and that tradition did not fit his purpose. Since the biblical text of Gen 5:24, however, mentions that Enoch pleased God, the author seized on that aspect of the tradition in order to say something about the quality of Enoch's faith. It is curious that the author had to go to such lengths, if it were adequate to portray Enoch as one who lives and is therefore righteous. If anything, the focus on Enoch pleasing God would argue against him as someone who embodies Hab 2:2-3.

The final example in this section is Noah. The biblical account of Noah and the flood does not really attend to Noah's faith. Rather, he is presented as a righteous and blameless person, for which reason he and his family are spared the devastation of the flood. The tradition of his righteousness may be the reason why he is included here, as he would be an example of the righteous person who lives by faith (Hab 2:2-3). The final verse confirms that interpretation, since his righteousness is seen as a product of his faith.

However, the author provides additional qualifying information in the notice that Noah was warned by God about things unseen. Part of the definition of faith given above is that it is proof of things not seen. Thus the fact that Noah heeded God's warning seems to be an adequate demonstration that he had faith. Again it is the question of how Noah demonstrated his faith that has captured the author's imagination; it is faith in action. As a person warned about what is yet unseen, he is like the readers, who must anticipate salvation under the rubric of what is unseen (Koester, 483).

The issues of faith and faithfulness are prominent in Hebrews. In this chapter the author begins a lengthy exposition of faith that relies not on definition alone, even though that is his point of departure. Locating himself within the tradition of the Hebrew Bible and Hellenistic Judaism, the author knows that examples are necessary to make faith concrete. To avoid an extended theological exposition on faith, he presents portraits of faith evident in the heroes who have embodied it. Through each of the examples he presents, the author tries to show the relationship between faith in the unseen and how one lives a life pleasing to God. This is the witness of the heroes presented in this part of the chapter.

FOR REFERENCE AND FURTHER STUDY

Cosby, Michael R. *The Rhetorical Composition and Function of Hebrews 11 in Light of Example Lists in Antiquity.* Macon, GA: Mercer University Press, 1988.

Grässer, Erich. *Der Glaube im Hebräerbrief.* MTS 2. Marburg: Elwert, 1965.

Hamm, Dennis. "Faith in the Epistle to the Hebrews: The Jesus Factor," *CBQ* 52 (1990) 270–91.

Hughes, Philip E. "The Doctrine of Creation in Hebrews 11:3," *BTB* 2 (1972) 64–77.

Kendall, R. T. *Believing God: Studies on Faith in Hebrews 11.* Grand Rapids: Zondervan, 1981.

27. *The Faith of Abraham, Sarah, and Their Descendants* (11:8-12)

8. By faith Abraham obeyed when he was called to set out for a place that he was to receive as an inheritance; and he set out, not knowing where he was going. 9. By faith he sojourned in the land of the promise, as in a foreign land, living in tents, as did Isaac and Jacob, who were heirs with him of the same promise. 10. For he looked forward to the city that has foundations, whose architect and builder is God. 11. By faith he received power of procreation, even beyond the normal age—with Sarah, who was barren—since he considered him faithful who had promised. 12. Therefore from one person, and this one as good as dead, descendants were born, "as many as the stars of heaven and as the innumerable grains of sand by the seashore."

NOTES

8. *By faith Abraham obeyed when he was called to set out for a place that he was to receive as an inheritance:* Abraham's faith is legendary in the scriptural tradition and in Hellenistic Judaism, so, unlike the previous two examples, he is someone known especially for his faith (LXX: Gen 15:6; Sir 44:20; Philo, *Migration of Abraham* 43, 44, 132; *On Abraham* 262, 269, 270, 273). Abraham is also known for his righteousness (Philo, *Migration of Abraham* 121–24; *On Abraham* 232). According to the LXX, the first person Abraham explicitly obeyed was his wife Sarah in 16:2, where the same verb as in Heb 11:8, *hypakouein*, is used. Of course, he is shown as obedient to God in Gen 12:4, "And Abraham went, as the LORD had told him." Elsewhere in the narrative Abraham obeys God in Gen 22:18 and 26:5. The author follows the LXX account of Abraham's migration to Canaan in his notice that Abraham set out for the land of Canaan (Gen 12:5). Hebrews identifies the destination as the "place," *topos*, that was to be his "inheritance," a concept that has deeper meaning in the sermon (1:14; 6:12, 17). In 11:10 the author will draw out the symbolic significance of Abraham's destination.

not knowing where he was going: The Genesis account leaves the impression that Abraham knew where he was going. Genesis 11:31 says that Terah's family set out for the land of Canaan. The symbolic significance of this remark shows the author's purpose. Faith is the assurance of things not seen (11:1), and thus the object of faith is not readily apprehended.

9. *By faith he sojourned in the land of the promise:* The verb "sojourn," *paroikein,* echoes the LXX account of Abraham's stay in Canaan (Gen 12:10; 18:8). He also sojourns in Gerar and other Philistine lands (20:1; 21:23, 34). The expression "the land of the promise" does not occur in the LXX and is the author's formulation of what is implicit in the biblical account (Gen 12:7; 13:14; 18:19).

   as in a foreign land, living in tents, as did Isaac and Jacob, who were heirs with him of the same promise: Genesis 15:13 contains a divine oracle that Abraham and his descendants will sojourn in a land not their own (*en gę ouk idią*). The verb "dwell," *katoikein,* contrasts with "sojourn," *paroikein.* Genesis 4:20 (LXX) uses the simple verb *oikein* when describing Jabal, "the ancestor of those who dwell in tents." The same verb occurs in relation to Abraham in Gen 16:3; 20:1; 24:3. Since, however, *katoikein* appears in reference to Abraham in 13:6, 12, 18; 14:13; 20:15; 22:19, probably not too much should be made of the choice of verbs here. See Gen 26:2-3; 37:1; 47:4, where both verbs are synonymous. The mention of Abraham, Isaac, and Jacob together is common in the biblical tradition (see, e.g., Exod 3:6, 15; 4:5; Matt 22:32; Mark 12:26; Luke 20:37; Acts 3:13).

10. *For he looked forward to the city that has foundations, whose architect and builder is God:* The imagery shifts from the land that was promised to a city. "Looked forward," *ekdechesthai,* should probably be taken as eschatological, as in 10:13. The tradition in *2 Bar* 4:1-7, where a heavenly Jerusalem is shown to Adam, Abraham, and Moses, may have influenced the author (cf. *2 Enoch* 55:2; Attridge, 324; Koester, 486). In *4 Ezra* 10:27 the city is said to have huge foundations (Rev 21:14, 19). The heavenly Jerusalem and an earthly city that does not remain are mentioned in 12:22 and 13:14. Confirmation of this city's location comes in the identification of its architect, *technitēs,* and builder, *dēmiourgos,* as God. The LXX uses *technitēs* in relation to God only at Wis 13:1. Philo uses both terms synonymously in the same order of God in *Unchangeableness of God* 30–31 and, in reverse order, of Bezalel in *On the Giants* 23. He also uses each term to refer to God, but not in tandem, within the same book (*technitēs: On Creation* 135; *Allegorical Interpretation* 1.18, 31; *Change of Names* 31; *demiourgos: On Creation* 10, 36, 68, 72, 138, 139, 146; *Allegorical Interpretation* 1.77; *Change of Names* 18, 29, 32).

11. *By faith he received power of procreation, even beyond the normal age:* The text is problematic at this point. Grammatically it is possible to take Sarah as the subject: "By faith Sarah herself received power to conceive" (RSV). Perhaps the greatest obstacle to that translation is that the expression "power of procreation" is about the power to deposit seed, which cannot refer to a woman's role in procreation (Epictetus, *Dissertations* 1.13.3; Philo, *On Creation* 132; *On Drunkenness* 211; *On the Cherubim* 49; Otfried Hofius, *katabolē EDNT* 2:255–56). Eisenbaum, following Sowers, appeals to Philo's allegorical interpretation of Sarah as "virtue," sowing good counsels and excellent words analogously to Abraham's sowing seed (*On Abraham* 100), to suggest that this is how one might think of Sarah as the subject of the verse. One problem she overlooks, however, is that

Philo does not use the idiom "sow seed," *katabolē spermatos*, but rather the verb *speirei*. More problematic still is the fact that Philo is discussing an allegorical interpretation of Abraham and Sarah that others have appealed to but that Philo himself rejects as false because it gives the wife an active role that is not her due (*On Abraham* 101–102).

One way around the problem is to take the phrase "Sarah herself was barren" as a parenthetical remark (Koester, 488). It is also possible to translate the phrase as "with Sarah, who was barren." The latter option takes the pronoun *autē*, "herself," as a dative, "with Sarah" (Attridge, 325). The advantage of this translation is that the text then refers to both Abraham and Sarah, who together conceived Isaac. The expression "beyond the normal age" takes into account the biblical narrative about Abraham's and Sarah's advanced years and the impossibility of their conceiving a child (Gen 18:9-15; Philo, *On Abraham*, 111).

since he considered him faithful who had promised: Hebrews presents God as faithful (see the Notes at 10:23), and here the author relates that fidelity to God's promise. The verb *epangellesthai* is used also at 10:23 and 12:16, again with God as its subject. The noun *epangelia* is more frequent (4:1; 6:12, 15, 17; 7:6; 8:6; 9:15; 10:36; 11:9 [bis], 13, 17, 33, 39).

12. *Therefore from one person, and this one as good as dead, descendants were born, "as many as the stars of heaven and as the innumerable grains of sand by the seashore":* The author returns to Abraham, as the grammatical gender of "one person" is masculine. Paul has a similar reference to Abraham as "as good as dead" in Rom 4:19. Here the author reiterates in a different form the sentiment expressed in the previous verse, that Abraham was beyond the normal age for procreation. The verse concludes with an allusion to Gen 22:17, where God speaks of the future fulfillment of the promise to Abraham in metaphors that express the abundance of the blessing given to him and Sarah.

Interpretation

The author turns his attention to Abraham, who is certainly a model of faith in the biblical tradition (Gen 12:1-3; Rom 4:9-11; Gal 3:6-9). He gives Abraham a rather large role to play in this chapter. Although vv. 13-16 appear to be about a group of ancestors larger than just Abraham and Sarah, their experience as "strangers and aliens" in the lands they resided in shapes the passage as a whole. In vv. 17-19 the story of the binding of Isaac will conclude the reflection on Abraham's exemplary faith. The passage under consideration here divides into two parts: vv. 8-10 describe Abraham's call, response, and rationale for answering the call; vv. 11-12 explain how the promise was fulfilled in Abraham and Sarah.

Faith has a motivating and guiding role in this passage. Faith causes Abraham to trust in God and is the agent that brings him to his destination (v. 8). Furthermore, faith plays a sustaining role, nurturing Abraham and his heirs during the time when they await the promise's fulfillment (v. 9). Earlier, Hebrews described Abraham as someone who possessed the virtue of endurance and obtained the promise (6:15). Although it is not explicit in the text, Hebrews may have seen Abraham's "patient endurance," *makrothymia*, as a byproduct of his faith, a condition the author would hope for in his readers. He says as much in 6:11-12: "And we want each one of you to show the same eagerness with respect to the fullness of hope to the very end, so that you may not become sluggish, but imitators of those who through faith and patience (*makrothymia*) inherit the promises."

Also in chapter 6 the author included himself and the readers among the heirs of Abraham (6:18). Here the more immediate heirs of Abraham—Isaac and Jacob—are shown to possess a similar endurance as they sojourned in the land of the promise, living in tents. When the author, then, presents the reason for Abraham's faith as well as that of his heirs in v. 10, he is also including the readers. They, like Abraham, look forward to a city built by God, an anticipation that is repeated in 11:14-16 but is more fully developed in 12:18-24 and echoed in 13:14. Like Abraham, they too need to be nurtured and sustained by faith.

Perhaps there was no greater sign of God's fidelity to Abraham and Sarah than the fact that in their old age they would live to see the immediate fulfillment of God's promise to them in the birth of a son, Isaac (Gen 15:1-6; 17:15-22; 18:9-15; 21:1-3). God promised Abraham descendants as numerous as the stars of heaven and the sands of the seashore (Gen 22:17), to show the extent to which the promise would be fulfilled. But Abraham would see only a partial fulfillment of what was promised. The notice that Abraham considered "him faithful who had promised" connects the readers to Abraham's story as the author recalls his exhortation to them in 10:23 to hold fast to confidence, "for he who promised is faithful." Whereas their stories are linked, they are not exactly the same. The author understands Abraham to have seen the fulfillment of the promise only in the short term. Ultimate fulfillment of the promise comes for the descendants of Abraham, who await the future realization of the fullness of the promise. They, like Abraham, are on a pilgrimage to a destination promised by God (3:1, 12; 4:1-2; 6:11-12; 10:35-39; 11:13-16; 12:18-24, 28-29; 13:14).

It may not be out of the question to see the reference to Abraham as "as good as dead" from whom "descendants were born" as an anticipation of 11:18-19. There the text mentions Abraham's descendants again in relation to his belief that God was able to raise up descendants "even from the dead." In both instances the way Abraham thought of God (the verbs *logizesthai* and *hēgeisthai* are synonyms: Philo, *On the Cherubim*, 73; *Sacrifices of Cain and Abel* 49-50) becomes an important factor in his faith. In the first instance he saw God as faithful, and in the second he understood God as capable of doing something wondrous. For the readers, then, Abraham becomes an exemplar of faith as defined in 11:1, since by faith he was assured of what he had hoped for and he had looked forward to the unseen.

The author's presentation of Abraham in this part of the chapter captures how completely his life was a life of faith, from his origins to his destiny.

From Abraham's call and his response to God to his sojourn in Canaan and his desire for the city of his final destination, his faith is depicted as constant. Uncertainty did not inhibit Abraham on his faith journey because he had a more distant goal in sight that guided him on his way. Whatever intermediary setback or inconveniences he endured, he accepted these in view of the promise God had made to him and the hope he had of reaching his final destination. To this extent Abraham is a true exemplar of faith for readers of Hebrews in every generation.

For Reference and Further Study

Daniélou, Jean. "Abraham dans la tradition chrétienne," *CSion* 5 (1951) 68–87.

Greenlee, J. Harold. "Hebrews 11:11—'By Faith Sarah Received Ability,'" *Asbury Theological Journal* 54 (1999) 67–72.

Harrington, Daniel. J. "Abraham Traditions in the Testament of Abraham and in the 'Rewritten Bible' of the Intertestamental Period," in G. W. E. Nickelsburg, ed., *Studies in the Testament of Abraham.* SBLSCS 9. Missoula: Scholars, 1976, 165–71.

Mercado, Luis Fidel. "The Language of Sojourning in the Abraham Midrash in Heb. XI, 8-10: Its Old Testament Basis, Exegetical Traditions and Functions in the Epistle to the Hebrews" (Dissertation abstract), *HTR* 60 (1967) 494–95.

Siker, Jeffrey S. *Disinheriting the Jews: Abraham in Early Christian Controversy.* Louisville: Westminster John Knox, 1991.

28. *The Desire for a Better Country* (11:13-16)

13. In faith all of these died without having received the promises, but they saw and greeted them from afar, and confessed that they were strangers and foreigners on the earth, 14. for people who speak in this way make it clear that they are seeking a homeland. 15. If they had been thinking of the land that they had departed, they would have had opportunity to return. 16. But as it is, they earnestly desire a better country, that is, a heavenly one. Therefore God is not ashamed to be called their God; indeed, he has prepared a city for them.

Notes

13. *In faith all of these died without having received the promises:* Varying his opening, the author comments on the mortality of the witnesses thus far presented. He is, however, vague about whom to include. Since Enoch is the only one who did not die, the author may mean all the others mentioned. Genesis records Abel's death in 4:8, Noah's in 9:29, Abraham's in 25:8, Sarah's in 23:1-2, Isaac's

in 35:29, and Jacob's in 49:33. In view of the mention of the promises, which began with Abraham, the author probably has him, Sarah, and their descendants in view. To say that these individuals did not receive the promise is to look beyond the earthly fulfillment of the promises, which they did indeed receive in their lifetimes. The author has already said as much of Abraham in 6:15. The truth of the author's claim lies in the fact that they did not receive the promises in a final sense, as the rest of the passage seeks to explain.

but they saw and greeted them from afar, and confessed that they were strangers and foreigners on the earth: Genesis 13:14-17 recounts the story of God's showing the land to Abraham and reiterating the promise of many descendants. Abraham had already settled in the land (Gen 13:13), but he and his descendants had not taken possession of it, and so he still wandered and considered himself a "stranger" and an "alien" (Gen 23:4). Without the final realization of the promise before their deaths these ancestors could only see and greet them from afar. This reference to the earthly status of the ancestors in their unfulfilled state contrasts with the real object of their yearning in v. 16. The verb *homologein*, "confess," here in the form of a participle, links the ancestral generation to the readers, who also have a "confession" (3:1; 4:14; 10:23). This verb means "acknowledge the truth," or "profess" (BDAG, 708–709; Otto Michel, *homologeō, ktl., TDNT* 5:199–220). It occurs again in Hebrews at 13:15.

14. *for people who speak in this way make it clear that they are seeking a homeland:* The verb "make clear," *emphanizein*, occurred in 9:24 to describe Christ's appearance before God. Here the sense is "make evident" (BDAG, 325–26; Dieter Lührmann, *emphanizō, TDNT* 9:7). There is nothing remarkable about the language of seeking a homeland in a culture in which citizenship was restricted and cities and towns were brimming with resident aliens. The expression is polyvalent, as the question of a heavenly homeland returns in 13:14, where now Christians seek a city that is to come. On the heavenly Jerusalem see the Notes at 11:10.

15. *If they had been thinking of the land that they had departed, they would have had opportunity to return:* The statement is contrary to fact, designed to set up a comparison (see 4:8; 7:11; 8:7). "Think of," *mnemoneuein*, has the same meaning in 11:22 and 13:7 (Otto Michel, *mimnēskomai, ktl., TDNT* 4:682–83). The land they had departed was initially Ur of the Chaldees, and then Haran (Gen 11:31). "Opportunity," *kairos*, means "time," but not in the sense of *chronos*, "measured time" (BDAG, 497–98; Gerhard Delling, *kairos, ktl., TDNT* 3:455–64). There is no biblical record that Abraham's family ever returned to Ur or to Haran.

16. *But as it is, they earnestly desire a better country, that is, a heavenly one:* "Desire," *oregein*, connotes something deeper than a mere wish. "Better," *kreittonos*, is the author's term of choice for comparisons (1:4; 6:9; 7:19, 22; 8:6; 9:23; 10:34; 11:35, 40; 12:24). "Country" is supplied for a smoother translation; the text literally says "they earnestly desire a better." The ultimate goal is the "heavenly" homeland, which the author sees as his readers' final destination (12:22, 28; 13:14). As with other NT authors, the author of Hebrews presents Christians as heirs of Abraham (6:17), who share a heavenly call (3:1) and gift (6:4).

Therefore God is not ashamed to be called their God: In 2:11 it was said of the Son that he is not ashamed to call his fellow humans brothers and sisters. So also with God, who in Israel's tradition had been called by names other than Elohim and Yнwн. God is the God of Abraham, Isaac, and Jacob (Exod 3:6, 15; 4:5). The language is covenantal, where the formula "I will be their God" is standard (Gen 17:8; Exod 29:45; Jer 24:7; 32:38; Ezek 11:20; 14:11; 37:23, 27; Zech 8:8).

indeed, he has prepared a city for them: The author concludes this section with another mention of the ultimate goal, the heavenly Jerusalem (11:10; 12:22-24). The verb "prepare," *hetoimazein*, means "make something ready" (BDAG, 400; Walter Grundmann, *hetoimos, ktl., TDNT* 2:704–706). The only place in the LXX where the noun "city" is the object of this verb is in Hab 2:12 in the negative context of "founding a city on iniquity" (cf. Josephus, *Life* 86). In the papyri this verb is a technical term for preparing something in anticipation of a person's visit (MM, 258; Phlm 22). The New Jerusalem is also a city "prepared" by God (Rev 21:2).

INTERPRETATION

The author briefly interrupts the catalogue of witnesses at this point in order to develop the idea expressed in v. 10, which he had passed over. The passage begins with a thematic assertion about the nomadic generation (v. 13), followed by a supportive rationale (v. 14) and demonstrated by a contrary-to-fact proof (v. 15). The section closes with a conclusion about the ultimate goal of the ancestors and what God has prepared for them in order that they might reach it (v. 16). The author's goal seems to be to provide an eschatological interpretation of 11:10.

These verses appear at first to apply to all the heroes mentioned thus far, but it becomes clear that Abraham, Sarah, and their descendants are in view. All the ancestors mentioned have died except Enoch, but not all confessed that they were strangers and foreigners on earth. Still, the history of the ancestors in Canaan is a history of people who resided there as aliens. God had identified Abraham as an alien in Canaan, even as the land was being promised to him (Gen 17:8). Abraham himself confessed that he was a stranger and an alien (Gen 20:1; 21:23, 34; 23:4), as did Joseph, speaking for himself and his family (Gen 47:4). Jacob claimed alien status when he lived with Laban (Gen 32:4), and he settled in Canaan as an alien, as had his father Isaac (Gen 35:27; 37:1). Psalm 105(104):12 refers to the ancestral generation as aliens in the land of Canaan and all of Israel as aliens in Egypt (v. 23).

The author exploits this nomadic history as proof that the ancestral generation could only greet the promises from afar. Reflecting on the experience of wandering people, he draws the conclusion that they would never have called themselves strangers and aliens if they were not in some way yearning for a homeland. Despite the fact that the ancestral generation had been given the promises, they were nevertheless displaced people even while they were in Canaan, because they had not taken possession of the land. They exemplify those who are unsettled and are on the move, but they are not wandering aimlessly.

The author then places a sensitive reading of the biblical narrative in service of yet another purpose. Any people that departs from a homeland has the opportunity to return to the place of their origin. The ancestral generation, however, had no real homeland to begin with, and even the one they were promised was not to become their homeland in their own lifetime. Abraham never really considered a return to Ur of the Chaldees. Like him, his descendants had not been thinking of the land from which they had come. He and his descendants were destined to wander, and so they saw themselves as strangers and aliens. Still, they had been promised a land, and within the confines of the Genesis narrative that land was their desired destination. Hebrews interprets their desire differently in order to show what their final destination would be. They are still included in those who will ultimately receive the fulfillment of the promises.

Exercising some license, the author reflects on the fact that Abraham and Sarah and their immediate descendants never really resided in Canaan as though it were their homeland. Even the homeland they originally had did not factor into their musings about a place to settle. The conditional clause in v. 15 is contrary to fact, by which the author indicates that the ancestors were thinking of another place rather than their place of origin. He concludes that their hope was directed to a better, heavenly country. They now become the types of individuals longing for an eternal inheritance (9:15). At this point in the text the story of the wandering ancestors becomes the story of the readers, for indeed they are the ones seeking a heavenly homeland, a city not made with hands, which has been prepared for them (12:22, 28; 13:14).

The previous passage gave as a rationale for Abraham's faith the fact that he considered God faithful. This passage ends on a note that presumes God's fidelity by recalling the specific formula of the covenant: "I will be their God" (Gen 17:8; Exod 29:45; Jer 24:7; 32:38; Ezek 11:20; 14:11; 37:23, 27; Zech 8:8). Also, the notice that God is not ashamed to be called their God echoes the attitude of the Son in the midst of his brothers and sisters (2:11). Resident aliens did not generally have citizen status where they resided, and so they were not equals in those cities or lands to the native population. This was no cause for shame, but seemed rather to be the basis for God's covenant with the ancestors. That the ancestral generation were a wandering people was in fact a defining characteristic of Israel's polity. The ancient confession in Deut 26:5 proclaimed Jacob a wandering Aramean and an alien. Indeed, it was God who had initially called Abraham to leave his land and to wander. In faith he answered that call. Consequently God was not ashamed to be the God of a wandering people, for in the author's view God is always a God of people moving toward their inheritance. In this instance it is a heavenly inheritance, the city prepared for them, which both the readers and the ancestors will one day possess.

The author has actualized the wandering of Israel's ancestors for his readers by reinterpreting the meaning of the land they had longed to possess as a city prepared for them by God. Since the readers long to make that city their final destination as well, the story of the ancestors has become their own story. The intertwining of the two narratives is bolstered by the shared confession of the two groups. The observation that the ancestors "confessed" that they were strangers and aliens on earth joins their story to that of the readers, who "have no lasting city," but are looking forward "to a city that is to come" (13:14). The connection is closed by the concluding observation that this city had been prepared for them by God. Hebrews revitalizes the scriptural tradition for all who feel as Israel's ancestors did: they are unsettled in their present circumstances and feel as though they are strangers and aliens in this world (1 Pet 2:11). In so doing, Hebrews encourages its readers of all generations to keep the ultimate goal in view.

For Reference and Further Study

Ernst, Josef. "Die griechische Polis—das himmlische Jerusalem—die christliche Stadt," *TGl* 67 (1977) 240–58.

Étienne, P. "Estrangeiros e Peregrines na Terra . . . em Busca de uma Pátria: Epistola aos Hebreus 11, 13-14," in *Actualides Bíblicas-Castro*. Rio de Janiero: Vozes, 1971, 610–15.

Johnsson, William G. "The Pilgrimage Motif in the Book of Hebrews," *JBL* 97 (1978) 239–51.

Moxnes, Halvor. "God and His Promise to Abraham: First-Century Appropriations," in idem, *Theology in Conflict: Studies in Paul's Understanding of God in Romans*. NovTSup 53. Leiden: Brill, 1980.

Swetnam, James. "Hebrews 11: An Interpretation," *MelT* 41 (1990) 97–114.

29. *Abraham to Joseph* (11:17-22)

17. By faith Abraham, when put to the test, offered up Isaac. He who had received the promises was ready to offer up his only son, 18. of whom he had been told, "It is through Isaac that descendants shall be named for you." 19. He considered the fact that God is able even to raise someone from the dead—and he did receive him back as a symbol. 20. By faith Isaac

blessed Jacob and Esau concerning things to come. 21. By faith Jacob, when dying, blessed each of the sons of Joseph, "bowing in worship over the top of his staff." 22. By faith Joseph, when he was dying, made mention of the exodus of the Israelites and gave instructions concerning his bones.

Notes

17. *By faith Abraham, when put to the test, offered up Isaac:* The author returns to the opening "by faith." Before the interlude of vv. 13-16, Abraham and Sarah were the topic of discussion. Now, another chapter of the Abraham/Sarah saga resumes the discussion of his faith. Genesis 22:1-19 tells the story of the binding of Isaac, and how God, responding to Abraham's faith, allowed Abraham to "redeem" Isaac by substituting a ram for his son. It is first noted by the author that God was testing Abraham, an allusion to Gen 22:1. The motif of God's testing of individuals or of Israel as a whole is common in the Hebrew Bible and in the LXX (e.g., Exod 15:25; 16:4; 20:20; Deut 8:2; 13:3). It was also possible to put God to the test (e.g., Exod 17:2, 7; Num 14:22; Deut 9:22). The Hebrew verb *nasah*, translated in the LXX by *peirazein*, means to "test." The object of God's testing Israel or any individual is articulated in Deut 8:2, something that is well illustrated by the Abraham narrative, "to see what is in your heart, whether or not you would keep God's commandments."

    The verb "offer up," *prospherein*, has been used extensively in Hebrews in relation to the cult (see the Notes at 5:1). One problem is that the verb is in the perfect tense here, which suggests that Abraham actually sacrificed Isaac. Erich Grässer follows Rose (*Die Wolke der Zeugen*, WUNT 60 [Tübingen: Mohr Siebeck, 1994] 236–46) in claiming that the author of Hebrews knew of traditions in which Abraham actually sacrificed Isaac (*Hebräer* 3:145–46). The verb *prospherein* does mean "bring an offering," without necessarily implying that the offering was actually sacrificed (Konrad Weiss, *prospherō*, TDNT 9:65). These same traditions claim that God raised Isaac from the dead.

    He who had received the promises was ready to offer up his only son: Abraham is described as "he who had received the promises," *ho tas epangelias anadexamenos* (see 6:13). The verb *anadechesthai* is rare in the LXX and the NT (2 Macc 6:19; 8:36; Acts 28:7). The tense of *prospherein*, "offer," is imperfect, indicating Abraham's readiness to offer Isaac (Attridge, 334).

18. *of whom he had been told, "It is through Isaac that descendants shall be named for you":* The citation from Gen 21:12 replicates the LXX. The quotation functions as a reminder that Abraham, in his readiness to offer Isaac, was about to sacrifice not only his flesh and blood, but the fulfillment of the promise as well. This serves as yet another example of the extent to which Abraham believed in God and trusted.

19. *He considered the fact that God is able even to raise someone from the dead:* The notion that God "is able," *dynatos*, is biblical (LXX: Job 36:5; Pss 23:8; 88:9; Jer 39:19; Dan 3:17; NT: Matt 3:9; 19:26; Mark 10:27; Luke 3:8; 18:27; Rom 11:23). The expression

"to raise from the dead," with the verb *egeirein*, is rare in the LXX. It is used about Elijah in Sir 48:5. The concept is present in Dan 12:2, but the verb is *anistanai* (see also 2 Macc 7:9, 14), not *egeirein*.

and he did receive him back as a symbol: The verb *komizein*, "receive back," does occur with the sense of receiving someone back from the dead in 2 Macc 7:29. Here, however, Isaac is received back as a symbol, *en parabolē*. Since the sacrifice was never completed, he was received from the brink of death, but for Hebrews that "rescue" stands as a symbol for the resurrection of believers. Elsewhere in Hebrews *en parabolē* has this meaning of "as a symbol" at 9:9.

20. *By faith Isaac blessed Jacob and Esau concerning things to come:* Having completed his treatment of Abraham, the author naturally turns to Isaac and his descendants. The LXX *Vorlage* for this verse is Gen 27:27-40, where Isaac blesses Jacob and Esau. The author does not discuss Jacob's ruse or Esau's outrage. The important thing for Hebrews is that the blessings were future oriented. "The things to come" is one of the author's terms for the prospect of eschatological fulfillment (1:14; 2:5; 6:5; 9:11 [*v.l.*]; 10:1; 13:14).

21. *By faith Jacob:* The next in line of the great male ancestors is Jacob. As with earlier examples, Jacob is not singled out in the Hebrew Bible for his faith. He is known as a trickster who can be tenacious in pursuit of God's blessing. This tenacity may be a sign of his faith, but faith is not predicated of him in the narratives. Wisdom 10:10 calls Jacob a righteous man, so once again it may be his righteousness seen in relation to the Habakkuk citation in 10:38 that placed him in this catalogue of heroes of faith.

when dying, blessed each of the sons of Joseph, "bowing in worship over the top of his staff": The allusion is to Gen 48:8-22, where Jacob blesses Joseph's sons Ephraim and Manasseh. As with Jacob and Esau, the author bypasses the interesting details of intrigue in the narrative and focuses on a single point. Here it is a recollection of Gen 47:29, where Jacob's impending death is mentioned. The author appends another verse from Gen 47:31, where Joseph bows himself on the head of his staff. The MT has "bed" instead of the LXX's "staff."

22. *By faith Joseph, when he was dying:* Again the author's interest seems to be in another ancestor as he is about to die. The verb "die," *teleutan*, is frequent in the LXX, but not in the NT, appearing only here in Hebrews. The author alludes to Gen 50:24, where Joseph speaks of his coming death.

made mention of the exodus of the Israelites: The verb *mnemoneuein* means "remember," but it cannot mean that here since the Exodus has yet to occur (BDAG, 655; Otto Michel, *mimnēskomai, ktl., TDNT* 4:675–83). In 11:15 its meaning is "think of." As the allusion is to Gen 50:24, where Joseph actually predicts the Exodus, the meaning is conveyed by the translation "he made mention of the exodus." The author may have understood this prediction as a sign of his faith that God would indeed rescue Israel from Egypt.

and gave instructions concerning his bones: In Gen 50:25 Joseph instructs his brothers to carry his bones out of Egypt when the exodus takes place. On the verb "give instructions," *entellesthai*, see the Notes at 9:20.

INTERPRETATION

Perhaps no story about Abraham captures the depth of his faith as does the Binding of Isaac. The author naturally includes it here in this fourth subdivision of chapter 11. The motif of divine rescue runs through this section, which begins with Abraham and moves to a brief consideration of the faith of his descendants, Isaac, Jacob, Esau, and Joseph. Interest in the death of these great ancestors pervades the passage, extending the immediate meaning of v. 19 beyond Abraham to include the other figures featured in these verses.

Like the Genesis narrative of the Binding of Isaac (Gen 22:1-19), Hebrews focuses on the divine request as a test of Abraham's faith. Omitting many of the details of the original narrative, the author stresses the meaning of the test and its potential consequences for the promises Abraham had received (vv. 17-18). Had Isaac actually been sacrificed, the promises would never have been fulfilled, since he was the divinely designated heir to bring them to completion. This fact is as plain in the original story as it is in Hebrews, with its inclusion of the verbatim LXX citation from Gen 21:12. As Paul noted in Rom 9:7-8, where he cited the same verse, Isaac is the child of the promise and represents the rightful descendants of Abraham. Thus the author highlights the relationship between faith and the promise for the benefit of his readers.

Curiously, the story of the Binding of Isaac has the ability to challenge faith as well as to confirm it. Other stories in the Abraham/Sarah cycle show how Abraham puts God to the test by placing the promise in jeopardy when he takes matters into his own hands. The narratives of Abraham and Sarah before a foreign ruler demonstrate God's fidelity in seeing the promise to completion, as Abraham and Sarah have to be rescued from an Egyptian Pharaoh (Gen 12:10-20) and a Philistine king (Gen 20:1-18). These stories inspire readers to faith in a God who remains constant against all odds. The Binding of Isaac, on the other hand, catches the reader off guard. A natural question arises: Why, after rescuing these ancestors before, would God now choose to put the promise in jeopardy by asking Abraham to make this ultimate sacrifice?

The simple answer supplied, even by the original story, that God was testing Abraham, belies the deeper complexity of the narrative. In this story a divine test is met by exemplary faith, which appears to remove any of Abraham's earlier tendency to exhibit impulses to try to rely on himself to see the promise to completion. By its nature, the promise itself rests on Isaac's survival of the test as much as Abraham's, which suggests that the Binding of Isaac is as much a story of hope as it is of faith. From the time he spied Mt. Moriah from afar on the third day, at the moment when he assured the young men who accompanied him that he and Isaac would return, to the point where he assured his only son that God would provide for the sacrifice, Abraham's faith was tempered by hope that the God who rescued him before would not fail him now. Hebrews believes that Abraham was assured of this hope because he considered that God could raise the dead (v. 19). The motif of rescuing the dead here recalls that Isaac was born to Abraham when he himself was as good as dead (11:12). The original Genesis narrative does not posit this as the cause for Abraham's compliance with God's request. For Hebrews, however, it is an attempt to explain what would have prevented Abraham from wavering. It also functions to draw the readers into the story by recalling that they, too, must endure hardships that may test their own faith.

The message to the readers is evident and recalls the opening verse of the chapter, "Faith is the assurance of things hoped for." What else could explain the endurance of Abraham in this moment of trial? The author interprets the cause of Abraham's steadfastness with his readers in mind. In 2:3 the readers were invited to consider how they could escape if they neglected the salvation that was promised. As the wilderness generation was subject to its own "day of testing," when it had put God to the test (3:8-9), so also are the readers exhorted not to fail the test (3:12–4:13). The example to follow is that of Jesus, who himself was tested (2:18; 4:15).

Isaac's invocation of future blessings over Jacob and Esau is recounted in Gen 27:27-29, 39-40. Since Jacob received a blessing and Esau the exact opposite, one wonders how the author could think that both were blessed (Eisenbaum, *Jewish Heroes*, 164). The Genesis text distinguishes between what each received by clearly indicating that Isaac blessed Jacob (*ēulogēsen* [27:27]), but answered Esau (*apokritheis* [27:39]) in response to his request for a blessing. Even later the author acknowledges that Esau was rejected and did not inherit the promises (12:16-17). For Hebrews it is enough to note that both were blessed by Isaac with regard to future things, as he himself was on the verge of death. An element of hope, then, is included in Isaac's blessing of his sons, since in Hebrews "things to come" refers to things promised and awaited (1:14; 2:5; 6:5; 9:11 [*v.l.*]; 10:1; 13:14). Again the author provides his readers with an entry into the story.

The evidence of Jacob's faith comes in the blessing of Joseph's sons, Ephraim and Manasseh. The original narrative is found in Gen 48:8-22, a story that echoes Isaac's blessing of Jacob and concession to Esau. Jacob's eyesight is poor and he can barely distinguish between the brothers. As he is about to bless Ephraim first, Joseph removes his father's hand and places it on the elder son's head so that the firstborn will be first blessed. Jacob, however, refuses Joseph's request and blesses the younger son first. Hebrews alters the story when the author imports the LXX of Gen 47:31 into the text. After Jacob blesses the boys, he bows in worship over the head of his staff. This for the author must be the sign of his faith in rendering the blessings. The original setting of this verse is Jacob's response to Joseph's promise that he will not bury his father in Egypt. Since there is no mention of Jacob's faith in the narrative of the blessing of Ephraim and Manasseh, the author of Hebrews has transposed this verse from the earlier chapter as a demonstration of the faith he wished to exemplify in the figure of Jacob.

The final example of faith in this section is Joseph himself, also about to die. The mention of the Exodus from Egypt represents the quality of his faith, as it shows the assurance of something hoped for. So also do the instructions about his burial, which indicate how assured he was that the exodus would take place (cf. Koester, 500).

All the examples of the ancestors in this section of chapter 11 witness to faith while at the same time demonstrating that they have hope for future realities that were unseen by them. Abraham hoped that God would provide a sacrifice with which to redeem his son Isaac from death. Isaac blessed his twin sons and prophesied the things to come, i.e., that Jacob would be greater than his elder twin Esau. While Esau did not receive a blessing per se, Jacob also prophesied his future fate. Jacob blessed Ephraim and Manasseh, prophesying, too, that the younger son would be greater than the elder. Joseph predicted the Exodus and confirmed the assurance of his faith by giving instructions about carrying his bones out of Egypt. Each of these ancestors, then, illustrates that aspect of faith in Hebrews, which is assurance of things hoped for.

For Reference and Further Study

Daly, Robert J. "The Soteriological Significance of the Sacrifice of Isaac," *CBQ* 39 (1977) 45–75.

Davies, Philip R., and Bruce D. Chilton. "The ʿAqedah: A Revised Tradition History," *CBQ* 40 (1978) 514–46.

Hayward, Robert. "The Sacrifice of Isaac and Jewish Polemic against Christianity," *CBQ* 52 (1990) 292–306.

Swetnam, James. *Jesus and Isaac: A Study of the Epistle to the Hebrews in Light of the Aqedah.* AnBib 94. Rome: Pontifical Biblical Institute, 1981.

Wilcox, Max. "The Bones of Joseph: Hebrews 11:22," in Barry P. Thompson, ed., *Scripture: Meaning and Method. Essays Presented to Anthony Tyrrell Hanson for his Seventieth Birthday.* Hull: Hull University, 1987, 114–30.

Wood, J. Edwin. "Isaac Typology in the New Testament," *NTS* 14 (1967–68) 583–89.

30. *Moses and the Exodus Generation* (11:23-31)

23. By faith Moses was hidden by his parents for three months after his birth, because they saw that the child was beautiful, and they were not afraid of the king's edict. 24. By faith Moses, when he was grown up, refused to be called a son of Pharaoh's daughter, 25. choosing rather to share ill-treatment with the people of God than to have the temporary enjoyment of sin. 26. He considered the reproach of Christ to be greater wealth than the treasures of Egypt, for he was looking ahead to the reward. 27. By faith he left Egypt, unafraid of the king's anger; for he persevered as if he had seen the invisible one. 28. By faith he kept the Passover and the pouring of blood, so that the destroyer of the firstborn would not touch their firstborn.

29. By faith the people passed through the Red Sea as if it were dry land, but when the Egyptians attempted to do so they were drowned. 30. By faith the walls of Jericho fell after they had been encircled for seven days. 31. By faith Rahab the prostitute did not perish with those who were disobedient, because she had received the spies in peace.

Notes

23. *By faith Moses was hidden by his parents for three months after his birth:* The author takes the next logical figure after the ancestors whose stories were restricted to Genesis. The source of the details about Moses' birth and rescue from the Pharaoh's edict is Exod 2:1-4. Moses, like Abraham, has already been featured in Hebrews in 3:1-6, where his fidelity as a servant was compared with the fidelity of the Son. Here in v. 23, however, it is really not Moses' faith that is under discussion, but that of his parents. The Exodus account in the MT says that Moses' mother hid him for three months (Exod 2:2); his father is mentioned only as a Levite who married a Levite woman. The LXX, however, has "they" for the verb's subject (see Philo, *Moses* 1.9-11; Josephus, *Antiquities* 2.217-21). Hebrews also describes the time differently. The LXX has "three months," *treis mēnas*, instead of *trimēnon* as Hebrews does. This adjective is biblical (Gen 38:24; 4 Kgdms 23:31; 2 Chr 36:2, 9).

    because they saw that the child was beautiful: This part of the text is faithful to the Exodus account. The adjective *asteios* occurs elsewhere in the LXX to describe physical beauty (Num 22:32; Jdg 3:17; Jdt 11:23; Sus 7). For Philo *asteios* is a term for the virtuous person who consistently chooses good over evil (*Allegorical Interpretation* 1.93; 2.23, 53; 3.167, 190-91; *The Worse Attacks the Better* 66; *Posterity and Exile of Cain* 32; *Noah As Planter* 176; *Confusion of Tongues* 109; *Flight and Finding* 18; *Change of Names* 193, 204, 252; *On Dreams* 1.171, 176; 2.24, 230; *On Abraham* 22; *Every Good Person Is Free* 27, 53, 72) and describes a state that is pleasing to God (*Allegorical Interpretation* 1.77; *The Worse Attacks the Better* 4).

    and they were not afraid of the king's edict: The biblical account is silent on this detail. Perhaps the author was thinking of the Hebrew midwives, of whom the LXX says "they feared God," using exactly the same verb, *ephobēthēsan*, as Heb

11:23 (cf. Attridge, 339). Implicit in the biblical account is the idea that the mid-wives feared God more than they did the Pharaoh. Hebrews attributes this courage to Moses' parents. The noun "edict" is found in the LXX at 2 Esdr 7:11; Esth 3:13ᵈ; and Wis 11:7, where it describes the edict of the Pharaoh ordering the death of the Israelite children.

24. *By faith Moses, when he was grown up, refused to be called a son of Pharaoh's daughter:* Only now is Moses the subject of faith. The Exodus account speaks of Moses "when he was grown up," *megas genomenas,* as the time when he joined his own people and observed their plight under the Egyptians. It says nothing of his refusal to be called the son of the Pharaoh's daughter.

25. *choosing rather to share ill-treatment with the people of God than to have the temporary enjoyment of sin:* This verse is closer to what the Exodus account says happened when Moses had grown up than the previous one. Moses did not actually share the ill-treatment, but he seemed to sympathize with the plight of his people (LXX: *tous huious Israēl*). In defense of a fellow Israelite he killed an Egyptian taskmaster (Exod 2:12). The verb for "share ill treatment," *synkakoucheisthai,* is *hapax,* and several commentators have suggested it was a coinage of the author (Attridge, 340; Koester, 96, 502). For the simple form, *kakoucheisthai,* see 11:37; 13:3. Curiously, even though the simple form is used in 13:3 the call to share the suffering of those ill-treated would have been an appropriate instance for using the compound. At the very least the readers may have made a connection with the compassion of Moses for his kin. The reference to the people of God (*tǭ laǭ tou theou*) confirms that the author may intend to actualize the story of Moses for his readers (4:9; 8:10).

   The Exodus narrative makes no mention of Moses bypassing the enjoyment of sin in favor of suffering. The author appears to be shifting the focus of the text more toward the circumstances of his readers (6:1-8; 10:26-31). In Hebrews, the fact that the enjoyment of sin is "temporary" contrasts with what is lasting (10:34; 13:14).

26. *He considered the reproach of Christ:* On reproach, *oneidismos,* see the Notes at 10:33. The exact meaning of the expression is difficult to ascertain. Many com-mentators see in this verse the influence of Ps 89(88):51-52, "Be mindful, Lord, of the reproach (*oneidismou*) of your servant, how I carry in my breast the re-proaches of many peoples, with which your enemies reproach, with which they reproach the surrogate of your anointed one (*christou*)." Westcott (*Epistle to the Hebrews,* 372) understood the term to apply to Moses as an anointed one who had to bear the reproaches any "envoy" of God would be subject to. In this sense a figure like Moses, who prefigures Christ, is subject to reproach. Others see Moses as a prophetic seer who had some knowledge of Christ and thus of the reproaches his followers suffered for their association with him (D'Angelo, *Moses,* 95–149; Anthony Tyrrell Hanson, "The Reproach of the Messiah in the Epistle to the Hebrews," *SE* 7 [1982] 231–40). Yet another view seems more ap-propriate in light of the actualization of the text for the readers in the previous verse, namely that the author is making a connection between their suffering of reproach and his own, which he endured by faith (Koester, 503).

to be greater wealth than the treasures of Egypt, for he was looking ahead to the reward:
The noun "wealth," *ploutos*, occurs only here in Hebrews. The fact that Moses
was fixed on "greater" wealth reflects the author's interest in comparing material things in relation to more lasting and eternal things. Thus what Moses had
set his sights on was naturally greater than anything that could be had even in
the storehouse of Egypt (see Koester, 503, on Egyptian wealth). On "reward"
see the Notes at 2:2.

27. *By faith he left Egypt, unafraid of the king's anger:* Which part of the biblical narrative serves as the source for the beginning of v. 27 is unclear. The LXX of Exod
2:15 recounts that Moses "withdrew," *anachōrein*, from Egypt to Midian because
he feared the Pharaoh would learn about the incident with the Egyptian taskmaster. The MT tells of a more urgent departure, using the verb *barah*, "flee."
Despite the fact that his fear is a motivating factor, some commentators believe
Exod 2:15 to be the source of v. 27 (Attridge, 342; Braun, 382; Lane 2:374–75).
Others take the actual exodus, Moses' second departure from Egypt in Exod
15:22, as the source (Bruce, 321–22; Hughes, 497–99; Montefiore, 204). A third
option tries not to tie a particular biblical text to this verse and interprets it as
a general statement about or a midrashic paraphrase on Moses' departure from
Egypt, sometimes with the help of Hellenistic Jewish tradition (Eisenbaum,
Jewish Heroes, 170; D'Angelo, *Moses*, 59–62; Grässer 3:173; Koester, 503–504;
Weiss, 608–609). Ellingworth (615) proposes yet another and rather creative
option. In Exod 11:8 Moses leaves the Pharaoh in a rage (*thymos*). He believes
the author has conflated this text in his mind with Exod 2:14. As ingenious a
suggestion as it is, even by his own admission there is no way to know that this
was what the author did. The fact that commentators have proposed so many
different solutions should be taken seriously, for they have genuinely grappled
with the problems in this verse. In this instance, however, perhaps function
should take precedence over form. The author has the biblical stories of the
individuals present in this chapter in mind. He is not doing exegesis of texts,
but presenting models of faith. One ought not expect that all the details are
going to be faithful to an original text. As seen in the previous examples, sometimes what he writes generally conforms to the LXX, whereas some of the details
do not.

for he persevered as if he had seen the invisible one: The verb *karterein* means "endure," "be steadfast," or "persevere" (LSJ, 880; BDAG, 510; Walter Grundmann,
kartereō, ktl., TDNT 3:617–20). It occurs only here in the NT and infrequently in
the LXX (Job 2:9; Sir 2:2; 12:15; Isa 42:14; 2 Macc 7:17; 4 Macc 9:9, 28; 10:1, 11; 13:11;
14:9). It is extant in Hellenistic Judaism (Philo, *On Agriculture* 152; Josephus,
War 1.535; 3.316; 4.590; 5.487; 7.232, 378; *Antiquities* 3.208; 5.321, 360; 7.310; 9.287;
11.52; 14.70; 16.208). The one Moses has continually in view is God, described
here as the "unseen one," *aoratos*, an adjective that occurs only three times in the
LXX (Gen 1:2; Isa 45:3; 2 Macc 9:5) and five times in the NT (Rom 1:20; Col 1:15,
16; 1 Tim 1:17; cf. Wilhelm Michaelis, *horaō, ktl., TDNT* 5:315–82). Philo applies
it to God (*On Creation* 69; *Allegorical Interpretation* 3.206; *On the Cherubim* 101;
Sacrifices of Cain and Abel 133; *The Worse Attacks the Better* 31, 86; *Posterity and
Exile of Cain* 15; *Noah As Planter* 18; *Moses* 2.65; *On the Decalogue* 60). In Hebrews

the unseen is the realm of the eternal (11:1-3, 13). Moses could persevere throughout his life because by faith he transcended the visible world in which he lived.

28. *By faith he kept the Passover and the pouring of blood, so that the destroyer of the first-born would not touch their firstborn:* The author invokes a normal term for observing the Passover (LXX: Exod 12:48; Num 9:2; Josh 5:10; 2 Kgdms 23:21; NT: Matt 26:18). Earlier in the sermon the author had used *rantizein* for the "sprinkling of blood" (9:13, 19, 21; 10:22). Here he chose the noun *proschysis*, which is not extant in the LXX, although the verb *proschein* is. Its meaning is closer to "pour" than to "sprinkle" (e.g., Exod 24:6; 29:16, 21; Lev 1:5, 11; 3:2, 8, 13; 7:4; 8:19; 9:12, 18; 17:6; Num 18:7; Deut 12:27 [A R]). The LXX of Exod 12:22 has *kathizein*, "touch," for the action of marking the lintels and doorposts of the Hebrew households. The author is making a connection here with the earlier discussion of the rituals of the old covenant as opposed to the new. The purpose of the pouring is to preserve the firstborn among the Israelites from the tenth and final plague in the Exodus narrative (Exod 12:29-32). In Exod 12:23 the verb *patassein*, "strike down," is used for the action of the Destroyer, whereas Hebrews uses *thinganein*, "touch." The verse concludes with a genitive plural pronoun, "of them," referring to the Israelites, whose firstborn were spared.

29. *By faith they passed through the Red Sea as if it were dry land:* Faith is now attributed to those who came out of Egypt with Moses. The subject of the verb "pass through," *diabainein*, is unexpressed; it is supplied by the third person plural form of the verb. The source of the verse is Exod 14:22, 29. The location is specified as the "Red Sea," *tēn erythran thalassan*, the same term used in the LXX (Exod 10:19; 13:18; 15:4, 22; 23:31). The "sea" was as if it were dry land, close to the description in the LXX (Exod 14:21, 29). Implicit in this verse is that God protected the Israelites, and that somehow their faith was involved. Some of the NT miracle narratives stress the necessity of faith for the recognition of a miracle (Matt 9:2, 22, 28-29; 14:31; 15:28; Mark 5:34; 9:24; 10:52); perhaps this tradition has influenced Hebrews.

but when the Egyptians attempted to do so they were drowned: The source of this part of the verse is Exod 14:27-28. The report of the Egyptians' failure to pass as the Israelites had is meant to show the role of faith in the previous part of the verse. The curious thing is that in the original narrative the Egyptian army exhibits more faith than do the Israelites. In Exod 14:25 they proclaim, "Let us flee from the Israelites, for the Lord is fighting for them against Egypt."

30. *By faith the walls of Jericho fell after they had been encircled for seven days:* The faith in question is implicitly Israel's. The verse is drawn from Josh 6:14-16, 20. Presumably the element of faith lies in the method of the city's destruction, merely a shout on the part of the people, after it had been encircled for seven days.

31. *By faith Rahab the prostitute did not perish with those who were disobedient, because she had received the spies in peace:* The story of Rahab is told in Josh 2:1-21. She exhibits faith when she hides the Israelite spies, and when she confesses that the Lord had given the land to the Israelites (v. 9). More telling still is her remarkable confession in v. 11, "The Lord your God is indeed God in heaven

above and on earth below." She and her family were spared because of her cooperation with the divine plan. The mention of "peace" is missing from the LXX narrative, but it may anticipate the exhortation on the "peaceful fruit of righteousness" in 12:11 and on the pursuit of "peace" in 12:14 (Attridge, 344; Koester, 505–506).

INTERPRETATION

The previous section focused on the notion of faith as "assurance of things hoped for." Now the author turns to heroic figures from the past who exemplify faith by not "shrinking back" in the face of hardship. The examples recall the citation from Hab 2:2-4, which the author has "re-scriptured" in a particular way that highlights the righteous individual awaiting the one who is to come. The righteous one lives by faith and does not shrink back, lest that individual displease God through lack of endurance. The examples here make concrete the exhortation of 10:32-39, with its closing reminder that "we are not of those shrinking back to destruction, but of those of faith for the preservation of the soul."

There are four divisions in this passage: (1) vv. 23-28, the faith of Moses; (2) v. 29, the faith of the Exodus generation; (3) v. 30, faith at the battle of Jericho; and (4) v. 31, the faith of Rahab.

The opening section does not begin with an example of Moses' faith but with that of his parents. Philo has a strikingly similar account about Moses' parents secluding him for three months: "Now the child from his birth had an appearance of more than ordinary goodliness (*asteioteran*), so that his parents as long as they could actually set at naught the proclamations of the despot. In fact we are told that, unknown to all but a few, he was kept at home and fed from his mother's breast for three successive months" (*Moses* 1.9; *Preliminary Studies* 131-32). The LXX speaks only of his mother's role in hiding him. In the face of peril, Moses' parents opted to keep him safe by hiding him, directly contravening the edict of the Pharaoh. Thus they are examples of courage as well as of faith. Illustrative of the righteous ones who live by faith, they did not shrink back, preserving Moses' life because he was pleasing to God, and thus they became pleasing to God themselves for not shrinking back.

The second example recalls Moses' position in the household of the Pharaoh as a grown man, who now is the subject of faith. His refusal to be called the Pharaoh's daughter's son is a refusal to stand apart from his own people. He rather chose solidarity with them in their suffering over what the author styles as "the temporary enjoyment of sin." Two things are operative here. First, the fact that he was *asteios* at birth is now confirmed in his moral choices, for as Philo indicates, being *asteios* is the mark of the virtuous person. Second, by observing that he preferred to share ill-treatment with the people of God over the temporary enjoyment of sin, the author indicates that Moses chose what was lasting over the transient. Ultimately, the author notes, Moses endured reproach suffered for the Christ because he looked to a reward (v. 26). The description of Moses in his proximate and remote choices and motivations offers an important witness to the readers.

The depiction of a mature Moses acting out of proper moral choices exemplifies the person who has moved beyond an elementary to a more advanced level in progress toward salvation (6:1-2). The fact that he was able to calculate what was more valuable to him in the long run demonstrates the kind of faith the readers need for their own journey. Moses endured reproaches for the Christ because he looked to a reward. In 3:5 his fidelity as God's servant was attributed to his willingness to attest to things spoken of later. Here the future reward motivates him to endurance and to the sacrifice of wealth that he could have had in the short run. The readers themselves have suffered and sacrificed their own relative wealth because they had a better and more lasting possession (10:32-34). The exhortation not to throw away their confidence in 10:35 was offered with the motivation that confidence brings with it a great reward. It would be hard not to see the connection between the example of Moses and the reality of the readers' own struggles, which require faith to endure (cf. Koester, 509).

The fourth example of Moses' faith appeals to his behavior during the difficult moment of the Exodus itself. In this example he represents those who by faith endure because they have the "proof of things unseen" (11:1). For Moses the world had become, like the burning bush, a place that discloses the presence of the unseen God. By faith he lived a life marked by belief in God, even though God was unseen. He exemplifies the believer described in 11:6, who affirms the existence of the unseen and is rewarded accordingly. Faith, then, sustained him when he decided to go against the dictates of the Pharaoh, and like his parents he did not succumb to fear. Opposition to unjust authority requires faith like that. It is unlikely that the author is encouraging his readers to action against public authorities in their day (cf. Koester, 509). Rather, the positive side of Moses' example takes precedence, namely that he endured by seeing "him who is invisible."

Last, Moses' faith led him to carry out the instructions he had been given for the observance of the Passover (Exod 12:1-12, 21-28). Moses' action, dictated by God, was undertaken on behalf of the people for their protection. And so the Israelites were spared the final plague in order to be led out of Egypt to the land that was promised them. Moses could not foresee the consequences of his actions but, acting in faith, he made possible the fulfillment of the promises given to Abraham. His example is important for the readers, who seek and await a heavenly homeland (11:14-16; 12:22-24) without being able to foresee the circumstances they may face before reaching it.

The faith of the Israelites (11:29) allowed them to cross through the sea to dry land, whereas the Egyptians, lacking such faith, perished. Another situation of fear and hardship is overcome by faith. When they set out to cross through the sea, the Israelites had risked the possibility that they would not survive, as the goal they sought was not immediately obtained. Only faith to endure the hardship could make possible the attainment of what they had hoped awaited them on the other side. The Egyptians failed because they could only attempt to do what the Israelites had done. Success is attributed to faith.

Similarly, the victory at Jericho was fueled by faith. By divine dictate the Israelites were instructed to march around the city for seven days, accompanied by seven priests blowing trumpets of rams' horns. On the seventh day at the sound of a trumpet the people were to make a loud shout in order to bring the walls down. Their trust in Joshua and God sustained them in their weeklong effort, and by faith they succeeded.

Perhaps the battle of Jericho prompted the author to reflect on yet another figure in that story. The final example brings Rahab, a non-Israelite prostitute, into the picture. She confesses to the spies that "The Lord your God is indeed the God of heaven above and the earth below" (Josh 2:11). She may have been motivated by self-interest in seeking the preservation of her family, but she sought assurance from the spies on the basis of a confession that their God would protect her and her family, along with anyone else who believed in that God. She and her family were spared (Josh 6:17, 22-25). The other inhabitants of Jericho are described as disobedient, like the wilderness generation who lacked faith (Heb 3:18; 4:6, 11). Rahab exemplifies the relationship between faith and works, alongside Abraham in Jas 2:18-25. The observation that she offered hospitality to the Israelite spies with peace looks ahead to 12:14 and 13:2, 20 (Attridge, 344).

The examples of faith presented in this section all encounter urgent and extreme situations in which endurance required faith. Each of the situations involved trust in the face of peril and an uncertain outcome. The individuals who exemplified faith in these instances chose something of lasting value over the exigency of the moment. Hebrews believes they were able to act in faith because they remained steadfast in their trust in God, even when confronted by an imminent threat to their well-being and security. In the end, each received a short-term reward, even if they did not ultimately receive the full benefit of what was promised (11:39).

This section of chapter 11 continues the author's portrayal of the heroes of faith by presenting biblical figures who acted out of faith for the sake of a greater purpose. Even though this greater goal lay outside their immediate grasp, they endured the tribulations of the moment in order to advance toward it. The examples offered here have a timeless character that inspires readers of Hebrews to appropriate the courage and endurance necessary to stay the course toward one's final destination. In each of the cases included in this passage, persevering through adversity resulted in preservation that brought the subjects closer to their goal. The author's message is both enduring and sustaining.

FOR REFERENCE AND FURTHER STUDY

Barber, C. J. "Moses: A Study of Hebrews 11:23-29a," *GJ* 14 (1973) 14–28.

Bittner, Wolfgang. "Der Umgang mit Gott, dem Unsichtbaren (Hebr 11,27)," *TBei* 16 (1985) 1–4.

Hanson, Anthony Tyrrell. "Rahab the Harlot in Early Christian Theology," *JSNT* 1 (1978) 53–60.

Hay, David M. "Moses through New Testament Spectacles," *Int* 44 (1990) 240–52.

Lehmann, K.-P. "Die messianischen Leiden des Propheten Mose. Exegetische Anmerkungen zu Hebräer 11,23-31," *Texte und Kontexte* 22 (1999) 95–114.

31. *The Faith of the Persecuted* (11:32-40)

32. And what more should I say? For time would fail me to tell of Gideon, Barak, Samson, Jephthah, of David and Samuel and the prophets—33. who through faith conquered kingdoms, administered justice, obtained promises, shut the mouths of lions, 34. quenched the power of fire, escaped the edge of the sword, were made powerful out of weakness, became mighty in war, put foreign armies to flight. 35. Women received their dead by resurrection. Others were tortured, refusing to accept release, in order to obtain a better resurrection. 36. Others suffered mocking and flogging, and even chains and imprisonment. 37. They were stoned to death, they were sawn in two, they were killed by the sword, they went about in skins of sheep and goats, destitute, afflicted, tormented—38. of whom the world was not worthy. They wandered in deserts and mountains, and in caves and holes in the ground.

39. Yet all these, though they were attested for their faith, did not receive what was promised, 40. since God had provided something better for us so that they would not, apart from us, be made perfect.

NOTES

32. *And what more should I say? For time would fail me to tell of Gideon, Barak, Samson, Jephthah, of David and Samuel and the prophets:* The verse opens with a rhetorical question instead of the *anaphora* "by faith," *pistei*. There are seven instances of

similarly worded questions in Josephus (*War* 1.425; 2.366, 379; 4.177; 5.395; *Antiquities* 16.53; 20.257; cf. 16.384) where the main verb is *dei*, "be necessary" (*chrē: War* 2.366) with the complementary infinitive *legein*, "say." Hebrews uses a deliberative subjunctive in the first person, which is usual in the NT (BDF §366). "For time would fail me" is a standard rhetorical device. Philo uses it in a form close to Hebrews with "time," *ho chronos*, as the subject of "would fail," *epilepsei*, in *Special Laws* 4.238 (see also *Sacrifices of Cain and Abel* 27; *On Dreams* 2.63; *Moses* 1.213).

The heroes listed are not in the chronological order of the biblical narrative, where Barak precedes Gideon, Jephthah precedes Samson, and David precedes Samuel. The order should be Barak (Judg 4:4–5:31), Gideon (Judg 6:11–8:35), Jephthah (Judg 11:1–12:7), Samson (Judg 13:24–16:31), Samuel (1 Sam 1:21–28:3), and David (1 Sam 16:12–1 Kgs 2:10). One may question the wisdom of including some of these figures, since they are not representative of the kind of faith Hebrews is generally interested in. Barak, for example, was somewhat diffident about fighting Jabin's general, Sisera. He reluctantly agreed to go on the condition that Deborah would go with him (Judg 4:7-8). In response to an angelic visitor who proclaimed the Lord to be with him, Gideon said, "But sir, if the LORD is with us, why then has all this happened to us? And where are all his wonderful deeds that our ancestors recounted to us . . . ? But now the LORD has cast us off, and given us into the hand of Midian" (Judg 6:13). He even asked for a sign from the Lord to confirm the message he was receiving (Judg 6:17). Jephthah was known for having made a vow that he would sacrifice whoever from his household would greet him as he returned from battle, if the Ammonites were given into his hand. Ironically, he first meets his daughter, whom he then loses in the fulfillment of his vow (Judg 11:29-40).

David, the man of valor, put an end to Israel's wars with the Philistines (1 Sam 17:50-51; Sir 47:7). He was a great king who received an oracle that someone from his house would rule on the throne of Judah in perpetuity (2 Sam 7:12-16). Despite his failings, David was known for his dedication to the Lord (2 Sam 22:51). Acts 2:30 identifies him as a prophet, as does Hebrews (4:7).

Samson was a mighty warrior who followed the plan of the Lord against his parents' wishes (Judg 14:1-4). Despite his affair with Delilah, which brought about his death, his own self-sacrifice was redemptive (Judg 16:30-31).

Samuel was the last judge of Israel, instrumental in making kings. As a boy under the tutelage of the priest Eli at the shrine of Shiloh he responded to the Lord in faith and in return received an oracle concerning the house of Eli (1 Sam 2:18–3:18). Sirach 46:15 describes him as faithful. In 2 Chr 35:18 and Sir 46:13, 15 he is identified as a prophet. Perhaps this is why the author appends "and the prophets" to the end of the verse.

33. *who through faith conquered kingdoms, administered justice, obtained promises, shut the mouths of lions,* 34. *quenched the power of fire, escaped the edge of the sword, were made powerful out of weakness, became mighty in war, put foreign armies to flight:* The author now condenses his subject in these two verses by cataloguing the actions for which these heroes and others are remembered. The nine clauses would seem to apply to more individuals than the six just mentioned. Gideon, Barak, Samson, Jephthah, and David qualify, as individuals who had overcome

the kingdoms of Israel's enemies, and so "conquering kingdoms" may apply to them. The expression *eirgasanto dikaiosynēn* is ambiguous, as it can mean "they practiced righteousness" or "they administered justice." The latter sense is found in 2 Sam 8:15, referring to David who "administered judgment and justice to all his people." The LXX (2 Kgdms 8:15) translates this as "he did [or worked] judgment and justice" for all his people. Since the judges on the list also administered justice, this is likely the meaning here.

How the individuals listed "obtained promises" is not specified. Perhaps, as with Abraham earlier (11:11; cf. 6:15), the author understands them to have received some fulfillment of the promises, but in a final sense (see 9:15). Even in this section of the chapter there appears to be a distinction as to how promises are obtained. Those mentioned in v. 34 receive something different from the ultimate fulfillment of the promise of resurrection in v. 35.

That the list extends beyond the six individuals mentioned is evident in the next clause, "they stopped the mouths of lions," which is a quotation from Dan 6:19 and 23 [Θ]. Samson and David also had encounters with lions (Judg 14:6; 1 Sam 17:34-35; cf. Sir 47:3). The expression "quenched the power of fire" alludes to the Prayer of Azariah in the Greek additions to the book of Daniel (LXX: Dan 3:50, 88), in which the three young men praise God for delivering them from the fiery furnace.

The term "the edge of the sword" is common in the Hebrew Bible (e.g., Josh 6:21; 8:24; 10:28, 30, 32, 35, 37, 39; Job 1:15, 17; Jer 21:7; Sir 28:18; 1 Macc 5:28, 51). The reference here is to those who had escaped that fate, but it is too general to know how it may apply to the individuals on the list. More curious is how the author understands the role of faith in bringing that rescue about. Of those listed, Gideon and Samson are examples of individuals who were made powerful out of weakness. The former had only a small army, coming from the least of the tribes (Judg 6:15), and the latter, when shorn, brought the house down on the Philistines (Judg 16:30). David, as a youth who slew the giant Goliath, may also be an example (Sir 47:5). Some commentators see Esther and Judith as examples of women who were empowered, as both are so mentioned in *1 Clem* 55:3-6 (Attridge, 349; Koester, 513).

Echoing the acquisition of strength in the previous clause is the phrase "became mighty in war." This epithet can certainly be applied to the judges on the list. Gideon, for example, is called "powerful in might" (Judg 6:12). Sirach 47:7 lauds David for crushing the power of his enemies. Joshua is "mighty in war" in Sir 46:1 and "able at war" in Sir 47:5.

The final clause in the series, "put foreign armies to flight" is syntactically different from the previous eight. The verb does not lead as in the previous eight instances, and its voice is active, rather than passive as in the two previous clauses. The object of the verb *parembolē* can mean "camp" or "army," and both meanings are extant in the LXX (camp: Gen 32:3, 9, 22; Exod 29:14; army: Judg 4:16; 8:11; 1 Kgdms 14:16; BDAG, 775). Hebrews uses the noun with the meaning "camp" in 13:11-12, but here it means "army." Any of the judges listed are examples of those who routed foreign armies, as is David.

35. *Women received their dead by resurrection:* Following the list of heroes in Sirach 48, where one finds the mention of Elijah raising a corpse from the dead (v. 5),

one might surmise that the author has in mind here the widow of Zarephath (1 Kgs 17:17-24). She really does not come to faith, however, until her son is restored to life (1 Kgs 17:24); in fact, she accuses Elijah of causing the death of her son (v. 18). Although she is not mentioned in Sirach 48, it is natural to think, too, of the Shunammite woman whose son Elisha restored to life (2 Kgs 4:18-37).

Others were tortured, refusing to accept release, in order to obtain a better resurrection: More explicit persecution forms the theme of the rest of this passage. As the root of the word indicates, the verb "torture," *tympanizein*, means to use an instrument called a *tympanon*. This was a drum that was part of a rack on which a person was slowly beaten to death (2 Macc 6:19, 28, 30; BDAG, 1019; Attridge, 349). Josephus uses the compound *apotympanizein*, "beat to death" (*Against Apion* 1.148). Those in question did not accept release, *apolytrōsis*, which the author has used in 9:15 in the sense of redemption. The story of Eleazar in 2 Maccabees 6 noted that he was urged to feign eating pork to gain release, but he refused to compromise his principles (cf. 4 Macc 9:16). Sometimes the motive of the Maccabean martyrs for accepting death willingly is that they hope for the resurrection (2 Macc 7:14, 23; 4 Macc 16:25; 17:18; 18:23). The telling note for the author is that the expected resurrection is described as "better," meaning the one he and his readers look forward to, as distinguished from what the Maccabean martyrs and those revived by Elijah and Elisha expected.

36. *Others suffered mocking and flogging:* Another group of "others" endure yet two more forms of persecution. The text says that they received a test of "ridicule and lashes." A variation on this expression occurs in 11:29, where it means "attempt." "Mocking" describes what the seven brothers suffered in 2 Macc 7:7-19. As a form of verbal abuse it may be likened to what some of the readers had experienced according to 10:32. It also calls to mind the mocking that Jesus suffered at his crucifixion (Heb 13:13; Matt 27:29-31, 41-42; Luke 23:11). "Flogging" was a common and especially brutal form of punishment in the ancient world. All four gospels relate that Jesus was flogged before his crucifixion, but Matt 27:26 and Mark 15:15 have the verb *phragellein*, whereas Luke 23:16 uses *paideuein*. John alone has *mastigein* in Pilate's offer to have Jesus flogged and released (19:1). The synoptic Passion predictions, however, use *mastigein*, the verbal form of the noun employed in this verse, *mastigos* (Matt 20:19; Mark 10:34; Luke 18:33). Paul is nearly flogged in Acts 22:24, where it is not a punishment in itself but a means of interrogation, "examination by flogging" (*mastixin*). Paul himself claimed to have endured "countless floggings" (*plēgais*) (2 Cor 11:23).

and even chains and imprisonment: Among those listed as models of faith, the prophets were often imprisoned (Jer 20:2, 7; 29:26; 37:15; 1 Kgs 22:27; 2 Chr 16:10). The seventh Maccabee brother asked to be released from his chains, whereupon he cast himself into the braziers ending his life (4 Macc 12:2, 8, 19). There may also be a link here with the imprisonment some community members had suffered (10:34).

37. *They were stoned to death:* Perhaps aware that he really is running out of time, the author brings the catalogue to a conclusion with a series of references without

elaboration, somewhat like those of the previous verse. Stoning was Judaism's capital punishment (Lev 20:27; Deut 22:21). The NT knows of it (Luke 20:6; John 8:59; Acts 5:26; 7:58-59) even if it is not clear whether under the Romans it was permissible to Jews. According to 2 Chr 24:21 the prophet Zechariah was stoned (cf. Matt 23:35; Luke 11:51). The history of stoning prophets is mentioned in the NT (Matt 23:37; Luke 13:34; cf. Matt 21:35).

they were sawn in two: The verb *prizein* occurs only here in the NT and is infrequent in the LXX (Amos 1:3; Sus 59 [Θ]). The best known example of a victim suffering this fate in the tradition is Isaiah (*Martyrdom of Isaiah* 5.11-14). Variant readings in a number of manuscripts add *epeirasthēsan*, "they were tested" before or after "they were sawn in two." This is probably due to a scribal error known as dittography, where something that was supposed to be copied once was actually copied twice (Attridge, 346).

they were killed by the sword: Uriah, the son of Shemaiah, was a prophet who was killed by the sword (Jer 26:23; LXX: 33:23). Elijah claims in 1 Kgs 19:10 that apostate Israelites have killed the Lord's prophets with the sword (cf. Jer 2:30). Many people, however, meet this end in the Hebrew Bible, so whether the author has only prophets in mind is not certain (Lev 26:7, 8; Num 14:3, 43; Judg 4:16; 1 Sam 2:33; 2 Sam 1:12; 3:29; 2 Kgs 19:7; 2 Chr 29:9; Job 36:12; Ps 78:64; Isa 1:20; 3:25; 13:15; 14:19; 22:2; 37:7; Jer 11:22; 14:12, 18; 16:4; 18:21; 19:7; 20:4; 21:9; Ezek 32:20-31; Lam 2:21; 4:9; 1 Macc 4:15; 7:38, 46; 10:85).

they went about in skins of sheep and goats, destitute, afflicted, tormented: If this part of the verse also refers to prophets, then Elijah and Elisha come to mind for their garb (LXX: 3 Kgdms 19:13; 4 Kgdms 2:8, 13, 14; cf. Zech 13:4). "Destitute," *hysteroumenoi*, was used in 4:1 and will appear again in 12:15. It basically means to suffer a deficiency. "Afflicted," *thlibomenoi*, is related to the word *thlipsis*, "affliction." Both are used in the NT to describe suffering, persecution, and social dislocation (1 Thess 1:6; 3:4; 2 Thess 1:4, 7). "Tormented," *kakouchoumenoi*, recalls the compound in 11:25, *synkakoucheisthai* (see the Notes at 11:25). The verb *kakouchein* is rare in the LXX (3 Kgdms 2:26; 11:39[A]).

38. *of whom the world was not worthy:* The author makes a parenthetical remark to the effect that people so treated are denigrated by the world, but in reality the world pales in comparison to them. John 15:18, "If the world hates you . . ." speaks of a similar worldly sentiment.

They wandered in deserts and mountains, and in caves and holes in the ground: The reference may be to the Maccabees, who celebrated at the time of the purification of the sanctuary and recalled how long they had wandered in mountains and caves (2 Macc 10:6). Also, 1 Macc 1:29 reports that in an attempt to escape the Antiochene persecution many pious Jews fled to the wilderness, where they had hiding places (1 Macc 2:31; 2 Macc 5:27). Or there may be an allusion here to Elijah, who in despair fled to the wilderness after his life was threatened by Jezebel (1 Kgs 19:4). He also stood on a mountain (1 Kgs 19:11) and at the entrance to a cave (1 Kgs 19:13). Israel is said to have hidden from the Midianites in mountains and caves in Judg 6:2. They also hid from the Philistines in caves, holes, rocks, tombs, and cisterns (1 Sam 13:6). David fled to the wilderness (1 Sam 22:14) and to a cave (1 Sam 22:1; 1 Sam 24:3) to escape Saul. Revelation

6:15 has *spēlaion*, "cave," in an apparent allusion to Isa 2:19. John 11:38 uses it to describe Lazarus' tomb.

39. *Yet all these, though they were attested for their faith, did not receive what was promised:* The verb "attest" is *martyrein*, which the author used in his presentation of the first heroes of faith (11:2), thus forming an *inclusio* for this section of the sermon (Attridge, 352). The observation that "they did not receive" what was promised recalls the statement that the first heroes described: Abel, Enoch, Noah, and Abraham died without receiving the promises (11:13). Abraham was said in 6:15 to have obtained the promise, meaning that God had indeed given the promise to him (Gen 12:1-3), including an heir who was born to him and Sarah (Heb 11:8-12). Still on another level he did not receive the fulfillment of the promise, which is given to those who are of the new covenant, founded on better promises (8:6).

40. *since God had provided something better for us so that they would not, apart from us, be made perfect:* The verb "provide," *problepein*, means "look ahead" or "foresee." In secular Greek it does mean "provide for" (BDAG, 866; MM, 538). It occurs only here in the NT and is used once in the LXX in Ps 36:13. This verse effectively explains why the heroes of faith did not receive the fulfillment of the promises. It was because God had intended to provide something better (*kreitton*) for the readers who come after them. These are the better things that belong to salvation (6:9), the better hope (7:19), a better covenant (7:22; 8:6), better sacrifices (9:23), a better and lasting possession (10:34), a better, heavenly country (11:16), and a better word (12:24). The author has developed this plan of God to provide something better throughout the sermon. The ancestors and heroes of faith could not have come to completion before the sacrifice of Christ made that possible. Perfection is a matter of purifying the conscience, and this could not be done effectively under the old covenant (7:11; 9:9). Such purification, according to the author, comes from the self-offering of Christ (9:14; 10:22). The heroes of faith who precede those who are brought to completion in Christ could not have been perfected apart from the readers, who receive completion in their eternal inheritance (9:15) in the heavenly Jerusalem (12:22-24). Ultimately, Hebrews believes these individuals received what was promised them.

INTERPRETATION

The previous section presented faithful witnesses who risked their well-being and security to act by faith for a greater goal. This section offers the examples of judges, a king, and prophets, as well as martyrs, whose accomplishments and endurance of suffering were actualized by faith. The section differs from the fuller examples of the heroes presented previously in the chapter. Here the author chooses to summarize a wide range of varied experiences of things achieved by faith, substituting the prepositional phrase "through faith" (*dia pisteōs*) for the earlier anaphora "by faith" (*pistei*). Individuals are named only in v. 32, where five judges, one king, and unnamed prophets are grouped together. In the subsequent six verses the tribulations of the martyrs are catalogued impersonally. Presumably the author trusts his readers to know which individuals he has in mind in the brief summary he offers. The readers must also know that the experiences catalogued here were undergone through faith. The passage closes with a summation (vv. 39-40) that links the figures in this section with those already catalogued earlier in the chapter and with the readers, who are given an advantage over everyone else already mentioned.

This section, as ambiguous as it is, addresses the sufferings and tribulations of the readers and intends to exhort them to a faith similar to that exhibited by the people who endured the forms of suffering and persecution listed. Thus it looks back to 10:32-39, where the critical punch line from Hab 2:2-3 stresses the faith of the righteous, who persevere and endure suffering without shrinking back because they live by faith.

One might have expected that perfect models of faith would be presented, but the individuals listed here represent a mix of talents and abilities (cf. Eisenbaum, *Jewish Heroes*, 174–75). Some of these individuals may actually have gotten in the way of the divine will, but they were nonetheless instruments of accomplishing it despite their shortcomings. Fuller treatments of the foibles of these individuals can be found in the Notes above, so here they can be summarized. Gideon's doubt, Barak's diffidence in war, Samson's weakness in strength, Jephthah's rashness, and David's sins were not insurmountable obstacles for God's grace to be at work in such imperfect vessels. Thus they become valuable examples for individuals who themselves are less than perfect (5:11–6:8; 10:25-31).

Similarly, the general catalogue of sufferings and tribulations seems rushed by comparison to what precedes it in this chapter, yet there may be some appeal in not overspecifying the examples, so that there is some room left for the readers genuinely to identify their own circumstances with those of the hero-martyrs of the past. Even if they themselves have not had to witness to the point of bloodshed (12:4) their own tribulations are as real as some of those presented in this passage (10:32-34). Deeds of faith and courage take precedence over individuals in the bulk of this passage, effectively emphasizing what any person of faith can accomplish by remaining steadfast in the face of difficulties. Some of the actions taken yielded positive results, as in the cases of the women who received back their dead. Others made more complete sacrifices on the basis of an assurance that they would receive a better resurrection. Eventually, as the list unfolds, it appears that the individuals mentioned are aliens without a homeland, forced to wander and even to live in caves and holes. The author says explicitly that they are destitute, afflicted, and tormented (v. 37). No longer at home in this world, these individuals appear to be closer in their plight to the readers than to the people listed by name earlier in this chapter, untimely born for the ultimate fulfillment of God's promises (11:13-16). The fact that these unnamed heroes lived in a world that was not worthy of them may mitigate to some extent the futility of their suffering, and that alienation places them among those who have no lasting city here on earth (13:14). Both groups are destined ultimately to receive what was promised, but the readers in particular are encouraged to embody the confidence and endurance needed to surmount the difficulties they face in their own alienation from the society of their day.

This is the effective meaning of the concluding two verses. Despite the apparent greatness of the heroes of faith in chapter 11, they did not receive immediately what they were promised. Regardless of the way the Bible has told their stories, emphasizing as it does the glory of God on Israel's behalf, they were not positioned historically to see the completion of the divine plan. Nothing willful on their part had prevented them from seeing this, for, as the author has already noted, they could only greet it from afar (11:13). This lack of fulfillment, nevertheless marked by faith and hope, is what all the heroes of this chapter have in common (cf. Eisenbaum, *Jewish Heroes*, 178). For the author of Hebrews the end of history is in Christ (12:2; see Peterson, *Hebrews and Perfection*, 156–59); the hopes of the heroic generation are thus proleptic. They could not be perfected apart from those who would find completion in Christ. This is the something better that God has foreseen for the author and the readers.

The phrasing of v. 40 envisions the possibility of the eschatological fulfillment of the promises for the heroes of faith catalogued in this chapter (Braun, 401). The author writes that "God had provided something better for us so that they would not, apart from us, be made perfect." Although the readers may have had a temporal advantage in that they lived after Christ, they do not necessarily have an eschatological advantage over those who lived before Christ. If anything, the stress on the history of faith in chapter 11 has linked the readers to previous generations. The examples of figures of faith show continuity and discontinuity (Eisenbaum, *Jewish Heroes*, 180; Koester, 520), but the discontinuity is not of the sort that would prevent those who lived before Christ from being numbered among the "assembly of the firstborn" and "the spirits of the righteous made perfect" (12:23-24). In fact, the completion brought about by the sacrificial death of Christ would seem to necessitate their inclusion.

Bringing this chapter to a close, the author shows his purpose: to include the great biblical figures of faith along with the readers in the pilgrimage toward their final common destiny. Despite the many comparisons between the old and the new covenants and the stress on the "better" promises, priesthood, and covenant, those figures who exercised faith in a less complete way because of a determination of history still share in the ultimate eschatological fulfillment of what God has promised them. In that way their faith is shown to be not only exemplary, but sufficient. In presenting these heroic figures as exemplary and sufficient, the author's paraenetic purpose in encouraging his readers to match the endurance of these legendary individuals emerges. This purpose is facilitated by the invitation to the readers to include themselves in the stories of the faith heroes and heroines and by the observation that in the end all of them together will find the same completion.

FOR REFERENCE AND FURTHER STUDY

Barrett, C. K. "The Eschatology of the Epistle to the Hebrews," in W. D. Davies and David Daube, eds., *The Background of the New Testament and Its Eschatology*. Cambridge: Cambridge University Press, 1964, 363–93.

Cockerill, Gareth Lee. "The Better Resurrection (Heb. 11:35): A Key to the Structure of Rhetorical Purpose of Hebrews 11," *TynBul* 51 (2000) 215–34.

Grässer, Erich. "Exegese nach Auschwitz? Kritische Anmerkungen zur hermeneutischen Bedeutung des Holocaust am Beispiel von Hebr. 11," *KD* 27 (1981) 152–63.

Hofius, Otfried. "*Stomata machairēs*, Hebr 11,34," *ZNW* 62 (1971) 129–30.

Schatkin, Margaret A. "The Maccabean Martyrs." *VC* 28 (1974) 97–113.

32. *Looking to Jesus* (12:1-3)

1. Therefore, since we are surrounded by so great a cloud of witnesses, let us also lay aside every encumbrance and the sin that easily besets us, and let us run with perseverance the race that is set before us, 2. looking to Jesus the pioneer and perfecter of our faith, who for the sake of the joy that was set before him endured the cross, disregarding its shame, and has taken his seat at the right hand of the throne of God. 3. Consider, then, him who endured such hostility against himself from sinners, so that you may not grow weary or lose heart.

NOTES

1. *Therefore, since we are surrounded by so great a cloud of witnesses:* The conjunction *toigaroun*, "therefore," resumes the topic of chapter 11. On the verb *perikeisthai*, "wrap around" or "surround," see the Notes at 5:2. The noun "cloud" has the metaphorical meaning of "host" or "crowd" (BDAG, 670; Albrecht Oepke, *nephelē, nephos, TDNT* 4:902–10).

let us also lay aside every encumbrance and the sin that easily besets us: The verb "lay aside," *apotithenai*, means to "put aside" or "lay aside," and it appears often in hortatory contexts in the NT (Eph 4:22, 25; Col 3:8; Jas 1:21; 1 Pet 2:1; cf. 2 Pet 1:14). Josephus uses it for "putting aside habits" (*Antiquities* 6.259). Philo has it in relation to casting off a burden (*Posterity and Exile of Cain* 48; *On Giants* 16; *Special Laws* 1.102). The noun "encumbrance," *onkos*, occurs only here in the Bible. Philo uses it metaphorically in a comparison of Hagar and Rebecca drawing water from a spring. Hagar brings a waterskin, whereas Rebecca brings a pitcher. The waterskin is an "encumbrance," *onkos*, but the "pitcher," a vessel of reason, is not. Regarding the process of progressing toward virtue, Philo likens the body to the waterskin, which weighs one down and must be discarded in favor of reason if one is genuinely to pursue virtue and spiritual realities (*Posterity and Exile of Cain* 137). As the author will use an athletic metaphor in the last part of this verse, it is likely that he has in mind the image of an athlete shedding extra weight.

and the sin that easily besets us: The definite article may indicate that the author has a particular sin in mind, like apostasy, but it can be generic, too (Attridge, 355). The peculiar description of sin in this context, where the readers are surrounded by these great witnesses to faith, is curious. The adjective *euperistatos*, "easily besetting," (LSJ, 726; cf. BDAG, 410), occurs nowhere else in Greek literature. The author may have coined it (Spicq 2:385). The sense here is that sin is an encumbrance that needs to be thrown off.

and let us run with perseverance the race that is set before us: The reason for casting off the burden of sin is to be able to run the race more easily. The author has used athletic imagery in 10:32. Here he invokes more explicitly the race that is before them. The noun for "race" is *agōn*, which means an athletic contest (BDAG, 17; Ethelbert Stauffer, *agōn, ktl., TDNT* 1:134–40). The race metaphor is used elsewhere in the NT, as is athletic imagery in general (Acts 13:25; 20:24; 1 Cor 9:24-27; Gal 2:2; Phil 2:16; 3:13-14; Col 2:1; 1 Tim 6:12; 2 Tim 2:5; 4:7). For the expression "set before us" see Epictetus, *Dissertations* 3.25.3; Josephus, *Antiquities* 16.19. The race has to be run with perseverance (on *hypomonē* see the Notes at 10:36), for as Epictetus says, "No contest is held without turmoil" (*Dissertations* 4.4.31). The model is Christ in v. 2.

2. *looking to Jesus the pioneer and perfecter of our faith:* The verb "look to," *aphoran*, means to look intently at someone or something (BDAG, 158). Epictetus has an interesting parallel in which he, as teacher, exhorts his students to help him complete his purpose, which is to bring them to maturity (*apotelesthai*) (cf. Heb 6:1). At one point he encourages them to look (*aphoran*) to God in things small and great (*Dissertations* 2.19.29; see 3.24.16; cf. 4 Macc 17:10; Josephus, *Antiquities* 20.48; *Against Apion* 2.166). On Jesus as the "pioneer," *archēgos*, see the Notes at 2:10; he is also called the "forerunner" in 6:20. He cannot be the "pioneer" of faith in the sense that faith was nonexistent before him. The author has just catalogued other witnesses to faith. The pioneering function must reside in the fact that he has reached the goal of faith, the presence of God. Thus as pioneer he has made it possible for others to approach God. The author calls him the "perfecter," *teleiōtēs*, of faith as well. As perfecter he has brought faith to a new

expression in his own obedient submission to the will of God (3:2-6). Thus he is a faith role model. Only a faithful one can enter into God's rest (3:18). As both pioneer and perfecter, then, Jesus makes this kind of faith possible for others and offers an example to follow.

who for the sake of the joy that was set before him endured the cross: There is some ambiguity in the preposition *anti*, translated here as "for the sake of." It can also mean "instead of." If that is the case, Jesus is letting go of joy to endure suffering (cf. 2 Cor 8:9; Phil 2:6-7). The author has said as much of Moses, who let go of royal status in order to share the suffering of his people (11:24-25). This interpretation would fit with the earlier statements about Jesus being made like his brothers and sisters in every respect so that he might experience the suffering they experience in order to save them (2:10-18). The translation "for the sake of" changes the picture a bit, making the "joy" a goal or reward like what the martyrs expect for their endurance. Then, like Moses, Jesus suffered for the sake of the joy that lay ahead of him (Attridge, 357).

disregarding its shame: The verb *kataphronein* has the meaning of "look down on," "despise," "scorn," or "treat with contempt." It can also carry the sense of "not valuing" or "disregarding" (BDAG, 529). "Shame," *aischynē*, was an important cultural concept, as was its opposite, "honor." A fair amount of recent NT criticism has paid special attention to both values in the NT (see Bruce J. Malina, *The New Testament World: Insights from Cultural Anthropology* [Louisville: Westminster John Knox, 1993]). In this verse most modern translations prefer "despising shame" (NAB; NASB; NIV), as did the KJV and the Rheims NT. The NEB has "making light of its disgrace." The Amplified Bible opted for both meanings in "despising and ignoring shame." The NRSV chose "disregarding shame."

The only extant parallel for the use of the verb *kataphronein* with *aischynē* as its object is in Dio Chrysostom's Oration 7.139 (Wettstein 2:434; David A. de Silva, *Despising Shame: Honor Discourse and Community Maintenance in the Epistle to the Hebrews*. SBLDS 152 [Atlanta: Scholars, 1995] 169). Dio discusses the decline of sexual mores, particularly in the matter of adultery with outcasts, and he concludes that, unchecked, the immorality might spread to victims in respectable families. He reasons that such immoral activity results "when shame is commonly disregarded." The sense of his remark is that people no longer feel the restraint of shame because the moral value of modesty is no longer important to them. In a world where the pursuit of honor was everywhere evident, one would not expect to find many literary references to individuals who disregarded shame. If anything, the countercultural example of a person who disregarded honor might be more compelling. Certainly among philosophers who espoused moral autonomy or self-sufficiency the enslavement of the pursuit of honor might be seen as more threatening to one's moral life than the disregard of shame. It is no surprise, then, that the ideal philosopher would be presented as someone unconcerned with the pursuit of honor (Diogenes Laertius, *Lives of Eminent Philosophers* 9.36; Epictetus, *Dissertations* 3.15.11; 3.22.106; 4.1.70, 87, 162-67; *Enchiridion* 19.1; 24.1). That kind of concern could only inhibit and compromise one's moral purpose. As with the example of Jesus in this verse, things like "honor" and "shame" are really not important in view of a larger goal. "Shame" in this verse is a metaphor for suffering and death, so texts portraying individuals who disregard death may be more relevant for understanding this verse than the one cited above on disregarding shame (on the shame associated with crucifixion see Jerome Neyrey, "'Despising the Shame of the Cross,'" *Semeia* 68 [1994] 113–37). The notion of disregarding death is evident in the Maccabean martyrs, who were earlier presented as heroes of faith (4 Macc 6:8-9, 20-21; 13:1; 14:11; 16:2; cf. Philo, *Every Good Person Is Free* 30; Lucian, *The Passing of Peregrinus* 23, 33). Perhaps the author has their example in mind here, too.

and has taken his seat at the right hand of the throne of God: The author writes of Jesus' session at the right hand of God, with one last allusion to Psalm 110. One difference is evident: the tense of *kathizein* is perfect here, which commentators take as a more definitive statement than the earlier allusions or citations (e.g., Attridge, 358). See the Notes at 8:1 and 10:12.

3. *Consider, then, him who endured such hostility against himself from sinners:* The particle *gar*, "then," introduces a self-evident conclusion (BDAG, 190). The verb "consider," *analogizesthai*, has a deliberative sense. It occurs only here in the NT and is rare in the LXX (Wis 17:13 [S]; 2 Macc 12:43 [A]; 3 Macc 7:7). The verb "endure" was used earlier, in 10:32, to refer to how the readers had endured their own struggles (see the Notes at 10:32). The author is making a connection here between the sufferings of Christ and their own. This is helped by the use of the noun "hostility," *antilogia* (see the Notes at 6:16 and 7:7). If this verse is referring to Jesus' earthly life, the hostility may be the things he suffered at the time of his death. These are recounted in the various Passion narratives (Matt 26:45; Mark 14:41; Luke 24:7; cf. Acts 2:23) and Passion predictions (e.g., Mark 10:33-34). Variant readings of "themselves," *autous* ($\mathfrak{P}^{13,46}$ $\aleph^2$ Ψ 048. 33. 81. 1739* *pc* lat sy^p bo) and *heautous* ($\aleph$* D*) are better attested than "himself," but do not fit the context (Metzger, *A Textual Commentary*, 675).

so that you may not grow weary or lose heart: The verb "grow weary," *kamnein*, is joined here with *psychē*, soul, which means that the author does not have the usual meaning of the verb in view (LXX: Wis 4:16; 15:9; 4 Macc 3:8; 7:13) but intends the sense found in Job 10:1, "weariness in the soul." The sense of *eklyein*, "give up," is to lose one's nerve (Epictetus, *Dissertations* 2.19. 20; Philo, *On the Virtues* 88; Josephus, *Antiquities* 5.134; 13.233). The example of Christ's steadfastness in suffering is supposed to inspire the readers to endure their own.

INTERPRETATION

The author returns to more direct exhortation of the readers in this part of the sermon. The chapter as a whole is divided into five parts. The first (12:1-3) employs the athletic metaphor of a race and the motivating image of the perfected and exalted Christ to spur the readers to victory. The second part (12:4-13) addresses the role of discipline in the development of endurance. The third part (12:14-17) speaks to community order and the pursuit of peace with one another, while the fourth (12:18-24) employs the image of the Sinai theophany as the backdrop for introducing the notion of the heavenly Jerusalem. The fifth part (12:25-29) concludes with a warning not to refuse God, so as to reassure the readers that they will receive the unshakeable kingdom, their ultimate goal.

The first part (vv. 1-3) opens with a link to the previous chapter, an emphatic "therefore." The readers are invited to consider themselves surrounded by the witnesses who testified to the power of faith in the previous chapter, but their example now recedes as the model of Jesus as the pioneer and perfecter of faith emerges. His example forms the heart of this brief introductory section, anchoring the readers' preparation for their own race (v. 1) and their imitation of his endurance (v. 3). They are asked to "look to" and "consider him" above all the others they had considered in chapter 11. The fact that he is exalted at the right hand of God demonstrates that, unlike the witness of the previous chapter, he ultimately received what was promised (11:39).

As this section opens, then, the great witnesses to faith are gathered in an arena or a stadium where the readers are competing in an athletic context (*agōn*). The idea of a contest carries an implicit struggle, and so, in order to compete well, the readers are encouraged to cast off whatever might weigh them down and affect their ability to compete. It becomes clear that the burden that must be cast off is anything that might inhibit the readers' progress forward. The athletic imagery and the casting off of extra weight are stock items in moral exhortation among Hellenistic moral philosophers (Diogenes, *To Monimus* in *The Cynic Epistles*, ed. Abraham J. Malherbe, SBLSBS 12 [Missoula, MT: Scholars, 1977] 156; Epictetus, *Dissertations* 1.18.21-23; 3.25.1-6; Philo, *Posterity and Exile of Cain* 137; *Allegorical Interpretation* 3.47). Such metaphors liken the moral life and progress in virtue to a struggle that calls for steadfast determination toward reaching a goal (Heraclitus, *To Hermadorus* in Malherbe, *Cynic Epistles* 192; Epictetus, *Dissertations*, 1.4.20-23; 1.24.1-5; 4.12.15-17). Individuals involved in moral development can fall back from time to time, and so philosophers played a role like that of a coach encouraging an athlete not to lose heart when setbacks occur (Epictetus, *Dissertations* 4.9.15-18; *Enchiridion* 29.1-2; Seneca, *Epistles* 51.1-9).

The use of example was standard in moral exhortation among Hellenistic philosophers (Benjamin Fiore, *The Function of Personal Example in the Socratic and Pastoral Epistles*. AnBib 105 [Rome: Pontifical Biblical Institute, 1986] 45–163). The truly virtuous person was supposed to embody the moral ideal and demonstrate it in deeds as well as in words. To this extent the manner of one's life and death was capable of disclosing a person's character and worth (Lucian, *Demonax* 1-2; Pliny, *Letters* 8.13; Plutarch, *Demetrius* 1.4-6; Malherbe, *Moral Exhortation*, 38–40; 135–41). It was not uncommon for philosophers to offer the examples of individuals who succeeded in reaching their moral purpose (Seneca, *Epistles* 51:1-9; Pseudo-Isocrates, *To Demonicus* 9-15; Malherbe, *Moral Exhortation*, 62–64, 125–26, 135–41).

The example of Jesus as pioneer and perfecter of faith shows both continuity and discontinuity with the heroes and heroines of the previous chapter. Like them, he endured hardships, trials, suffering, and death. Unlike them he completed the course and received what had been promised. From his example the readers learn the power and value of endurance in the face of suffering. They also see how his disregard of shame enabled him to persevere in his tribulations, because he had his sights set on something of lasting rather than transient value. The fact that he attained the goal of his endurance is expressed by the author's final allusion to Psalm 110.

As the final verse of this section shows, Jesus' example functions as a model for the readers to imitate in their own struggle. They, too, are drawn into the history of faithful endurance by joining the heroes and heroines of the previous chapter in order to benefit from their example. They are, however, to imitate more closely the example of Jesus so that like him, they too might receive what was promised. It is his example that will keep them on track to the goal and prevent them from being discouraged and from losing heart.

The scope of Christ's life and salvific work in v. 2 combined with the example of his own endurance forms a powerful image, capable of supporting and sustaining readers who find running the race arduous and difficult. The author's pastoral approach emerges clearly here, showing that he knows his audience very well and is concerned that they renew their stamina so that they will not become weary or fainthearted. Preaching that kind of encouragement is always difficult, because the preacher's words can easily shade into platitudes that ring empty to the listeners and may even trivialize their struggle. Often image and metaphor achieve the desired end more than direct speech. Connecting with the imagination of his readers, the author of Hebrews presents the picture of Christ who knows the sufferings of the human heart and yet perseveres to the end. His victory is the victory of all who can follow in his way.

FOR REFERENCE AND FURTHER STUDY

Black, David Alan. "A Note on the Structure of Hebrews 12,1-2," *Bib* 68 (1987) 543–51.
Croy, N. Clayton. *Endurance in Suffering: Hebrews 12:1-13 in its Rhetorical Religious and Philosophical Context*. SNTSMS 98. Cambridge: Cambridge University Press, 1998.
Littleton, Boyce Johnny. "Exposition of Hebrews 12:2," *Faith & Mission* 16 (1999) 22–29.

Moessner, Jeanne Stevenson. "The Road to Perfection. An Interpretation of Suffer-
    ing in Hebrews," *Int* 57 (2003) 280–90.
Pfitzner, Victor C. *Paul and the Agon Motif: Traditional Athletic Imagery in the Pauline
    Literature.* NovTSup 16. Leiden: Brill, 1967.

33. *The Discipline of Suffering* (12:4-13)

4. In your struggle against sin you have not yet resisted to the point of shedding your blood. 5. And you have forgotten the exhortation that addresses
you as children—"My child, do not regard lightly the discipline of the
Lord, or lose heart when you are punished by him; 6. for the Lord disciplines those whom he loves, and chastises every child whom he accepts."
7. Endure trials for the sake of discipline. God is treating you as children;
for what child is there whom a parent does not discipline? 8. If you are
without discipline, in which all children share, then you are illegitimate
and not his children. 9. Moreover, we had human parents to discipline us,
and we respected them. Should we not be even more willing to be subject
to the Father of spirits and live? 10. For they disciplined us for a short time
as seemed best to them, but he disciplines us for what is beneficial, in order
that we may share his holiness. 11. Now, discipline always seems painful
rather than pleasant at the time, but later it yields the peaceful fruit of
righteousness to those who have been trained by it.

12. Therefore straighten your drooping hands and strengthen your
weak knees, 13. and make straight paths for your feet, so that what is lame
may not be put out of joint, but rather be healed.

Notes

4. *In your struggle against sin you have not yet resisted to the point of shedding your
blood:* Following on the example of Jesus who endured the hostility of sinners,
the author takes up the circumstances under which his readers have endured
in their own lives. The verb "struggle against," *antikathistanai*, occurs only here
in the NT. It is used thrice in the LXX (Deut 31:21; Josh 5:7; Mic 2:8 [A]). The verb
"resist," *antagōnizesthai*, also is found here alone in the NT. There is one instance
in the LXX at 4 Macc 17:14, where it refers to Antiochus IV Epiphanes. The fact
that they had not resisted to the point of shedding blood indicates that no one
in the community had been so persecuted that bloodshed or death were involved. This may mean that the struggle they were engaged in involved other
kinds of harassment associated with social dislocation, already mentioned in
10:32-34 (see Introduction, 3. *Date*). Second Maccabees 13:14 offers an interesting

parallel where the cognate verb *agōnizesthai* is joined to the prepositional phrase "to the point of death." In contrast, of course, is the example of Jesus, whose suffering was complete to the extent that it did involve bloodshed and death. This is not to say that the author is encouraging his readers to engage in the struggle to the same point. Some commentators provide parallel texts that use similar language to describe athletic or boxing contests, such as one from Seneca (*Epistles* 13.2) where the truly tested boxer fights to the point of blood (see Attridge, 360; Koester, 525). Given the use of similar metaphors earlier in the sermon, the comparisons are interesting. But even these commentators prefer the images drawn from the martyrological tradition.

5. *And you have forgotten the exhortation that addresses you as children:* This part of the verse could actually be a question, although it has commonly been taken as a statement. The verb "forget," *eklanthanesthai*, is used only here in NT and is not at all extant in the LXX. Both Josephus (*Antiquities* 4.53; 7.318) and Philo (*Allegorical Interpretation* 3.92; *On Joseph* 99) employ it. "Exhortation," *paraklēsis*, is the same word used to describe Hebrews as a whole (13:22). In 6:18 it meant "encouragement." Earlier the author prodded his readers on to maturity, chiding them for wanting to remain at the level of the elementary things (5:11-13). Here he addresses them literally as "sons." He does this in view of the role discipline has to play in their lives, and such discipline naturally begins in the family, with children. The choice of the term "sons" is no doubt dictated by the quotation from Prov 3:11-12, which begins with the address "son." These words are addressed to men and women alike; hence the translation "children."

   The citation follows the LXX text closely. The author has added the pronoun "my" at the beginning, perhaps wanting to personalize the text for his readers. The noun for "discipline," *paideia*, encompasses a rich educational tradition in Greek culture (Werner Jaeger, *Early Christianity and Greek Paideia* [Harvard: Belknap Press, 1961]; Georg Bertram, *paideuō, ktl., TDNT* 5:596–625). The translation of the word is "discipline" and shows affinity for the proverbial *pathein mathein*, "to suffer is to learn." The tradition of God disciplining Israel as a parent disciplines a child is also evident in Deut 8:5-6.

   As the tradition of psychagogy among the philosophers shows, at times students needed harsh discipline, even verbal reproach according to the custom of *parrhēsia*, "frank speech." But the discipline was always tailored to the needs of the student (Philodemus of Gadara, *On Frank Criticism* Frag. 2). In Hebrews this aspect of the educational process is represented by the verb *elenchein*, "reproach" and its corresponding noun, *elenchos*. So also is it represented in the wisdom tradition of the LXX (Prov 1:23, 25, 30; 6:23; 9:7, 8; 15:10, 32; 16:17; 18:17; 19:25), where it is often synonymous with "discipline" (Prov 5:12; 12:1; 13:18; 15:10; Wis 1:5; Sir 18:3) that might require frank speech (Prov 10:10).

   The encouragement "not to lose heart" echoes 12:3, where the same verb, *eklyein*, encourages the readers not to give up or lose their nerve in their own struggle against sin. It is bolstered by the notice that the Lord loves those whom he disciplines, a common notion in Israel's wisdom tradition. Such chastisement should not be taken as a sign of punishment or divine disfavor (2 Macc 6:12-17; Isa 53:5; Ps 94[93]:12-13).

7. *Endure trials for the sake of discipline. God is treating you as children:* The verb "endure" resumes the author's exhortation and recalls 12:3 (that Christ endured the hostility of sinners precisely as God's Son). He, too, was disciplined [instructed] by what he suffered, and the example of his "endurance" is decisive. The readers are now more closely linked with the Son by the reminder that God is "treating" them as children. The author has already used the verb *prospherein* eleven times (5:1, 3; 8:3, 4; 9:7, 9; 10:1, 2, 8, 11) with its usual meaning having to do with sacrifices or offerings. Here it means "treat" (see Philo, *On Drunkenness* 69; *On Joseph* 47; Josephus, *War* 7.254). The verse ends with a commonplace: that every parent disciplines his or her child, preparing the reader for the conditional argument that follows.

8. *If you are without discipline, in which all children share, then you are illegitimate and not his children:* Now the focus is sharpened as the need for discipline is placed in a new light. Those "without" it are not genuine children of God. The author prefers the preposition "without," *chōris* (4:15; 7:7, 20; 9:7, 18, 22, 28; 10:28; 11:6, 40; 12:8, 14) for the power it has in making distinctions and bringing to the fore what is truly important, e.g., "without the shedding of blood there is no forgiveness of sins" (9:22). Now, without discipline there is no true "sonship," and the result is illegitimacy (*nothoi*). As in the case of Christ, suffering is necessary for sonship (2:10).

9. *Moreover, we had human parents to discipline us, and we respected them. Should we not be even more willing to be subject to the Father of spirits and live?:* Another *qal wahomer* argument concludes to the important point of the citation from Prov 3:11, that the readers should take the discipline of God seriously, even more seriously than that of their parents. Appealing to their own familial experience, he now transforms the function of *paideia* from the realm of the flesh (*tēs sarkos hēmōn pateras:* "parents of our flesh") to the realm of the spirit (*tō patri tōn pneumatōn:* "to the Father of spirits"). Paul sees himself in the role of paternal discipliner in 1 Cor 4:15, "For though you may have ten thousand instructors (*paidagōgous*) in Christ, you do not have many fathers (*pateras*)." The author of Hebrews does not see himself or the leaders of the community in such a quasi-parental role.

   Entrepein in the middle voice can mean "cause shame," "be ashamed," and in the active voice "respect," i.e., "show deference to." Both meanings are extant in the LXX ("shame": Num 12:14; Pss 34:4, 26; 39:15; 68:7; 69:3; 70:24; 82:18; Sir 4:25; "respect": Exod 10:3; Lev 26:41; Wis 2:10; 6:7; Sir 4:22; 41:16) and the NT ("shame": 1 Cor 4:14; 2 Thess 3:14; Titus 2:8; "respect": Matt 21:37; Mark 12:6; Luke 18:2; 20:13). *Hypotassein* means to "subject" or "submit to" (BDAG, 1042). The verb is frequent in the LXX (3 Kgdms 10:15; 1 Chr 22:18; 29:24; 2 Chr 9:14; Pss 8:7; 17:48; 36:7; 46:4; 59:10; 61:2, 6; 107:10; 143:2; Wis 8:14; 18:22; Hag 2:19; Ep Jer 1[A]; Dan 7:27; 11:37; 2 Macc 4:12; 8:9, 22; 9:12; 13:23; 3 Macc 1:7; 2:13). Elsewhere in the NT it is found in Col 3:18; Titus 2:5, 9; 3:1; 1 Pet 2:13, 18; 3:1, 5; 5:5. The phrase "father of spirits" occurs only here in the Bible. The author may allude to Num 16:22; 27:16, where the expression "the God of the spirits of all flesh" occurs. A similar wording occurs in *Jub.* 10:3. To call God "father" was common in Judaism and Christianity (e.g., 2 Sam 7:14; Matt 6:9; Luke 11:2; Rom 8:15-16; Gal 4:6). Who the "spirits" are cannot be determined. The author's point is comparative. One may respect a father whose activity is in the realm of the flesh, but one must submit to a Father whose realm of activity is primarily the spiritual world. The argument recalls a similarly structured one in 9:13-14, where the author argued for the purification of conscience that resulted from Jesus' self-offering to God through the eternal Spirit. There the contrast was between earthly sacrifices and a heavenly one; here it is between an earthly discipline and a heavenly one, in which one understands that the purpose of suffering serves a higher goal. The basic argument is completed by the final note, "we shall live." The last instance of this verb was in the Habakkuk citation in 10:38. The connection in this chapter between discipline and faith (12:1) makes it likely that the use of the verb "live" is not merely coincidental here.

10. *For they disciplined us for a short time as seemed best to them, but he disciplines us for what is beneficial, in order that we may share his holiness:* The first expansion of the argument of the previous verse follows the same pattern of speaking of parental discipline at the outset and then concluding to the advantage of divine discipline. The differences between the two extend to the motivations and goals of each. As for motive, parents discipline as the need arises, "as seems best to them" (see Josh 9:25; 1 Esdr 8:11; Luke 1:3; Acts 15:22; Josephus, *Antiquities* 16.163), whereas God disciplines *epi to sympheron*, "for what is beneficial" for bringing about the stated goal, i.e., holiness. Regarding goals, "for a short time," *pros oligas hēmeras*, shows that the child's discipline is limited to the time of basic education. In God's purpose the end result extends beyond a given time period until "we may share in his holiness." For the Stoics anything that was good was beneficial (Diogenes Laertius, *Lives of Eminent Philosophers* 7.98-99; Epictetus, *Dissertations* 1.28.5-7). "Holiness," *hagiotēs*, occurs only here and in 2 Cor 1:12 as a variant (LXX: 2 Macc 15:2). It is a synonym for *hagiōsynē* (Rom 1:4; 2 Cor 7:1; 1 Thess 3:13; MM, 4).

11. *Now, discipline always seems painful rather than pleasant at the time:* Another expansion on the basic argument draws on the commonplace that discipline is difficult when it is being administered. Eventually, when one sees the benefits, the suffering is valued for a greater good (Prov 23:13-14; Wis 3:5; Diogenes Laertius, *Lives of Eminent Philosophers* 5.18). Common, too, is the opposition between "sorrow" and "joy" (e.g., Prov 14:13; John 16:20; 2 Cor 6:10).
    but later it yields the peaceful fruit of righteousness to those who have been trained by it: The goal of discipline is "the peaceful fruit of righteousness." The expression sounds a bit like Jas 3:18, "the fruit of righteousness sown in peace." In the LXX the expression "fruit of righteousness" occurs in Amos 6:12 and Prov 11:30. In Phil 1:11 the "fruit of righteousness" comes through Jesus Christ. "Bearing fruit" is a common metaphor in NT exhortation (Matt 3:10; 7:19; John 15:2; Gal 5:22; 2 Tim 2:6). The adjective "peaceful" anticipates 12:14, where the readers are exhorted to strive for peace. Discipline and training contribute to that goal. The expression "to those who have been trained by it" extends the athletic metaphor. On "to train," *gymnazein*, see the Notes at 5:14. Here "discipline" is the trainer.

12. *Therefore straighten your drooping hands and strengthen your weak knees:* The exhortation draws to a close with an allusion to Isa 35:3 (cf. Sir 25:23), with a few modifications. "Straighten," *anorthoun*, is related to "discipline" in Ps 17:36

(LXX): "your discipline has straightened me at last." Elsewhere in the LXX this verb connotes the help God gives to the weak (e.g., Pss 144:14; 145:8; Sir 11:12). "Be weak," *paralyein*, refers mainly to bodily weakness in the NT (Luke 5:18, 24; Acts 8:7; 9:33; LXX: Jer 6:24; Ezek 7:27; 1 Macc 9:55; 3 Macc 2:22), but it may be used metaphorically as in the LXX (Wis 17:14, 18; Sir 25:23; Jer 26:15; 27:15; Ezek 21:12).

13. *and make straight paths for your feet, so that what is lame may not be put out of joint, but rather be healed:* The allusion is to the LXX of Prov 4:26, where the goal is the acquisition of wisdom. The author applies it here to the avoidance of sin (12:4). "Put out of joint," *ektrepein*, also means to "turn aside" or "avoid." Here the medical meaning is preferred (BDAG, 311). The alternative to being "put out of joint," to "be healed," *iasthai*, is the desired goal. Thus the author completes the section with a medical metaphor of healing that comes from corrective straightening rather than from further dislocation. In the tradition of psychagogy, medical imagery is often invoked for correcting moral failures (see Philodemus of Gadara, *On Frank Criticism* Frags. 30; 39; 63; 64; 69; 86; Col. XVIIa; Tab. XII M; Malherbe, *Letters to the Thessalonians*, 323–24).

INTERPRETATION

A direct appeal to the readers' experience of suffering leads off this section. Having exhorted them in the previous section to cast off the burden of sin, the author now acknowledges that they have been engaged in a struggle against sin—but it is the sin of others, who have imposed suffering on them. The reference recalls the earlier reference to their "struggle with sufferings" in 10:32-34. Whatever form the persecution took, it most likely involved some form of social dislocation or harassment. The readers may have been treated harshly in Rome in the aftermath of the destruction of the Temple in 70 C.E. (see Introduction, 3. *Date*). Thus the author can say that they had not resisted to the point of bloodshed. As they were exhorted to endurance in that previous section (10:36), so also here.

Their struggle is not necessarily explained, nor is it dismissed, but the author attempts to place it in the context of the tradition of discipline. Perhaps he feels that were the readers to understand their sufferings as discipline they would be more likely to endure them. To that end the citation of Scripture may help. The text from Prov 3:11-12 elevates ordinary parental discipline to the level of divine discipline in an effort to show that discipline does not preclude love. Rather, the fact that the readers suffer so is a manifestation of their status as children of God. To deny the importance of discipline or to escape it altogether would be tantamount to accepting the status of illegitimate children. This, of course, is not possible for the readers, who have already been joined in fictive kinship with one another as brothers and sisters of Christ (2:11-17; 13:1).

The argument is advanced in a way typical of the author's style. Interweaving parental and divine discipline, he constructs an a fortiori argument to show the inherent worth of divine discipline. Even though he appeals to the readers' former relationship to their parents, he does so in the past tense. They "had" parents and they "respected" them. It is as if they have left the natural parental relationship behind in order to enter into fictive kinship in the Christian community, where God now functions as the spiritual parent. If natural children respect their parents because as children they are subjected to them, then the spiritual parent, God, is worthy of much more respect, as holiness is a goal superior to any object of mere parental discipline. The analogy between parental and divine discipline is designed to enhance the image of God in the readers' minds as well as to encourage them to endure their sufferings for a greater good. Parents may discipline their children at will and perhaps according to their own whim, but God's discipline is always for the person's good in advancing the individual toward holiness. Were there a simple correspondence between parental and divine discipline, the readers' sufferings might have been trivialized as nothing more than what any child would have to endure in the normal course of his or her relationship with a parent. The author constructs the argument, however, to show God's care for them, which exceeds the obligation of a parent to the extent that it is also an invitation to share in God's holiness.

The argument regarding discipline concludes in v. 11 with an observation from human experience. It is a commonplace that discipline is painful at the time it is being administered. With hindsight, however, a lesson can be drawn and the hardship may be seen to have produced some good. As with the example of Jesus, who endured suffering for the sake of the joy that was set before him (12:2), the readers are encouraged to look forward to the goal of discipline, specified here as the peaceful fruit of righteousness. The author returns to the athletic metaphor by specifying that the ones who receive the peaceful fruit of righteousness are those who have trained for it. The blending of athletic training and discipline is natural in moral exhortation, since both require the endurance of hardship for the sake of a future goal.

This section of the chapter closes with further scriptural allusions to Isa 35:3 in v. 12 and to Prov 4:26 in v. 13. The image of drooping hands and weak knees suggests the picture of someone who has been worn down by an athletic contest (Koester, 540). "Straightening" in the LXX comes in the form of divine aid. Here, however, the readers are to straighten themselves, somehow to lift themselves out of their weakened state. They need also to straighten the paths on which they walk so as not to do further harm to their limbs, but rather to progress on the path of healing. There may be an allusion to the athletic metaphor in the image of keeping on the straight path to the goal (Koester, 540), but it is more likely that the author is shifting to images associated with righteousness and moral virtue at this point. As indicated in the Notes above, moral exhortation among Hellenistic philosophers employed medical metaphors of treatment, surgery, and healing in their efforts to help individuals advance in progress toward achieving their moral purpose.

The role of suffering in our lives is hard to understand, especially when the innocent suffer. This question was no less difficult to answer in Hellenistic Judaism in the post-exilic era (Job 2:11-13; 33:29-33). Like Judaism, Christianity found meaning in suffering based on noble examples, in the case of Christians the example of the suffering and death of Christ. Hebrews contributes to that tradition by presenting Jesus "who learned obedience through what he suffered" (5:8). Alluding, then, to his example, the author engages the readers' real sufferings so as not to trivialize them. Speaking of them as a form of "discipline," he wants his audience to know that they are not the cause of what they have to suffer. Rather, he places their hardship in a wider context that was shared by Jesus as well. As suffering was constitutive of his sonship, so also it is a sign that the readers are sons and daughters of God. Knowing that one cannot explain another's suffering, the author prefers to show how suffering is related to God and to Christ. The readers, then, are drawn to understand the meaning of their own suffering in view of a larger goal.

FOR REFERENCE AND FURTHER STUDY

Costé, J. "Notion grecque et notion biblique de 'la souffrance éducatrice,'" *RSR* 43 (1955) 497–508.

Lenglet, A. "À la suite de l'initiateur (He 12, 1-4)," *AsSeign* 51 (1971) 56–61.

Marrou, Henri Irénée. *A History of Education in Antiquity*, trans. George Lamb. New York: Sheed and Ward, 1956.

Mende, Theresia. "'Wen der Herr liebhat, den züchtigt er' (Heb 12,6). Der alttestamentliche Hintergrund von Hebr 12,1-11; 1,1-4; 2,6-10," *TTZ* 100 (1991) 23–28.

Vanhoye, Albert. "La souffrance éducatrice: Hé 12, 5-7. 11-13," *AsSeign* 52 (1974) 61–66.

V. Warnings and Exhortations (12:14–13:19)

34. *A Warning Against Godlessness* (12:14-17)

14. Pursue peace with everyone, and the holiness without which no one
will see the Lord. 15. See to it that no one fails to obtain the grace of God,
lest a root of bitterness arise and cause trouble, and through it many become defiled. 16. See to it that no one becomes like Esau, an immoral and
profane person, who sold his birthright for a single meal. 17. You know
that later, when he wanted to inherit the blessing, he was rejected, for he
found no opportunity to repent, even though he sought the blessing with
tears.

Notes

14. *Pursue peace with everyone, and the holiness without which no one will see the Lord:*
This brief hortatory section begins by recalling the mention of peace in 12:11.
The injunction to pursue peace most resembles Ps 33:15 in the lxx, "seek peace
and pursue it," which is actually cited in 1 Pet 3:11. Peace as a goal is found in
other nt books (Matt 5:9; Mark 9:50; Rom 12:18; 2 Cor 13:11; 1 Thess 5:13).
"Holiness" echoes *hagiotētos* in 12:10, although here the author uses a less
peculiar noun, *hagiasmos*, a standard term in nt exhortation (Rom 6:19, 22;
1 Cor 1:30; 1 Thess 4:3, 4, 7; 2 Thess 2:13; 1 Tim 2:15; 1 Pet 1:2). The word is used
only here in Hebrews, but the idea of holiness has been invoked before in the
sermon (2:11; 9:13-14; 10:14). Failure to pursue peace and holiness will prevent
one from seeing the Lord. "Lord" can refer to God (7:21; 8:8-11; 10:16, 30; 12:5-6)
or Christ (2:3; 12:14). The goal is eschatological (Matt 5:8).

15. *Take care to see that no one fails to obtain the grace of God:* The verb "fall back,"
hysterein, was used in 4:1 with the meaning of "fall behind." The author has
affirmed that through Christ the readers may approach the throne of grace,
where they will find grace in time of need. The assumption is that grace has
been offered. Still, it is possible for people not to "approach," but to "fall back"
from it, preventing individuals from reaching the goal.

lest a root of bitterness arise and cause trouble, and through it many become defiled: A
citation from Deut 29:17 forms the next part of the warning. The lxx of the text
is not the same as the author's citation. Perhaps he was working with a different
version (Attridge, 366). Whereas Hebrews has "lest a root of bitterness arise
and cause trouble," the lxx reads "lest there is among you a root rising up in
gall and bitterness." Basically, what seems to have happened in some manuscript traditions is that the two words for "in gall," *en cholē*, were transcribed
by a scribe who read the verb "cause trouble," *enochlē*. The Hebrew Bible (Deut
29:18) has yet another reading: "it may be that there is a root among you bearing
poisonous and bitter fruit." The sense of the Hebrew fits the context better, since

12:11 offered as the goal of discipline a yield of "the peaceful fruit of righteousness." Throughout the sermon, however, it is clear that the author relies on a particular version of the lxx for his Scripture texts.

The root of bitterness has the power to infect other members of the community, whom it can "defile," *miainein*. The lxx usage normally has to do with ritual defilement (Exod 20:25; Num 5:14; Ezek 4:14; 23:13). It can have the same meaning in the nt (John 18:28; Jude 8). In Tit 1:15 it is used metaphorically for the defilement of the mind and conscience. The author's concern with the purification of the conscience makes it likely that the defilement he is speaking of here is sin, which defiles the conscience.

16. *See to it that no one becomes like Esau, an immoral and profane person who sold his birthright for a single meal:* The negative example in this regard is Jacob's brother Esau. The allusion is to Gen 25:29-34, where Esau sells his birthright to Jacob in exchange for a meal of lentil stew. He is first described as "immoral," *pornos,* an adjective related to *porneia,* which often in biblical texts has to do with sexual immorality (see 1 Cor 5:9-11; Eph 5:5; 1 Tim 1:10; Rev 21:8; 22:15; Friedrich Hauck and Siegfried Schulz, *pornē, ktl., TDNT* 6:579–95). It will be used again in Heb 13:4. There is nothing in the Genesis account that would suggest that Esau was a fornicator, but later legends (*Jub.* 25:1, 7-8; Philo, *Sacrifices of Cain and Abel* 81, 120, 135; *Allegorical Interpretation* 3.2; *Migration of Abraham* 153; *The Worse Attacks the Better* 45; *On Flight and Finding* 39; *On Drunkenness* 9-10; *Special Laws* 4.40; Attridge, 368; Koester, 532; Weiss, 666) suggested that there was something irregular about his marriage to two Hittite women (Gen 26:34-35). Esau is also called "profane," *bebēlos,* an adjective associated with ritual defilement, in the lxx (e.g., Lev 21:9; 1 Kgdms 21:5-6; 2 Macc 5:16; 3 Macc 2:2, 14; 7:15). The fact that he sold his birthright for a single meal indicates what is important to him. The birthright would have brought him a double portion of inheritance (Deut 21:17), which contrasts with a single meal. The noun "birthright," *prōtotokia,* is cognate with the noun for "firstborn," *prōtotokos,* which referred to the Son in 1:6, a connection the readers probably made. The readers hope to be among the "assembly of the firstborn" (12:23), so the story of Esau is polyvalent and is capable of drawing them into the text.

17. *You know that later, when he wanted to inherit the blessing, he was rejected:* The reference is to Gen 27:30-40, recounting Esau's return with game for Isaac, and how he learned of his brother's ruse. Esau tried to get another blessing from Isaac, but that was not possible. This is what Hebrews alludes to when it says Esau tried to inherit (*klēronomein*) a blessing. The verb "be rejected," *apodokimazein,* is extant in the lxx (e.g., Jer 6:30; 7:29; 8:9; 14:19; 38:35; Sir 20:20; Ps 117:22). The sense is that he was rejected by Isaac, not by God.

for he found no opportunity to repent, even though he sought the blessing with tears: This part of the verse contains another instance of the noun *topos,* "place," used metaphorically for "opportunity" (see the Notes at 8:7). Genesis 27:38 says that Esau wept. Perhaps more poignantly for Hebrews, Gen 27:34 recounts that Esau cried out with a loud and bitter (*pikran*) cry. The connection to the lack of opportunity for Esau's repentance was undoubtedly not lost on the readers in light of 6:4-8 and 10:26-31.

INTERPRETATION

These four verses form the third part of the chapter, taking the shape of a direct exhortation to pursue peace within the listeners' community followed by a warning and an example. This exhortation follows on the comparison of parental and divine discipline and fits within a consideration of familial relationships. The example of Esau, whose sibling relationship with his brother Jacob was marked by anything but peace, provides motivation. The emphasis on his regret over failing to obtain a blessing from Isaac functions as a warning for the readers, lest they end up in a similar situation. His example bolsters the warning in v. 15 about failing to obtain the grace of God and becoming defiled.

The author relies heavily on traditional material in this part of the chapter. The opening verse echoes the Beatitudes, where those who are pure of heart will see God (Matt 5:8) and those who pursue peace will become children of God (Matt 5:9). The allusion to Ps 33:15 (LXX) places the pursuit of peace within the biblical tradition. The warning against defilement depends on an allusion to Deut 29:17, and the example of Esau is drawn from Gen 25:29-34 and 27:30-40. The author's imagination is thoroughly biblical, and he is at home in a world of metaphor, imagery, and thought that is centered in the LXX. The way he relies on and adapts the biblical tradition in this section illustrates his interest in "re-scripturing" the tradition for his readers.

The actualization of these traditions for the readers encourages them to realize the values of peace and holiness within their community (Attridge, 367; Ellingworth, 661–62; Grässer 3:286–88; Lane 2:449–50; Weiss, 661). The earlier section (vv. 4-13) presented a share in God's holiness as the eschatological goal of divine discipline. Here the author turns to the more immediate pursuit of peace and holiness, which anticipates a final fulfillment as part of their eternal inheritance (9:15). The example of Esau (vv. 16-17), who sold his birthright and jeopardized his inheritance, is sufficient to make the author's purpose clear to his readers. That example is anticipated by the biblical allusion to the root of bitterness. The metaphor acts as a warning to the readers not to turn away from God's grace lest there arise in the community someone who has a defiling effect on the purity of the group as a whole.

The concern for possible internal dissension, which will compromise the group's holiness, is prominent here. Should a root of bitterness arise and cause trouble, many in the group will be defiled. The author has already addressed a form of division among the readers over the issue of absence from the communal meeting (10:25). Immediately afterward he reminds them that there is no longer a sacrifice for willful sinning (10:26). Any deliberate attempt to sow bitterness and cause trouble falls under the same category of judgment as intentional sinning.

The "re-scripturing" of the story of Esau goes beyond the original Genesis narrative. The Genesis account does not portray a sinful and repentant Esau; rather, he is characterized as a victim of Jacob's guile. In response to his bitter cry Isaac attempts to give him a blessing, but since the words are the exact opposite of those spoken to Jacob they are tantamount to a curse (Gen 27:39-40). Jacob is the one who actually initiates reconciliation with his twin in Genesis 32–33. For Hebrews, Esau becomes the symbol of an attitude of heart that threatens the unity of the community.

The parallel structure of the opening of vv. 15 and 16, "see to it that no one . . ." renders the verses mutually interpretive. Esau is a person who failed to obtain grace, who caused trouble in the family of Isaac and Rebekah, and who brought defilement on their household. He exemplifies the problematic root of bitterness, and so he is called immoral and profane. However much Hellenistic Jewish tradition about Esau has influenced the author, he functions in this context as a model not to be emulated. Apart from that, he becomes a flesh-and-blood example of the apostate who is unable to be restored to repentance (6:4-8) and of the person who willfully persists in sin, for whom there is no sacrifice for sins (10:26). Despite his tears he received only the prospect of judgment (10:27). The author depicts this root of bitterness as reaping what he had sown, becoming a broken and despondent man. A similar fate awaits any from among the readers who fail to heed the example.

The antidote to the root of bitterness is the pursuit of peace and holiness and the reception of God's grace. Only these things have the power to protect the community from defilement. The readers received their initial sanctification in baptism (6:2), and the source of that sanctification is Christ himself, who made it possible by his once for all self-offering (2:11; 9:13-14; 10:14). Sanctification is maintained by endurance in suffering, understood as a manifestation of divine discipline, which grants a share of God's holiness (12:10). Internal turmoil or dissension among believers threatens holiness and inhibits the action of God's grace in the community. The reinterpreted example of Esau warns against any possible dissolution of community coherence along these lines.

Striving for holiness requires that individuals live in peace with their fellow human beings, Christian and non-Christian alike. Even though the warning here may be directed primarily to the way Christians live within their own communities, it cannot avoid affecting their behavior in the wider world. The sense of the text is that rancor within the community is a form of contagion that can spread if it is unchecked. Such dissension can affect the Christian's relations with all people. Hebrews counsels care and diligence in the pursuit of peace and holiness so that nothing will inhibit the readers from reaching their final destination.

For Reference and Further Study

Käsemann, Ernst. "Hebräer 12:12-17," in idem, *Exegetische Versuche und Besinnungen.* Göttingen: Vandenhoeck & Ruprecht, 1970, 1:307–12.
McKnight, Scot. "The Warning Passages of Hebrews: A Formal Analysis and Theological Conclusions," *TJ* 13 (1992) 21–59.
Mugridge, Alan. "Warnings in the Epistle to the Hebrews," *RTR* 46 (1987) 74–82.
Oberholtzer, Thomas K. "The Warning Passages in Hebrews," *BSac* 146 (1989) 67–75.

35. *A Comparison Between Mount Sinai and Mount Zion* (12:18-24)

18. You have not come to something tangible, a blazing fire, and darkness, and gloom, and a whirlwind, 19. and the sound of a trumpet, and a voice with words whose hearers begged that not another word be added to them. 20. For they could not endure the order that was given, "If even an animal touches the mountain, it shall be stoned to death." 21. Indeed, so fearsome was the sight that Moses said, "I tremble with fear." 22. But you have come to Mount Zion and to the city of the living God, the heavenly Jerusalem, and to myriads of angels in festal gathering, 23. and to the assembly of the firstborn who are enrolled in heaven, and to a judge, the God of all, and to the spirits of the righteous made perfect, 24. and to Jesus, the mediator of a new covenant, and to the sprinkled blood that speaks a better word than the blood of Abel.

Notes

18. *You have not come to something tangible, a blazing fire, and darkness, and gloom, and a whirlwind:* On "come to," *proserchesthai*, see the Notes at 4:16. Here the author makes another comparison with the wilderness generation. Earlier their rebellion was the focus of his reflections (3:7–4:10); now he takes up the theophany at Sinai recounted in Exod 19:7–20:21. The Israelites were not supposed to "ascend," the mountain, *anabainein* (Exod 19:12; *prosanabainein* in 19:23) or to "touch" it, *thinganein*. For the author the approach is more important than an ascent because of his preference for this verb (4:16; 7:25; 10:22; 11:6), which expresses his interest in access to God. In Deut 4:11 the verb does occur in a speech of Moses, where he reminds the people that at Sinai they "approached and stood at the foot of the mountain" without the cultic sense of the word in Hebrews (Attridge, 372). What the readers have approached differs from the concrete reality of Sinai, which the wilderness generation faced. They were forbidden to touch the mountain precisely because they could have. As with previous

comparisons between the old and the new covenant, the author stresses the material over the spiritual. The verb *psēlaphan* means "touch by feeling," but without the object in view (BDAG, 1097–98). It is the verb used for blind grop-ing (LXX: Gen 27:12; Judg 16:26; Deut 28:29; Job 5:14; 12:25; Isa 59:10). Perhaps the author chose this verb because of the mention of "darkness" in the list of other phenomena that follows. The expression "tangible darkness" is found in the plague narratives at Exod 10:21.

The other visual phenomena described here—fire, darkness, gloom, and a whirlwind—are influenced by the description of the Sinai theophany in Deut 4:11 (absent "gloom") rather than the description in Exod 19:7–20:21. The nouns "darkness," *gnophos*, and "whirlwind," *thyella*, occur only here in the NT. "Gloom," *zophos*, is used in 2 Pet 2:4, 17 and Jude 6, 13.

19. *and the sound of a trumpet, and a voice with words whose hearers begged that not another word be added to them:* The author now describes the aural phenomena surrounding the Sinai theophany. The trumpet sound is part of the description in Exod 19:13, 16, 19; 20:18, where the LXX uses *phonos*, as in this verse, instead of *ēchos*. *Phonos* can describe the voice of God, "the voice with words" (cf. Deut 4:12). In Exod 20:19 the people are so frightened that they ask that God not speak to them lest they die (cf. Deut 5:25). Hebrews heightens the sense of their fear in the choice of the verb "beg," *paraiteisthai*, which also has the sense of "refuse" (Heb 12:25; cf. Luke 14:18-19; Acts 25:11; 1 Tim 4:7; 5:11; 2 Tim 2:23; Titus 3:10; Gustav Stählin, *aiteō, ktl., TDNT* 1:191–95).

20. *For they could not endure the order that was given, "If even an animal touches the mountain, it shall be stoned to death":* This verse and the next form a parenthetical remark explaining the people's fear. The author's source seems to be Exod 19:12-13, where humans and animals alike are forbidden to touch the mountain. The verb for "endure" here is *pherein*, "carry" or "bear" (1:3; 6:1; 9:16; Konrad Weiss, *pherō, ktl., TDNT* 9:56–87), not *hypomenein*, which the author uses for the endurance of hardship and suffering (10:32; 12:2, 3, 7). *Pherein* has this sense of enduring hardship only in 13:13. The apparent quotation is a paraphrase of the Exodus text. The sense of "even" is clear: if the animal is liable, how much more so will a human be.

21. *Indeed, so fearsome was the sight that Moses said, "I tremble with fear":* The conclu-sion of the parenthetical remark attends to the fear of Moses. The adjective "fearsome," *phoberos*, used only in Hebrews in the NT, has occurred in 10:27 and 31. Fear is not associated with Moses in the Exodus account of the Sinai theoph-any. Rather, one finds it mentioned in Deut 9:19, where he recounts to the Isra-elites how he discovered the golden calf on his descent from Mount Sinai. He says there, "and I am afraid (*ekphobos*) of the anger and fear" (LXX), referring to God's anger over the calf. "Trembling," *entromos*, is used to describe Moses' fear in Acts 7:32 (cf. Acts 16:29).

22. *But you have come to Mount Zion and to the city of the living God, the heavenly Jeru-salem:* The second half of the comparison begins as did the first, with the verb "come to," *proserchesthai*. Attention is given to the spiritual nature of what the readers can approach; it is the heavenly Jerusalem. Its earthly name is Mount

Zion, which was the name of the stronghold David took as his city (2 Sam 5:7; 1 Kgs 8:1). "Zion" is equated with Jerusalem (2 Kgs 19:21, 31) and often in the Psalms is identified as the dwelling place of God (e.g., Pss 2:6; 48:2; 50:2; Eduard Lohse, *Siōn, ktl.* [B, C], *TDNT* 7:319–38). According to Joel 4:16-17 (LXX) God would be manifested there with powerful signs. In Hellenistic Judaism, Zion and Jerusalem are synonyms (*Jub.* 1:28; 4:26; 8:19). The designation "city of the living God" locates it as the dwelling place for God under one of the author's favorite epithets for the divinity (3:12; 9:14; 10:31). The "heavenly Jerusalem," *Ierousalēm epouraniǭ,* is the ultimate goal set before the readers (13:14; on the term "heavenly Jerusalem" see the Notes at 11:10).

and to myriads of angels in festal gathering: In contrast to the terrifying sights associated with the Sinai phenomenon, the heavenly Jerusalem will be a place of festivity, filled with angels beyond counting. In Greek a "myriad," *myrias,* equals ten thousand. Angels were part of the tradition of the Sinai theophany (Deut 33:2), but they are also frequent in the literature of Hellenistic Judaism, where their number is extraordinary (*1 Enoch* 60:1; 71:8-13; *2 Enoch* 40:3; *Appendix to 3 Enoch* 22:4-7). The "festal gathering," *panēgyris,* occurs only here in the NT. In Amos 5:21 such a gathering is the object of God's contempt (cf. Hos 2:11; 9:5). In Ezek 46:11 it refers to Israel's regular festivals (Josephus, *War* 5.230; *Antiquities* 2.45; 5.170; Philo, *On the Cherubim* 91-92; *Migration of Abraham* 92; *Moses* 2.159, 226).

23. *and to the assembly of the firstborn who are enrolled in heaven:* The key to the identity of those comprising the "assembly of the firstborn" lies in the relative clause "who are enrolled in heaven." Commentators note that the "registration" referred to here may be either legal or eschatological (Attridge, 375; Koester, 545). The legal sense of *apographein* (MM, 60) is attested in Luke 2:1, 3, 5, the only other places where the verb occurs in the NT (LXX: Judg 8:14; 1 Esdr 8:30; 3 Macc 2:29; 4:14; 6:34, 38). The eschatological sense refers to those whose names are written in a heavenly registry, where the verb is rather *graphein* or *engraphein* (Exod 32:32; Ps 69:28; Dan 12:1; Luke 10:20; Phil 4:3). The latter is preferred as a reference to the righteous living, who await the vindication of God's judgment (Braun, 437; Bruce, 376–77; Ellingworth, 680; Lane 2:468–69).

and to a judge, the God of all: The phrase is ambiguous and can be also translated as "and to God, the judge of all." Either way the judgment of God is in view; only the emphasis changes. The image of God as judge is common in Judaism (e.g., Isa 66:16; Ezek 18:30; 24:14; 34:17; 35:11; Joel 3:12; Job 21:22; Pss 7:8, 11; 9:8; 50:6; 58:11; 82:8; 94:2; 96:13; Eccl 3:17) and early Christianity (e.g., Rom 2:2, 3, 16; 3:6; 1 Pet 4:5; Rev 20:12). Hebrews has already referred to God as a judge in 10:30 and will again at 13:4.

and to the spirits of the righteous made perfect: At the beginning of this verse part of the citizenry of the heavenly Jerusalem were described as the assembly of the firstborn enrolled in heaven. Here the dead are included as well. "Soul," *psychē,* and "spirit," *pneuma,* are synonymous in Heb 4:12. That the souls of the righteous dead were with God was a belief held by some Hellenistic Jews (*1 Enoch* 22:3-9; Wis 3:1; *2 Bar* 3:20; *4 Ezra* 7:99). Being made "perfect" is an important concept in Hebrews. Here it means that the spirits are brought to completion, or reach their goal, which means they are eternally with God and have entered into God's rest (4:9-10) (see Peterson, *Perfection*, 163–65).

24. *and to Jesus, the mediator of a new covenant, and to the sprinkled blood that speaks a better word than the blood of Abel:* The description of Jesus as the mediator of a new covenant was an important aspect of the central argument of the sermon (see the Notes at 8:6). The notion of sprinkled blood was featured in 9:19-21 in particular, but the notion of sacrificial blood was present throughout that chapter. Here the blood is compared to the blood of Abel. The reference to "speaking" recalls 11:4, where the blood of Abel crying out from the ground is alluded to in the notice that it is still speaking. How exactly Jesus' blood speaks a better word or message is a point of debate. Some commentators propose that Abel's blood cried out for revenge, whereas Jesus' blood on the basis of 4:16 speaks a word of grace (Braun, 440; Bruce, 361; Hughes, 552; Lane 2:473–74; Weiss, 682–83; Westcott, 417). For Erich Grässer (*An die Hebräer* 3:324), the distinction is between heaven and earth. As priest and sacrificial victim, Christ carried his own blood into the heavenly sanctuary, where he intercedes for others, whereas Abel's blood could only cry out from the ground. For Harold Attridge the difference is in the quality of the atonement. Abel's blood could bring only limited atonement, whereas Christ's is more complete (Attridge, 377). In view of the reference to the souls of the righteous made perfect in the previous verse, the notion of Christ's blood accomplishing complete atonement is preferred.

Interpretation

The fourth section of this chapter is vivid in its imagery and language, appealing to sight and sound to conjure up realistic images of Mount Sinai and Mount Zion for comparison. A contrast is drawn again between old and new, with the old symbolized by the Sinai theophany and the new by the city of God, the heavenly Jerusalem, Mount Zion. Both images call for the full involvement of the readers' imagination, which places them in the scenes so that they can conclude to the relative value of each for their salvation. The main theme of the passage is access to God and the advantage the readers have over the wilderness generation as they respectively approach God. They have been compared to this generation earlier (3:17-19) and warned not to fall into a similar kind of disobedience, which had prevented them from entering into God's rest.

This section divides into two parts: Mount Sinai (vv. 18-21) and Mount Zion (vv. 22-24). The two sections are demarcated by the antithesis "You have not come to . . ." (v. 18) and "But you have come to . . ." (v. 22), and each catalogues a series of phenomena and things associated with the experience of two groups. The main point is that the readers have better access to God than the wilderness generation had. Not only is the location of divine access better, but they themselves make a better approach than the wilderness generation made when they are characterized by steadfastness and obedience.

The visual and aural elements of the Sinai phenomena capture the might of God's power and the fear it was capable of generating. The fear is so palpable in the passage that the reader gets a real sense of the terror experienced by those at Sinai, communicated by the notice that they begged the voice to stop speaking. How little they could bear the divine demands and the warning that they should not approach the mountain lest they should die! For Hebrews this is a significant difference (v. 19). The entire experience was so terrifying that even Moses, who mediated between the people and God, trembled. The prohibition against approaching the mountain recalls the restricted access to the Holy of Holies, preventing even Aaron, under penalty of death, from approaching the divine presence had he entered it on any day other than the Day of Atonement (Lev 16:2). The entire scene in vv. 18-21 confirms that under the Sinai Covenant access to God was limited by design. It is almost as if its purpose was to prevent people from having such access. Of course, it was because of the overwhelming holiness of God that the people had to keep their distance.

The readers of Hebrews, on the other hand, have already been invited to live (12:9) in order to share in the holiness of God (12:10). They have been given unprecedented access to God through the self-offering of Christ (9:6; 10:19-22). The way to God in Hebrews does not lead to death, but to life (12:9), and it is indeed called "a new and living way" (10:20). So the images associated with Mount Zion in this passage are images of life and joy in festal gatherings, the assembly of the firstborn, spirits of the righteous made perfect, and Jesus, the mediator of a better covenant, whose own lifegiving blood speaks a better word than Abel's. These images lead the readers to the conclusion that they find completion and full access to the living God in a city that is alive and marked by the vitality of a people destined to inhabit it. In this city dwells the assembly of the firstborn, who, unlike Esau, did not throw away their birthright for a transient meal (12:16), but through suffering and patient endurance completed the race to claim their eternal inheritance (12:1-2, 12-13).

In this brief passage the author has skillfully painted graphic images of two mountains, Sinai and Zion, to express the differences in access to God granted under the covenants associated with each. The old covenant aimed at limiting access to God by preventing people from freely approaching the deity. The sights and sounds associated with the giving of the covenant at Sinai created a barrier between the people and God that could only be breached by a legitimate mediator, Moses. The people were so terrified by what they saw and heard that they begged the voice to stop speaking. The mediator himself was so terrified that he trembled in fear. The controlling images are darkness, gloom, fear, and trembling. God's location under the

old covenant was foreboding, and the character of this location was transferred from the mountain to the sanctuary and eventually to the Temple,
with the result that access to God was limited and restricted ritually.

Mount Zion, on the other hand, is a location of an entirely different sort.
It is the place where one meets the living God in festal gatherings, as members of the assembly of the firstborn. The mediator of a better covenant,
Jesus, has not restricted access to God, but through his own self-offering
has opened up a new and living way to come into the presence of God.
Under the new covenant the living God does not dwell on a mountain to
keep people at a distance, but rather lives together with them in a city,
where they have the status of firstborn and perfected righteous, both the
living and the dead. The controlling images are myriads of angels, the
sounds of festal gatherings, and a mediator whose blood has removed any
obstacle between God and people because of its ability to purify the consciences of those who now reside in the city of the living God (9:11-14; 10:22).
Whereas a sense of fear and foreboding characterized Mount Sinai, a sense
of joy and promise imbues Mount Zion.

The reader encounters in this passage one of the most remarkable teachings of Hebrews: that Christians have already "come to" their final destination. All the wonderful things associated with the city of the living God are
present to them as a result of Christ's self-offering, which inaugurated the
new covenant. These things they now possess, even before the ultimate
realization of them in the final time. Preaching a realized eschatology, the
author of Hebrews invites his readers to know the effects of having full
access to God: the new covenant mediated by Christ becomes immediate
and their future destination is now present, allowing them to taste "the
goodness of the word of God and the powers of the age to come" (6:5).

For Reference and Further Study

Betz, Otto. "The Eschatological Interpretation of the Sinai Tradition in Qumran and
    in the New Testament," *RevQ* 6 (1961) 89–108.
Caird, George B. "Just Men Made Perfect," *LQHR* 35 (1966) 89–98.
Casey, J. M. "Christian Assembly in Hebrews: A Fantasy Island?" *TD* 30 (1982) 323–
    35.
Jones, Peter Rhea. "A Superior Life: Hebrews 12:3–13:25," *RevExp* 82 (1985) 391–405.
Spicq, Ceslas. "La Panégyrie de Hébr. xii,22," *ST* 6 (1952) 30–38.

36. *A Consuming Fire* (12:25-29)

25. See that you do not refuse the one who is speaking; for if they did not escape when they refused the one who warned them on earth, how much less will we escape if we turn away from the one who warns from heaven! 26. At that time his voice shook the earth; but now he has promised, "Yet once more I will shake not only the earth but also the heaven." 27. This phrase, "Yet once more," indicates the removal of what is shaken—that is, created things—so that what cannot be shaken may remain. 28. Therefore, since we are receiving a kingdom that cannot be shaken, let us give thanks, by which we offer to God an acceptable worship with reverence and fear; 29. for indeed our God is a consuming fire.

NOTES

25. *See that you do not refuse the one who is speaking:* The warning in 3:12 began with the same imperative, *blepete*, "see." The author uses the verb *paraiteisthai* again, but here it has the meaning of "refuse" (see the Notes at 12:19). The periphrastic "the one who speaks" refers to God. In the immediate context it recalls the previous section of the chapter, where God spoke at Sinai (12:19). Hebrews, in general, has been about a God who speaks anew, so the readers may hear an echo of other parts of the sermon where the author stressed that aspect of God's revelation (1:1; 2:2; 3:5; 5:5).

    for if they did not escape when they refused the one who warned them on earth, how much less will we escape if we turn away from the one who warns from heaven: The author has made a fortiori arguments earlier in the sermon (2:1-3; 9:14; 12:9). He returns to the disobedience of the wilderness generation (3:16–4:11). The verb "escape," *ekphygein*, was used with the object "judgment" in 2:3, a similar comparison between the readers and the wilderness generation. In fact, the disobedience of the wilderness generation was confirmed by the just penalty they received (2:2). The author reiterates the point in a new context that cautions the reader not to refuse God. The purpose of the contrast becomes evident in the difference between the warnings. The warning issued at Sinai was earthly, whereas the warning the readers receive in their theophany is from heaven (on the verb *chrēmatizein*, "warn," see the Notes at 8:5). As with the contrast between the theophanies in the previous section of the chapter, a distinction is drawn between the material and the spiritual. The readers are cautioned not to "turn away" or "reject," *apostrephein* (LXX: Gen 31:3; Exod 4:21; Num 32:15; 1 Kgdms 30:22; 31:9; 2 Kgdms 5:23; Pss 43:25; 73:11; Job 10:9; Jer 15:6; NT: Matt 5:42; Acts 3:26; Rom 11:26; 2 Tim 1:15; 4:4; Titus 1:14). *Apostrephein* is a stronger verb than "refuse," *paraiteisthai*, which the author applied to the wilderness generation (12:19). Thus the readers' offense would be more serious. The way God speaks from heaven has been developed by the author throughout the sermon. It has been primarily through Scripture (1:1, 5-13; 2:6-8; 3:7-11, 15; 7:17, 21; 8:8-12; 10:37-38; 12:5-6), through the Son (1:2; 2:11-13; 10:5-7), and through the Holy Spirit (6:4-5; 10:15-17).

26. *At that time his voice shook the earth:* In Exod 19:18 (MT) the shaking is restricted to Mount Sinai, but in Ps 68(67):8 it is the earth that quaked (see Ps 77:18). Judges 5:5 uses the verb *saleuein*, as here, to describe Sinai shaking.

but now he has promised, "Yet once more I will shake not only the earth but also the heaven: The citation is from Hag 2:6, interpreted here as a promise rather than an oracle. The author has modified the simple quotation from the prophet by inserting "not only," *ou monon*, and "but also," *alla*, into it. He has also shortened the citation by leaving off "and the sea and the dry land" and the end of the verse in Hag 2:6. Since the contrasts he has been developing are between heaven and earth, he probably deemed the remainder of the citation superfluous. The changes have heightened the eschatological tone of the citation, and so the heavenly sanctuary is not included in the locus of the turmoil, as the next verse confirms (cf. Braun, 443; Grässer 3:331–35; Weiss, 689–91).

27. *This phrase, "Yet once more," indicates the removal of what is shaken—that is, created things—so that what cannot be shaken may remain:* The author explains his reason for including the LXX citation. The stress on the temporal is evident in the attention given to the adverbial expression "yet once more," *eti hapax*. The noun "removal," *metathesis*, was used in 7:12 when the author spoke of the "change" in the Law that resulted from the change in the priesthood. It was also used to describe Enoch's disappearance from earth in 11:5. The implication is that the material world will pass away so that the eternal may remain. "What cannot be shaken" is the eternal, for it remains (*menein*). There may be a parallel here with the author's thought in 1:10-12, where Ps 102(101):26-28 is cited. In 1:11 the citation from the Psalm confirms that God remains (*diamenein*). The perishing of earth and heaven (1:10) may be likened to the shaking of the heaven and the earth. Each captures the sense of the transient by highlighting what remains (cf. Wilfried Eisele, *Ein unerschütterliches Reich: die mittelplatonische Umformung des Parusiegedankens im Hebräerbrief.* BZNW 16 [Berlin: de Gruyter, 2003] 123–24; Attridge, 381). The verb "shake," *saleuein*, is used eschatologically in the NT (Matt 24:29; Mark 13:25; Luke 21:26; Georg Bertram, *saleuō, salos, TDNT* 7:65–70).

28. *Therefore, since we are receiving a kingdom that cannot be shaken, let us give thanks:* The conclusion is hortatory. The readers are receiving, *paralambonontes* (present participle) a kingdom, in the final sense (see Dan 7:18 [LXX]). That the kingdom cannot be shaken places it in the eternal realm, on the basis of the comparison drawn from the Haggai quotation, and it is an eschatological reality the readers now possess (Attridge, 382). The appropriate response to what they are receiving is gratitude.

by which we offer to God an acceptable worship with reverence and fear: The verb "offer worship," *latreuein*, has been used to refer to cultic matters (8:5; 9:9; 10:2; 13:10), and so it can apply to acts of worship. The adverb *euarestōs*, "acceptable," connotes what is "pleasing" and qualifies the kind of worship. Pleasing God will be a concern of the author in the next chapter (13:16, 21). He may also anticipate the exhortation to his readers in 13:1-6 (Koester, 557).

Such worship is further qualified by the expression "with reverence and fear," *meta eulabeias kai deous* (12:28). Ancient authors distinguished *deos* from *phobos* in that the former was durative. Thus the word has a strong sense of fear associated with it. Rudolf Bultmann sees *eulabeia kai deos* as synonymous with *phobos kai tromos*, "fear and trembling" in Phil 2:12 (*eulabēs, ktl., TDNT* 2:753; see Raymond F. Collins, *First Corinthians*. SP 7 [Collegeville: Liturgical Press, 1999] 119 on 1 Cor 2:3, where he speaks of Paul's dread before the Corinthians). The context of chapter 12, which deals with the Sinai theophany and includes the exclamation of Moses in 12:21, "I am terrified and trembling," supports the interpretation of *meta eulabeias kai deous* as a strong warning that encompasses actual fear of the power of God over humans (cf. Patrick Gray, *Godly Fear: The Epistle to the Hebrews and Greco-Roman Critiques of Superstition*. SBLAB 16 [Atlanta: Society of Biblical Literature, 2003] 206–209). As Lane (1:487) notes, "*eulabeia* signifies the fear that is appropriate 'before an imminent peril, namely, before the judgment of God' (Andriessen, *NRTh* 96 [1974] 284)." *Deos* is *hapax* in the NT, but it is found in the LXX in 2 Macc 3:17, 30; 12:22; 13:16; and 15:23. The author has already used the noun "reverence" in 5:7 in reference to the earthly Jesus (cf. 11:7). There it characterized his own "service" in obedience to the will of God. So he is the model for the readers. The two nouns "reverence" and "fear" occur together only here in the NT.

29. *for indeed our God is a consuming fire:* The author cites Deut 4:24; 9:3 in the conclusion to this warning. The expression comes from warnings to Israel not to abandon the covenant. Here the image of a purging fire functions to motivate the readers to upright behavior as it did in 6:8 and 10:27. As commentators note, "fire" is a manifestation of God's judgment in the Hebrew Bible (Isa 33:14; Wis 16:16; Ps Sol 15:4; NT: 2 Pet 3:7; see Attridge, 383).

Interpretation

The final section of this chapter warns the readers to remain steadfast and not refuse God as the wilderness generation had. Following on the promise of Mount Zion (12:22-24), the warning reminds the readers what is at stake in their response to God's word to them. The section has three parts: the warning itself (v. 25), the warning's rationale supported by a scriptural citation (vv. 26-27), and a concluding invitation to a worship of thanksgiving (vv. 28-29).

The warning is structured as a *qal wahomer* argument that proceeds from the lesser to the greater. The author has used this kind of argument before (2:1-3; 9:13-14), and the sentiment here is similar to the argument in 10:26-34, where the warning is bolstered by scriptural citations and concludes with a supportive statement about God. As with the comparison between Mounts Sinai and Zion (12:18-24), the earthly is contrasted to the heavenly, the transient with the permanent, in an effort to stress the seriousness of the warning and the qualitative differences between the respective refusals involved. The inability to escape recalls the failure of the wilderness generation to escape God's judgment (2:3).

As in 3:12, where the readers were sternly warned against apostasy, the warning in 12:25-29 begins with the imperative "see," *blepete*, and a negative particle to exhort the readers not to refuse God, expressed in the periphrasis

ton lalounta, "the one who is speaking." The author envisions a serious offense involving a willful and culpable refusal to listen. It is an offense that
will be punished more severely than the offense of those who disregarded
"the one who warned them on earth." The contrast is drawn between the
recipients of the sermon in the present and the wilderness generation at
Sinai in the past, as described in the previous section (12:18-24) and earlier
in 3:7-19. Whereas the past generation was warned on earth, the present
generation is warned from the heavens; thus they are under greater obligation to obey. This difference is confirmed by the use of the stronger verb
apostrephein, "reject," at 12:25 in reference to the present generation, and
the use of *paraiteisthai*, "refuse," for the wilderness generation. Any refusal
by the Hebrews community to listen now has become nothing less than a
rejection of God.

The "re-scripturing" of Hag 2:6 develops the author's interest in contrasting the earthly to the heavenly. Additions to the verse render a stronger
antithesis between Sinai and Zion. The oracle, interpreted as promise,
focuses on the entire created order, including the portion of the heavens
that is created. Perhaps a good commentary on the author's interpretation
of Hag 2:6 is Heb 1:10-12 (= Ps 101:26-28, LXX). That allusion to the creation
narrative in the opening of Genesis stresses, as does the original, that God
created earth and heaven, and as created entities they are not permanent.
Thus they will perish, wear out, be rolled up, and change (1:11-12). Only
the eternal will remain. The author links this section to what he had written
in the first chapter by returning to the notion of what "remains." Here it is
explained as what cannot be shaken, i.e., the eternal.

The tradition of heaven and earth being shaken and passing away is
eschatological (Matt 5:18; 24:29; Mark 13:25, 30; Luke 21:26). The Gospel of
Mark may have influenced the author here (Mark 13:25), since in his thirteenth chapter Mark also gives eschatological warnings that begin with
blepete (13:5, 9, 23, 33), whereas Matthew and Luke use this verb only once,
when they replicate Mark 13:5 (Matt 24:4; Luke 21:8). Additional uses of
blepete in his gospel indicate that Mark seems to prefer this imperative (4:24;
8:15; 12:38). It is not clear which LXX texts Mark chose for composing the
citation in Mark 13:25. The first half of the verse appears to be taken from
Isa 34:4, but the second half could have been drawn from Isa 13:13, Joel
2:10, or Hag 2:6, 21. Each of these LXX texts uses the synonymous verb *seiein*,
"shake," which Mark then changed to *saleuein*, "shake." So the author of
Hebrews may have intended to interpret the citation from Hag 2:6, 21 in
light of Mark 13:25 to draw out the eschatological meaning of what must
transpire in order that the unshakeable may remain. Hence he uses *saleuein*
in 12:26, 27 to bracket the citation from Hag 2:6, 21 in which he retains the
verb *seiein* from the LXX.

Gratitude is the appropriate response to the promise of an unshakeable
kingdom, and it is expressed in fitting service to God. The verb "worship,"

latruein, has been used consistently in relation to the sacrificial cult under the old covenant. Here the author adopts it to describe the community's ritual service under the new covenant. The fact that it is offered with "reverence and fear" indicates that God's holiness is not lessened under the new covenant, even as access to God becomes freer. In 5:7 "reverent submission" characterized Jesus' priestly service as he offered himself to God. He is the model worshiper in that sense, and the use of the term "reverence" here intends to apply Jesus' cultic disposition to the readers. The sense of the noun *deos* as "fear" in v. 28 is also reinforced by the reminder that God is a consuming fire. The image is of course drawn from Deut 4:24 and 9:3, where Israel is warned to keep the covenant and avoid idolatry (Attridge, 383). Here it recalls the warning of 6:8 and the "fiery zeal" of 10:27. In Hebrews the image stands for God's judgment and punishment. As such it is an appropriate conclusion to the warning that began in 12:25.

The author closes the twelfth chapter of his sermon with a stern eschatological warning (vv. 25-27) that is nevertheless tempered by liturgical language designed to encourage a positive response of the readers to the God who speaks to them (vv. 28-29). This warning, like the one in vv. 14-17, brackets the reminder of what the readers already possess in the heavenly Jerusalem (vv. 18-24). By placing both warnings around the joyful description of Mount Zion, the author highlights precisely what may be lost should the readers waver in their fidelity to God. This concern is what drives the strong and fearsome language of this passage. Having shown his readers what they now have under the new covenant, he wants them to respond accordingly, with the gratitude that is appropriate to the gift they have received, i.e., an unshakeable kingdom.

For Reference and Further Study

MacRae, George W. "A Kingdom that Cannot Be Shaken: The Heavenly Jerusalem in the Letter to the Hebrews," *TY* (1978–79) 27–40.

Oberholtzer, Thomas K. "The Failure to Heed His Speaking in Hebrews 12:25-29," *BSac* 146 (1989) 67–75.

Rhee, Victor (S.-Y.). "Chiasm and the Concept of Faith in Hebrews 12:1-29," *WestTheolJourn* 63 (2001) 269–84.

Thompson, James W. "'That Which Cannot Be Shaken': Some Metaphysical Assumptions in Hebrews 12:27," *JBL* 94 (1975) 580–87.

37. *Final Exhortations* (13:1-6)

1. Let love for brothers and sisters remain. 2. Do not neglect to show hospitality to strangers, for by doing that some have entertained angels without knowing it. 3. Remember those who are in prison, as though you were bound together with them; those who are being tortured, as though you were in the same body with them. 4. Let marriage be held in honor by all, and let the marriage bed be kept undefiled; for God will judge the immoral and adulterers. 5. Keep your lives free from the love of money, and be content with what you have; for he has said, "I will never leave you or forsake you." 6. So we can say with confidence, "The Lord is my helper; I will not be afraid. What can anyone do to me?"

NOTES

1. *Let love for brothers and sisters remain:* The first in a series of brief exhortations addresses the question of love for brothers and sisters, *philadelphia*. In Greek literature and among the philosophers the term refers to the kind of love found among blood relatives (Hans von Soden, *adelphos, ktl., TDNT* 1:144–46). Plutarch has an entire treatise devoted to it, *On Brotherly Love* (*Moralia* 478A-492D). A portion of Hierocles' treatise *On Duties* (4.27.23) is devoted to the topic (see Malherbe, *Moral Exhortation*, 96–97). The emblematic pair of siblings embodying this virtue are the *Dioscuri*, Castor and Pollux (Plutarch, *Moralia* 478D; Lucian, *Dialogues of the Gods* 286). Interest in *philadelphia* extended beyond Greek literature and philosophy. The noun *philadelphia* and the adjective *philadelphos* are extant in the LXX (*philadelphia*: 4 Macc 13:23, 26; 14:1; *philadelphos*: 2 Macc 15:14; 4 Macc 13:21; 15:10). Models of *philadelphia* in Josephus are Jacob's son, Joseph (*Antiquities* 2.160-161) and Moses (*Antiquities* 4.26). Elsewhere in Josephus there is one use of the noun (12.189) and two instances of the adjective *philadelphos* (*War* 1.275, 485). Philo's single reference to *philadelphia* echoes the exemplary character of the *Dioscuri* but also shows that the concept extends to sisters as well as brothers (*Embassy to Gaius* 87). He uses the adjective *philadelphos* twice (*On Joseph* 218; *Embassy to Gaius* 92). In the *Testament of the Twelve Patriarchs* the antonym *misadelphia*, "hatred of brothers and sisters" is used twice (*T. Benj.* 7:5; 8:1), where the example of the vice is Cain. While the noun *philadelphia* does not occur among these Testaments, Joseph speaks of honoring his brothers (*T. Jos.* 10:6; 11:1; 15:3; 17:1-3, 5). New Testament authors have adopted the term because of their preference for it over the concept of *philia*, friendship, which was accompanied by a strong reciprocity ethic. Since Christians formed fictive kinship with one another, *philadelphia* was apt for describing Christian love. So, for example, Paul never uses the terms *philia* or *philos* (friend), but does use *philadelphia* (Rom 12:10; 1 Thess 4:9; see Mitchell, "'*Greet the Friends By Name,*'" 226). Elsewhere in the NT, *philadelphia* is found in 1 Pet 1:22 and 2 Pet 1:7. The exhortation to let *philadelphia* remain grounds the recommendations that follow. The author has already referred to the love evident among community members (6:10; 10:24, 32).

2. *Do not neglect hospitality, for by doing that some have entertained angels without knowing it:* The verb "forget," *epilanthanein*, had the sense of "overlook" in 6:10 and will take the meaning "neglect" (13:16). "Hospitality," *philoxenia*, (literally love of strangers) was an important practice in the ancient world (Gustav Stählin, *xenos, ktl., TDNT* 5:1–36) and especially among Christians, given how much they traveled and how dangerous the environment of inns was (see John Stambaugh and David Balch, *The New Testament in its Social Environment*. Library of Early Christianity 2 [Philadelphia: Westminster, 1986] 38; Wayne A. Meeks, *The First Urban Christians: The Social World of the Apostle Paul* [New Haven: Yale University Press, 1983] 109). The noun occurs only here and in Rom 12:13. The adjective "hospitable," *philoxenos*, is found in 1 Tim 3:2; Titus 1:8; 1 Pet 4:9. The latter part of the verse may refer to the paradigm of hospitality in the Hebrew Bible, i.e., Abraham entertaining the divine visitors (Gen 18:2-15). The legendary nature of his welcome is attested to in Philo (*On Abraham* 107; cf. 114; *On the Virtues* 108) and Josephus (*Antiquities* 1.196; cf. *Life* 142), who both prefer the noun *xenia* to *philoxenia*. However, others who entertained angels may qualify: Lot (Gen 19:1-14), Gideon (Judg 6:11-18), Manoah and his wife (Judg 13:3-22), and Tobit (Tob 12:1-20) (see Attridge, 386).

3. *Remember those who are in prison, as though you were bound together with them; those who are being tortured, as though you were in the same body with them:* The injunctions not to forget are now followed by more positive ones. The author has already commented on the readers' compassion for prisoners in 10:34. The sentiment here seems to reflect the same kind of compassion marked by empathy. The verb "bind together," *syndein*, connotes the sharing of another's plight. Such *syn*-compounds are common within the language of friendship in the ancient world. This particular verb, for example, describes the friendship between David and Jonathan in 1 Kgdms 18:1. In Philo it refers to the bond all humans share by nature, but in comparison with a deeper and more lasting bond (*The Eternity of the World* 13). He also uses it for the bond of kinship (*Moses* 1.324; *Special Laws* 2.240). The participle "those who are mistreated," *kakouchoumenoi*, recalls the maltreatment suffered by the martyrs mentioned in 11:37. A compound form of the verb, *synkakoucheisthai*, was applied to Moses, who shared the suffering of his fellow Israelites in 11:25. Both examples from chapter 11 understand the motivation for such acceptance of suffering and commiseration with those who suffer to be a byproduct of faith.

4. *Let marriage be held in honor by all, and let the marriage bed be kept undefiled; for God will judge the immoral and adulterers:* Marriage is a common topic for exhortation among Hellenistic moralists, and in Judaism and early Christianity (e.g., Maximus of Tyre, *Discourse* 36.6b; Hierocles, *On Duties* 4.22.21-24; Plutarch, *Advice to the Bride and Groom*; Musonius Rufus, *Fragments* 12; Lev 19:20, 29; 20:9-21; Philo, *Posterity and Exile of Cain*, 116; *On Abraham* 133-34; 1 Cor 7:1-16; 1 Thess 4:3-7; Eph 5:3-5, 22-33). The "immoral" and "adulterers" are mentioned together elsewhere in the NT only in 1 Cor 6:9, where Paul lists the unrighteous who will not inherit the kingdom of God. The two terms are not equal (Koester, 558).

5. *Keep your lives free from the love of money, and be content with what you have:* Another standard topic among moralists was the pursuit of money (*philargyros, philargyria*),

sometimes treated in conjunction with sexual immorality (Lucian, *Nigrinus* 16). After a discussion of carnal incontinence Epictetus takes up the desire for money, which he links to general moral lassitude in which, unless the vices are checked, the condition only worsens (Epictetus, *Dissertations* 2.18.6-18; cf. 2.16.45; 3.7.21). The injunction to be content is an oblique caution against the vice of "covetousness," *pleonexia*. Dio Chrysostom, in an oration he dedicates to the topic, calls it the cause of the greatest evils (*Orations* 17). Philo cautions self-control against the vice (*Allegorical Interpretation* 3.166), and counsels overcoming it (*On Agriculture* 83; *Moses* 2.186). The antidote for it is justice (*Every Good Person is Free* 159). He advises self-control to defeat the love of money, too (*On the Change of Names* 226–227), calling it a serious illness (*Special Laws* 1.24) and unholy (*Special Laws* 1.281). First Timothy 6:10 describes it as the root of all evil.

for he has said, "I will never leave you or forsake you": The motivation for following these two injunctions is given in a quotation from Deut 31:6, 8 (cf. Josh 1:5). In the original, Moses speaks the words twice, once to all Israel (v. 6) and once to Joshua (v. 8). Since he is recounting God's word the verbs are in the third person, "he will not leave you or forsake you." The form of the saying with the verbs in the first person directs it to the readers as though God were speaking directly to them. Since Philo (*Confusion of Tongues* 166) has the same form of the saying, it is likely that there was an alternate version of the LXX in which the change had already been made (Attridge, 388; Koester, 559; cf. Friedrich Schröger, *Der Verfasser des Hebräerbriefes als Schriftausleger* [Regensburg: Pustet, 1968] 194–96). Trusting God is the antidote to the love of money.

6. *So we can say with confidence, "The Lord is my helper; I will not be afraid. What can anyone do to me?":* The section is completed by another citation from Scripture, Ps 117:6 (LXX). The wording is exactly the same as in the LXX. The verb *tharrein*, "have confidence," introduces the citations (cf. 2 Cor 5:6, 8; 7:16; 10:1, 2). It is related to *tharraleotēs*, a synonym for "confidence," *parrhēsia*, used elsewhere in Hebrews (3:6; 4:16; 10:19, 35; Epictetus, *Dissertations* 3.22.93-96; Lucian, *Demonax* 50; Philo, *Who Is the Heir* 19-30; *On Joseph* 222; Josephus, *Antiquities* 2.52, 131-33; Walter Grundmann, *tharreō*, TDNT 3:25–27). Further motivation for following the author's injunction against the love of money is the ability to live without earthly fear, having confidence in the Lord. According to 10:31, rather than fearing humans the readers should fear God (cf. 12:28).

INTERPRETATION

The final chapter of Hebrews has been the subject of some very interesting studies on its relationship to the rest of the sermon. Commentators who have found peculiarities in the form and content of the chapter have raised questions about the integrity of Hebrews and have proposed that the chapter may not have been part of the original composition. William L. Lane gives a helpful summary of three main issues that have led scholars to examine the chapter in relation to what precedes it. First, there is a lack of transition between the opening of the chapter and the end of chapter 12. Second, the form of the chapter—general admonition—differs from the forms employed in the first twelve chapters, particularly the hortatory sections. Third, the chapter's content differs significantly from the rest of the sermon's content, conforming less to the character of the first twelve chapters and more to general NT teaching, and in particular to what may be considered Pauline (Lane 2:496). Similar analyses of the problems in chapter 13 are shared by other commentators (Attridge, 384; Ellingworth, 692–93; Grässer 3:344–45; Weiss, 697–98). Therefore some scholars see the chapter as a later addition to Hebrews by the author himself (Montefiore, 237–38; Héring, 119; Hughes, 561; Thurén, 51–53; Westcott, 429) in the form of an appendix, postscript, or adaptation of the sermon to a letter form. Others see it as something added by an editor or a committee (Buchanan, 243–45, 267–68; Charles C. Torrey, "The Authorship and Character of the Epistles to the Hebrews," *JBL* 30 [1911] 137–56; E. D. Jones, "The Authorship of Hebr. xiii," *ExpTim* 46 [1934–35] 562–67; Franz Overbeck, *Zur Geschichte des Kanons, 2 Abhandlungen* [Chemnitz: Scheitzner, 1880] 16). There are good reasons, however, to see the chapter as highlighting themes already articulated in the sermon, and thus to consider it an integral part of Hebrews (Attridge, 384–85; de Silva, 484; Koester, 554; Lane 2:496–507).

Yet another instance of "love for brothers and sisters" follows in the injunction to remember those in prison. The author has already complimented the readers on their past compassion toward prisoners (10:34), which apparently is still needed. No specific mention of the circumstances of those imprisoned is included. The exhortation here is bolstered by a form of the Golden Rule (Matt 7:12), which may have been implicit in the recollection of the compassion they had for prisoners in the earlier reference. Remembrance of those who are ill treated need not refer only to the situation of prisoners, although it is not unlikely that prisoners would have been ill-treated as well. The motivation is the same: empathy as though they were in the same body, as they are. This verse looks back to the mistreated martyrs in 11:37 and to the example of Moses in 11:25. Paul has the idea of suffering together with one another in his theology of the Body of Christ in 1 Cor 12:26. Since Hebrews does not develop such a theology, it is likely that the author is not alluding to that part of the Pauline tradition. In light of 2:17-18 (cf. 4:15) the model of compassion is Christ, who understands what it means to suffer as a human (Schierse, *Verheissung*, 105).

The exhortation to honor marriage looks like a stock topic and need not presume a problem with immorality and adultery among the readers (cf. Tob 4:12-13). There is really nothing else in Hebrews that would support the view that the author is addressing a particular moral problem in the community he addresses. Hellenistic moral philosophers associated marriage with honor and sexual morality (Malherbe, *Letters to the Thessalonians*, 229), so the treatment of the topic here seems to reflect the common social mores of the day. Distinctive in Hebrews is the warning about divine judgment of those who fail to honor marriage, or who defile the marriage bed.

The final exhortation against the "love of money" also reflects a stock topic among pagan and Jewish moralists (see the Notes above). Greed and the desire for money were treated together with sexual immorality (cf. Tob 4:12-14; Rom 2:21-22; 1 Cor 5:9-11; 6:9-10). First Timothy 6:10 gives a global scope to the love of money, associating it with apostasy and considering it a root vice that gives rise to others (Raymond F. Collins, *I & II Timothy and Titus: A Commentary*. NTL [Louisville and London: Westminster John Knox, 2002] 158–59). In 10:34 the author recalls that under earlier persecution the readers did not cling to their property, but gladly gave it up in view of a greater possession that lay ahead of them. In that instance they were content with what they had, even after they had lost some of their possessions. The motivating clause from Deut 31:6, 8 indicates that reliance on God rather than money is the antidote to greed.

The concluding citation from Ps 117:6 (LXX) reprises a favorite theme of Hebrews, the ability to speak with confidence. The introduction is peculiar to the extent that the author has chosen the verb *tharrein* over *parrēsiazesthai*, since he has favored the noun for "confidence," *parrhēsia*, throughout the sermon (3:6; 4:16; 10:19, 35). The psalm citation is a natural complement to the text of Deuteronomy cited in the last verse. The original setting of the psalm is a celebration of God's covenant love for Israel, manifested in the deliverance of Israel from its enemies. The psalm proclaims that placing one's trust in God is better than putting confidence in mortals and princes. The setting of the citation here transposes that purpose now to encompass placing one's trust in God over trusting in material things like possessions and money. When the author recalled the readers' tribulations in 10:32-39, he exhorted them not to throw away their confidence and to continue to endure (vv. 35-36). The thought is echoed here with reference to their present circumstances. They need to be confident and to rely on God, who will help them to overcome their fear, which otherwise might drive them to rely on money and possessions or, in the thought of 1 Timothy, to fall away from their faith.

Exhortations to love are frequent in the NT and early Christian literature. As the author brings his sermon to a close he invites his readers to focus on the importance of knowing what to love and what not to love. Their love for brothers and sisters should take many forms, such as sharing hospitality, visiting those in prison, and honoring their spouses. Contrasting with the positive manifestations of love is the love of money. Relying on the Lord in all things for help and aid in time of need precludes greed, in the author's view. If concern for money and possessions derives from fear and insecurity, it is only love that can drive those emotions out.

For Reference and Further Study

Fascher, Erich. "Zum Begriff des Fremden," *TLZ* 96 (1971) 161–68.
Koenig, John. *New Testament Hospitality: Partnership with Strangers as Promise and Mission.* Philadelphia: Fortress Press, 1985.
Lane, William L. "Unexpected Light on Hebrews 13:1-6 from a Second-Century Source," *PRSt* 9 (1982) 267–74.
Matera, Frank J. "Moral Exhortation: The Relation between Moral Exhortation and Doctrinal Exposition in the Letter to the Hebrews," *TJT* 10 (1994) 169–82.
Vanhoye, Albert. "La question littéraire de Hébreux xiii. 1-6," *NTS* 23 (1976–77) 121–39.
Wedderburn, A. J. M. "The 'Letter' to the Hebrews and its Thirteenth Chapter," *NTS* 50 (2004) 390–405.

38. *Offering a Sacrifice of Praise* (13:7-19)

7. Remember your leaders, those who spoke the word of God to you; consider the outcome of their conduct, and imitate their faith. 8. Jesus Christ is the same yesterday, today, and forever. 9. Do not be carried away by diverse and strange teachings; for it is well for the heart to be strengthened by grace, not by foods, which have not benefited those who observe them. 10. We have an altar from which those who minister in the tent have no right to eat. 11. For the bodies of those animals whose blood is brought into the sanctuary by the high priest as a sacrifice for sin are burned outside the camp. 12. Therefore Jesus also suffered outside the gate in order to sanctify the people by his own blood. 13. Let us then go to him outside the camp, bearing his abuse. 14. For here we have no lasting city, but we are seeking the city that is to come. 15. Through him, then, let us continually offer a sacrifice of praise to God, that is, the fruit of lips that confess his name. 16. Do not neglect to do good and to share what you have, for such sacrifices are pleasing to God.

17. Obey your leaders and submit to them, for they are keeping watch over your souls and will give an account. Let them do this with joy and not with sighing—for that would be harmful to you.

18. Pray for us; we are sure that we have a good conscience, desiring to act honorably in all things. 19. I urge you all the more to do this, so that I may be restored to you very soon.

Notes

7. *Remember your leaders, those who spoke the word of God to you:* Again the exhortation begins by asking the readers to "remember," this time their leaders. They

are identified only by the designation *hēgoumenōi*, a common term for "leader" in the Hellenistic world (Hermann M. F. Büchsel, *hēgeomai, ktl., TDNT* 2:907–909). In this verse the participle of the verb *hēgeisthai* occurs, but there is a corresponding noun, *hēgemōn*, which is applied to individuals in prominent leadership capacities, political, military, civic, or religious (LSJ, 763; MM, 277). In the NT the noun refers to administrative officials in Palestine (Matt 2:6) or to provincial governors (Matt 10:18; Mark 13:9; Luke 21:12; 1 Pet 2:14). It is also used for Roman prefects like Pontius Pilate (Matt 27:2, 11, 14; Luke 20:20), Felix (Acts 23:24, 26, 33; 24:1, 10), and Festus (Acts 26:30). The leaders intended here are the ones who had originally preached to the community members, as indicated by the relative clause "who spoke the word of God to you" (Acts 8:25; 11:19; 13:46; 14:25; 16:6; Phil 1:14). Since the current leaders are referred to in v. 17, it may be that these former leaders are deceased. The term is used of Christian leaders in Acts 15:22.

consider the outcome of their conduct, and imitate their faith: The "outcome," *ekbasis*, can be the final result of one's life (Wis 2:17) or the result of a particular action (Wis 8:8; 11:14; BDAG, 299). As their "conduct" or "behavior," *anastrophē*, is the object of consideration, the former meaning is preferred. The parallelism of this noun with faith suggests that it, too, has to do with how the leaders conducted themselves in faith rather than what they believed (Grässer 3:370).

8. *Jesus Christ is the same yesterday, today, and forever:* An important notice of the constancy of Christ recalls that he is the eternal Son and High Priest, now exalted at the right hand of God. The affirmation that Jesus Christ is the same echoes the citation from Ps 102(101):28 in 1:12. "Yesterday and today" is a biblical expression connoting duration of time (LXX: Exod 5:14; 1 Kgdms 20:27; 2 Kgdms 15:20; Sir 38:22; 1 Macc 9:44). Hebrews adds "forever" in light of Christ's eternal status as Son and High Priest. Otherwise the author mainly uses the adverb "today," *sēmeron*, in relation to scriptural citations (1:5; 3:7, 15; 4:7; 5:5; cf. 3:13).

9. *Do not be carried away by diverse and strange teachings; for it is well for the heart to be strengthened by grace, not by foods, which have not benefited those who observe them:* The verb "be carried away," *parapherein*, can have the sense of being led astray by a particular teaching. An example from Lucian, *Hermotimus*, where Hermotimus refers to having become enamored of Stoicism, is instructive. After being confronted by his friend Lycinus, and having decided to change philosophical schools, Hermotimus exclaims: "You are right. I am going away to do just that—to make a change—of dress as well. . . . So it is no small favor that I owe you, Lycinus: you came and pulled me out when I was being carried away (*parapheromenon*) by a rough turbid torrent, giving myself to it and going with the stream" (86). The danger comes from "teachings" (*didachais*), which in the NT can mean the activity of teaching (Mark 4:2; 12:38; 1 Cor 14:6; 2 Tim 4:2) or its content (Matt 16:12; Mark 1:27; John 7:16; 18:19; Acts 2:42; 5:28; 13:12; 17:19; Rom 6:17; 16:17; 1 Cor 14:26; 2 John 9; Rev 2:14, 24; BDAG, 241). The noun was used in 6:2 in reference to elementary instruction of the community. The teaching is qualified by the adjectives "diverse," *poikilais*, and "strange," *xenias*, two pejorative terms in the context (see Josephus, *War* 2.113, 414; 4.150; 5.402).

The verb "strengthen," *bebaioun*, is rare in the LXX (Pss 40:13; 118:28; cf. 3 Macc 5:42), found in supplications for strength or confirmation. New Testament usage reflects the sense of "confirmation" or "strengthening" (Mark 16:20; Rom 15:8; 1 Cor 1:6; 2 Cor 1:21; Col 2:7). The earlier instance in Heb 2:3 had more a sense of "legitimation." The contrast of strengthening the heart by grace rather than by food (see Pss 104(103):15; 105(104):16) focuses the issue (Thurén, *Lobopfer*, 194–96). Again, it seems to be a matter of the internal as opposed to the external, as it was in the discussion of the new covenant (8:8-13). Although the issue is different here, the function of food in relation to God as described by Paul in 1 Cor 8:8 is similar: "Food will not bring us any closer to God" (cf. Rom 14:17). The foods in question are not clearly identified. The noun *brōma* can refer to food governed by Jewish dietary regulations (Lev 11:34; 25:6; Deut 2:6; 1 Macc 1:63; 4 Macc 1:34; cf. 4 Macc 6:15; Johannes Behm, *brōma, brōsis*, *TDNT* 1:642–45). This interpretation is supported by the relative clause that follows. The expression "those who observe them" is participial, from the verb "walk about," *peripatein*, which is used to describe someone who is Law-observant (LXX, *peripatein*: Prov 8:20; Eccl 11:9; *poreuesthai*: Deut 19:9; 26:17; 30:16; 3 Kgdms 2:2-3; 3:14; 8:58; Pss 84:11; 101:6; 119:1; 128:1; Mic 4:5; Tob 1:3; 3:5; Bar 1:18; 2:10; 3:13; 4:13). These individuals have not benefited (*ōphelein*) from such foods, as those of the wilderness generation were not benefited by the message they received (4:2), because they did not receive it in faith.

10. *We have an altar from which those who minister in the tent have no right to eat:* By way of contrast the author calls attention to what the readers have (see 4:15; 6:19; 8:1; 10:19). "Altar" is the same noun used in relation to the sacrifices of the old covenant (7:13). To what exactly the altar refers is not stated. This has led to a variety of interpretations. Some see it as a reference to the Eucharist (de Silva, *Despising Shame*, 275; Swetnam, "Christology and the Eucharist in the Epistle to the Hebrews," 74; Vanhoye, *Old Testament Priests*, 228–29), others to the cross (Attridge, 396; Hughes, 575; Helmut Koester, "Outside the Gates," 313; Lane 2:538; Montefiore, 244; Spicq 2:425), and still others to the heavenly sanctuary (Ronald Williamson, "The Eucharist and the Epistle to the Hebrews," *NTS* 21 [1975] 308–309; Floyd V. Filson, *"Yesterday,"* 48–49; Gerd Theissen, *Untersuchungen zum Hebräerbrief*, 76–79; James Thompson, *Beginnings of Christian Philosophy*, 146). The following verses referring to the suffering of Christ and to meeting him in his suffering make it probable that "altar" is a metaphor for the suffering and death of Christ, i.e., the cross. The phrase "those who minister in the tent" looks back to chapter 9 and the Levitical priesthood. The Levitical priests were able to eat of the sacrifices (Lev 7:5-6), except on the Day of Atonement. Those ministering at this altar have no authority to eat at it. Some commentators see a reference here to the fact that just as the sacrifices were not consumed on the Day of Atonement (Lev 6:30; 16:27), these individuals are not permitted to eat at the Christian altar because Christ's self-offering was an atoning sacrifice (Braun, 463; Lane 2:539). Those who serve are not identified, but it is likely the author has in mind the Levitical priests, who function here to facilitate the comparison in vv. 11-13 (Attridge, 397).

11. *For the bodies of those animals whose blood is brought into the sanctuary by the high priest as a sacrifice for sin are burned outside the camp:* The author refers to two texts, Lev 6:30 and 16:27, which prescribe the ritual for the disposition of the sacrificial offerings on the Day of Atonement. The animals in question are the bull (Lev

16:11-14) and goat (Lev 16:15-19). Their blood was carried into the Holy of Holies to be sprinkled on and before the mercy seat over the Ark of the Covenant (Lev 16:14-15). Hebrews has referred to the sanctuary earlier (9:2-3, 8, 12, 25). The carcasses were to be taken outside the camp to be burned (Lev 6:27; cf. Exod 29:14; Lev 9:11).

12. *Therefore Jesus also suffered outside the gate in order to sanctify the people by his own blood:* The second half of the comparison presents Jesus as the victim of an atoning sacrifice on the analogy that he suffered outside the gates of Jerusalem. The only other place where the expression "outside the gate" occurs in the NT is in Acts 16:13, where it is simply descriptive. As long as the Temple stood, the prescription of Lev 16:27 would have been fulfilled by taking the carcasses of the sacrificial animals outside the city to be burned. The gospel tradition places Jesus' death outside the city of Jerusalem (Matt 27:31; Mark 15:20; John 19:20). Again, the purpose of Christ's sacrifice is to sanctify the "people," a designation in Hebrews for Christians (4:9; 8:10; 10:30). On the verb "sanctify" see the Notes at 2:11. The author also alludes to Christ's function as High Priest, as the high priest under the old covenant had to offer sacrifice for the people (5:3; 9:7, 19).

13. *Let us then go to him outside the camp, bearing his abuse:* The comparison complete, the author now exhorts his readers to imitate Christ by sharing in his sufferings, under the metaphor of "going outside the camp," recalling the noun *parembolē*, "camp," from the LXX version of Lev 16:27. He does this so as not to confuse his readers when in the next verse he talks about the city on earth that they do not have. They are invited, too, to bear the "abuse," *oneidismos*, that was inflicted on him. The expression "his abuse" is similar to "the abuse of Christ" in 11:26. On "abuse" see the Notes at 10:33. Sharing in the sufferings of Christ was a standard element of early Christian exhortation, and Hebrews places itself within that tradition (Matt 10:38; Mark 8:34; Luke 14:26-27; Rom 6:8; 8:17; 1 Cor 2:2; 2 Cor 4:10; Gal 3:1; Phil 3:10).

14. *For here we have no lasting city, but we are seeking the city that is to come:* The author recalls 12:22-24, where "the city of the living God" was equated with the heavenly Jerusalem. This is the city the readers are moving toward, and here is where they will enter into rest (4:1, 11). "Lasting city," *menousan polin*, echoes other places in the sermon where "abiding" or "remaining" played a role. The city that is to come is the abiding possession (10:34) that cannot be shaken (12:27). The readers are seeking a city that is to come, as Abraham looked forward to the city with foundations built by God (11:10). The verb *mellein*, "be about to," or "to come," is used frequently in Hebrews for salvation (1:14), the world (2:5), the age (6:5), and the good things (9:11; 10:1). Now it is referred to the readers' final destination.

15. *Through him, then, let us continually offer a sacrifice of praise to God, that is, the fruit of lips that confess his name:* The expression "sacrifice of praise" is found in the LXX at Lev 7:12, 13, 15; 2 Chr 29:31; 33:16; Pss 27:6 [S²]; 49:14, 23; 106:22; 115:8; Sir 32:2; 1 Macc 4:56. These offerings are animal or grain sacrifices. Among the LXX examples Ps 49:14 is the closest to the formulation in this verse. Sacrifice here has been spiritualized to prayers or hymns of praise. The qualification of

this worship as "the fruit of lips" is an allusion to Hos 14:3 (LXX). On the meta-phorical use of the language of sacrifice in the Hellenistic world see Attridge, 400. On the verb "confess," *homologein*, see the Notes at 11:13. The verb is used in the NT for professing faith in Jesus (1 John 2:23; 4:2, 3, 15; 2 John 7). In Rev 3:5, Christ confesses the name of anyone who perseveres and is included in the book of life. The expression "to confess with the lips" is found in Rom 10:9-10.

16. *Do not neglect to do good and to share what you have, for such sacrifices are pleasing to God:* Yet another metaphorical use of "sacrifice" forms the next part of this exhortation. The chapter began with a similar injunction not to neglect hospital-ity. Here the more general term under which hospitality would fall is the object (cf. 12:14; 13:1-5). "Good deed," *eupoiïa*, occurs only here in the NT, but doing charitable works was characteristic of early Christians. The noun is singular in Greek and may be translated more literally as "well-doing" (BDAG, 410). Fre-quently before closing his letters Paul exhorted his readers to similar conduct (2 Cor 13:11; Gal 6:2; 1 Thess 5:14-18; Phil 4:4-7). These actions are likened in 12:28 to the worship that pleases God.

17. *Obey your leaders and submit to them, for they are keeping watch over your souls and will give an account:* The early exhortation to remember their leaders referred to those who first preached to them and who may no longer be alive (13:7). Here the author turns to their actual leaders. Curiously, they are not mentioned by name. An interesting text from Sir 10:20 portrays a leader (*hēgoumenos*) as some-one deserving honor in the midst of his "brothers." Paul refers to those who do not obey the truth in Rom 2:8 (cf. Jas 3:3). The wilderness generation suffered from "disobedience," *apeitheia*, which prevented them from entering into God's rest (4:6). The sentiment is echoed in 1 Pet 5:1-5, but this need not be construed as a problem isolated to Roman Christians. The paraenesis is general here. The leaders are not exempted, as the indirect reference to them is tantamount to an exhortation that they do for the community what they are required to do. The verb "keep watch," *agrypnein*, is infrequent in the LXX. In 1 Esdr 8:59 it refers to guarding the sacred vessels for the Temple until they can be given over to the priests and Levites, the clearest instance in which the notion of safekeeping occurs. The leaders will have to account for the safekeeping of the souls en-trusted to them. Doubtless this is a reference to the day of judgment, when all will have to render an account of what they have done and said (Matt 12:36; 25:31-46; 1 Pet 4:5). On the noun *logos* as an "account" see the Notes at 4:13.

Let them do this with joy and not with sighing—for that would be harmful to you: The presumption is that if the leaders give an account joyfully, without sighing, the readers will benefit more than if it is given and received grudgingly. The expres-sion "with joy," *meta charas*, recalls 10:34; 12:2, 11. The contrasting response, "sighing," *stenazein*, could be taken as a sign of discontent (Jas 5:9). This is the preferred meaning in light of the conclusion that it might be harmful.

18. *Pray for us; we are sure that we have a good conscience, desiring to act honorably in all things:* The author requests prayers for himself, preferring the plural pronoun "us" to the singular "me." Such a request for prayers is found in other NT letters (Rom 15:30; 2 Cor 1:11; Phil 1:19; Eph 6:18-19; Col 4:3; 1 Thess 5:25; 2 Thess 3:1;

Phlm 22). The appeal to a good conscience is an expression of the author's sincerity in writing to this community (cf. 2 Cor 1:12). In Paul's letters his own personal example and motivation for preaching factor into his paraenetic purpose (Malherbe, *Letters to the Thessalonians*, 82–84, 126).

19. *I urge you all the more to do this, so that I may be restored to you very soon:* The verb "urge" or "encourage," *parakalein*, occurs frequently in Paul's letters (Rom 12:1; 15:30; 16:17; 1 Cor 1:10; 4:16; 16:15; 2 Cor 2:8; 10:1; Phil 4:2; 1 Thess 4:1, 10; 5:14; Phlm 9), but it also occurs in deutero- and non-Pauline letters (Eph 4:1; 1 Tim 2:1; 1 Pet 2:11; 5:1). The author hopes to be "restored"; *apokathistanai* can mean "return" (BDAG, 111–12). And so the author may have belonged to the community he addresses. Otherwise he is expressing a wish to make a return visit. Longing to be with a letter's addressee is a feature of the friendly letter in antiquity (Stanley Stowers, *Letter Writing in Greco-Roman Antiquity*. Library of Early Christianity 56 [Philadelphia: Westminster, 1986] 61, 65, 68, 69, 76, 82, 159). It is also a feature of NT letters (Rom 15:22, 24, 29; 1 Tim 3:14; 2 Tim 4:9; Titus 3:12).

Interpretation

The second part of chapter 13 continues the concluding exhortations. Framed by references to past (v. 7) and present (v. 17) leaders, the heart of the passage examines the "altar" Christians have (vv. 10-14) in order to elucidate the meaning of Christ's sacrifice in their own lives (Attridge, 391). The final part of the text takes up matters of Christian conduct (vv. 16-17) before turning to the author's request for prayers for himself and a wish to see the readers again (vv. 18-19). Exactly how everything in this passage fits together is problematic, and the text does not yield an easy interpretation. The author moves quickly through a number of items that are not naturally related to one another. Thus the passage has the character of a compendium of exhortations and teachings as Hebrews comes to a close.

A concern for continuity marks the passage's opening. Recalling the now-deceased leaders who had instructed the readers in the initial stages of their conversion to Christianity is a paraenetic device intended to keep them on track. The force of the exhortation in v. 9 "not to be carried away" relies on the readers' past fidelity to what those leaders had taught them. Sandwiched between vv. 7 and 8 is what appears to be a liturgical proclamation that defines the desired constancy and continuity in terms of the model the author has presented throughout Hebrews, namely Jesus Christ. The constancy of Christ is eternal; it spans past, present, and future. The leaders themselves had exemplified a similar kind of constancy in the conduct of their own lives. The call to imitate their faith is also a call, then, to imitate their lives (Grässer 3:370). "The outcome of their conduct" is probably a reference to the end of their lives and could possibly be an oblique reference to martyrdom (Attridge, 392).

The exhortation not to be carried away by diverse teaching carries with it the reference to foods that had not benefited the observant. It invokes technical language and appears to refer to some type of ritual involving food. "Foods," however, is probably a euphemism for anything associated with the old covenant. Earlier, in 9:9-10, food and drink were associated with gifts and sacrifices that could not purify the conscience. These means could not compare with the "once for all" self-offering of Christ. Jukka Thurén has made a strong case for a reference to Jewish ritual meals as the problem being addressed in this verse (*Lobopfer*, 194–200). The reference to eating at the altar, however, seems to refer to the consumption of sacrificial animals in rituals other than those on the Day of Atonement. Therefore it is not necessary to conclude that the readers were participating in ritual observances involving certain foods. Rather, the author is likening these rituals to diverse teachings. Just as the food and drink rituals associated with the old covenant were ineffective in purifying the conscience, so also are diverse teachings ineffective in strengthening the hearts of the readers. Both are ineffective means. Consequently, grace is more effective for strengthening the heart.

In support of the analogy between diverse teachings and foods, the author turns to the importance of the atoning and purifying sacrifice of Christ by discussing the altar of the cross. Here is where the self-offering of Christ made possible the purification of conscience that was not possible under the ritual of the old covenant (7:11, 19). Various aspects of the ritual for the Day of Atonement that were already mentioned earlier in Hebrews are alluded to in this part of the passage in order to draw out the significance of the relationship of Christian worship to the service of Christ at the altar of the cross. Using the same word for altar (*thysiastērion*), the author had already noted in 7:13 that on earth Christ was not entitled to serve at the Levitical altar because he was not born into a line of priests. Now he makes clear that the Levitical priests are not entitled to eat at the altar of Christ's sacrifice. The allusion to eating refers to the fact that the priests could eat of certain sacrifices (Lev 7:5-6). On the Day of Atonement, however, there was no consumption of the sacrificial animals (Lev 6:30; 16:27), which may explain the author's reference to the priests not being entitled to eat at the Christian altar, since Christ's was an atoning sacrifice (Braun, 463; Lane 2:539). Rather, the carcasses of these animals were burned outside the camp (Lev 6:27; cf. Exod 29:14; Lev 9:11). While the Temple stood, those animal carcasses were taken outside the city of Jerusalem for burning.

The author believes that the location of Jesus' self-offering, outside the city of Jerusalem, adds yet another sign that his death was an atoning sacrifice (7:11, 25, 27; 9:11-14, 24-26; 10:11-14). The analogy is less than perfect since, on the Day of Atonement, the sacrifices were performed within the camp or the city and the remains were immolated outside of it. Perhaps the author was thinking more about the spatial movement required by the two sacrificial acts, where the actual location of the altar was secondary (cf. Koester, 576). On the Day of Atonement the animals were sacrificed on an altar outside the Tabernacle. Their blood was then carried *into* the sanctuary, and their bodies were burned *outside* the camp (v. 11). Jesus suffered *outside* the city and carried his own blood *into* the heavenly sanctuary (9:12). As the blood of the sacrifices associated with the Day of Atonement allegedly effected atonement for the people of the old covenant, the blood of Christ sanctifies the people of the new covenant.

The analogy between the atoning sacrifices of the old and the new covenants provides a basis for the exhortation that follows in v. 13. The readers are encouraged to participate in the sufferings of Christ by going to him outside the camp. The location, "outside the camp," does not mark the place where Jesus now is; rather it signifies the manner in which the readers are to approach the exalted Christ. Whenever they imitate him in bearing abuse, they go outside the camp. This symbolic movement may be especially poignant because they really have no earthly home. They are somewhat disenfranchised as aliens in the world they live in. Therefore they seek a city yet to come, where they will realize the fulfillment of what had been promised. Just as the author reminded them in 12:24 that when they come to Mount Zion they come to Jesus, so also here, as they seek to enter the heavenly city, they must go to Jesus. They do this by means of their faith (Koester, 577).

As the author reminded the readers that they have an altar (v. 10), he exhorts them to offer their own sacrifice of praise (v. 15) and to do good and share what they have, which he also calls "sacrifices" (v. 16). At this point the text alludes to Ps 50(49):14, since the author found in that text an appropriate source to support his exhortation. The psalm contrasts animal sacrifices with thanksgiving offerings, sacrifices of praise. In it the psalmist has God declare a preference for the latter over the former. Interestingly, the psalm opens with the image of a God who speaks and who shines forth from Zion. The third verse has God accompanied by a "consuming fire," followed by the introduction of God as a judge. The ninth verse shows God rejecting sacrificial bulls and goats, and the thirteenth depicts God as someone who does not partake of sacrificial food. The unrighteous in v. 16 are portrayed as paying only lip service to the covenant, and as hating discipline. The psalmist stresses God's preference for a sacrifice of praise (vv. 14, 23). The images and ideas of this psalm are quite compatible with Hebrews in general, and here the option for worship that prefers praise instead of sacrifice is especially appropriate (see 12:28-29).

The second half of the exhortation in v. 16 stresses that worship has a practical counterpart in good works and sharing possessions. Previously the author had described their "work and love" in "serving the saints"

(6:10). Now that service is incorporated into their worship, so that the readers' worship is constituted by praising God and charitable works. Like "sacrifices," both are "offered." The sacrifice of praise was qualified by the expansion of v. 15, "the fruit of lips that confess his name."

The opening of the passage invokes the example of Jesus' constancy in order to encourage constancy among the readers (v. 8). In like manner, Jesus is an example of the proper worshiper, who proclaims God's name in the midst of the assembly (2:12) and helps others (2:16, 18). Jesus, however, is more than just an example to be imitated; he is actually the means by which worship can be offered to God. "Through him" in v. 15 echoes others places in Hebrews where his instrumentality in aiding the reader's approach to God was stressed (2:14; 7:19, 25; 10:10, 20; 13:20). A main theme of Hebrews has been that the readers now have unprecedented access to God by means of Jesus' high-priestly service. His once for all self-offering has made that access possible for all time, *eis to panteles* (7:25). Similarly, their worship of praise to God is offered through him continually, *dia pantos*.

An exhortation to obey their present leaders in v. 17 forms a bracket around the center of the text with a reference to their former leaders in v. 7. The point of encouraging obedience is continuity. The author recalls the readers' past obedience in order to encourage their present obedience. Since diverse teachings were likened to foods that did not benefit those who observe them, it is likely these diverse teachings are the object of the author's intention here. What exactly the teachings were cannot be determined, since no specific information about them is given.

What can be known, however, is how the leaders serve the community. They are charged with the care of souls and with giving an account of the community. Why they give an account rather than the individual members themselves is not clear. Elsewhere Hebrews gives the impression that such an account will be required of each person (4:12-13). The sense here is that the leaders are called to additional accountability regarding how well they led. If the readers do not follow obediently, the leaders may be judged failures in carrying out their responsibility in maintaining the community. Such a requirement places an added burden on them, and the author appeals to the readers not to make the leaders' job more difficult than it need be. Thus they should be obedient so that the leaders do not have to "sigh" about their charges. It is preferable if the leaders can render the account of their stewardship joyfully, because the readers themselves benefit more from a good account than a bad one.

For Hebrews the proper attitude of the Christian is joy. The readers were complimented in 10:34 for accepting the loss of their possessions "with joy." Jesus endured suffering on the cross for the sake of the "joy" that was set before him (12:2). Even discipline properly accepted passes from "sorrow" to "joy" (12:11), and so the leaders should make their accounting "with joy."

The passage closes with the author's request for prayers. Such requests are found among other NT letters (see the Note to v. 18 above). Joined to the request is a statement of confidence that the author has discharged his duty faithfully and well. The previous verse encouraged the readers to allow their leaders to make their account of them before God with joy. Now the author assures his readers that he has conducted himself honorably. If he includes the community leaders among the readers he may be assuring them, too, that he has given them no cause for "sighing." The appeal to his honor is not self-serving. Rather it serves to assure the readers that he has written to them honestly and forthrightly and with no regret. Such assurances are common in the psychagogic tradition of Hellenistic moral philosophy. The personal example of a teacher or philosopher is an important validating and authenticating feature.

A further object of their prayer is the return of the author to them. The desire to see them soon expresses the genuine affection the author has for his readers, and may mitigate some of the harsher things he has written to them. Expressing a desire to see his readers again is a common element of the friendly letter in antiquity, which functions to bind the writer and the audience together more closely. For similar expressions in other NT letters see the Note at v. 19 above.

References to the community leaders, living and dead, and to the author himself show that those entrusted with the care of souls in Christian communities have a responsibility that cannot be shouldered alone. Dynamic leadership requires mutuality of respect and support, including prayer and good wishes. Hebrews concludes, then, on a note that recalls how much the author included himself in the instructions and exhortations he offered to his readers (2:1, 2-3, 8-9; 3:6, 14; 4:3, 13, 14-15, 16; 6:3, 18-19; 7:19, 26; 8:1; 10:10, 19, 21, 26, 39; 12:1, 9-10, 25, 28; 13:6, 10, 14) presumably as an example to the current leaders of the community. Leaders must elicit support of those they lead by means of their style of leadership, and the author of Hebrews is exemplary in the many ways he has shown in his sermon that he is a fellow pilgrim on the way to the same destination as his readers.

For Reference and Further Study

Andriessen, Paul. "L'euchariste dans l'Épître aux Hébreux," *NRTh* 94 (1972) 282–92.
Koester, Helmut. "'Outside the Camp': Hebrews 13:9-14," *HTR* 55 (1962) 299–308.
O'Neill, J. C. "Who Killed Whom (4Q285) Without the Camp (Heb 13:12-13)?" *JHC* 9 (2002) 125–39.
Saunders, Landon. "'Outside the Camp': Hebrews 13," *ResQ* 22 (1979) 19–24.
Young, Norman H. "'Bearing His Reproach' (Heb 13.9-14)," *NTS* 48 (2002) 243–61.

Postscript

39. *Benediction and Farewell Greetings* (13:20-25)

20. Now may the God of peace, who brought our Lord Jesus up from the dead, the great shepherd of the sheep, by the blood of the eternal covenant, 21. supply you with everything good so that you may do his will, working among us that which is pleasing in his sight, through Jesus Christ, to whom be the glory forever and ever. Amen.

22. I urge you, brothers and sisters, bear with my word of exhortation, for I have written to you briefly. 23. I want you to know that our brother Timothy has been set free, and if he comes in time, he will be with me when I see you. 24. Greet all your leaders and all the saints. Those from Italy send you greetings. 25. Grace be with all of you.

Notes

20. *Now may the God of peace, who brought our Lord Jesus up from the dead:* The author concludes his homily with a benediction not unlike ones found in other NT letters; he returns here to an epistolary form (see the comparative chart in Attridge, 405). The epithet "God of peace" does appear in other NT epistolary benedictions and farewell greetings (Rom 15:33; 16:20; 2 Cor 13:11 [God of love and peace]; Phil 4:9; 1 Thess 5:23). The author may know it as a formula or it may have been prompted by the exhortation to pursue peace in 12:14.

A basic tenet of Christian faith is that God raised Jesus from the dead. Usually the verb in such expressions is *egeirein* (Acts 3:15; 4:10; 5:30; 13:30; Rom 4:24; 8:11; 1 Cor 6:14; 15:15; 2 Cor 4:14; Gal 1:1; Eph 1:20; Col 2:12; 1 Thess 1:10; 1 Pet 1:21) or *anistanai* (Acts 2:24, 32). Here, however, the verb is *anagein*, "bring up" (cf. Rom 10:7). There is an echo here of the same verb in 2:10, where God brings up many sons and daughters to glory when Jesus himself is perfected. The author refers not only to the resurrection but also to Christ's exaltation (Attridge, 406).

the great shepherd of the sheep, by the blood of the eternal covenant: Early Christians thought of Jesus as a shepherd (Matt 26:31; John 10:11, 14; 1 Pet 2:25; 5:4; Rev 7:17). The term closest to "great shepherd" is "chief shepherd" in 1 Pet 5:4. The epithet "great" recalls that he is the great high priest in 4:14 and the great priest in 10:21. "The blood of the eternal covenant" is the means of purifying the conscience (9:14) and is what purifies the heavenly sanctuary (9:22-23). Here it is a reminder that Christ's exaltation followed on his own self-offering (2:14; 9:12; 13:12), through which he carried his own blood into the sanctuary (9:25). Christ's blood made it possible for others to enter the sanctuary after him (10:19). That God made an eternal or everlasting covenant was a common belief in Hellenistic Judaism (LXX: Ps 104:10; Isa 24:5; 55:3; 61:8; Jer 32:40; 50:5; Ezek 16:60; 37:26; Sir 45:7, 15; Bar 2:35; 2 Esdr 3:15). The author has used the adjective "eternal" throughout the sermon to indicate the permanent effect of Christ's sacrificial death (5:9; 6:2; 9:12, 14, 15) under the new covenant.

21. *supply you with everything good so that you may do his will:* The verb *katartizein* means "prepare" or "provide" (cf. 10:5; 11:3). Doing God's will was a value in Judaism and Christianity (Pss 40:9; 143:10; *Odes* 14:43 [LXX]; Mark 3:35; John 4:34; 5:30; 7:17; 9:31). The use of Ps 40:6-8 in Heb 10:5-7 indicated that God had supplied the human Jesus with a body so that he could make his self-offering. In that context he proclaimed, "I have come to do your will." Now the readers will be supplied with whatever is necessary for them to do God's will. God's will is otherwise referred to in 2:4; 10:7, 9, 10, 36.

    working among us that which is pleasing in his sight: The will of God will be accomplished by the good works done among the readers, the acts that are pleasing to God. In chapter 11 the worship of Abel pleased God on the basis of his faith. So now the readers may do likewise (10:24-25, 38-39; 13:1, 7, 15-16).

    through Jesus Christ, to whom be the glory forever and ever: It is not clear whether the glory is attributed to God (Lane 2:559; Ellingworth, 731; Weiss, 759–60) or to Jesus (Attridge, 408; Bruce, 389; Braun, 480). The end of the verse is a standard doxological formula (4 Macc 18:24; Pr Man 15; Rom 11:36; 16:27; Phil 4:20; 1 Tim 6:16; 2 Tim 4:18).

22. *I urge you, brothers and sisters, bear with my word of exhortation, for I have written to you briefly:* On the verb "urge" or "encourage," *parakalein*, see the Notes at 13:19. The author describes what he has written as a "word of exhortation," *logos tēs paraklēseōs*, playing on the opening verb. The expression appears elsewhere in the NT in Acts 13:15 to describe Paul's speech in a synagogue. This has led some to think of Hebrews as a synagogue sermon (see Introduction, 5. *Genre*). The author of 1 Peter claims something similar about the length of his work: "I have written briefly encouraging and witnessing. . . ." Both documents stem from the Roman church, so the form may reflect a custom among Roman Christians. Since Hebrews is not as brief as 1 Peter, the author is being ironic in the claim (cf. Attridge, 408).

23. *I want you to know that our brother Timothy has been set free, and if he comes in time, he will be with me when I see you:* Timothy is not clearly identified. He could be a member of the Roman community to whom the author writes or another Christian whom they know. Most likely it is the Timothy known as a coworker of Paul (Rom 16:21; 1 Cor 4:17; 16:10; 2 Cor 1:1, 19; Phil 1:1; 2:19; 1 Thess 1:1; 3:2, 6; 2 Thess 1:1; Phlm 1). He is frequently mentioned in Acts as a companion of Paul (16:1, 3; 17:14, 15; 18:5; 19:22; 20:4); his mother was Jewish and his father was Greek. Timothy is the ideal Pauline coworker who represents both the Jew and the Gentile. To him two of the Pastoral letters (1 and 2 Timothy) are addressed. The notice that he has been set free suggests that he has been released from prison. He may have been imprisoned with Paul at one time (Phlm 1). Since Hebrews was written after the Pauline letters, the reference may be to an imprisonment that is nowhere else mentioned in the NT. The verb "release," *apolyein*, frequently refers to being set free from prison in the NT, but it can also mean "be healed," "be set free from an illness," or "be dismissed" or "sent away" (BDAG, 117–18).

24. *Greet all your leaders and all the saints. Those from Italy send you greetings:* Such greetings often closed ancient letters, and this is true of those found in the NT

(Rom 16:3-16; 1 Cor 16:19, 20; 2 Cor 13:12; Phil 4:21, 22; Col 4:10-15; 1 Thess 5:26; 2 Tim 4:19, 21; Titus 3:15; Phlm 23; 1 Pet 5:13-14; 2 John 13; 3 John 15). How to understand "those from Italy" (*apo Italias*) is debated. The preposition "from" can refer to someone's native land (BDAG, 105–106) without indicating their actual location. Some commentators understand the greeters to be residing outside of Italy (Attridge, 410; Brown and Meier, *Antioch and Rome*, 146–47; Ellingworth, 735–36; Lane 2:571; Montefiore, 254; Weiss, 765). Others prefer to leave the expression ambiguous (Bruce, 391; Koester, 583–84). Given the ambiguity of the prepositional phrase, it cannot be decisive and the sermon's destination must be decided on other factors. When those factors are accounted for, the best destination is Rome.

25. *Grace be with all of you:* The final greeting is standard among NT letters (e.g., Rom 16:20; 1 Cor 16:23; 2 Cor 13:13; Eph 6:24; Phil 4:23; Col 4:18; 1 Thess 5:28; 2 Thess 3:18; 1 Tim 6:21; 2 Tim 4:22; Phlm 25).

INTERPRETATION

The final verses of Hebrews constitute the benediction and farewell in epistolary form. Ancient letters normally included a farewell without a benediction. Here the forms reflect NT usage. This passage divides into two parts: vv. 20-21, the benediction; vv. 22-25, the farewell.

One notices allusions in v. 21 to important themes in Hebrews. The author has stressed the need to do God's will, something exemplified by Christ himself (10:7, 9, 10, 36). The covenant was featured prominently throughout the sermon (7:22; 8:6, 8, 9, 10; 9:4, 15, 16, 17, 20; 10:16, 29; 12:24), as was the blood of Christ (9:12, 14; 10:19; 12:24) and the exhortation to please God (11:5, 6; 12:28; 13:16). The agency of Christ is an essential theme in the author's christology (2:14; 7:19, 25; 10:10, 20; 13:20). Although the expression "the God of peace" occurs only here, the notion of peace has been mentioned in relation to Melchizedek (7:2), Rahab (11:31), and the readers (12:11, 14). Novel to the benediction is the reference to the resurrection of Jesus and the designation of him as "the great shepherd of the sheep." The adjective "great," however, was applied to him in 4:14 and 10:21 in relation to his priesthood. The author may have recalled the image of Christ as a shepherd because of his own role in writing to the readers or because he has spoken of the community's leaders in this chapter (Attridge, 406). The benediction closes with a brief doxology to Christ, whose glory has been mentioned earlier in 1:3; 2:7, 9, 10; 3:3. The presence of familiar themes of Hebrews in this passage may argue for the authenticity of the epistolary conclusion (Attridge, 405).

The final farewell (vv. 22-25) asks for forbearance among the readers with what the author has written. It is identified as a "word of exhortation," which may have been the name for a synagogue homily (see the Note at

v. 22 above). This designation has prompted study and discussion on the literary form of Hebrews. The homiletic and hortatory characteristics of Hebrews as a whole show that the designation sermon is apt.

The ambiguous mention of Timothy leaves open the question whether it refers to the well-known companion of Paul to whom two of the Pastoral Epistles are supposedly addressed or to someone else bearing that name. The range of meaning for the verb *apolyein*, "release," may allow for the possibility that Timothy has recently been freed from imprisonment, or that he has recovered from an illness, or that he has been sent away. Whatever the circumstances, he appears to be known to the readers. The author is genuinely hopeful that Timothy may accompany him on his return visit to Rome.

Final greetings are sent to the leaders and the saints, thus the entire community receiving the sermon. The ambiguity of the reference to those "from Italy" has prompted speculation about its meaning. The most natural reading is that there are Italians in the location from which the author is writing (Attridge, 410). This may mean that although he writes to Rome he is not there, or anywhere else in Italy (Lane 2:571). As commentators are quick to point out, there is really no way of telling where the author or these Italians are located (Attridge, 410). All we know is that he has included greetings from some Italians to those receiving the sermon (Bruce, 391).

In his final words the author of Hebrews situates his work by offering a benediction and a doxology, along with personal greetings. His sermon is complete and in good pastoral style he offers his own wishes that his readers may be strengthened by God to accomplish all that the author hopes they will bring to fruition. Since God is identified as the God of peace, he ends on a note of hope that indeed the community will experience "peace" as they now must digest his words and apply them to their lives. This was his purpose in sending the sermon to them, and this is his sincere hope for all who read it.

For Reference and Further Study

Attridge, Harold W. "Paraenesis in a Homily (*logos paraklēseōs*): The Possible Location of and Socialization in the 'Epistle to the Hebrews,'" *Semeia* 50 (1990) 21–26.

Black, C. Clifton. "The Rhetorical Form of the Hellenistic Jewish and Early Christian Sermon: A Response to Lawrence Wills," *HTR* 81 (1988) 1–18.

Gelardini, Gabriella. "Hebrews, an Ancient Synagogue Homily for *Tisha be-Av:* Its Function, its Basis, its Theological Interpretation," in eadem, ed., *Hebrews: Contemporary Methods—New Insights*. Leiden and Boston: Brill, 2005, 107–27.

Siegert, Folker. *Drei hellenistisch-jüdische Predigten*. WUNT 61. Tübingen: Mohr Siebeck, 1992.

Thyen, Hartwig. *Der Stil der jüdisch-hellenistischen Homilie.* FRLANT 47. Göttingen: Vandenhoeck & Ruprecht, 1955.

Willis, Timothy M. "'Obey Your Leaders': Hebrews 13 and Leadership in the Church," *ResQ* 36 (1994) 316–26.

Wills, Lawrence. "The Form of the Sermon in Hellenistic Judaism and Early Christianity," *HTR* 77 (1984) 277–99.

INDEXES

SCRIPTURE AND OTHER ANCIENT WRITINGS

22:10	106	20:27	298	*4 Kingdoms*	
22:18	272	21:5-6	278	2:8	260
24:31	140	23:31	249	2:13	260
27:22	140	30:22	287	2:14	260
28:6	106	31:9	287	4:43	160
28:13	173			5:5	202
29:24	272			5:7	202
		2 Kingdoms		5:18	77
		4:23	99	6:15	160
2 Chronicles		5:23	287	9:33	189
5:10	175, 179	8:2	38	10:1	202
6:9	141	8:6	38	10:6	202
7:5	188	8:15	258	10:7	202
9:4	160	11:5	99	17:13	173
9:14	272	11:7	99	17:37	173
13:11	174	11:9	99	19:31	216
14:2	89	11:14	202	20:17	168
15:8	124, 188	12:11	105	22:19	169
16:10	259	13:18	160	23:31	249
19:8	140	15:20	298	24:4	77
20:32	89	22:4	105		
23:4	99	22:8	105	*Additions to the*	
23:20	140	23:21	252	*Book of Esther*	
24:11	105			4:8	111
24:21	260				
25:2	89, 211	*3 Kingdoms*		*Baruch*	
26:11	59	2:2-3	299	1:18	299
26:12	140	2:3	83	2:10	299
26:19	174	2:26	260	2:35	170, 202,
29:2	89	3:14	299		307
29:9	260	7:48	201	3:13	299
29:31	300	8:28	110	4:13	299
29:35	145	8:30	110		
33:16	300	8:38	110	*1 Esdras*	
34:9	105	8:45	110	4:54	161
35:18	257	8:49	110	5:40	75
36:2	249	8:52	110	5:51	201
36:9	249	8:54	110	7:13	231
		8:58	299	8:11	273
		8:63	188	8:16	224
1 Kingdoms		9:7	169	8:24	217
1:22	194	10:5	160	8:30	283
2:11	161	10:15	272	8:50	231
2:19	50	11:39	260	8:59	301
2:31	168	13:14	169	8:70	75
6:6	75	18:28	190	9:8	81
11:14	188	19:13	260	9:9	224
14:16	258	19:18	96	9:45	202
17:36	218	20:8	202		
18:1	293				

82.16	75	7:13	225	22:44	44
102.26	75	7:19	273	23:35	230, 260
		7:21	224	23:37	260
Suetonius, *Claudius*		8:20	65	24:3	195
25.4	8	9:2	252	24:4	290
		9:22	252	24:29	59, 288, 290
Xenophon, *Memorabilia*		9:27	147	24:50	224
1.4.4	100	9:28-29	252	25:19	98
2.1.1	117	10:2	81	25:31-46	301
		10:7	149	25:31-34	195
		10:18	298	25:34	97
Papyri		10:38	298	25:41	120
		10:40	81	25:46	120
BGU		11:3	224	26:18	252
4.1138.13	228	11:20	59	26:28	153, 189,
		11:21	59		190, 217
P. Lond.		11:23	59	26:31	307
370	163	12:5	98	26:36-46	110
		12:32	51	26:42	202
P. Oxy.		12:36	301	26:45	218, 267
2.237.7.17	228	12:41-42	231	26:64	44, 65
		12:42	132	27:2	298
		12:50	224	27:11	298
New Testament		13:22	37, 90, 229	27:14	298
		13:35	97	27:24	96
		13:39	195	27:26	259
Matthew		13:40	195	27:29-31	259
1:1	147	13:49	195	27:31	300
1:6	147	13:54	59	27:34	223
2:6	298	13:58	59	27:35	74
2:12	162	14:2	59	27:39	74
2:22	162	14:31	252	27:41-42	259
3:2	149	15:5	96	27:43	74
3:7	51	15:22	147	27:46	74, 110
3:9	244	15:24	81	27:48	223
3:10	273	15:28	252	28:20	195
3:11	224	16:12	298		
4:1-11	77	16:26	96	*Mark*	
4:17	149	17:9	146	1:4	190
5:8	277, 279	18:8	120	1:5	149
5:9	277, 279	18:14	224	1:13	77
5:12	57	18:17	57	1:27	298
5:13	217	19:23	146	1:32	38
5:18	290	19:26	244	1:44	38
5:42	287	20:19	146, 259	2:3	38
6:9	272	21:9	224	2:27	98
6:19-21	223	21:35	260	3:14	81 [bis]
7:6	217	21:37	272	3:29	217
7:12	295	22:32	236	3:35	224, 308

AUTHORS

Abernathy, D., 46
Aitken, E. B., 9, 29
Anderson, C. P., 7, 29
Andriessen, P., 25, 29, 289, 306
Attridge, H. W., 3, 7, 16, 17, 18, 19, 22, 28, 35, 36, 37, 38, 41, 42, 44, 45, 47, 54, 60, 62, 64, 65, 66, 67, 69, 72, 73, 74, 75, 78, 81, 83, 87, 88, 89, 90, 91, 96, 97, 98, 101, 104, 106, 111, 115, 116, 117, 118, 119, 121, 132, 133, 134, 141, 142, 145, 146, 147, 148, 153, 154, 155, 156, 160, 161, 164, 166, 168, 170, 174, 176, 177, 178, 179, 182, 184, 188, 194, 195, 199, 200, 204, 211, 212, 217, 219, 223, 228, 229, 230, 232, 236, 237, 244, 250, 251, 253, 255, 258, 259, 260, 261, 265, 266, 267, 271, 277, 278, 279, 281, 283, 284, 288, 289, 291, 293, 294, 295, 299, 301, 302, 307, 308, 309, 310

Bachmann, M., 63
Backhaus, K., 26, 29
Balch, D., 293
Balz, H., 84
Barber, C. J., 256
Barrett, C. K., 264
Bartlet, J. V., 7, 29
Bateman, H., 55
Bauernfeind, O., 134
Baumgartner, W. (HAL), 75, 153
Becker, E.-M., 104
Behm, J., 299

Berényi, G., 192
Bertram, G., 271, 288
Betz, O., 286
Billerbeck, P., 156, 166
Bittner, W., 256
Black, C. C., 309
Black, D. A., 3, 30, 269
Blass, F. (BDF), 123, 127, 145, 194, 257
Bleek, F., 28, 194
Brady, C., 71
Brändle, R., 28
Braun, H., 11, 15, 28, 47, 62, 67, 81, 87, 90, 177, 199, 200, 228, 233, 251, 263, 283, 284, 288, 299, 303, 308, 309
Brooks, W., 159, 186
Brown, J. V., 7, 30
Brown, R. E., 6, 8, 10, 30, 55, 309
Bruce, F. F., 7, 8, 12, 28, 37, 41, 47, 64, 73, 87, 153, 194, 200, 228, 251, 283, 284, 308, 309
Buchanan, G. W., 6, 16, 28, 295
Büchsel, H.M.F., 148, 298
Bultmann, R., 98
Burch, V., 7, 30

Caird, G., 286
Caragounis, C. C., 28
Carlston, C., 79
Casey, J. M., 286
Cavallin, H.C.C., 227
Charlesworth, J. H., 30, 101, 162, 233
Chilton, B. D., 248